THE ROUGH ROAD TO RENAISSANCE

Creating the North American Landscape

Consulting Editors   Gregory Conniff

Bonnie Loyd

David Schuyler

JON C. TEAFORD

The Rough Road to Renaissance

o URBAN REVITALIZATION IN AMERICA, 1940–1985

The Johns Hopkins University Press

Baltimore and London

The Johns Hopkins University Press, 701 West 40th Street, Baltimore, Maryland 21211
The Johns Hopkins Press Ltd., London

∞ The paper used in this book meets the minimum requirements of American National
Standard for Information Sciences—Permanence of Paper for Printed Library Materials,
ANSI Z39.48-1984.

Photography credits: Photograph 1 by George Ruark; photographs 1–4 and 6 courtesy of the
Carnegie Library, Pittsburgh. Photograph 5 courtesy of the Pittsburgh Chamber of Commerce
and the Carnegie Library. Photographs 7–9 and 13–15 courtesy of the Cleveland Public
Library. Photographs 10–12 courtesy of the Cincinnati Historical Society.

Library of Congress Cataloging-in-Publication Data

Teaford, Jon C.
    The rough road to renaissance : urban revitalization in America, 1940–1985 / Jon C. Teaford.
        p.   cm. — (Creating the North American landscape)
    Includes bibliographical references.
    ISBN 0–8018–3971–8 (alk. paper). — ISBN 0–8018–4134–8 (pbk. : alk. paper)
    1. Urban renewal—United States—History—20th century.   2. Inner cities—United
States—History—20th century.   3. Central business districts—United States—
History—20th century.   4. Gentrification—United States—History—20th century.
I. Title. II. Series
HT175.T43   1990
307.3′416—dc20   89-49001   CIP

CONTENTS

Illustrations are found in a gallery between pages 314 and 315.

TABLES

THE ROUGH ROAD TO RENAISSANCE

INTRODUCTION ○ The Road to Renaissance

During the early 1980s, stark contrasts confronted visitors to Saint Louis, Chicago, Detroit, or New York. In any of the older major American central cities one found blocks of abandoned houses and apartment buildings with hollow windows overlooking the rubble of demolished neighbors. Not far from these ruins gentrified neighborhoods boasted fashionable restaurants and rehabilitated townhouses that brought smiles to chamber-of-commerce boosters eager for evidence of the city's renaissance. On the horizon one could catch the glint of glass-sheathed downtown office structures rising forty, fifty, and sixty stories, and the steel framework of soaring towers under construction visibly testified to the faith of private capital in the future of urban America. Yet visitors to downtown could walk one block from these monuments representing an investment of billions of dollars and come across rows of shabby storefronts, some empty, others specializing in "adult literature" or fire-damaged merchandise. Nearby, fast-food outlets lined once-fashionable shopping streets, where the remaining retailers struggled to stay in business. But along the waterfront throngs of tourists and local shoppers crowded the new "festival marketplace," sampling its array of boutiques and restaurants.

The rehabilitated townhouses a short distance from abandoned apartment hulks, the sleazy porn shops in the shadow of slick office towers, and the decayed retailing streets a few blocks from the exciting marketplaces all symbolized the mixed signals of rebirth and decline that characterized urban development during the four decades following World War II. Throughout these years the older cities struggled to capture their share of

1

American affluence and to polish their tarnished image. But at the same time Americans could read in their newspapers and see on television tales of inner-city slums, of senseless violent crime, and of rioting in the urban core. It was obvious that wealth and poverty, vitality and decay, stood shoulder to shoulder in the older central cities. Cries of urban crisis alternated with boasts of urban renaissance, and observers could point to ample signs of both hope and despair. Bold new office-hotel-apartment complexes seemed to mark a reversal of urban fortunes, but the census figures and municipal account books told another story, a story of shrinking population, declining sales, and a contracting tax base.

This study charts the treacherous course toward the seemingly elusive goal of urban renaissance. It examines the period 1940 to 1985 and focuses on twelve large central cities in the northeastern quadrant of the nation: Boston, New York, Buffalo, Philadelphia, Pittsburgh, Baltimore, Cleveland, Cincinnati, Detroit, Chicago, Saint Louis, and Minneapolis. Each of these cities had over half a million residents in 1950, and each, with the exception of New York, declined in population during every decade from 1950 to 1980. And even New York lost population both in the 1950s and the 1970s and gained only slightly in the 1960s. Moreover, none of these cities annexed substantial tracts of territory during the four decades after World War II. Instead, suburban municipalities ringed each of the cities, siphoning both population and commerce from the urban hub. All were largely products of the nineteenth century, and together they faced an uncertain future in the second half of the twentieth century. Given the American devotion to growth and bigness, the common threat of stagnation and decline appeared especially serious. To be branded a has-been city would be devastating in a nation dedicated to success. None of these older central cities had lost population during any decade of the nineteenth or twentieth centuries prior to the 1930s. Most at some time in their past had actually enjoyed a reputation as a boomtown, doubling in population every ten years and luring the capital of go-getters eager to strike it rich. By the 1940s, however, they had entered a new phase of their histories, and the following pages will describe how they reacted to the unfamiliar prospect of decline.

This book focuses on the localities and their public policies and not on the development of federal programs in Washington. Others have investigated the federal response to the problems of troubled central cities. They have traced the origins of federal policies, the legislative history as bills passed through congressional chambers, and the administrative developments in various Washington bureaucracies. And they have described the urban proposals of every president from Franklin Roosevelt to Ronald Reagan.[1] But I look at what was happening in Buffalo, Saint

Louis, and the other aging cities; how leaders there were coping with obsolescence; what policies local bureaucrats, politicians, and civic chieftains were initiating and realizing; and how these local notables reacted to and implemented federal programs. This acccount is, then, a view of the older central cities and their problems from the vantage point of city hall rather than Capitol Hill.

Social scientists have been more eager to tackle this subject than historians; in fact, during the 1980s, economic development in older urban centers became a "hot" topic among political scientists. Paul Peterson ignited scholarly fires when he argued that economic growth was a primary goal of city government, and one that garnered local consensus; pro-growth policies were a necessary product of the competition among cities for jobs and investments. According to Peterson, redistributive functions inevitably had to assume a secondary position on the municipal agenda.[2] John Mollenkopf saw politics as increasingly important in urban economic development, writing of pro-growth coalitions of business and political leaders seeking support from the federal government.[3] Meanwhile, neo-Marxists regarded urban revitalization policies as manifestations of the inevitable contradictions underlying twentieth-century capitalism; during the 1950s and 1960s, the state had to underwrite faltering capitalism through massive investments that would lead to the fiscal crisis of the 1970s.[4]

With the penchant of social scientists for generalizations these authors have each sought the essence of urban development policy. Yet in the eyes of a historian the supposedly glittering analyses of the political scientist often appear to be gross generalities, explanations that distort reality by a too radical pruning of details in the search for an answer. The social scientists have identified pertinent themes and issues, yet I do not attempt such a neat formulaic interpretation of the renaissance initiatives. This book describes what happened and recognizes that many people with many goals and interests participated in the revitalization saga and that the story's plot was less structured than a social scientist might desire. The history of the older central cities should not be shoved into a theoretical straitjacket. Boston, Baltimore, and New York did not proceed along the road to renaissance on automatic pilot with the course set by the inherent contradictions of capitalism or the inevitable interest in economic growth. Instead, changing local leadership and emerging demands at all levels of society did shift the direction of policy.

To understand the development of policy, however, it is necessary to recognize the marked changes in technology, demographics, and settlement patterns that threatened the aging urban giants. Molded largely by the needs and desires of nineteenth-century Americans, cities like Philadelphia, Baltimore, Cleveland, and Minneapolis were growing increasingly obsolete in the uncongenial climate of the mid-twentieth century. New modes of transportation, an influx of poor migrants, and the unprecedented competition from the suburbs now placed these older urban centers at a disadvantage in the struggle for businesses and residents who would pay more in taxes than they required in services. The revitalization policy discussed in the following pages had to respond to these troubling realities.

Changes in transportation and the advent of an automobile-dependent culture posed one of the most serious challenges to the central cities. During the postwar decades, the building stock, street layouts, and patterns of land use in older cities still largely reflected a bygone dependence on the streetcar. At the beginning of the twentieth century, offices and stores had found it necessary to cluster downtown, where the web of streetcar lines was densest. This was the location most accessible to employees and customers, and thus many businesses had to vie for space in the crowded urban core. Moreover, this central concentration of employment together with the slow pace of streetcar travel forced most city workers to reside within a five-mile radius of the downtown. To commute any further was too time-consuming, inconvenient, and costly for the vast majority of employees. The introduction of the automobile and truck, however, freed businesses, employees, and shoppers from the centripetal bonds of the past and offered a suburban alternative to the clustering of commerce and population around a single dominant hub. By the mid-twentieth century, downtown employees could buy homes far beyond the central-city boundaries in new suburban municipalities, and businesses could locate at any one of the multiple hubs of stores, offices, and factories that developed near suburban freeway interchanges or along the major highways. The dominant mode of transportation no longer ensured central-city supremacy. With its narrow thoroughfares and lack of parking space the central city was, in fact, out of step with the times.

Meanwhile, changing population patterns also seemed to undercut the competitive position of central cities. Throughout their histories the older urban centers had attracted poor migrants both from rural America and abroad. In the mid-twentieth century this influx of poor newcomers continued as millions of black and white Southerners and immigrants from Latin America moved to New York, Detroit, and Chicago. Yet unlike in the past a movement of middle-class residents out of the city accompanied this influx of poor migrants. With new automobiles plus low-interest home mortgages subsidized by the federal government, middle-class city dwellers, and many of their working-class colleagues, could now settle in their suburban dream houses and abandon the aging, obsolete residences of the central city to impoverished blacks, Puerto Ricans, and Appalachian newcomers. The result was a central-city population with decreasing resources and increasing problems.

By the 1960s and 1970s the central city seemed synonymous with poverty, crime, and general social decay. Moreover, in white eyes it was simply becoming a black domain and thus off limits. As such it appeared less and less attractive to many prospective investors and residents as well as to many businesses and homeowners remaining within the city. Because of the automobile, the earlier centripetal pattern of metropolitan life no longer was necessary; because of the burgeoning symptoms of social disintegration, the older central cities no longer appeared desirable.

By the mid-twentieth century the advantages offered by suburban governments further undermined the position of older municipalities. In the minds of many Americans suburban municipalities seemed better suited to meet the demands of the diverse metropolitan population. Whereas central-city governments had to balance the public service expectations of downtown business leaders, large and small manufacturers, impoverished ghetto residents, and the residue of middle-class homeowners, each of the small suburban municipalities catered to a narrower social fragment. In homogeneous suburbs officials could tailor programs to the needs and desires of the citizenry; in the heterogeneous central city policy was often an ugly patchwork of compromises and bargains that was intended to accommodate everyone but too frequently satisfied no one. An outlying municipal haven for the wealthy, for example, could offer government especially suited for the affluent, providing the most restrictive residential zoning and first-class schools specializing in college preparation. Such a municipality need not accommodate fast-food franchises or malodorous chemical plants. Likewise, working-class suburban cities could serve the special interests of that class, and industrial suburbs could guarantee manufacturers low taxes and minimum local interference. Each could offer a fragment of metropolitan society insulation from its enemies and public protection and nurture. Moreover, special metropolitan authorities or contractual agreements among adjacent municipalities guaranteed small suburban cities such services as water delivery and sewage disposal that required massive public investment and operated most efficiently on a large scale. In other words, by the 1950s and 1960s suburban dwellers enjoyed the benefits of both large and small governmental units whereas residents of the central city attempted to cope with their less flexible governmental structure, a structure that increasingly seemed to help the "other guy."

The older central cities were, then, out of step with the automobile age, burdened by an aging housing stock sheltering an impoverished population and handicapped by a political structure that did not satisfy the expectations of the diverse social groups of metropolitan America. By the mid-twentieth century these older urban hubs seemed to suffer from a serious case of obsolescence. The suburbs were gaining an ever increasing competitive advantage, and the central cities needed to adapt to the changing times. During the post–World War II era, the boom in office employment and the growth of the white-collar sector did appear to bode well for the downtown business district, offering one positive portent for the central cities. But suburban office complexes could blunt this advantage unless the central city adapted to the automobile, curbed crime and general disorder, retained white, middle-class residents, and pursued a public policy friendly to commercial real estate development. Even the remaining assets of the central city might disappear unless leaders did something to overcome urban shortcomings or at least compensated for them.

By the 1940s central-city businessmen, politicians, planners, and journalists clearly recognized that something needed to be done. If the older central cities were to pursue the path to renaissance and achieve social and economic revitalization, then it was necessary to adopt public policies that would make the central city a better place in which to live and to do business. The threat was clearly perceived, and programs of physical renewal seemed imperative.

Complicating the struggle for revitalization, however, was the disruption of traditional politics after World War II. Before the 1940s in most cities American municipal politics had been partisan politics with party organizations being significant as intermediaries and brokers between elected officials and the citizenry. In some cities an authoritative party machine had served this function whereas in others two competing party organizations existed, neither with the power to dictate policy or even the selection of candidates but still with an important brokerage role. The party could mediate among racial and nationality groups to ensure that each got what it wanted and could maintain an ethnic balance of power. It could broker difficulties between elected officials and city employees and guarantee that partisan appointees toed the line. Moreover, through its ward organization it could keep the channels open between city hall and the neighborhoods and squelch grass-roots discontent. Party loyalty also imposed some order on the relationship between mayors and council members, with many executives enjoying a reliable bloc of support among municipal legislators from their own party. Yet after World War II party government disappeared in most of the older central cities. The Republican party vanished, and the Democratic organization was seriously weakened. Many mayors ran on their own, proudly proclaiming their independence, and a fragmented political structure developed.

Thus the underlying political structure did not necessarily facilitate a successful attack on urban problems. Fewer mayors could rely on an effective party organization to put out the fires igniting among municipal employees, ethnic minorities, and neighborhood groups. In most of the older urban hubs officials were attempting to shore up the city at the same time the local political foundations were shifting. The result was a collapse of some promising careers and vaunted programs.

This study describes some of the manifold difficulties that developed and demonstrates that the road to renaissance was not a straight course without twists or detours. Instead, during the four decades after World War II, urban leaders headed in a number of different directions in search of the goal of revitalization. Moreover, I show that at some times the search proceeded with much optimism and vigor whereas at other times it almost seemed a lost cause.

During the late 1940s and early 1950s, for example, expectations of success were especially strong and hopes of renewal were high. The principal strategy of the older cities in their battle for continued supremacy was to beat suburbia at its own game. To maintain preeminence, the aging hubs had to adapt to changing transportation technology and lifestyles. They would thereby acquire the advantages that suburbia boasted and retain middle-class residents and customers to balance the onslaught of poor minorities. Cities emphasized the construction of highways and airports, the provision of new housing and more open spaces, and the creation of a cleaner environment by eliminating air and water pollution. Benefiting from record-low interest rates and a ready market for municipal bonds, such cities as Philadelphia, Pittsburgh, Cincinnati, and Detroit invested billions of dollars in expansive schemes of public improvements. During the first decade after World War II, these aging cities optimistically planned for a better future, assuming that a physical renovation of the city could erase the existing flaws in urban life. Moreover, urban leaders sought to unite the diverse elements of the city behind this program of physical amelioration, patching over social and political divisions with a booster rhetoric promising a better life for all. When confronted with the prospect of possible decline, city leaders did not, then, choose to cut back municipal responsibilities or retrench in preparation for a bleak future. Instead, they chose to defy the centrifugal drift toward suburbia and sought to perpetuate the central city's preeminent position in metropolitan America.

By the late 1950s and early 1960s, however, the optimism of earlier years was yielding to skepticism. New office buildings were rising along downtown streets, leading many to proclaim a central-city building boom.

But during these years, urban residents began to recognize the sometimes dismal and often disruptive consequences of the federal urban renewal and interstate highway programs. These well-meaning schemes to update the central cities and bring them into the mid-twentieth century too frequently produced results that fell far short of expectations. Despite billions of dollars invested in the physical plant of the city, the promised new era did not arrive.

Many believed that the answer was not continued investment solely in physical renewal but new programs of spending for human renewal. Thus during the 1960s, expensive schemes for rehabilitating human behavior joined those for reconstructing buildings, transportation facilities, and the general urban infrastructure. Financed largely by the federal government's War on Poverty, central cities assaulted the problems of the urban underclass with the same confidence in government action that characterized the physical renewal schemes. But as the number of federal programs mounted, Washington increasingly determined the direction and nature of the assault on social and physical decay. By the close of the 1960s the aging central cities pursued policies not simply because they could answer local problems but also because federal money was available and would be lost if the municipal authorities failed to act. Dollars from Washington were as much the determinants of public policy as local demands or desires.

In the 1970s, however, skepticism mounted as the human renewal schemes seemed if anything less successful and more destructive than the already criticized physical renewal programs. Racial tension produced rioting and backlash, crime rates soared, and the poor remained poor. Despite the volumes of reports from learned and costly consultants, despite the billions of federal dollars, despite the efforts of business moguls in the private sector, urban renaissance was more elusive than ever. In the battle for control of the cities, decay appeared to be advancing while revitalization was in retreat.

Moreover, by the late 1960s and early 1970s a new approach to revitalization was gaining the upper hand as cities stopped trying to become more like suburbia with its orientation to the automobile. Instead, the older hubs now sought to build on their own traditional strengths, emphasizing mass transit and rehabilitation of older structures rather than demolition and reconstruction. A new rhetoric of revitalization lavished praise on old-fashioned neighborhoods, renovated townhouses, and the density and diversity of urban life. Efforts to adapt to the automobile and reduce the competitive advantage of suburbia had reaped what some deemed disastrous results. A shift of direction appeared to be imperative.

The bankruptcy of New York City in 1975 marked the low point in the travails of the aging central cities. The wealthiest city in the world, the center of finance capitalism, had been unable to pay its debts and could no longer borrow. Moreover, other central cities also appeared to be on the brink of financial ruin. Retrenchment was imperative, and one city after another reduced its labor force and its investment in capital improvements. After three decades of increased spending, central cities were forced to admit their limitations as units of government and divest themselves of some responsibilities. Faced with the grim realities of the mid-1970s, even the most ardent believers in an urban comeback seemed to lose faith. Since cities could not even balance their books, it appeared unlikely that they could overcome the social and physical decadence engulfing them.

The 1970s represented, then, a new era of diminished expectations. Mayors no longer needed to battle poverty or rebuild vast urban tracts to win national acclaim. If they were simply able to pay the bills, they might well end up on the cover of *Time* magazine. Many urban experts no longer spoke of rebirth but urged the adoption of policies that would help the central cities grow old gracefully. Revitalization seemed too much to expect. But government leaders could at least soften the blows of aging and keep the urban hubs from dying too painful a death.

In the early 1980s the downtown building boom, the much-ballyhooed opening of festival marketplaces in the urban core, and the rehabilitation of some inner-city neighborhoods brought renewed hope to the central city, and the rhetoric of rebirth again surfaced in the pronouncements of journalists, politicians, and business leaders. Baltimore called itself Renaissance City, Detroit boasted of its Renaissance Center, and fortunate Pittsburgh claimed to be in the midst of its second renaissance, the first having transformed the city in the late 1940s and the 1950s. Even in beleaguered Buffalo and Cleveland there was talk of a comeback. But the problems of decay persisted, and skeptics remembered that they had heard the well-worn promises of rebirth before. The cities had pursued a rough course over the past four decades; whether they had overcome the perils of obsolescence was still in doubt.

Thus the following account is not a tale of unremitting triumphs or an unqualified testimonial to the efficacy of well-intentioned public policies. There were some achievements during the four and a half decades from 1940 to 1985, but the road to urban renaissance was not an easy one. Along that road there were enough pitfalls to warrant serious consideration whether the journey was worth the effort and whether the billions of dollars spent on physical and social renewal were wasted. To the perceptive observer the road was lined with ample monuments both to the possibilities and limitations of recent public policy.

CHAPTER ONE ○ The Problem Perceived

The census figures for 1940 confirmed the expectations of most urban experts. During the prior decade, Boston, Philadelphia, Cleveland, and Saint Louis had suffered a decline in population, and most of the nation's other major cities only had inched upward in number of inhabitants. Of the ten largest cities in the nation eight had either lost population or grown at a slower rate than the country as a whole. New York City had barely surpassed the national average, and among the top ten only Los Angeles could claim to be booming. Moreover, this sluggishness was in marked contrast with the pattern just two decades earlier. Whereas, during the 1930s, Cleveland's population had dropped 2.5 percent, between 1910 and 1920 it had risen 42 percent. In the 1930s Detroit had gained a mere 3.5 percent; twenty years earlier it had soared 113 percent. After more than a century of rapidly rising population the growth of the leading cities, especially those in the northeastern quadrant of the United States, seemed to be coming to a halt.

Many urban leaders recognized the dangers inherent in the new figures. A prominent planner in Cleveland ominously argued that "the beginning of an era when Cleveland will have to compete with all other major cities in a race for the 'survival of the fittest' is at hand."[1] Meanwhile, the Saint Louis City Plan Commission claimed that the Missouri metropolis was "fast becoming a decadent city" and with considerable prescience contended that the city of more than 800,000 residents in 1940 was "well on the way toward decline of its total population to 500,000 by 1980 or 1990."[2] Boston's mayor warned that "unless prompt measures are taken the contagion will spread until virtual decay and destruction of the whole city has taken place."[3] Throughout the country observers commented on the gradual disintegration of the urban giants, and few could muster much praise for the metropolitan core in the years immediately preceding World War II. Many wrote of economic "dry rot" in the downtown districts, of deterioration and abandonment in the surrounding slums, and of the threatening spread of decay in the remaining residential ring. No one sought to preserve the largest cities of the Northeast and Midwest in their existing form. Instead, by the close of the 1930s these aging metropolises were perceived as relics in radical need of rehabilitation and restructuring.

Local leaders and urban experts viewed this decline of the central cities largely as a physical rather than a social problem. Supposedly, it did not arise from racial conflict or discrimination, a maldistribution of economic or political power, or an absence of law and order. Thus the answer was not racial integration, social and economic revolution, or tougher police action. Rather, the commonly identified enemy of the late 1930s and early 1940s was "blight." When they spoke of blight, city officials, business leaders, and urban planners meant the process of physical deterioration that destroyed property values and undermined the quality of urban life. Moreover, blight was often referred to as a cancer, an insidious, spreading phenomenon that could kill a city if not removed or forced into remission. It was this malady destroying the physical tissue of urban America that appeared to be the archfoe of older central cities and that aroused fears for their future.

But civic leaders were not about to surrender to the forces of blight. When the Saint Louis City Plan Commission asked rhetorically, "Shall we gradually abandon St. Louis?" the expected answer was a resounding "no."[4] A Boston newspaper editorialized that "the population decline need not be accepted with apathy and resignation." Instead, it argued that "with ingenuity and energy the condition can be turned into an occasion for new progress.[5] Meanwhile, in Cincinnati a business leader announced that "obviously the citizens of this metropolitan area do not wish to see Cincinnati retrogress," and consequently "the time is at hand" for "the taking of those steps and the making of those improvements necessary to arrest decline and to assure progress."[6] In one aging central city after another, urban leaders both in the public and private sectors agreed with this conclusion. Decisive action could again put the cities on an upward path.

By the early 1940s, then, business chiefs and municipal officials not only recognized the problem confronting them but also began to make plans to do something about it. Since the perceived problem was one of physical structure rather than of social organization, the perceived answer was physical rejuvenation and reconstruction. The tonic that could revive the aging central cities had to include a healthy dose of new highway and sewer construction, the building of better housing and more modern commercial structures, and the elimination of environmental pollution. The engineer, architect, and contractor and not the social worker or agitator were to cure the city's ills. They were to mix the elixir that would bring new life to Boston, Buffalo, Cleveland, and Chicago.

Since the impetus for the campaign against decay came from businesspeople and public officials at the top of the social and political ladder, it was not surprising that physical solutions proved more attractive than a restructuring of society. Though the residents of decaying neighborhoods may have favored action to curb decline, the loudest crying about the signs of impending doom came from downtown real estate interests threatened by falling property values and harried mayors facing fiscal crisis because of the drop in assessed valuations. In their minds blight was a physical phenomenon, and the best means to combat it was increased investment in the construction of private and public facilities under their control. Physical rejuvenation would bolster their positions; social change would undermine them. Thus physical solutions seemed most desirable.

World War II diverted capital, labor, and materials to the battle abroad, thwarting immediate realization of the plans for physical renewal. But at home politicians, planners, and civil servants prepared for their upcoming battle for the rehabilitation of the city in the postwar era. By 1945 central-city decline had been the subject of discussion for a number of years, and urban revival was a recognized goal. Leaders of the older central cities were aroused to the dangers before them, and they made ready to take action.

The Emigration of Residents

Among the most serious phenomena facing the older central cities was the migration of residents to outlying suburban municipalities. None of the major metropolitan districts lost population during the 1930s, for in the Boston, Philadelphia, Cleveland, and Saint Louis areas gains in the suburbs more than compensated for losses in the central cities. From the beginning of the century the outward movement had accelerated with the suburban population in the nation's metropolitan districts growing at twice the pace of the central-city population during the 1920s and three times the rate of the urban core in the 1930s. "Decentralization" was the watchword of urban experts as millions of metropolitan Americans dispersed to homes beyond the central-city boundaries.

These migrants may have realized their dreams of a suburban house with a plot of grass and room for a garden, but those concerned for the future of the central city viewed the suburban trend with consternation. In fact, decentralization appeared to be a close ally of blight, clearing the city of residents and thereby preparing the ground for dreaded physical deterioration. In 1940 Harland Bartholomew, the distinguished city planner of Saint Louis, warned that "the whole financial structure of cities, as well as the investments of countless individuals and business firms, is in jeopardy because of what is called 'decentralization.' " If residents kept moving outward causing a depreciation of property in the urban core, the result, according to Bartholomew, could only be disaster for central-city treasuries dependent on property taxes and for central-city landlords unable to rent their holdings.[7] A year later a leading Cincinnati realtor argued that chief among the nation's urban problems was "the undue acceleration of population flight away from city centers causing rot and decay at their cores." This Cincinnatian warned, "If this movement is permitted to proceed unabated, the loss of wealth will be beyond comprehension, because region after region, still sound for good living, will become blighted."[8]

Especially serious was the migration of the wealthier classes to suburbia. Since World War I a steady stream of middle-class Americans had migrated to suburban municipalities, leaving the central city poorer and the suburbs richer. The growing disparity in wealth between the city and its suburbs was evident in the census statistics for twelve aging central cities in the nation's northeastern quadrant. As seen in table 1, in eight of the twelve the average monthly rent for housing was higher in the metropolitan area outside the central city than within. The gap between central city and suburbs varied among the metropolitan areas, but it was most notable in Boston, Philadelphia, Cleveland, and Saint Louis, the very cities that had recorded population declines during the 1930s. The extreme example of disparity was in the Cleveland metropolitan district, where the average rent for dwellings in the suburbs was 78 percent higher than in the central city. Whereas the suburban average was $51.42, the highest figure for any ward within the city was $41.77. In other words, the average suburban dwelling was considerably more expensive than the average housing in the "best" central-city neighborhood.

Moreover, in nine of the twelve metropolitan districts, the most exclusive and expensive area of residence was outside the central city. For ex-

Table 1. Economic Disparities between Central Cities and Their Suburbs, 1940

Metropolitan Area	Average Rents ($) Central City	Outside Central City	Political Subdivisions Ranking Highest in Average Rents ($) Central City		Outside Central City	
New York City	43.83	47.84	Manhattan Health Area 41	202.00	Scarsdale	155.19
Chicago	34.47	40.66	Community Area 72	70.81	Kenilworth	158.14
Philadelphia	31.22	38.57	Ward 8	70.62	Pine Hill	125.00
					Lower Merion	94.22
Detroit	35.88	33.71	Ward 2	55.49	Bloomfield Hills	254.32
Cleveland	28.93	51.42	Ward 33	41.77	Bratenahl	101.08
Baltimore	30.31	33.60	Ward 28	49.22	Baltimore County District 9	49.54
Saint Louis	25.75	31.15	Ward 25	52.92	Ladue	156.37
Boston	32.74	39.33	Ward 5	61.23	Hull	89.04
					Brookline	77.94
Pittsburgh	34.87	27.85	Ward 14	79.63	Fox Chapel	139.17
Buffalo–Niagara Falls	30.91	32.93	Ward 20	55.56	Amherst	48.33
Minneapolis–Saint Paul	33.55	30.78	Ward 13	54.38	Dellwood	126.49
					Edina	69.69
Cincinnati	31.54	29.60	Ward 13	59.63	Wyoming	58.50

Source: Sixteenth Census of the United States: 1940, Housing—Data for Small Areas (Washington, D.C.: U.S. Government Printing Office, 1943).

ample, the average rent in the elegant suburb of Fox Chapel was $139.17 as compared with $79.63 for Pittsburgh's most prestigious area, Ward 14 in the Squirrel Hill district. Likewise, the rental figure for posh Bloomfield Hills was more than four times that of Detroit's wealthiest ward, and suburban Edina ranked considerably higher on the economic scale than any ward in Minneapolis. All of these figures added up to the same conclusion: the wealthiest urbanites generally were not building homes within the central-city boundaries. Instead, many of the metropolitan elite had migrated to suburbia.

In some central cities there had been virtually no construction of upper-middle-class dwellings since World War I. Suburban Lakewood, Cleveland Heights, and Shaker Heights had drained Cleveland of much of its white-collar population, leaving that central city largely a working-class municipality. Similarly, in the Saint Louis, Chicago, and Boston areas builders had erected few new homes within the central city for upper-middle-class buyers during the previous twenty years. Managers and professionals in metropolitan Saint Louis were expected to live in Clayton, Webster Groves, and Ladue and not in the central city. The north shore suburbs along Lake Michigan and the well-heeled enclaves west of the city attracted most upper-middle-class Chicagoans. And the suburban municipalities of Brookline, Newton, and Wellesley were home to most of Boston's white-collar elite.

There were some exceptions to the general migration of residential wealth to the suburbs. For example, sooty industrial suburbs surrounded Cincinnati, housing thousands of working-class residents employed in the soap factories and machine tool plants. In contrast, the central city's east-side neighborhoods, such as Hyde Park and North Avondale, were the metropolitan hub of upper-middle-class life. As a result Cincinnati's average rent was higher than that of the suburbs, and its Ward 13 topped the economic ladder in the metropolitan area. In Pittsburgh and Buffalo the presence of a number of working-class industrial suburbs also meant that the generalization of residential wealth in outlying municipalities did not apply.

Yet the outward migration of the wealthier classes was prevalent enough to disturb many observers of the late 1930s and early 1940s. One critic, in an article on Saint Louis, was "astounded to find that much of what was until recent years the most substantial residential area of the city is being allowed to degenerate into semislums."[9] Even in Cincinnati an observer reported ominously, "During the past decade there has been a loss of approximately 6 percent of the substantial population, which has been supplanted by negroes, migrants from the Kentucky and Tennessee mountains, and persons seeking the relief bounty of the City."[10] Speaking before the National Conference on Planning, another reported that Philadelphia had lost 78,000 inhabitants between 1930 and 1940 in the inner-city area within a five-mile radius of city hall, and he claimed that the near north side neighborhoods had been hit by a "blitzkrieg of deterioration." In response to an advocate of decentralization who suggested that Philadelphia should grow horizontally rather than vertically, this gloomy prophet warned, "Just let this deterioration in the central areas continue, and spread in a vast, widening ring around the center of the city, and Philadelphia will be so darned horizontal that it won't even be able to sit up and take nourishment".[11]

This planner and many of his colleagues also noted that the outward migration of the middle class and the spread of blighted residential areas could add up to dire consequences for the municipal treasuries. Saint Louis's Harland Bartholomew reported that "the older residence districts almost uniformly received public services two and one quarter times in cost the amount paid in taxes." In contrast, "the newer residence district paid approximately twenty-five per cent more in taxes than the cost of city services received."[12] A few years earlier a study of a Cleveland slum found that the tax income from the district was $10.12 per capita whereas the public expenditure in the area amounted to $61.22 per person. "In other words," the study concluded, "the city of Cleveland subsidized each man, woman and child in this area to an amount of $51.10," which seemed to be "a rather large subsidy for the privilege of maintaining a slum area."[13] Throughout the country surveys computed the cost of slum dwellings to the municipal government, and everywhere the answer was the same. Blighted neighborhoods were a burden on the public treasury and could eventually doom the city to bankruptcy. Thus the central city needed new middle-class housing to boost a property tax base that was declining because of the depreciation of vast tracts of aged buildings.

Critics of decentralization not only recognized the impending drain on the city coffers, they also regretted the siphoning off of leadership talent. As the "best" people moved beyond the municipal limits, central cities lost the human resources that seemed necessary for civic improvement. A spokesman for the Chicago Association of Commerce warned of the "withdrawal from the city of many of the brains and voices best suited to help it help itself."[14] Likewise, a student of metropolitan Cleveland observed that "the lack of trained and efficient officials in the administration of urban affairs is also intensified by the migration of the more competent into the suburbs."[15] A Cincinnati businessman reiterated this sentiment when he claimed that "less and less of the better elements of the population . . . are living in the city proper, so that the political aspects of the older city are becoming dangerous to the ideals of good government."[16] If the central city lost its middle-class population, then the venal political bosses who based their machines on lower-class support would supposedly become even more powerful, and the political hacks in city hall would become even more numerous. To middle-class observers this would increase the problems of the central city and seriously hamper urban efforts at combating blight and obsolescence.

Some commentators even felt that suburban living made the wealthier classes callous and indifferent to the plight of the central city. According to one critic of Philadelphia suburbanites, "the most loyal upper-class Philadelphian will generally admit, freely and with a sort of perverse pride, that the city itself is only a necessary evil, incident to the pursuit of the more gracious life along the [suburban] Main Line."[17] Moreover, these uncaring suburbanites burdened the city treasury without paying their fair share of municipal expenses. Each workday suburban commuters crowded city streets, necessitating costly paving and widening projects and adding to police expenditures. Yet their expensive homes in outlying municipalities were not on the central-city tax rolls. Citing Boston as an example, one observer wrote disparagingly of "dwellers in parasitic dormitory cities" expecting much from the central city but giving little in return.[18] Likewise, the Saint Louis City Plan Commission argued that "the taxpayer of the central city is subsidizing the suburban dweller and that this subsidy continues to grow as the area of urbanization is expanded."[19] In 1937 the federal government's National Resources Committee expressed the mounting fears of many urban experts when it argued that no community "can long remain a sound functioning organism, if those . . . who gain the greatest benefits from it, escape from most of the obligations communal life imposes, and if those who obtain the least . . . amenities of life are left to bear the brunt of civic responsibility and taxation."[20]

Especially exasperating to those who perceived the dangers of decentralization were the roles of the federal government and private lending institutions in encouraging migration to the suburbs. In 1934 Congress had created the Federal Housing Administration (FHA) to insure low-interest, long-term mortgages, thereby encouraging lenders to extend more generous terms to prospective home buyers. If the buyer defaulted on an FHA-insured mortgage, then the FHA had to reimburse the lender for the loss. The administrators of the FHA, however, did not intend to lose money by insuring mortgages on risky properties, and they generally defined risky properties as those in older central-city neighborhoods endangered by blight. Thus the FHA encouraged the purchase of new homes in the suburbs but discouraged investment in central-city neighborhoods.[21] Moreover, private lending institutions usually adopted the same policy, preferring safe loans in the suburbs to possible defaults in the inner city.

In 1940 such policies were no secret to the business community nor to urban planners. *Business Week* observed that federal agencies "seemed resigned to the internal decay of the cities" and reported that the FHA had blacked out as ineligible for mortgage insurance "approximately 50% of Detroit and 33% of Chicago."[22] Planner Harland Bartholomew criticized the FHA for adopting a policy of "abandonment of the older slum districts and, also, of practically all the blighted districts." He argued that this had "the effect of accelerating decentralization and of undermining the values of property in three-fourths of the main body of the city." Though Bartholomew suggested a plan whereby 80 percent of FHA mortgage money would be allocated to the slums and blighted neighborhoods and 20 percent to the suburbs, officials in Washington paid little heed.[23] Instead, they continued to subsidize outward migration.

By 1940, then, urban leaders were fully alerted to the possible dire consequences of the decentralization of population and believed that the suburban trend would continue. If the central city was to hold its preeminent position in metropolitan America, it now had to compete with the suburbs as a place of residence. This was the challenge of the coming years.

The Specter of Commercial Decline

Even more threatening than residential migration was the likelihood of future commercial decline in the central city. Municipal treasuries needed the revenue from lucrative business properties to compensate for the deficit incurred in servicing tax-poor residential slums. If the owners of factories, stores, and office towers continued to find the central city a desirable location, then the ample property tax receipts from these businesses might well keep the aging municipalities solvent. Thus commerce might prove the needed anchor to keep the city safe and sound while middle-class residents drifted off to suburbia.

Unfortunately for central-city leaders, by the late 1930s and early 1940s there were few signs of commercial vitality in the older urban hubs. In fact, commercial decline seemed to be marching lockstep with residential decline. The central business districts were growing increasingly shabby, and traffic clogged their narrow thoroughfares. Lack of necessary capital during the Depression decade kept many factory owners from moving out of the central city and building new plants, but the growing reliance on truck transport and the emerging preference for expansive single-story facilities made the highways and wide-open spaces of suburbia seem increasingly attractive. By the close of the 1930s the prospects for marked commercial growth in Boston, Buffalo, Pittsburgh, and Cleveland were no brighter than the prospects for rapid population increase.

The downtown business district was especially vital to the future of the central city. With its soaring skyscrapers and massive department stores, it symbolized the wealth, excitement, and opportunity of urban life. More tangibly, its tax revenues kept the city operating. Though it generally encompassed only 1 percent or 2 percent of the city's area, the downtown accounted for anywhere from 12 percent to 20 percent of the city's total assessed valuation. In one city after another it was a golden asset that subsidized many of the other neighborhoods. For example, Saint Louis's central business district paid two and a half times more in taxes than it cost in municipal services.[24]

This valuable asset to the municipal treasury, however, seemed to be in danger. Between 1930 and 1940 the assessed valuation of the Saint Louis business district dropped $46 million, or 28 percent, whereas the valuation of the city as a whole fell only 19 percent. Likewise, from 1936 to 1946 properties in downtown Pittsburgh, known proudly as the Golden Triangle, decreased in valuation 28 percent whereas the decline for the entire city was only 21 percent. Throughout the country the figures were similar: from 1931 to 1945 the assessed valuation of central Baltimore declined 34 percent; from 1935 to 1944 downtown Boston's taxable worth dropped 24 percent; between 1936 and 1945 the value of Detroit's central business district fell 15 percent.[25] Even during the economic upturn of the early 1940s, downtown valuations did not rebound to earlier levels. For example, the figure for Chicago's central business district dropped from $552 million in 1939 to approximately $481 million in 1947, a fall of 13 percent. During these same years, the figure for Chicago as a whole declined only 3 percent, and the county areas outside of the city increased 6 percent in assessed value.[26] In each of the older urban hubs the downtown seemed to be slipping faster than the remainder of the city, and the possible consequences of this trend for the municipal tax base were ominous.

Many observers commented on the unhappy fate of the formerly prosperous urban core. "A visitor touring downtown St. Louis," wrote one commentator in a national magazine, "is amazed at the desolation and desertion characterizing scores of blocks in the business district."[27] In *Nation's Business*, the usually boosterish publication of the United States Chamber of Commerce, a writer claimed that the same was true of other big cities, all of which were, "economically speaking, . . . rotting at the core." According to this dismal observer, "New York, Chicago, Philadelphia, Boston, St. Louis and others show unmistakable signs of advanced decay in those central sections which 35, 50, or 75 years ago were the hubs of much of their activity."[28] A Philadelphian summed up the sentiments of many when he noted that business leaders had "become increasingly aware that the central business districts have not been pro-gressing" but instead "retrogression is very much in evidence."[29]

Numerous statistics supported this contention. Between 1926 and 1937 the number of persons daily entering the Saint Louis downtown area by vehicle dropped to 233,800 from 272,300. Likewise, between 1927 and 1942 the number of persons arriving daily in Pittsburgh's Golden Tri-angle fell to 247,000 from 297,000. Similarly, those entering and leaving downtown Detroit and Philadelphia declined 15 percent and 11 percent, respectively, between the late 1920s and the end of the 1930s.[30] Hundreds of thousands of commuters were still jamming the transit lines and thor-oughfares leading to the central business districts of the older cities. But their numbers were beginning to thin, and the attraction of downtown as a place of employment and shopping was waning.

Still other grim portents also heightened the fears of downtown de-cline. Throughout the 1930s the office building vacancy rate had been high, peaking at 27 percent nationwide in 1933. By 1940 it still averaged 17 percent to 18 percent nationwide, and in sluggish Philadelphia the rate was 23 percent, in Boston 25 percent, and in moribund Saint Louis 29 percent.[31] The office buildings of downtown Saint Louis had twenty acres of unleased floor space, and a local newspaper reported that "21 mercan-tile, loft and miscellaneous structures, with a total of 119 floors," were "completely vacant."[32] With the exception of Rockefeller Center in New York City, there had been no construction starts on major office buildings in the older central cities since the early 1930s. In 1940 the office towers accenting the skyline of major American cities were ironic monuments to the contrast between appearance and reality in the metropolitan down-town. Though they symbolized business success and the commercial might of the city, floor after floor of the office structures stood empty.

Not only was downtown construction at a standstill, in many cities demolition seemed to be the wave of the future. Rather than pay taxes on empty buildings, many landlords during the 1930s chose to tear them down and convert the space to parking lots. In 1927 less than 9 percent of the lots in Detroit's downtown were vacant; ten years later almost 24 per-cent had no buildings on them. From 1936 through 1939, ninety-six downtown buildings were demolished in the Motor City, and by 1940, 107 of the 140 blocks in the central business district contained one or more vacant lots. Meanwhile, the number of privately owned downtown parking lots rose from 110, with a total capacity of 7,720 cars in 1927, to 265 lots holding 17,251 cars in 1933. And during the next seven years, the in-crease in parking spaces continued. In 1940 a national magazine observed that "ten years ago a search for vacant land in downtown Detroit would have gone largely unrewarded; . . . today in the same area, a similar search would be satisfied at almost every turn."[33]

Similarly, in downtown Philadelphia there were between 125 and 375 demolitions each year during the 1930s, and the percentage of the parcels being cleared for rebuilding gradually dropped during the decade, falling to only 9 percent in 1939. Moreover, according to one survey of downtown Philadelphia, a number of merchants viewed "with considerable alarm the increase in the number of parking lots, . . . a few of which occupy almost a city block, and that these parking lots have not been confined to the streets of lesser importance but have invaded the main business thoroughfares."[34]

In Philadelphia, Detroit, and throughout the nation more and more gaps appeared in the downtown streetscape. Once valuable properties on major avenues could no longer attract anyone to build on them, and they were relegated to the storage of idle automobiles. Detroit's Temple Theater, for many years the most successful vaudeville house in the city, fell to the wrecker's ball after only thirty-five years of use, and a parking lot took its place. New York City's famed Hippodrome Theater likewise gave way to a parking lot. Demolition and abandonment of downtown real estate, in the words of one observer, was "a fast spreading epidemic" and was "rapidly becoming Real Estate's No. 1 problem."[35]

Even though the number of parking lots was increasing, parking remained one of the most serious downtown problems, and many urban leaders believed that lack of adequate space for automobiles was a prime source of the perceived decline of the central business district. Whereas the number of persons daily entering downtown Philadelphia dropped 11 percent between 1928 and 1938, the number of passenger automobiles making the trip soared 52 percent.[36] Likewise, the number of persons arriving in downtown Detroit plummeted 30 percent between 1925 and 1936, but the number of cars entering the city's core increased 6 percent.[37] And 7 percent fewer persons converged on the Boston central business district in 1938 than in 1927, but the use of the automobile by downtown visitors and workers rose 47 percent.[38] Thus fewer people but more cars were making the journey downtown, worsening central-city traffic jams and heightening the competition for parking spaces. The traffic congestion and parking problems resulted, in turn, in still fewer downtown customers, exacerbating the downward spiral of business activity. Yet the onslaught of cars continued to mount, for commuters were abandoning the streetcar for the automobile faster than they were abandoning the downtown as a place of employment and shopping. Ironically, by 1940 there were fewer people and buildings in the central business district but more congestion.

Traffic was the chief complaint of downtown business interests, but a close second on the list of criticisms was inequitable taxation. Repeatedly in the late 1930s and early 1940s, leaders in the real estate industry claimed that municipal property taxes were speeding the decline of the central business district. Owing to the optimism and real estate speculation of the 1920s, downtown land values soared to unprecedented heights by 1929, and assessed valuations likewise rose markedly. With the onset of depression and the new glut in office space, however, the market value of downtown office structures plummeted more rapidly than that of residential property. Yet to the consternation of downtown property owners, the drop in assessed valuations usually did not keep pace with the decline in market values. Moreover, office buildings traditionally were assessed at a higher proportion of their sale price than were residences.

According to downtown real estate interests, the result was an overburdened central business district, carrying an inordinate tax bill while also suffering from the ill effects of the automobile. In a report on central Boston a distinguished appraiser complained that "the present combination of excessive valuations with the highest tax rate among the large cities of the United States is gradually sucking all the value out of downtown business property."[39] A member of the Philadelphia Real Estate Board claimed that the same was true in his city and argued that "unquestionably, the large proportion of the city taxes borne by the central city business properties . . . is one of the factors leading to decentralization."[40] In Detroit a leading realtor found that a drop of 50 percent in downtown rental receipts combined with a decrease of only 30 percent in taxes increased the proportion of rental income used to pay taxes from 14 percent in 1929 to 20 percent in 1940.[41] Such facts aroused little concern among the thousands of rank-and-file urban dwellers who did not own office buildings or department stores. But the real estate industry viewed grimly the evidence from Detroit, Philadelphia, and Boston. Prominent downtown business interests recognized that municipal governments needed to attract other tax-rich properties and develop new sources of revenue if the financial burden was to lift from the beleaguered central business district.

The statistics, however, all pointed to commercial decentralization, offering little solace to central-city business leaders. Central-city retailing, for example, was lagging seriously behind the outlying areas in rate of sales growth. As seen in table 2, in the New York, Chicago, Philadelphia, Detroit, and Cleveland metropolitan areas the percentage increase in

Table 2. Percentage of Increase in Retail Sales, 1935—1939

Metropolitan Area	Central City	Outside Central City
New York City	12.1	27.1
Chicago	26.8	45.3
Philadelphia	16.4	31.7
Detroit	22.4	50.0
Cleveland	18.9	42.0

Source: Leverett S. Lyon, "Economic Problems of American Cities," American Economic Review 32 (March 1942 Supplement):310.

suburban retail sales was approximately double that in the central cities. Throughout the 1930s and early 1940s, retail business in Manhattan, the nation's preeminent shopping district, remained sluggish, and the largest New York stores began to seek greater profits through establishment of suburban branches. In 1937 Peck and Peck founded a branch in Garden City in suburban Long Island, and the following year it opened a store in the posh Connecticut suburb of Greenwich. In 1941 Bonwit Teller sought to tap the lucrative Westchester County market by establishing a branch in suburban White Plains, and in 1942 Best and Company expanded into both northern Long Island and Westchester County when it opened stores in Manhasset, White Plains, and Bronxville. Whereas major New York City retailers founded only eight branch outlets from 1930 through 1936, from 1937 through 1942 they established twenty-four outlying stores.[42] If a shopper wanted to patronize Macy's, Gimbel's, or Bloomingdale's, he or she still had to go to the central city, for these retail giants had not yet moved to suburbia. Moreover, sprawling shopping centers were not yet a feature of the suburban landscape. But the decentralization of retailing had begun.

Even more advanced was the decentralization of manufacturing. Since the very beginning of the twentieth century, heavy manufacturing firms had sought to locate at outlying sites, drawing thousands of industrial workers away from the urban core. From 1899 to 1937 manufacturing employment in New York City rose 35 percent, but in the surrounding metropolitan district it had increased 100 percent.[43] New York retained its preeminence in such light industries as apparel manufacturing and printing, but in heavy industries the migration was marked. Between 1900 and 1933 the number of heavy-metal workers in the southern half of Manhattan had dropped by more than 50 percent, and Manhattan had lost all but five of its former sixty-five foundries.[44]

The Chicago Plan Commission claimed that "industrial decentralization began in earnest" in the Illinois metropolis when the Western Electric Company left the central city in 1903 and built a giant plant in suburban Cicero.[45] In 1910 the creation of the Clearing Industrial District just beyond the Chicago city limits gave new impetus to the outward migration of industry. This suburban trend in manufacturing accelerated during later decades, and in the five years before 1941 forty-three manufacturing plants employing 6,800 workers left Chicago for suburban sites whereas only eighteen firms, with 2,800 employees, located within the city limits.[46]

The pattern was the same in virtually all of the aging metropolitan areas in the northeastern United States. As shown in table 3, in eleven of these twelve older metropolitan districts the number of manufacturing employees in suburbia increased at a faster rate or decreased at a slower pace between 1929 and 1939 than the number of industrial workers within the central city. In the Baltimore area suburban employment soared 251 percent whereas the figure for the city itself dropped 10 percent. Similarly, in the Detroit area the suburban increase was 90 percent, and the central-city decline was 18 percent. Only in Cincinnati did the central city fare better than the suburbs. Elsewhere the economic depression of the 1930s took a much heavier toll on the aging urban core than on the

Table 3. Percentage of Change in Manufacturing Wage-Earner Employment, 1929–1939

Metropolitan Area	Central City	Outside Central City
New York City	−8.1	+2.0
Chicago	−11.2	+0.6
Philadelphia	−20.5	+3.9
Detroit	−17.7	+89.7
Boston	−23.9	−11.1
Pittsburgh	−29.1	−4.2
Cleveland	−23.6	+13.7
Saint Louis	−13.8	−10.4
Baltimore	−10.4	+251.3
Buffalo	−29.8	+4.4
Cincinnati	−17.0	−23.6
Minneapolis– Saint Paul	−28.1*	+1.6

Sources: *Fifteenth Census of the United States, Manufacturers: 1929* (Washington, D.C.: U.S. Government Printing Office, 1933); and *Sixteenth Census of the United States: 1940, Manufactures, 1939* (Washington, D.C.: U.S. Government Printing Office, 1942).
*Figure for both Minneapolis and Saint Paul.

younger and more resilient outlying suburban municipalities.

Moreover, the return to prosperity during World War II did not reverse the centrifugal trend. If anything, the outward migration of industry accelerated as new defense plants located on the metropolitan fringes. The giant Willow Run aircraft plant employing more than forty-two thousand workers was twenty-five miles from downtown Detroit, McDonnell Aircraft located its massive works far beyond the Saint Louis city limits in suburban Saint Louis County, and suburban Long Island was the site of the greatest airplane factories in the New York City area. The situation was similar in Chicago, where only three of the area's eight major war plants located within the central city. By 1944 the Chicago Plan Commission could report that the central city had become "the hub of a vast semicircle of huge manufacturing plants, most of which [were] located at varying distances outside the corporate rim of Chicago."[47]

Thus in the early 1940s the evidence of commercial decentralization was mounting, and no intelligent observer of urban America failed to note the signs of economic decline in the older central cities. The automobile and truck seemed to be forcing the downtown business district and central factory zones into obsolescence. And as centrally located properties depreciated in value, the municipal tax base shrank. Clearly, if this trend were to continue, the aging central cities would be in trouble. They needed tax-rich properties to support municipal services, for a marked increase in the existing tax rates did not seem feasible. Commercial real estate interests were already complaining loudly and bitterly about ruinous local taxes. The answer to the central city's problems appeared to be commercial revival. To many Americans this was essential for the future of the urban hub.

Responding to Decline

Faced with the symptoms of decline, civic leaders did not resign themselves to inevitable decay and deterioration. Instead, during the early 1940s urban Americans began to fashion the strategy for a grand assault on the forces that were sapping the vitality of the central city. In 1940 the *Saint Louis Post-Dispatch* editorialized, "People will live in St. Louis if St. Louis is made livable," and in the following years proposals for creating a livable city abounded.[48] Leaders in the aging central cities did not expect a return to the days of soaring population growth. Rather, they sought to stabilize the city and halt its downward course by making it an attractive place to live and to conduct business. The *Post-Dispatch* admitted that "St. Louis cannot expect to stop the migration to the county that has come with quick transportation," but "it can slacken that migration by checking its major cause, the spreading blight of the metropolitan center."[49] A Cleveland newspaper summed up the views of many when it observed: "Even if Cleveland is not to be a bigger city, it at least can become a far better city."[50]

To most urban leaders a better city was a physically rejuvenated city. Rather than sponsor programs that tampered with the metropolitan social structure or that redistributed wealth and power, planners, politicians, and the business community believed physical changes were the appropriate weapons against blight. Thus brick, mortar, and asphalt constituted the artillery in this initial offensive against the decline of the central cities. A renewed infrastructure would supposedly save the city from blight and limit the inroads of decentralization.

Leading the initial effort at revitalizing the older cities were central-city real estate interests. Residential neighborhood clubs, labor groups, and political party organizations did not spearhead the movement for renewal. In fact, in the early attack on urban decline their role was minimal or nonexistent. Instead, it was the real estate broker and those with large investments in commercial properties who were in the vanguard. No group had more to lose than the real estate interests if the perceived decline continued. Downtown properties were bringing prices lower than their assessed values, and commercial blight seemed to be robbing landlords of millions of dollars each year. If leaders of the real estate industry wanted to prevent central-city properties from spiraling downward in value, they felt that a program of improvements was necessary. Unless they took some action, their investments appeared doomed.

Recognizing this grim fact, in 1940 the Urban Land Institute, a nonprofit research corporation sponsored by the National Association of Real Estate Boards, began to examine closely the older American cities. The institute was dedicated to discovering the causes of urban decline and to prescribing cures for the malady. According to its statement of purpose, the organization was concerned "not only with means for assuring sound city growth but also with means for conserving values in our present business and residential areas and for opening the way toward sound reconstruction of those areas where decay is far advanced."[51] But it did not expect to solve the problem by itself. Instead, the leaders of the institute believed that the threat of decentralization demanded "action with scope enough to ease the transition and prevent huge unnecessary losses," which would require the "coordinated effort of business groups, owners of residential property, and governmental bodies."[52] This group of leading real estate figures from throughout the nation thus envisioned a joint public-private initiative to curb the consequences of debilitating decentralization.

Among the institute's first projects was a series of reports on downtown problems in a number of cities throughout the country. By September 1942 leading brokers and appraisers had completed surveys of the central business districts of Boston, Cincinnati, Detroit, Louisville, Milwaukee, New York, and Philadelphia.[53] Included in each report were proposals for reviving the downtown. Though these differed somewhat from city to city, a common denominator was the emphasis on traffic and parking. In the opinion of the nation's leading real estate brokers the automobile lay at the root of much central-city decay, and successful revitalization required the adaptation of the downtown business district to the new automotive age. Improved traffic circulation, more parking garages, and expressways feeding into the central business district seemed at least a partial answer to downtown problems. And it was clear that the real estate industry's revitalization program would encompass major improvements to accommodate the growing army of automobiles.[54]

Throughout the country a variety of local groups also shared the Urban Land Institute's concern for the future of the central city. In 1940 the Boston chapter of the American Institute of Architects proposed "a nonprofit, non-political, non-partisan private association" including representatives of various interest groups to study the approaching "crisis of ruinous deterioration."[55] In New York City the Merchants Association drafted an urban redevelopment bill and presented it to the state legislature. The measure proposed government incentives for large-scale private investment in urban redevelopment because, according to the association, it had "already become obvious that sufficient public funds [could not] be made available to do all of the necessary rehabilitation work."[56]

In 1940 a group of downtown businesspeople in Saint Louis began to meet informally to plan the rehabilitation of their central business district. Including the presidents of two of the largest downtown department stores and of one of the city's leading banks, this group retained Harland Bartholomew as a consultant in their incipient effort to revive central Saint Louis. Concerned Saint Louis leaders proposed such concrete improvements as more parking facilities, express highways, and new middle-income housing close to downtown.[57] In 1941 businesspeople on the north side of Saint Louis organized the Civic Committee on Conservation and Rehabilitation because of fears that the city was "on the decline at a speed that eventually will mean destruction, abandonment, bankruptcy and a ghost city." It too suggested more downtown parking and improved traffic flow as well as an easing of FHA restrictions on loans for the repair and construction of houses in run-down neighborhoods.[58]

That same year the Downtown Committee of Baltimore issued a report that spelled out measures necessary to achieve the group's goal of guaranteeing "the attraction of Downtown Baltimore for shopping, business and amusement—to the end that its economic usefulness and its value to the city will be preserved." This organization of prominent merchants, bankers, and property owners and managers proposed the standard list of new "parking terminals," building face-lifts, tax relief, and reforms to improve traffic circulation.[59] But in Philadelphia the Penn Athletic Club felt that such changes were not sufficient and opted for a policy of boosting local morale. Sponsoring "Talk Philadelphia Week," the club took the offensive against fifth columnists within the city who "sold short" their hometown, and club speakers exhorted the citizenry of the flagging metropolis to be "boosters and builder-uppers."[60]

Not only were business groups and boosters becoming increasingly concerned with curbing central-city decline, so were the private planning organizations in the older metropolises. With a membership drawn largely from the city's elite, these groups now lobbied for improved urban planning as a tool for excising blight. In March 1940 New York's Regional Plan Association helped sponsor a conference in support of the Merchants Association proposal for urban redevelopment.[61] The Buffalo City Planning Association likewise dreamed of a renewed city and discussed proposals for an ideal downtown of the future. The group's president expressed the views of worried Buffalo residents when he noted, "We must plan far ahead . . . to control or avoid decadence."[62]

Similarly, the publications of the Regional Association of Cleveland observed: "The movement of decentralization has already begun. How far will it go? How far ought it to go? How can we control it, for the greater benefit of all concerned?"[63] Imitating its regional planning counterpart in New York, the Cleveland group issued a series of reports and proposals on the creation of a better city, a city that would attract rather than repel people. Like the Saint Louis leaders, Cleveland's private planning organization proposed freeways "designed for the fast car of 1940" and inner-city housing projects serving as a "walk-to-work residence for white-collar workers" employed downtown.[64] Through such physical renewal the regional association hoped to successfully harness the forces of decentralization that were transforming Cleveland and every other major city.

By 1940, then, there was the beginning of a nationwide movement to revitalize the central city. Aware of the statistical signs of decline and unable to escape the obvious physical decay surrounding them, urban leaders were meeting and organizing for the purpose of studying what could be done. The private sector was becoming aroused and was confronting the public sector with demands for action. Physical rehabilitation through the construction of highways, garages, and inner-city middle-class housing ranked high on the agenda of the private groups, but all this meant millions of dollars in public investment.

After a decade of economic depression that had devastated many municipal treasuries, the leaders of local government were finally emerging from the fiscal doldrums and were now ready to consider seriously demands for physical renewal. During the 1930s, municipal leaders were forced to cope with declining tax revenues coupled with heavy interest payments on debts incurred in the 1920s for lavish public works programs. Further capital improvements had been out of the question unless funded by federal public works or relief agencies. By 1940, however, most major municipalities had backed off from the brink of bankruptcy and were reducing their bonded debt. Moreover, the war in Europe was stimulating an economic upturn in America and offering hope of increased tax revenues. Optimistic city officials also believed that prospects for continued aid from Washington were good. Therefore, the time had come for municipal governments to make plans for the rehabilitation of the central city.

Although most municipal governments were in a more promising financial position than they had been for a decade, big-city officials recognized that the long-term prognosis for fiscal health would not be good unless rebuilding began soon. At the close of 1940 New York City's planning commission reported, "A leveling off of population and declines in actual real estate values, with a simultaneous increase . . . in demand for city facilities and services, have created a grave situation never before experienced by the community." The commission observed that the city's current finances were "in excellent condition," but it warned that New York was faced "with exceptional difficulties in financing both its expense and capital budget requirements in the near and not-so-near future."[65] Similarly, the Saint Louis City Plan Commission claimed that central areas had to "be reconstructed if eventual municipal bankruptcy" was "to be avoided."[66] Just as blight and urban deterioration threatened downtown business interests, they endangered the solvency of those governments dependent on tax revenues from downtown. Thus it was increasingly clear that the downtown department store president and the big-city mayor were natural allies in the war on urban obsolescence. Municipal governments and real estate interests both had to start taking action if they were to preserve their financial positions. By 1940, mayors not only felt that they could finally act; they also realized that they had to act.

Responding to this imperative, a number of the aging central cities began drafting plans for new traffic arteries. For example, in June 1940 Mayor Maurice Tobin's Conference on Traffic, including representatives of twenty-four leading civic organizations, reported on its six-year, $20 million program for the construction of expressways in Boston. Basic to the plan was the conference's belief that "relief of downtown traffic congestion" was of "primary importance to the taxpayers of the entire city."[67] In conformity with this view the plan outlined a network of highways that, according to a Boston newspaper, would "take long-distance traffic off the Hub's narrow streets and . . . make the downtown section quickly accessible to the suburbs." This would supposedly be "a major step toward halting the decline in activity and the shrinkage of property values in the downtown area."[68] Moreover, the Off Street Parking and Terminals Committee of Mayor Tobin's Conference on Traffic recommended construction of municipal parking garages costing $8 million and accommodating three thousand cars.[69]

New York City's Mayor Fiorello La Guardia and Park Commissioner Robert Moses had already begun a system of limited-access parkways crisscrossing their metropolis, but they had miles more in the planning stages. Especially important to La Guardia and Moses was a proposed "Circumferential Parkway" ringing the city, and by 1941 construction was under way on the Brooklyn-Battery Tunnel, an essential, and expensive, link in this monumental expressway. Meanwhile, in February 1940 Chicago's commissioner of subways and superhighways presented detailed recommendations for a sixty-three-mile, $207 million expressway system. The plans called for four 8-lane depressed highways emanating from the central business district and a crosstown route cutting through the city's west side.[70]

Elsewhere city leaders were also beginning to loosen the municipal purse strings in order to improve the urban environment and upgrade the reputation of the older metropolises. Whereas traffic was the bane of Boston, a poor water supply had long embarrassed Philadelphia, seriously damaging the prestige of an aging city that could ill afford any further black marks on its record. Drawing its supply from the polluted Schuylkill and Delaware rivers, the city could make its water safe for consumption only by adding liberal quantities of chemicals. The result was a foul-tasting, malodorous liquid known locally as the "chlorine cocktail."[71] In 1940, however, the municipal leaders finally took action, winning approval from the voters for an $18 million bond issue to finance renovation of the water system. Not since 1929 had the bankrupt city won authorization for a loan, but now it seemed ready to make a new effort to improve urban life.

While Philadelphia was beginning to battle water pollution, Saint Louis was embarking on a crusade against befouled air. Heavy palls of smoke were commonplace in Saint Louis especially during the colder months, when thousands of furnaces burned bituminous coal. According to one local opponent of air pollution, on "black Tuesday," November 28, 1939, the city "was visited with the worst smoke pall that had ever been experienced. Visibility was reduced to a matter of a few feet. One could not see across the main thoroughfares."[72] Many Saint Louis residents regarded this air pollution as one of the chief causes of urban decline in the Missouri metropolis. When the census returns for 1940 reported a population loss in Saint Louis, the city's leading newspaper responded with a cartoon of billowing smokestacks captioned "Going Down in Smoke."[73] And the editorial page told readers that the flow of population to suburbia could be reversed "by ridding us of our smoke palls."[74] Moreover, Mayor Bernard Dickmann was confident that middle-class residents would choose to live in the inner city if the smoke were eliminated. According to His Honor, "When we solve the smoke problem, there would be no prettier place to live in the city than that."[75]

Seeking to revive Saint Louis by clearing it of smoke, in 1940 the city council passed a tough ordinance requiring those who burned smoky, high volatile fuel to use mechanical fuel-burning equipment, and those who did not employ such equipment could burn only smokeless fuel. In other words, the city outlawed the emission of heavy smoke by regulating the fuel and the equipment that could be used. Within a year the ordinance had proved so successful that it was winning national attention. According to a writer for the *Christian Science Monitor*, during the winter of 1940–41 in Saint Louis, "there were but 17 hours of thick smoke, a reduction of 85 per cent, and a drop from 610 to 186 hours of moderate smoke." Moreover, supposedly as a result of the cleansed atmosphere, "one hotel . . . had a 30 per cent increase in occupancy."[76] Some of those hotel rooms may have been occupied by eight visiting members of the Pittsburgh city council, who in February 1941 observed the effects of the Saint Louis smoke-control program. Mayor Dickmann told the visiting council members that sooty Pittsburgh could become clean as well, "if you have the courage of your convictions."[77] Rising to the mayor's challenge, in October 1941 the Pittsburgh lawmakers adopted their own smoke ordinance closely modeled on that of Saint Louis.

Thus by the fall of 1941 two of the grimiest of the older central cities were seeking to reverse the forces of decay and deterioration by ridding their atmosphere of smoke. Others were also eager to follow this lead. The Regional Association of Cleveland summed up the prevailing view when it argued that heavy soot-fall could drive out "population and enterprise, injuring land values and encouraging blight and slum conditions." The clearing of the skies could open up "the possibility of offering good living conditions downtown" that would "encourage the rebuilding of blighted residential areas, restoring land values, checking depreciation and increasing taxable values."[78] With smoke abatement the central cities could supposedly become as desirable a locale as the suburbs, providing a healthy environment free of filth.

Improvements in traffic circulation, water supply, and air quality all seemed necessary if the benighted central cities were going to survive the wave of decentralization. But some planners believed it was also necessary to reach down to the neighborhood level and build grass-roots bulwarks against blight and centrifugal migration. The federal Home Owners' Loan Corporation (HOLC) pioneered neighborhood conservation in the Waverly district of Baltimore. Waverly was an old inner-city neighborhood of thirty-nine blocks and seven thousand residents with four out of every five families owning their own homes. The HOLC program included three elements: first, the physical restoration of deteriorated housing; second, the drafting of a long-term neighborhood plan; and third, the creation of the Waverly Neighborhood Conservation League, a community organization dedicated to ensuring that the upgraded neighborhood did not once again deteriorate.[79] Promoters of the scheme claimed, "Just as the application of curative remedies will preserve the vigor and delay the eventual death of the human body, so can definite preventive measures be taken, in the case of the urban community, measurably to extend its period of usefulness and long postpone its final disintegration." Moreover, to replicate the slum-prevention measures applied in Waverly, the HOLC looked forward to "the establishment, in every large city, of a 'Department of Conservation' whose sole function it will be, by precept, example, and inspirational activity, to promote community stabilization projects in potentially and partially depreciated sections."[80]

Attracting considerable attention nationwide, the Waverly experiment was repeated in Chicago's Woodlawn neighborhood. With aid from the HOLC and the University of Chicago, whose campus was just north of the endangered neighborhood, the Chicago Plan Commission collected data on the condition of properties in the Woodlawn area and made recommendations for restoration or demolition. Moreover, as in Baltimore the goal was to activate the neighborhood to protect itself against the threat of blight.[81] To Chicago's planners, strong neighborhoods dedicated to self-preservation would supposedly brake the downward slide of the city as a whole.

Some districts, however, seemed unworthy of conservation and more deserving of demolition. As early as the late 1930s and early 1940s a number of cities were already planning the clearance and redevelopment of such tracts in the hope of bolstering urban fortunes. Following the passage of the Wagner-Steagall Housing Act in 1937, local governments had broken ground for thousands of public housing units on the site of former slums. Though this did not attract middle-class residents to the central city, at least it eliminated some of the most squalid remainders of residential decay.

But clearance for public housing was only part of the dream of a redeveloped city. By 1940 Saint Louis was clearing forty blocks of its downtown waterfront for a proposed national park commemorating westward expansion, and Pittsburgh was negotiating with the National Park Service for the creation of a park to replace ugly railroad yards and warehouses at the tip of the Golden Triangle, where the Allegheny and Monongahela rivers meet.[82] Moreover, in December of that year the Saint Louis City Plan Commission held its first forum on "Reconstruction and Rehabilitation of Central Urban Areas" with speakers from throughout the nation commenting on the prospects for urban redevelopment.[83] In Detroit, Mayor Edward Jeffries appointed the Mayor's Blight Committee to investigate the possibility of reclamation in the Motor City, and at the mayor's behest the City Plan Commission prepared a brochure encouraging private housing developers to invest in the reconstruction of the inner city.[84]

Meanwhile, Boston was mapping especially extensive plans for redeveloping and renovating its aging neighborhoods. At the request of the City Planning Board, in 1940 Mayor Tobin appointed a seventeen-member Advisory Committee on Community Rehabilitation, including delegates representing the Chamber of Commerce, organized labor, social welfare agencies, two life insurance companies, two real estate exchanges, the local housing association, and the professional societies of architects and landscape architects. Together with the City Planning Board this committee embarked on a "study of depreciated areas," "for the purpose of finding methods by which tremendous losses in real estate values may be recaptured, especially in areas close to the downtown district."[85] By the beginning of 1941 the board and committee had agreed to pursue detailed investigations of South Boston, the South End, and the West End, and they had adopted a "working definition of rehabilitation" that included "the demolition of buildings, street replanning and the construction of new buildings, as well as repairs and remodelling."[86]

As in other cities a basic goal was to stem the tide of decentralization, and the Boston planners, like their counterparts throughout the country, believed that this could be accomplished if Boston offered "within the center neighborhood environments which attempt to capture some of the attractions which pull people to the suburbs." This would be achieved "by providing adequate open space for recreation, rehabilitation of the buildings, replanning of the street pattern to obtain freedom from heavy traffic dangers and lessening the nuisance of smoke, dirt and noise."[87] Here was a formula for supposed success that was basic to the thinking of the pioneer redevelopers and that influenced plans for urban revitalization for the next thirty years. A revitalized city would offer more open space, better highways, and a cleaner life. This was the lure that suburbia offered, and now Boston and the other central cities had to fight fire with fire and become more like suburbia.

Especially encouraging to planners and boosters in Boston, Detroit, Saint Louis, and elsewhere was the passage of a series of state redevelopment laws in the early 1940s. In April 1941 the Merchants Association's urban redevelopment law passed the New York legislature. The following July, Illinois lawmakers enacted a Neighborhood Redevelopment Corporation Law originally sponsored by the Chicago building industry. And that same year the Michigan legislature adopted an urban redevelopment law modeled after the New York statute but drafted by the Detroit City Plan Commission and the Corporation Counsel.[88] Each measure authorized public aid to private corporations willing to invest in the reconstruction of the urban core. If the plans of a private corporation won the city's approval and the developer already had obtained more than half of the property necessary for the redevelopment project, then the private party would be able to exercise the power of eminent domain and condemn the remainder of the holdings in the project site. Thus recalcitrant slumlords could not block the rebuilding of decayed areas by refusing to sell their properties.

The New York law also authorized cities to exempt from local real estate taxes for ten years any increase in the value of the property improved by the developer. For a decade the developer's taxes would be assessed on the basis of the valuation at the time of purchase, not the actual value following redevelopment. During this period of tax limitation, however, the redevelopment corporation could not pay dividends totaling more than 5 percent of the development costs minus the interest payments. The New York law was not intended to appeal to speculators interested primarily in the prospect of quick, tax-exempt profits. Instead, the

New York, Illinois, and Michigan statutes were supposed to lure private enterprise into a partnership with the public sector in a serious assault on the decline of the central city.

Municipal leaders proved eager to exploit their newly gained authority and quickly set to work to publicize the redevelopment laws. Mayor La Guardia began a hard-sell campaign to win the cooperation of insurance companies with money to invest. Detroit's Mayor Jeffries also appealed to insurance companies, and by 1942 the Detroit City Plan Commission had prepared a proposal for rebuilding an 111-acre site near downtown and had submitted it to interested investors.[89] One week before the legislators in Springfield even passed the Illinois law, the Chicago Plan Commission had approved the outline of a proposed clearance and redevelopment program. Moreover, by October 1941 the commission had already published a booklet entitled *Rebuilding Old Chicago* describing the new law, the economics of redevelopment, and the accepted principles of neighborhood planning. Located in a Near South Side slum area, the Illinois Institute of Technology promptly requested the plan commission to study the possibility of redevelopment in its environs.[90] According to a national magazine, the new state laws gave private enterprise "the long-awaited green light to slum clearance," and urban leaders like Jeffries and La Guardia wanted to make sure that the business community saw the signal and started moving.[91]

During 1940 and 1941, then, the combatants in the war on urban decline were drafting their initial strategy. Leaders in the real estate industry working through the Urban Land Institute were investigating how to save their downtown investments. Other private parties were likewise considering how best to boost their cities, and municipal leaders and planning commissions were taking the first steps in an effort to make the central city a more attractive environment for living and working. By the summer of 1941 three of the states with the largest urban populations had also authorized city governments to join with private enterprise in the reconstruction of decaying areas. Ideas for urban rehabilitation abounded, and planners, business leaders, and politicians seemed ready to turn their aging cities around.

In December 1941, however, all plans for reconstructing the city were shelved. America's entry into World War II meant that defense efforts took top priority. Construction materials and manpower had to be diverted to the task of defeating the armies of Germany and Japan; by comparison, the forces of urban blight and decay seemed unimportant. Thus Boston did not build its traffic arteries in the early 1940s; construction of the Brooklyn-Battery Tunnel was halted; as late as 1946 only $7 million of the authorized $18 million of Philadelphia water bonds had been issued; Pittsburgh's city council suspended enforcement of the new smoke ordinance until war's end; Chicago's Woodlawn neighborhood continued to deteriorate; and city governments were unable to implement the new redevelopment laws. Schemes for curbing decentralization and thwarting blight were placed on hold, and the long-expected rehabilitation of the older central cities was delayed for at least four years.

In fact, during the war years, cities could do little but maintain existing services. Even repairs of streets and sewers were undertaken only if absolutely necessary. City officials and concerned citizens, however, did make plans for the future, and the drafting of postwar schemes for renewal and reconstruction was to occupy the time of many planners and scores of bureaucrats in the various city agencies. In one major city after another, municipal leaders used the wartime lull to prepare lists of improvements to be realized in the postwar era. Public officials in Washington and the state capitals warned of the need to plan for demobilization and the years following, and most of the older central cities responded to this advice. In 1944 Cleveland's planning commission summed up the views of many civic leaders when it observed that "now is the time to prepare for prompt post-war action, not only to remake the City's rotted core and improve unspeakably bad housing which threaten municipal bankruptcy, but also to set the stage for a vast volume of post-war private construction activity."[92]

New York City's Mayor La Guardia led the way in preparing for the return to peace. In September 1941, two months before the attack on Pearl Harbor, the foresighted mayor directed his city planning commission to draft a program of public works to be ready for construction following the war. Moreover, the 1942 city budget allocated funds for the acquisition of building sites for future public works and money to finance the drafting of preliminary plans as well as detailed blueprints. As of May 1942 the New York City Planning Commission had already compiled a long list of desired projects costing a total of $628 million, but by the close of the war the proposed postwar program had ballooned to $1,190 million.[93] Meanwhile, the city's civil servants set to work on drawings and specifications. At the beginning of October 1945, plans for 29 percent of the projects were complete, and the city was in the process of finishing blueprints for another 54 percent.[94] Throughout the four years of war, then, city officials, aided by paid consultants, identified thousands of needed projects, selected sites, and prepared working plans for an expected binge of postwar building.

La Guardia gave two reasons for this large-scale program of postwar preparation. According to New York City's chief executive, municipalities needed to create "a reservoir of public works to provide employment immediately after the war." Remembering the tragedy of the recent economic depression, the mayor predicted that the postwar "dislocation of industry" coupled with the "demobilization of millions of men from the armed forces" would produce "a picture just too terrible to contemplate."[95] Millions of veterans would supposedly be unemployed unless public projects were ready at war's end to take up the labor slack. But La Guardia admitted that the program was intended not only to ease hardships during the period of demobilization. Instead, it was also to "furnish the city and [his] successors for two or three succeeding administrations a complete, well-studied, well-rounded planned public improvement program."[96] In its effusive survey of the proposed projects published in 1945, the La Guardia administration expanded on this view, describing the postwar program as a means of transforming the city. "New York of Tomorrow, as envisioned by Mayor La Guardia," the administration's publicist wrote, "is to be a *new kind of city*—more beautiful, healthful and convenient; a more comfortable place in which to live, work and play."[97] Thus the postwar program was designed to create employment, but it was also intended to recreate the aging city.

The second largest city in the nation, Chicago, quickly followed New York's example, preparing postwar programs to combat the short-term problem of unemployment and to cure the long-term maladies of the urban environment. The Chicago Plan Commission reported that in compliance with the request of Mayor Edward Kelly it began "planning for peace by preparing . . . a 'shelf' of essential public works" so that the city could be ready "to put the thousands released from war positions back to work on improvements such as water and sewer systems, schools, streets, bridges, airports, recreational facilities, railroad improvements, subways, and housing." Moreover, this "long-range program for Chicago's future" was to conform to the emerging master plan that the commission had been developing for the city since 1939. In fact, during World War II, many of the older cities were drafting master plans that were supposed to serve as blueprints for future urban development and that plotted the public improvements needed for the coming generation. According to the Chicago commission, the master plan and long-range public works scheme together would allow the Windy City to "arrive at the end of the war with a comprehensive development program for the next twenty-five to fifty years" and ensure the "orderly and effective creation of a better Chicago in which to live and work."[98]

Other major cities were engaged in much the same effort. The Detroit

City Plan Commission prepared a public works program and a new master plan that together would cushion postwar unemployment and lay the groundwork for a renewed metropolis. By the close of 1943 the Motor City had a reserve list of programs costing an estimated $556 million that could be completed when funding was available.[99] Likewise, Cincinnati's Joint Improvement Program Committee compiled a list of projects estimated to cost $145 million, and at the same time the city planning commission was creating an updated master plan of the city to guide development in the postwar era.[100] Minneapolis relied on its Postwar Progress Committee to draft an agenda of desirable projects, whereas in December 1942 Saint Louis city planners summed up their proposals in a report entitled *Saint Louis after World War II*. This booklet specifically suggested "what should be done after the present war to solve the greatest economic and social problem that confronts St. Louis," the problem of urban decay and blight.[101]

Only a month after the attack on Pearl Harbor, Boston's Mayor Tobin spoke of the "men discharged from the service" when the war ended who would "create a problem of overwhelming magnitude and peril to our internal economy." Thus he warned the city council that "it would be flirting with economic disaster" not to prepare a program of public improvements to be "ready for immediate adoption at the termination of the war."[102] Even the city council of lethargic Philadelphia appropriated $700,000 for the planning commission to make specifications and blueprints for a citywide scheme of capital improvements that, according to a local planning group, would be ready "for the rebuilding era" that would probably follow the war.[103]

The Cleveland City Planning Commission offered an especially comprehensive scheme for placing itself in "a position to strike powerful blows at two of its greatest postwar problems—the achievement of high-level employment, and the development of its blighted areas into livable, economically sound neighborhoods."[104] The commission classified all residential areas within a four-mile radius of the center of the city, specifying some as zones requiring only protective measures, others as appropriate for neighborhood conservation, still other more deteriorated districts as suitable for conservation and partial clearance, and the worst areas as targets for total clearance and redevelopment. Moreover, the commission proceeded with two pilot studies, one in a conservation neighborhood and the other in a redevelopment area.[105]

Basic to the Cleveland approach was participation by neighborhood residents. In 1944, in words that anticipated fashionable planning thought of the 1970s, a Cleveland planner wrote: "Our effort is to discover what the community wants and to help it make its own plans and work for their realization, with the Commission acting as a technical adviser and liaison between the community and the local government." To realize this goal the commission tried if possible "to use existing local groups" and suggested that civilian defense organizations that had "begun to run out of things to do" could be reactivated as neighborhood conservation councils.[106] Thus in Cleveland the postwar ideal included not only massive public works but also a full-scale mobilization of the populace for the salvation of their neighborhoods.

Each of the varied plans for postwar development in the older central cities included a broad range of programs affecting every area of the city. For example, in New York City's program as revised in October 1942, the Board of Education won the largest share of the proposed capital improvements, receiving $118 million for school construction, but the Board of Transportation garnered $89 million for highways and mass transit, and the planning commission budgeted $83 million for sewage disposal, $81 million for hospitals, and $42 million for parks.[107] In fact, every department was to receive a share of the capital funds under the proposed program, and every borough and neighborhood would benefit. By October 1942 the office of the borough president of Manhattan had won $64 million in projects, a larger slice of the upcoming bonanza than any other borough executive. But the borough presidents of Bronx, Brooklyn, and Queens each could look forward to $30 to 38 million in promised projects, and the least populous borough, Richmond, was allocated $8 million.[108] The borough presidents were in charge of local street and sewer improvements, and their capital allocations were largely for these purposes. But it was evident both from the borough allotments and from the maps showing the location of promised parks, playgrounds, fire stations, and health centers that New York City was not concentrating its postwar program in any one department or in any one area of the city. Similarly, of the $947 million in proposed improvements for postwar Chicago, 18 percent was for mass transit and another 18 percent for expressways, 14 percent was for water supply, 12 percent for sewerage, and 8 percent for parks. Moreover, as in New York there was a liberal sprinkling of new schools, playgrounds, and sewer improvements in every geographic subdivision of the city.[109]

In each city that drafted a master plan or a long-range program of capital improvements the same pattern prevailed. Every department and district was to share in the largesse. The city government did not intend to invest only in downtown improvements or in visionary schemes to clear the slums. Instead, capital improvement budgets during and after the war attempted to give something to everybody. Any program of reconstruction or massive public improvements was to be wide ranging and diversified both in terms of the types of projects and their locations.

This pattern reflected the political realities of capital budgeting. The process began at the department level with each department deciding upon possible projects and then sending its request to the city planning commission or capital improvements committee. Thus each department was represented in the process, and each would expect a share of the benefits. Moreover, those department heads with the most clout were able to skew the budget allocations in their agencies' direction. After the planning commission or capital improvement committee drew up a preliminary budget, this budget had to win the approval of the city council. Most city councils consisted of representatives elected by wards who were expected to further the interests of their geographical subdivision of the city. In New York City the Board of Estimate, consisting of the mayor, comptroller, and the borough presidents, had veto power over the capital improvements budget, ensuring that each borough had a voice in the adoption of public works projects. Even if the council was not elected by wards, council members often identified informally with certain sections of the city or with ethnic groups concentrated in particular neighborhoods. Hence, each district within the city had to receive its fair share of proposed capital improvements if the budget was to win approval.

In most cities the voters also had to ratify bond issues needed to finance capital projects. On election day proposed capital improvements had to have broad enough appeal to elicit the support of at least a majority of the citizenry. The city could not use its credit exclusively for schemes that appealed only to downtown real estate interests. Rather, each postwar public works package had to placate as many interests as possible. It had to accommodate the various municipal departments and the bureaucrats in city hall; it had to appeal to the city council; and it had to prove attractive to the general electorate. This was a political fact of life that was to shape the postwar program of capital improvements. Moreover, this remained a factor in public improvement initiatives throughout the postwar era. Though critics of urban revitalization schemes often complained of the undue attention given downtown development, capital funding was never as concentrated in the central business district as they claimed. Public investment may have been most noticeable downtown, but politicians could never afford to ignore the remainder of the city.

By 1945 many city leaders were hopeful that all of the various segments of the body politic were rallying behind the proposed postwar projects. In August 1944 Saint Louis voters approved by more than a two-thirds margin a bond issue package of $43.5 million that was to finance postwar airport construction, waterworks and sewer improvements, and a broad array of lesser projects. According to Mayor Aloys P. Kaufmann, passage of the bond issue meant: "When our service men lay down their victorious arms they may pick up the implements of peacetime construction and begin the building of a greater city."[110] Three months later, in November 1944, Cincinnati voters likewise endorsed by an overwhelming majority a $41 million bond issue that supporters had billed as a program for "jobs and progress."[111] At the same time, Baltimore's electorate was approving a $10 million loan for highway construction.[112]

In slumbering Philadelphia there also were some stirrings of new life. A group of concerned leaders working through the Citizens' Council on City Planning held monthly meetings where they discussed possible postwar projects and considered downtown planning problems. Responding to some servicemen's suggestions for postwar improvements, the Citizens' Council sounded a typically activist note, arguing, "We must all overcome the inertia of complaisance and short vision," and "We must blast our way into a clean new future."[113] To the west, Pittsburgh's elite felt similarly, organizing in 1943 the Allegheny Conference on Post War Community Planning, which was dedicated to drawing the guidelines for a revival of the venerable and somewhat shabby steel capital.[114]

Yet during the war years, there were already signs that the battle for a new city might prove more difficult to win than the fight against the Axis. Though the ambitious postwar plans generally elicited a sense of civic euphoria in the central cities, when it came to preparing for actual implementation, the obstacles were becoming apparent. For example, in 1944–45 the Baltimore city council proved less than obliging when faced with plans drafted by New York's Robert Moses for a freeway cutting through the city's heart. A blue-ribbon committee selected to study the highway question reported, "Unless we are ready to see taxable values in the center of Baltimore continue to decline . . . , we have in our opinion no choice but to . . . see that a through-city route is built."[115]

The *Baltimore Sun* and the Downtown Committee wholeheartedly endorsed this conclusion, but some city council members had doubts. They challenged the scheme as excessively costly and suggested that less expensive street improvements might prove just as effective in solving the city's traffic problems. According to one municipal lawmaker, the council had the responsibility to protect citizens "against the levying of excessive taxes for building a fantastic project" that would "require them and their children and their grandchildren many years to pay for."[116] Council members also protested the displacement of twenty thousand residents by the proposed expressway. When questioning the chairman of the blue-ribbon committee, a council member complained of the destruction of "thousands of buildings, apartment houses, hotels, and lots of fine little homes" that might not be "good enough for some members of [the] Committee" but were "palaces to people occupying them."[117] The Baltimore expressway controversy would continue for more than thirty years, but these early shots in the battle warned of problems ahead. Drawing up lists of improvements was a relatively simple task; Baltimore leaders already knew that realizing these improvements was going to be a monumental job.

As yet, however, implementation remained largely a question for the future. The early 1940s was an era of proposals rather than results. After a decade of depression and four years of war, urban leaders were preparing to make up for lost time and drawing up ambitious plans to invest in public improvements necessary to protect the older central cities from the worst effects of blight and decentralization. Throughout the nation rehabilitation schemes were on the shelf, and city officials, business chiefs, and ordinary voters were mobilizing for a new battle after the last guns had been fired against the Japanese and the Germans. The goal of this postwar battle would be the modernization of the central city, the creation of a physical environment that might reverse the perceived tendency toward decay and decline.

Setting the Stage

During the decade before 1945, urban planners, municipal officials, central-city business leaders, and concerned citizens had perceived what they interpreted to be the incipient decline of the urban core. In their minds the dual villains responsible for this decline were decentralization and blight. Spurred on by a growing devotion to the automobile, decentralization drew residents and business from the older central cities, and blight followed closely behind destroying property values and tarnishing the reputation of the metropolis.

The solution most often proposed for this problem was the physical renewal of the city. New central-city expressways and parking garages would adapt the urban core to the automobile age; airports would preserve the role of New York City, Chicago, and Saint Louis as centers of transportation; middle-class housing in the inner city would ensure a ready supply of consumers for downtown retailers; and air pollution controls, sewage disposal plants, and new waterworks would eliminate environmental blight destructive to central-city prestige and commerce. Through such reforms the central city would also acquire some of the attractive attributes of suburban communities and thus trim suburbia's competitive advantage. Moreover, these projects would supposedly bolster the interests of the city's leading business figures and its chief public officials. Downtown department store owners and landlords would profit from improved access to the central business district and better parking facilities. Mayors could take political credit for rebuilding their cities while also shoring up the municipal tax base, and city planners and engineers could realize their dreams of a metropolis that conformed to the latest principles of their professions.

In the years before the attack on Pearl Harbor, private interest groups and city governments both had begun consideration of how specifically to counter the debilitating forces that were undermining the central city in its emerging competition with suburbia. World War II prevented the implementation of schemes for capital investment, but the interlude of war did give planners, politicians, and business people a chance to make copious plans for the future. These proposals included most of the elements of later revitalization schemes. New highways, slum clearance, parking facilities, neighborhood rehabilitation, and even participatory planning as espoused by Cleveland planners were all on the wish list for the postwar world. By 1945 the stage was set for urban America's campaign to renew the cities.

CHAPTER TWO ○ **Laying the Foundations for Renaissance**

With the coming of peace in August 1945, many civic leaders believed that a new era of opportunity was dawning for the nation's central cities. Postponed plans for rejuvenation could now be revived, and after a decade of debilitating economic depression and four years of war, the forward progress of urban America could be resumed. Blueprints for change lined the shelves and filing cabinets of city hall. Now was the long-awaited day of implementation.

The postwar era, however, did not neatly conform to the expectations of municipal officials, planners, and business leaders. There was no postwar economic depression nor any need for public works projects to take up the labor slack resulting from demobilization. Instead, the private sector shifted to the production of much-needed consumer goods, and wartime savings flowed abundantly into the cash registers of America's merchants. Labor problems did arise but in the form of labor unrest rather than labor surplus. City governments did not have to cope with deprived masses begging for employment; they had to cajole disgruntled employees who were demanding hospitalization, shorter work hours, and 20 percent to 30 percent pay raises. During the war, municipal wages had not kept pace with the rising cost of living, and in 1945 and 1946 city employees intended to dip deeply into municipal coffers as restitution for past sacrifices. One result of higher wages in both the private and public sectors was persistent inflation that undermined municipal buying power and raised doubts about the possibility of massive public construction schemes. Moreover, despite the exhortations of such dogged local officials as New York's Mayor La

Guardia, the federal government did not throw open its treasury and offer generously to fund the billion-dollar municipal programs for urban rejuvenation.[1] By the 1950s some federal money was available for local slum clearance, road building, and municipal airports, but in the immediate aftermath of World War II, Washington offered only limited help in realizing public works programs intended to cushion the expected harsh consequences of demobilization.

Expectations of unemployment and massive federal public works spending proved erroneous, but wartime planners were correct in anticipating a continued threat from blight and decentralization. Though each of the older central cities gained population between 1940 and 1950, the outward migration of the middle class accelerated, draining the urban hub of many of its white-collar inhabitants. By the 1950s the forces of decentralization were so strong that the aging central cities were again recording net losses in population. Newcomers were migrating to the urban centers, but these recent arrivals were impoverished blacks, Appalachian whites, and Puerto Ricans whose economic distress only added to the problems of New York, Cleveland, Detroit, and Chicago. Meanwhile, downtown retail sales lagged, and except in New York City and Pittsburgh, office building construction was virtually nonexistent until the mid-1950s. Thus the prewar phenomena of central-city decay and obsolescence persisted in the late 1940s and the 1950s, giving added urgency to cries for an urban rebirth.

To effectively respond to this need for revitalization, a new generation of business and municipal leaders had to lay the foundation for renaissance. They had to create private organizations dedicated to massing the clout of big business behind renewal efforts. They had to cleanse city hall of hacks and install a new breed of renaissance officials led by mayors devoted to a fresh vision of the city. And they had to build a solid fiscal base for urban redevelopment through able management of the municipal debt, creation of new sources of city revenue, and pressure on Washington and state legislatures for more funds. In other words, a prerequisite for renewal was a mobilized private sector, an energetic leadership in city hall, and a firm financial foundation. With these established, the older central cities could supposedly proceed toward the goal of revitalization.

Private Molders of the Urban Renaissance

Just as downtown business leaders had pioneered the revitalization effort immediately before World War II, in the late 1940s and the 1950s they were one of the principal engines of the renewal crusade. In one city after another they organized to ensure something was done to halt the detrimental effects of blight and decentralization, for in their minds drastic action was necessary. Their postwar diagnosis of the central city was just as grim as their gloomy predictions of the prewar years. The situation, if anything, was growing worse, and as leaders of the community it seemed natural to them that they should be prominent in sparking renewal. Thus they were ready to join with city officials and any other concerned citizens in a joint public-private initiative to save the aging metropolises.

Some commentators would write of the public-private partnerships in the older central cities during the postwar decades as if they were a new phenomenon. But from the beginning of American urban settlement business leaders had expected municipal cooperation in the boosting of local fortunes, whether through aid in attracting railroad lines in the nineteenth century or support for harbor projects or world's fairs in the twentieth century. Moreover, a sense of noblesse oblige and the desire for a good public image had traditionally encouraged business leaders to contribute money and energy to civic improvement schemes. City hall was expected to maintain a favorable business climate, and business chieftains were expected to raise the civic and cultural stature of the community. In postwar Pittsburgh, Saint Louis, and Baltimore, however, business needed to step up its commitment. Traditional boosterism and token generosity were not enough, for the central city appeared to need extraordinary aid from the corporate moguls.

The model for many of the private-sector organizations that developed in the late 1940s and the 1950s was Pittsburgh's Allegheny Conference on Community Development. With its reputation for soot, smoke, and little else, Pittsburgh seemed to be suffering from a classic case of urban decay. At the close of World War II corporate headquarters were purportedly planning to leave the city, and even the wife of the plutocratic Richard King Mellon, head of Pittsburgh's wealthiest clan, supposedly protested about returning to the grimy city after her husband's wartime sojourn in the armed forces.[2] Almost no one had anything kind to say about the city when the Allegheny Conference organized in 1943, and four years later *Fortune* concluded that the conference was possibly "Pittsburgh's last chance . . . to reverse the course of urban decay and industrial decline" and that it was "none too soon."[3]

No local organization represented greater wealth and corporate power than the Allegheny Conference. Not only did the group enjoy the patronage of Richard King Mellon, but its executive committee included the presidents or board chairmen of all the city's leading businesses. Moreover, at its founding the conference adopted the policy that members of this all-important executive committee had to participate personally in the meetings rather than act through lower-level corporate representatives. This rule ensured that the conference policymakers were figures who could make a commitment on the spot and not have to seek approval from some higher executive. When the presidents of U.S. Steel or Kaufmann's Department Store said their corporations would support an initiative, they were speaking with authority and the conference could count on their full backing. Only Mellon himself acted through representatives on the board, a prerogative that his unmatched wealth seemed to warrant. But he was loyal to the conference, using his formidable clout to secure compliance with the group's policies. Mellon not only controlled the Mellon Bank, but his family dominated Gulf Oil, Alcoa, Koppers, and Pittsburgh Consolidation Coal, four of the area's largest corporations, and he served as a director of scores of other firms.[4] As the chief bankroller of the Pennsylvania Republican party, the Mellon family could also ensure cooperation from a GOP administration in Harrisburg. No one could afford to ignore a telephone call from Richard King Mellon, and the Allegheny Conference was one of the chief beneficiaries of this fact of economic and political life.

None of the other older central cities could boast of a benevolent economic kingpin with the power of Mellon. But publicity about the Allegheny Conference stirred business leaders elsewhere to create imitations based on the Pittsburgh model. By the mid-1950s commentators throughout the nation were lauding environmental reforms and slum clearance projects in the steel capital, and the Pittsburgh Renaissance was the envy of other urban centers. If benighted Pittsburgh could give birth to a renaissance, then why not Cleveland, Baltimore, or Saint Louis? The secret of success seemed to be the Allegheny Conference, so the solution to ills elsewhere was to create local versions of the Pittsburgh organization.

For example, in the mid-1950s Baltimore's business elite followed the Pittsburgh lead. In 1954 a report of the Commission on Governmental Efficiency and Economy emphasized Baltimore's declining property tax base and warned of imminent disaster if no action were taken to reverse the trend. Responding to this dire prediction, developer James Rouse and some other prominent business leaders formed the Greater Baltimore Committee. The committee was intended to be an alliance of the chief executive officers of the one hundred largest firms in the Baltimore metropolitan area. As in the case of the Allegheny Conference executive committee, the members of the Greater Baltimore Committee could speak with authority for their corporations, committing them to action on the spot. Moreover, the same sense of emergency and the same belief in the need for immediate change underlay the creation of both the Baltimore committee and the Pittsburgh conference. In its statement of purpose the Greater Baltimore Committee observed: "Our watchword should be *action now* . . . We want sound planning, but we want action to implement the plans, and we want it now, not at some future time when we may not be around to see it."[5] Though the committee originally awarded freeway construction and harbor improvements highest priority, James Rouse was named to chair the Urban Renewal Subcommittee, which would be significant in promoting Baltimore's much-praised projects of downtown reconstruction.

Meanwhile, Saint Louis and Cleveland could claim their own versions of the Greater Baltimore Committee and the Allegheny Conference. In the early 1950s Saint Louis's mayor asked a group of the city's most prominent businesspeople to form Civic Progress, Inc., an organization dedicated to forcing action in the slumbering Missouri metropolis. The twenty-five members of this elite corps were the who's who of Saint Louis business and included the chief executives of Anheuser-Busch, Monsanto Chemical, McDonnell Aircraft, and Ralston-Purina as well as the owners of the two leading department stores and the presidents of the largest banks.[6] Together these moguls orchestrated the high-powered campaign to win approval for a $110.6 million bond issue intended to rebuild the aging city. Following this victory the Civic Progress member who acted as campaign chairman announced confidently: "Now we can move from a second-class city to a topflight community."[7]

The Cleveland Development Foundation hoped to achieve this same goal for its city. Inspired by the Allegheny Conference, in 1954 one hundred of Cleveland's largest corporations joined together to form the foundation. At its founding the group's sole purpose was "to advance urban development through joint leadership of Cleveland business," and to accomplish this end, the member corporations created a $2 million revolving fund and obtained pledges from five Cleveland banks to finance private investment in housing construction within the city.[8] Inner-city housing remained the focus of its attention during the 1950s, and as early as 1955 a government official claimed that the federal urban renewal bureaucracy was "hard pressed to keep up with the Foundation which [had] vitally aided municipal agencies to meet every deadline with the required voluminous paper work."[9]

As in Pittsburgh, Baltimore, and Saint Louis, the business elite of Cleveland seemed to be taking effective action to get its city off of dead center. The Allegheny Conference and its imitators regarded such dynamic efforts to stimulate the community and accelerate the engine of progress as essential. Business leaders had to forsake individualistic competition and unite in a common assault on the ills plaguing their city. In Cleveland the general manager of the May Company Department Store served with the president of Higbee's Department Store on the board of trustees of the Cleveland Development Foundation, joining with his mercantile foe in the common cause of urban revitalization. Similarly, Civic Progress included department store rivals Sidney Baer of Stix, Baer, and Fuller and Morton May of Famous-Barr, both recognizing the threat to downtown retailing that blight and decentralization posed. The united might of the monied elite was necessary to combat the enemies of the older central cities, and mobilization of these plutocratic recruits had to begin at once. This was the message of private revitalization groups throughout the Northeast and Midwest.

Though dominated by downtown businesspeople, the Allegheny Conference, the Greater Baltimore Committee, Civic Progress, Inc., and the Cleveland Development Foundation each were dedicated to revitalization throughout the central city. Other groups were forming, however, that were devoted specifically to the interests of the faltering central business district. Downtown retailers in some cities had organized even before the depression of the 1930s; for example, Chicago's State Street Council dated from 1927.[10] But plummeting sales figures and sluggish real estate values sparked the organization of a new wave of downtown groups in the 1950s. In 1954 J. Jefferson Miller, executive vice president of Baltimore's Hecht Company Department Store, heard that O'Neill's Department Store was closing. Responding to this latest sign of downtown Baltimore's sagging fortunes, Miller called the president of the Retail Merchants Association and warned him: "Look, time is running out. We'd better get started on an answer down here, or it's going to be impossible to catch up with the parade." The association president replied: "Okay, chairman, you have been selected as head of the committee to see what's going to be done about the downtown situation."[11] Thus was born the Committee for Downtown, which successfully urged the Greater Baltimore Committee to give higher priority to downtown renewal. During the following decade, the two groups and J. Jefferson Miller were to dominate the replanning of Baltimore's central business district.

Elsewhere downtown merchants saw the same signs of decay and responded similarly with new associations. For example, in 1955 Minneapolis business leaders organized the Downtown Council. Troubled by the blighting influence of an inner-city skid row zone, the council fought for demolition of this tawdry district. Moreover, Minneapolis's downtown group contracted for an economic survey of the central business district to discover what could be done to rejuvenate it. [12]

To the south Saint Louis business figures were stirred to action as well, forming Downtown in St. Louis, Inc., in 1958. The group's chairman described its mission as "a 'crusade' to renew downtown—to re-create it as an exciting, pleasant and accessible place for people—an area to which people will *want* to come to shop, to work, to live and to be entertained."[13] Toward this end Downtown in St. Louis lobbied for redevelopment of the core and improved parking and public transportation. Moreover, it sponsored an advertising blitz that spread the slogan "Downtown St. Louis Gives You *More*" to homes throughout the metropolitan area through newspapers, television, and radio.[14] It organized circus days, downtown sales days, and fashion festivals in the streets with models showing the latest styles. During the pre-Easter shopping season, it sent "four glamorous models, attired in furry, white bunny costumes," through the downtown streets to drum up business, and to cleanse the grimy core it "coordinated the program of downtown-wide pigeon and starling eradication, using the services of the Bird Repellent Company."[15]

Though the focus of the downtown groups was narrower than that of the Allegheny Conference and its ilk, the philosophy of cooperation in bailing out the sinking urban core was common to both types of organizations. The executive director of Downtown in St. Louis told his members that "more and more the great value of *collective* action is being realized" and commented on the growing belief that downtown interests could "do more by working *together* than they can possibly do working separately."[16] Moreover, the same sense of urgency prevailed. Complacency, self-satisfaction, and apathy were anathema to these boosters of renewal. "Action" was their favorite word.

The downtown organizations and the Allegheny Conference and its progeny were prime examples of the business activism that spurred revitalization campaigns in the late 1940s and the 1950s. These groups represented the economic elite and were intended to marshal the monied interests around the cause of rejuvenation. Other groups with a broader base, however, also lobbied for a program of revitalization and cooperated with corporate nabobs and city officials in their efforts to breathe life back into the central city. Though corporate cliques may have been leading organizers of the renewal cause, it was not their crusade alone. Groups claiming a more diverse constituency were also joining in the chorus calling for action.

In Philadelphia, for example, the Citizens' Council on City Planning was a key element in the coalition seeking rejuvenation of the Pennsylvania metropolis. Founded in 1943 "to facilitate citizen participation in city planning and to further the science of city planning in Philadelphia," as early as 1944 the council could claim sixty-four welfare, civic, and professional organizations on its membership rolls.[17] The Association of Philadelphia Settlements, Central Labor Union, City Business Club, North Penn Community Council, National Association for the Advancement of Colored People, and Inter-Racial Committee of Germantown were all among its members, and during the postwar era the Citizens' Council would welcome scores of other groups representing the diversity of interests in the City of Brotherly Love. The Greater Philadelphia Movement, the city's version of the Allegheny Conference, spoke for the business elite and was in the words of one local planner, "closer to the brass than the grass roots."[18] The Citizens' Council, in contrast, claimed a wider constituency, and though its most active participants never donned a blue collar, neither were they in the same class with Richard King Mellon. Instead, the director of planning of the Philadelphia Redevelopment Authority characterized them as "younger members of legal firms, architects, college professors, settlement-house directors, the second and third echelons of business executives, [and] advertising men."[19]

The Citizen's Council reviewed all proposals for capital improvements in the city and scrutinized every major planning initiative. Moreover, it organized town meetings so that neighborhood leaders could hear public officials explain planning policy and question the speakers from city hall. According to the council's executive director, the group sought "to provide the leaders of the interested community organizations with the latest factual information, and, conversely, to learn their observations and suggestions on the proposals."[20] Though it was a citizen's watchdog organization dedicated to grass-roots participation, it did not assume an adversarial stance toward bureaucrats in planning departments or "fat cats" in the Greater Philadelphia Movement. The Citizens' Council was a facilitator of the city's urban revitalization policy rather than a foe. Its leaders shared the renewal philosophy of the city's professional planners, and its executive director was senior redevelopment planner for the Philadelphia City Planning Commission. Its town meetings were intended to spread the gospel of modern planning and to educate neighborhood groups on the necessity of redevelopment and rehabilitation. In the words of one student of housing and renewal policy in Philadelphia, the Citizens' Council "became both a sounding board and an advertising agent for the planners' vision of the postwar city."[21]

Through its promotional efforts the council actually pioneered the cause of urban renewal. As early as 1947 an observer wrote that the group had agitated "the town to the point where people were talking seriously of 'the Renaissance.'"[22] That same year the Citizens' Council cosponsored the "Better Philadelphia Exhibition" at Gimbel's Department Store. Highlighting the exhibition was a scale model showing how the city center would look after the completion of a variety of redevelopment projects. The futuristic towers, airy open spaces, and broad, new traffic arteries all inspired thousands of visitors to support schemes of demolition and rebuilding.[23] The display seemed to demonstrate that Philadelphia could become better in the not-so-distant future if only the local electorate would rally around the modern notions of planning and redevelopment espoused by the Citizens' Council.

In 1957 the Citizens' Council expressed its basic outlook when commenting on a controversial redevelopment scheme. The group's newsletter observed that "the Citizens' Council will continue to encourage Urban Renewal with insistence that hardship to residents and businesses must be minimized in every way possible."[24] In other words, the council would work to protect grass-roots interests threatened by rebuilding schemes, but it would remain committed to the need for urban renewal. Throughout the 1950s the Citizens' Council had no doubts that the Philadelphia Redevelopment Authority and the Greater Philadelphia Movement were basically on the correct path in their pursuit of renaissance.

Taking the same stance was the Citizens' Planning and Housing Association (CPHA) of Baltimore. Created in 1941, the CPHA like its Philadelphia counterpart comprised a membership far broader than the Greater Baltimore Committee, including neighborhood, labor, and charitable organizations as well as chamber-of-commerce boosters. In 1954 its executive secretary explained that although CPHA had "a good business representation," it did not "speak for the business community."[25] In other words, it claimed to reach beyond the "brass roots" to the grass roots. Yet it was not a foe of the business moguls. Instead, it had encouraged the creation of the Greater Baltimore Committee and viewed that group as complementing CPHA efforts to renew the city. Moreover, the CPHA was an ally of the city planning bureaucracy; the executive secretary stated that one of the group's objectives was to interpret planning policy "to the community as a whole to help make it become a reality."[26] This was part of the organization's educational function. Reluctant Baltimoreans had to be made aware of the problem of blight and had to be taught the need to cooperate with city government in the battle against this debilitating foe.

With such an attitude the CPHA would be in the forefront of the renewal crusade. In the 1940s it fought for enforcement of the local housing code, and in the 1950s it was a loyal supporter of renewal initiatives. In 1956 a report evaluating local renewal policy found that the CPHA had been "squarely behind urban renewal, and its continued support, interest, and constructive criticism [were] indispensable elements in launching and sustaining a comprehensive urban renewal program."[27]

Chicago's version of the CPHA was the Metropolitan Housing and Planning Council (MHPC). Though well-to-do business leaders dominated its governing board, it was not an elite clique of Loop moguls. Instead, its director reported that her group maintained "liaison with 150 civic, labor, professional, welfare, women's, and community organizations to guide and coordinate their action on legislative and other relevant matters." Moreover, a typical MHPC committee of the early 1950s included a mixture of lawyers, professors, architects, and settlement house workers.

Like the Baltimore and Philadelphia organizations the MHPC was dedicated to preaching the planner's message, and according to its official statement of purpose it sought "to promote, stimulate and encourage public interest in, and understanding of, housing and neighborhood problems" and "the formulation and development of comprehensive long range planning."[28] Yet owing to the local political climate, the Chicago group proved more abrasive than its East Coast counterparts. In Chicago the council director observed: "Unlike Philadelphia, the public officials work as a closed corporation, and the watchword is 'no coaching from the audience, please.'" With "an atmosphere of skulduggery" prevailing, the MHPC had to guard against the legerdemain of partisan hacks indifferent to urban revitalization.[29] Chicago's friends of renewal not only had to educate the average citizenry, they had to ensure that the occupants of city hall learned the renaissance lesson as well.

Throughout the Northeast and Midwest, corporate chieftains, downtown merchants, and civic activists claiming to speak for a broad range of groups all agreed that the older central cities had to launch initiatives to overcome obsolescence and achieve rejuvenation. Though downtown business figures were to be disproportionately significant in the struggle for revival during the late 1940s and the 1950s, renewal schemes were not the product of small cabals of plutocratic overloads who foisted them on an unwilling public. A number of private groups were demanding action, and organizations like Chicago's Metropolitan Housing and Planning Council could prove feisty foes of public officials who dragged their feet. The Allegheny Conference and organizations modeled after it were mobilizing money on behalf of a new city whereas groups like the Citizens' Council on City Planning assumed responsibility for recruiting the general populace to the cause. Both types of associations were laying the private-sector foundation for the forthcoming assault. The cries for action were growing louder in corporate boardrooms and planning council seminars. It was time for politicians in city hall to respond.

The New Politics

A vital element in the postwar effort to remake the older cities was the movement to reform their politics and to create local governments conducive to rejuvenation. In the minds of major metropolitan newspapers, prominent business figures, leaders of civic organizations, and even many politicians, the central cities had to have a new leadership projecting a fresh image that proclaimed to the nation the revitalization of the shabby, tired urban hubs of the past. Portly, cigar-smoking bosses redolent in patronage but lacking in civic morality would only further blacken the already tarnished reputation of the city. Shortsighted hacks satisfied to address political banquets and cut occasional ribbons were likewise inadequate to guide the rebirth of the urban core. Moreover, ethnic politicians appealing primarily to ancient loyalties and animosities seemed out of touch with the need to unite the city in a crusade for renewal.

Thus the physical rehabilitation of the city appeared to demand a new breed of leader. The municipal chieftains of this new age especially had to appeal to the business community and the political and bureaucratic leaders in Washington, for these were the two most prominent potential sources of aid in the struggle to shore up the decaying urban hubs. If a city won a reputation for good government and efficient administration, it would have less difficulty dislodging money from administrators of federal urban renewal programs. And if the central-city mayors who testified before congressional committees were an articulate, intelligent contingent, then the House of Representatives and the Senate might prove more forthcoming in federal funding.

Similarly, if its local government earned the respect of business leaders, then a city might have a better chance for private-sector investment in its renewal schemes and its property tax base would benefit accordingly. Moreover, business support and the backing of elite organizations like Saint Louis's Civic Progress or the Greater Baltimore Committee was often essential in the bond issue elections and tax referenda necessary for funding programs of public improvements. The wholehearted endorsement of a corps of corporate moguls or the local chamber of commerce could mean thousands of dollars for advertising in support of a bond issue. Successful postwar mayors still had to appeal to their multiethnic constituencies and attend as many Sons of Italy dinners and St. Patrick's Day parades as their predecessors. Politicians who simply satisfied the grass-roots electorate, however, would not build the framework for the future physical rejuvenation of the city. The renaissance mayors of the mid-twentieth century needed a broader political reach so that they could command simultaneously the loyalty of the neighborhoods, the financial community, the real estate interests, and the national chieftains in Washington.

During the late 1940s and the 1950s, a new breed of urban leaders did, in fact, seize power, proving popular at the polls and building a broad political following. In Philadelphia, Saint Louis, Boston, and most of the other older cities, mayors dedicated to change and renewal took over city hall and sought to create a new urban politics. Though downtown business interests and the metropolitan newspapers generally were their most vocal and influential backers, the postwar mayors won landslide victories at the polls largely owing to the support of thousands of voters in the outer ring of central-city residential neighborhoods. In these districts housing the middle class and the more substantial members of the working class, the rejection of past politics struck a responsive chord. Like the downtown real estate interests, these homeowning taxpayers favored honest, efficient government that would not waste property tax dollars on salaries for corrupt political cronies. Moreover, schemes for broadening the tax base through central-city revitalization often appealed to these hard-pressed taxpayers eager for relief from local levies. Occasionally, when postwar mayors backed downtown schemes that might add to the tax burden of homeowners, voters in the outer ring of residential neighborhoods would rebel. But generally, central-city business leaders combined with homeowners to put the new regime into office.

Though the new political leaders who sponsored the rejuvenation of the older cities proved attractive to the business community, they were not invariably political conservatives nor pliant tools of big corporations. Two of the most notable of the postwar breed of mayors, Hubert Humphrey of Minneapolis and Joseph Clark of Philadelphia, earned a national reputation as quintessential liberals when later serving in the United States Senate. Another, Robert Wagner of New York City, was the son of the sponsor of the federal public housing law and the Wagner Labor Relations Act. As such he had inherited impeccable liberal credentials and the warm support of labor interests. Some postwar mayors, such as Albert Cobo of Detroit, did not hide their conservative sentiments nor their hostility toward left-wing labor groups. But the new political leaders did not need to be business spokespersons. Instead, they only had to be able to earn the respect of the business community. In the eyes of business leaders they had to appear energetic, honest, and able. This was the image that they had to project. A brogue, a highly visible clubhouse of working-class cronies, or an obvious devotion to following the well-worn paths of past politics was not acceptable.

In most cities the battle for new political leadership took the familiar form of a revolt against boss rule. Antiboss rhetoric had long been a part of city politics, and a loyal corps of middle-class, good-government advocates responded to antiboss rhetoric like Pavlovian dogs salivating at the sound of a dinner bell. Thus attacks on the political machine could galvanize a significant segment of the population, drawing the full forces of the citizen crusaders into the fray. Moreover, relevations of widespread corruption and gross incompetence could even shift working-class votes into the reform column, thereby ensuring victory at the polls. With the continuing migration of the middle class to suburbia, this appeal to the working class was increasingly important. By tarring the ward bosses and party committee members with the brush of corruption and incompetence, the metropolitan newspapers, civic leaders, and reform chieftains could, then, undercut the authority of these figures who seemed partially responsible for the debilitating mediocrity that plagued so many of the aging cities.

The crusade against "bossism" was especially vigorous in postwar Philadelphia. Since the Civil War, the Republican organization had dominated Philadelphia, and the city had not elected a Democrat to the mayor's office since 1884. At the turn of the century the muckraker Lincoln Steffens had labeled Philadelphia as "corrupt and contented," and by the close of World War II this description remained apt. Throughout the intervening decades the Republican organization had perpetuated the city's reputation for lethargy, and only rarely did the GOP leaders take action to stir the sleeping metropolis. In 1949 *Time* magazine reported: "For 65 years Philadelphia has suffered its Republican city government as it has the water it drank. Both gave off a faint but unpleasant smell, but a true Philadelphian got used to both."[30]

During the late 1940s, however, a reform movement began to arouse the city from its torpid state. Both the Citizens' Council on City Planning and the Greater Philadelphia Movement were manifestations of dissatisfaction with the status quo. But leading the revolt against Republican rule were a pair of Democratic patricians with Ivy League educations, Richardson Dilworth and Joseph Clark. Disgusted by the decline of their city and the indifference of the Republican leaders, they dedicated themselves to clearing city hall of the venal deadwood occupying its offices.

According to Clark, the "old Republican bosses were no angels, but they had boldness and they did something to build up the city. The men who came after them had nothing but a jackal's urge to peck over the carcass."[31] Challenging this "pathetic group of little men," the outspoken Dilworth ran for mayor in 1947 and promised, "[I'll] fight with the gloves off . . . I'm going to tell the people who is crooked and why."[32] He fulfilled his promise, but the voters seemed unconcerned and reelected the Republican mayor by a handsome margin of eighty-two thousand votes.

During the next four years, however, revelations of corruption in the Republican administration turned voters toward the Democratic camp. In 1948 the director of the city Department of Supplies and Purchases was indicted on two charges of embezzlement, nine of falsifying city records, ten of forgery, and twenty-eight of illegally making city purchases from his own florist firm. That same year the chief of the Amusement Tax Division committed suicide after confessing to the embezzlement of $250,000 of city funds. More indictments and suicides followed among the employees of the police department, the water department, the fire marshal's office, and the bureau of plumbing inspection.

In 1949 irate voters followed the advice of the city's two leading, and normally Republican, newspapers and elected Joseph Clark city controller and Richardson Dilworth treasurer. Two years later the Democratic victories continued with Clark winning the mayor's office and Dilworth the post of district attorney. Moreover, in 1951 the city adopted a new reform charter that gave Clark more authority than any previous chief executive of Philadelphia. In these elections Dilworth and Clark pieced together a victorious coalition of independent voters in outlying middle-class wards who were disgusted with corruption and black Philadelphians who increasingly cast a straight Democratic ticket. Meanwhile, the Republican organization retained the downtown and waterfront wards, the so-called Tenderloin, where inner-city residents voted according to orders of the machine committeeman.[33]

On taking office, Mayor Clark refused to kowtow to the Democratic ward leaders and charted an independent course. He filled city hall offices with his socially prominent reform friends and with persons recruited from out of town because of their reputation as top-notch administrators. Ability and expertise seemed to be the criteria for Clark's appointments and not local political credentials. Especially significant in the coming renaissance initiatives was Clark's city planning chief, Edmund Bacon.[34] With its officers chosen, the Clark administration presided over a capital improvement program of a magnitude unprecedented in Philadelphia history, and the new regime's vigor and rectitude won national applause as well as the close cooperation of the Citizens' Council and the Greater Philadelphia Movement. Winning the election in 1955, Dilworth succeeded Clark as mayor and lived up to Clark's description of him as "D'Artagnan in a double-breasted suit."[35] Together the crusading patricians seemed to bring Philadelphia into the mid-twentieth century and raised doubts about the city's traditional reputation as a moribund metropolis.

While Clark and Dilworth were dismantling the old order in Philadelphia, Boston voters were also turning away from their local symbol of old-fashioned bossism, James Michael Curley. First elected mayor in 1913, Curley had built a reputation both as an outspoken friend of "the little guy" and as one of the most disreputable politicians in urban America. In 1947, while serving his fourth term as Boston's chief executive, he finally paid the penalty for his past sins when he spent five months in federal prison for mail fraud committed during a recent term in Congress.

Not only were the federal authorities catching up with him, so was his age. In 1949, at the age of seventy-five, he ran for mayor once again, but Boston's voters rejected him, selecting instead the colorless city clerk, John B. Hynes, described in a friendly editorial as a "good honest" man, "who makes up in experience, integrity and administrative ability what he lacks by way of glamor."[36] Together with every major civic group each of the metropolitan newspapers backed Hynes, and one editorial expressed the exasperation of many who looked forward to a revival of the New England metropolis when it asked, "How long are the citizens of Boston going to tolerate a local regime which keeps the city in the municipal doghouse? How long is Boston to continue being the black sheep of American cities?"[37] As in Philadelphia the Boston election of 1949 revealed a split between the core and the periphery with the poor wards of East Boston, South Boston, Charlestown, Roxbury, and the West, North, and South ends favoring Curley, and the more affluent outlying areas of Mattapan, Hyde Park, Roslindale, West Roxbury, Brighton, and Allston siding with Hynes.[38]

In 1950 the mounting reform tide produced the New Boston Committee, a nonpartisan group of representatives from every ward, but which especially spoke for the younger generation of voters, who viewed Curley as a dangerous relic. The following year the New Boston Committee proved a powerful political force when its candidates won a majority on the city council and the school board. Moreover, Hynes again defeated Curley for mayor, after the old politician scored a new low, smearing the reform candidates as "friends of known supporters of communism."[39] Defeating the persistent Curley one more time in 1955, the lackluster Hynes remained in the mayor's office throughout the 1950s, largely ineffective in his efforts to spark the city's revival but at least doing nothing to further damage its repute.

Elsewhere the forces of reform and revival also tried to rid municipal government of the remnants of aging political machines. The leading booster for the rejuvenation of Saint Louis, Mayor Raymond Tucker, only won and retained office after doing battle with Democratic ward leaders and the organization of former Sheriff Thomas Callahan. A former engineering professor and a devotee of efficiency and nonpartisan expertise, Tucker defeated Callahan's candidate in the Democratic primary of 1953 and repeated this feat in 1957, smashing his opponent by a four-to-one margin.[40] Meanwhile, the former sheriff's brother had gone to prison for labor racketeering, and the ward leaders had divided among themselves, giving the mayor and his good-government allies the upper hand for the remainder of the 1950s. In an increasingly familiar pattern the Callahan forces in both 1953 and 1957 reaped the most votes in the low socioeconomic "delivery wards," where the party leader could deliver votes on demand. By contrast, Tucker proved most popular in the more affluent "newspaper wards," where the electorate voted on the basis of what they read in the *Post-Dispatch* or *Globe-Democrat* and not at the bidding of the local Democratic leader.[41]

In Cleveland, Mayor Anthony Celebrezze likewise won election in 1953 after defeating the candidate of the county Democratic organization in the primary. During his nine years in office, Celebrezze remained independent of the county party leader but repeatedly won reelection by promising freedom from boss rule and a program of slum clearance, urban renewal, downtown revival, transit improvements, and highway construction.[42]

Throughout the country there was an outcry against anything that smacked of boss rule. Though the local party organizations were relatively open and weak, Minneapolis experienced periodic outcries against the supposed "labor bossism" of the city's Central Labor Union. When that powerful organization's candidates finally met defeat in 1957, the *Minneapolis Tribune* editorialized that the vote was "an anti-bossism vote, a protest against boss-picked candidates and dubious boss-directed tactics."[43] Even the Chicago Democratic machine had to tolerate an antiboss mayor, Martin Kennelly, for eight years, from 1947 to 1955. Reacting to scandals in the last years of Mayor Edward Kelly's administration, voters sided with the antiboss Kennelly, an upright but colorless businessman who repeated the oft-heard promise of cleaning up Chicago.[44] Only in 1955 would the Chicago machine recapture the mayor's office with the election of Richard Daley, a man who knew how to combine traditional politics with the postwar imperative to recreate the physical structure of the central city.

Others working within traditional party organizations also had learned the wisdom of uniting with the forces of central-city revival rather than fighting them. Thus a few party leaders became known as "good bosses" and received plaudits rather than opprobrium from the metropolitan newspapers and the business community. Most notably, Mayor David Lawrence of Pittsburgh ruled his city's tight Democratic organization with a firm hand while cooperating closely with the Allegheny Conference in its efforts to revive the bleak steel city. Together the mayor and the business chieftains launched a well-publicized renaissance of the city that was to win Lawrence national recognition and to ensure his overwhelming victory in three reelection campaigns. In 1957 the business magazine *Fortune* named Lawrence one of the nation's ablest municipal executives, a rare honor for a Democratic party boss, and most rock-ribbed Republican Pittsburgh business moguls agreed with this acclaim.[45]

During the early 1950s, even New York City's traditionally notorious Tammany Hall Democratic organization won some laurels after its successful effort to place the "clean" candidate Robert Wagner in the mayor's office. Tammany boss Carmine DeSapio lectured at Ivy League colleges and reaped some praise in the pages of national magazines.[46] By the beginning of the 1960s he had become the bête noire of Manhattan reformers, and Mayor Wagner was abandoning the machine for an independent stance, but at least for a short time DeSapio too seemed to promise a new era of politics.

Baltimore's Mayor Thomas D'Alesandro, Jr., was a hybrid who sometimes appeared to be one of the new breed of executives and at other times seemed a tool of the so-called bosses. Though an old-fashioned ethnic politician with a loyal following among the city's Italians, D'Alesandro was not a product of a powerful party organization. According to the *Baltimore Sun*, in 1947 he entered the mayoral contest "almost as a lone wolf candidate," and that newspaper commended him for having "outmaneuvered" the "less admirable local leaders and bosslets" that had attached themselves to him.[47] Moreover, in 1951 at the close of his first term in office, the good-government devotees on the *Sun* editorial board lauded D'Alesandro for his "remarkable record of achievement" and pronounced him "an energetic and purposeful Mayor" who deserved "re-election by an overwhelming vote."[48]

Like all successful new-breed mayors, D'Alesandro was a builder, dedicated to the brick-and-mortar reconstruction of his aging domain. A local commentator referred to him as "the bustling man with the ground-breaking shovel" and observed, "His latest annual report has about 30 pictures of the Mayor with a shovel marking the start of building projects."[49] Yet by the mid-1950s the good-government forces had broken with D'Alesandro, and in 1955 the *Sun* was claiming that he had "ceased to be a leader and become something little better than a puppet" of political bosses and contractors.[50] During the late 1940s and the early 1950s, however, D'Alesandro seemed to usher in a fresh vigor, and his perpetual ground-breaking ceremonies appeared to mark the realization of plans for postwar improvement.

Though the *Sun* may have complained about D'Alesandro's apparent shift, overall the trend was in the opposite direction. In one city after another the Curleys and Callahans were losing their grip on urban politics, and if a politician wanted to survive he had to adapt to the new mood of the postwar era. The business elite and a majority of the electorate were tired of city administrations bogged down in partisan disputes over patronage and the spoils of office. They felt that the power of ward party leaders had to be curbed, and political figures had to reorient themselves to the broader issues of the central city's survival in the unfavorable climate of the postwar world. That superb political chameleon David Lawrence summed up this feeling when as a mayoral candidate in 1945 he exclaimed: "This city wants and needs leadership, we are tired of bickering; tired . . . of glory hunting . . . [and the] mossback thinking which retarded our city's progress." According to Lawrence: "A new spirit [is] abroad in the land and in the city. My program for Pittsburgh is a community program. When I am Mayor, we will work together and we will . . . let history worry about who gets the credit."[51] Moreover, Lawrence's words were not simply inflated campaign rhetoric, for a year after taking office the Democratic boss appointed Republican business representatives to a majority of the seats on Pittsburgh's first urban redevelopment authority. Lawrence admitted: "I never thought I'd live to see the day when I'd put my own Party in the minority."[52] But he knew that a Pittsburgh renaissance depended on cooperation and consensus among the Democratic administration and the Republican business community.

This political consensus for revitalization was evident in other older central cities as well. When launching a bond issue campaign for massive public improvements, Democratic mayor Raymond Tucker of Saint Louis could count on more cooperation from the Republican former mayor Aloys Kaufmann, who had become president of the chamber of commerce, than he could from his own party's ward leaders. Republicans who lined up solidly behind Thomas Dewey and Dwight Eisenhower in presidential contests would lend their support to Democrats Richardson Dilworth and Joseph Clark in their efforts to oust the archaic GOP organization and bring Philadelphia out of the dark ages. With the problems of urban blight and decentralization mounting, the divisive politics of the past seemed increasingly dysfunctional and obsolete. In Philadelphia and Saint Louis as in Pittsburgh, partisan loyalties seemed unimportant compared with the predicaments of downtown decline, clogged traffic arteries, and incompetent and ineffective government.

Yet divisions persisted, and in a few cities it seemed impossible to create a strong coalition to further the cause of urban rebirth. For example, in Buffalo old-fashioned ethnic politics continued to dominate city elections throughout the late 1940s and the 1950s, and feuds among nationalities drowned out talk of public improvements. In the particularly bitter Democratic primary election of 1949, opponents of mayoral candidate Steven Pankow began a whispering campaign to the effect that Pankow was not actually of Polish ancestry but was, in fact, Lithuanian. To allay suspicions among the large Polish electorate of Buffalo, Pankow publicly displayed his birth record showing his parent's place of nativity as Poland.[53] The *Buffalo Evening News* was indignant that "the question of racial background, a question that is offensive to the spirit of Americanism," played a role in the mayoral contest and claimed that "serious citizens must be outraged that such a question should be injected into the campaign."[54] But throughout the late 1940s and the 1950s Buffalo Poles voted for Polish candidates no matter whether they were Republican or Democratic, and ethnicity was the overriding concern in local elections. Thus while reform politicians elsewhere tried to build a consensus for revitalization, in Buffalo the voters were refighting the ethnic battles of the past.

Overall, the trend, however, was toward a politics that downplayed seething ethnic divisions and discarded old-fashioned partisan loyalties and the traditional party organization. The party clubhouses and ward leaders survived in many cities, but by the 1950s they no longer seemed to be as influential in municipal politics as they had been in earlier decades.

Reinforcing the decline in the significance of political parties and party organizations was the marked drop in Republican electoral strength in urban areas during the 1950s. In the 1940s the Republican party still wielded clout in a number of major cities, and competitive two-party politics was very much alive. At the beginning of 1946, ten of the twelve major central cities in the Northeast and Midwest had partisan contests for municipal office, and in five of the ten the mayors were Republicans. Moreover, in four of the ten, Republicans controlled the city council.[55] In 1945 Saint Louis voters reelected the Republican mayor by a record plurality and a two-to-one margin and chose Republicans for thirteen of the fourteen aldermanic seats that were up for election.[56] That same year Buffalo's voters were equally enthusiastic for the GOP, electing a Republican mayor and giving the Republicans a fourteen-to-one majority on the city council.[57] In 1947 Philadalphia's Republican mayor won a landslide victory, and all twenty-two of that city's council seats went to the GOP. Meanwhile, Cincinnati Republicans dominated their city's government from 1938 to 1947, and in Minneapolis control switched back and forth between the Democratic and Republican forces with the council split evenly thirteen to thirteen after both the 1943 and 1947 elections.

Even in some Democratic-controlled cities the Republicans still had a fighting chance for power and constituted a real opposition party. After the 1943 election Cleveland's Democrats held only a seventeen-to-sixteen edge over the Republicans on the city council, and the Democratic council leadership often had to depend on independent Republicans for necessary votes on important measures.[58] In Pittsburgh no Republican had occupied a council seat since 1939, and New York City had been overwhelmingly Democratic since the Civil War. But in most of the major cities there were still two significant parties.

During the late 1940s and the 1950s, however, middle-class Republicans moved out of the city and solidly Democratic blacks moved in. Moreover, those urbanites whose partisan loyalties had developed under the influence of the Hoover depression and the magic of Franklin D. Roosevelt grew proportionately larger as older dedicated Republicans who had withstood the lure of the New Deal died or retired to sunnier climes. Consequently, Republican fortunes nosedived in the major central cities, and most of the major metropolises became one-party towns. The decline in Republican representation on the city councils of Chicago, Cleveland, and Saint Louis (table 4) was indicative of the diminishing stature of the GOP. In 1945 Republicans enjoyed a three-to-one advantage over Democrats on the Saint Louis Board of Aldermen; by 1955 there were six times as many Democratic aldermen as Republican, and this ratio would remain the same into the early 1960s. Chicago's Republican contingent of council members dropped from seventeen to three between 1947 and 1959, and in Cleveland, Republican representation fell from fourteen in 1945 to six in 1961. Buffalo's GOP lost control of the council in the 1947 election, and in the 1950s the Democrats consistently remained in the majority. Likewise, after the 1951 election the composition of Philadelphia's council changed from twenty-two Republicans and no Democrats to fourteen Democrats

Table 4. Distribution of City Council Seats by Party, 1945–1961

Election Year	Chicago			Cleveland			Saint Louis	
	Dem.	Rep.	Ind.	Dem.	Rep.	Ind.	Dem.	Rep.
1945				19	14		7	21
1947	32	17	1	19	12	2	8	20
1949				22	11		15	13
1951	33	16	1	21	12		17	11
1953				20	13		20	8
1955	38	11	1	22	11		24	4
1957				24	9		24	4
1959	46	3	1	25	8		24	4
1961				27	6		24	4

Sources: Election results as reported in the *Chicago Tribune, Cleveland Plain Dealer,* and *St. Louis Post-Dispatch.*

and three Republicans, a distribution that was to persist until 1959, when the Republican share fell to only two seats.

The mayoral races offered similar evidence of a deterioration of two-party politics. By the mid-1950s all ten of the partisan central cities had Democratic mayors, and Republican opposition on election day was often token. In 1955 and 1957 Cleveland's Democratic Mayor Anthony Cele-brezze did not even face opposition in the general election, and in the 1959 and 1961 contests he won by a better than two-to-one margin.[59] Similarly, in 1957 Democratic Mayor Raymond Tucker carried all twenty-eight wards of Saint Louis and 77 percent of the vote in a contest against the Republican's sacrificial offering, a thirty-one-year-old attorney who had never before sought or held office.[60] Two years later Chicago's Demo-crat Richard Daley won reelection with 71 percent of the vote, and Demo-cratic Mayor Richardson Dilworth of Philadelphia crushed his opponent by almost a two-to-one margin.[61] Pittsburgh's David Lawrence also repeat-edly won reelection with ever larger percentages of the vote, and in each election the Democrats carried every council seat.[62] In 1953 the wealthiest patron of the Pennsylvania Republican party, Richard King Mellon, even put his imprimatur on the Democratic boss when he publicly praised Mayor Lawrence at a ground-breaking ceremony. According to one commentator, "At that dreadful moment the Republican pulse in Al-legheny County, long faint, became almost imperceptible."[63]

In fact, by the close of the 1950s the Republican pulse was dan-gerously weak in all but a few of the older central cities. In the 1959 elec-tion Cincinnati Republicans won five of the nine council seats, and they would continue to control that city through the 1960s. Minneapolis Republicans were also still viable and retained enough strength to possibly unseat the Democratic majority. And in Buffalo the GOP could threaten its foes as well, especially if it nominated a popular Polish candidate. But elsewhere there was no two-party system; the Republicans were only a shadow.

By the late 1950s, then, the Republican party was meaningless in most of the major central cities, and repeated antiboss campaigns had badly battered the Democratic party organizations. Independent Democrats ruled in the city halls of Cleveland and Saint Louis; and in Philadelphia, Richardson Dilworth and his appointees fought to minimize the influence of the Democratic ward leaders and the city's party chairman. Meanwhile, in Boston and Detroit city elections had long been nonpartisan, and party organizations never interfered in the choice of municipal candidates. Instead, a familiar Irish name seemed to be the chief criterion for election to Boston's council, and in less parochial Detroit a familiar name of any ethnic origin proved invaluable at the polls. Only in Chicago and Pittsburgh did a strong Democratic organization survive with powerful boss-mayors Richard Daley and David Lawrence in command.

Outside of these two cities the 1950s witnessed a marked decline in the importance of party organizations in municipal politics. With the demise of two-party competition and the rise of independent Democrats who ran without the party organization's endorsement, meaningful partisan politics was disappearing, giving way to factional contests and personal battles in which every candidate fought for his or herself. Unstable factionalism seemed to be the trend of the future with each faction or candidate having to build a winning coalition from among the diverse interests of the city rather than depending on a body of disciplined partisan voters responding loyally to the cues of a party machine. In the relatively tranquil Eisenhower era of the 1950s, such factionalism did not pose a serious threat to the peace of the city, but in the volatile 1960s, when blacks demanded increased privileges and militant unions threatened to drain municipal treasuries, the absence of an effective party organization could produce political crisis in the older urban hubs. Traditionally, the party machine had mediated between labor and business and among the city's hostile ethnic groups, thereby forming stable coalitions and keeping a lid on the social and economic hostilities of the heterogeneous central city. Without this stabilizing party mediator the prospects for a placid political future were not good.

Moreover, in the past the parties had screened candidates, recruiting leaders who could win votes and when in office avoid debacles that might prove disastrous to party fortunes. The weakening of party government meant an open door for the more volatile crusaders on both the left and the right who would run for office in the 1960s. A divisive critic of municipal bureaucracy or an outspoken foe of busing of students would not have passed through the sieve in the screening process under a strong party system.

Decline in party discipline and loyalty also could result in less cohesion among the various actors in the political arena. In a city with a strong party organization, Democratic mayors could count on the support of Democratic council members; the council members were expected to do as their boss said. Thus in both Pittsburgh and Chicago the overwhelmingly Democratic councils were rubber stamps for their boss-mayors David Lawrence and Richard Daley. But independents like Anthony Celebrezze and Raymond Tucker could not expect such cooperation nor could nonpartisan mayors in Boston or Detroit. With name recognition becoming a more important factor in winning election than the support of the party organization, it actually could be in the interest of an ambitious city council member to become a well-publicized opponent of the mayor. Again weakened parties could mean increased disarray.

During the 1950s, however, the decline in party politics had not produced a crisis in government. The independent Democrats had fashioned momentarily stable coalitions of downtown real estate interests, metropolitan newspapers, and reform-minded citizens, and these coalitions ruled over an inordinately placid political scene. Council members may have sniped at mayors and ward leaders may have felt little love for the rulers in city hall, but in most of the older central cities municipal politics was far from tumultuous. Newspaper accounts repeatedly characterized the municipal elections of the 1950s as "listless," "lackluster," and "lukewarm," and old-timers claimed that the reelection campaigns of independent Democrats were pale affairs compared with the partisan contests of the past. For the moment there did seem to be a consensus for the physical rejuvenation of the city guided by honest, efficient leaders like Raymond Tucker and Richardson Dilworth. But the population of the central city was changing, and its electorate was growing poorer and blacker. Moreover, if the much-publicized visions of a renewed metropolis were not realized and the central city continued to decay with serious fiscal consequences, then the consensus might well disappear, leaving a potentially disruptive political void.

Paying for the Postwar City

The promised postwar rejuvenation of older central cities required not only new leadership in city hall but also billions of dollars of public investment. Such capital improvements as highways, sewers, parks, and airports could not be built unless cities were able to raise vast sums of money. Yet decentralization and blight threatened the property tax base that traditionally had financed both operating expenditures and payments of interest and principal on debts incurred for massive building projects. Thus during the late 1940s and the 1950s urban leaders confronted the dilemma of building their revived cities on the sagging financial foundations of the past. Obviously, they needed to shore up this financial base before they could confidently remake their cities. Speaking in 1946 before a conference of the Municipal Finance Officers Association, Boston's city auditor summed up the view of many of his colleagues when he noted that "the liveliest question in municipal finance today" was "where are municipalities going to secure the revenues necessary to meet the rapidly expanding costs of post-war rehabilitation and reconstruction?"[64] In Philadephia, Pittsburgh, Cleveland, and Saint Louis, city leaders dreamed of an urban renaissance costing a Medici fortune but at the same time faced the fiscal realities that accompanied economic stagnation. It was their task to discover a financial formula by which dreams could somehow equate with realities.

In the past the chief source of money for capital improvements had been the municipal bond market. Cities had issued bonds to pay for their existing waterworks, sewers, and thoroughfares, and they intended to turn to the bond market for the financing of many postwar projects. Three factors, however, influenced whether cities would or could borrow. The first was level of indebtedness. When a city was already heavily indebted and possibly on the brink of bankruptcy, it would not be able to market its bonds on favorable terms, if at all. Moreover, state laws imposed debt limitations on cities, and if the municipality had already borrowed to its limit then further bond issues would be impossible. The second factor that influenced municipal borrowing was the prevailing interest rates in the bond market. If rates were high, then the city might defer borrowing until a later time when the market was more favorable. The third factor was the municipal tax burden. If payments for interest and principal on new indebtedness would require an intolerable rise in the tax rate, then urban officials and voters were unlikely to approve borrowing proposals. Thus city financial officers were most likely to recommend borrowing when existing indebtedness was considerably below the legal limit, when interest rates were down, and when the impact on tax rates would be minimal.

At the close of World War II the first two favorable conditions generally prevailed, and the final factor only delayed borrowing in some of the central cities. Levels of borrowing had been dropping for a decade, leaving cities without excessively burdensome debts. Moreover, interest rates had never been so favorable for municipal borrowers as during the postwar years. Only fears of higher taxes kept a few of the municipalities from exploiting the bond market, but these thrifty localities were outnumbered by those ready to embark on capital improvements.

The decline in indebtedness was especially encouraging to those eager to engage in capital spending. Throughout the war, shortages of material and men prevented cities from constructing costly capital improvements, and thus they had no reason to borrow. From 1942 through 1945 the net long-term debt of all cities having populations greater than 500,000 dropped 11 percent, leaving most cities well below their legal debt limit.[65] The downward trend in indebtedness had actually begun in the 1930s, when municipalities halted locally financed public works projects and tightened their belts in response to the economic depression. For example, Chicago's gross city debt had peaked at $141 million in 1931 and then dropped continuously to a low of $33 million in 1946.[66] Similarly, Philadelphia's gross debt declined 28 percent from a high in May–June 1934 to a low in 1947, the indebtedness of Saint Louis fell 46 percent from its 1937 high to 1946, and by the end of 1948 Buffalo's gross debt had plummeted 58 percent from its 1938 peak. Whereas in 1938 Buffalo was within $23,000 of its debt limit, by 1948 it had a borrowing margin of $54 million. Likewise, in 1935 Philadelphia was actually $42 million over its debt limit, but by 1946 it enjoyed a legal borrowing capacity of $69 million.[67] Throughout the nation the municipal ledgers showed an ample debt margin for the nation's largest cities, fulfilling one of the conditions for increased borrowing.

Meanwhile, bonds were selling at record-low interest rates, further enhancing the advantages of borrowing. In 1945 New York City borrowed at an annual interest cost of 1.873 percent, according to the municipal controller the lowest rate in the city's history.[68] As seen in table 5, bond rates move upward slowly during the postwar years, but throughout the late 1940s and early 1950s interest costs remained far below those prevailing in the 1920s and 1930s. The high level of federal taxes during the postwar era made the tax-exempt municipals especially attractive to investors and enabled cities to negotiate consistently favorable bond sales. In 1952 the city of Buffalo sold $8 million in municipal bonds at an inter-

Table 5. Bond Buyer's Index of State and Municipal Bond Yields, 1921–1956

Year*	Yield (%)	Year*	Yield (%)
1921	5.06	1948	2.36
1932	4.87	1950	2.07
1939	2.78	1952	2.11
1943	2.17	1954	2.54
1946	1.42	1956	2.56

Source: Carl H. Chatters, "Municipal Financial Needs versus Credit Restraints," *Municipal Finance* 30 (August 1957):16.
*As of January 2.

est rate of 1.5 percent, and as late as 1955 Cincinnati was able to market its securities at an annual interest cost of 2.0965 percent.[69] Other cities refinanced 4 percent bonds sold during the 1920s and 1930s with new issues bringing only 2 percent interest. Because of lower rates for new indebtedness and the advantageous refinancing of old bonds, the average rate of interest for the city of Chicago's debt fell steadily during the 1940s and early 1950s, dropping from 3.7 percent in 1940 to 1.9 percent in 1952.[70]

The combination of reduced levels of borrowing and record-low interest rates produced a marked decline in total debt costs during the 1940s. In 1939 Philadelphia's debt service amounted to $37 million, or an astounding 55 percent of the city's revenues; by 1947 this figure had fallen to less than $23 million, or 21 percent of the municipal income.[71] Similarly, the annual interest costs of Buffalo tumbled from $4.6 million in 1937–38 to $1.9 million in 1946–47.[72] In other words, by the late 1940s the nation's cities had climbed out from under the heavy debt burden of the prewar era and were in an excellent position to resume large-scale borrowing for capital improvements. Indirectly subsidized by federal tax policy, interest rates on municipal bonds were highly conducive to borrowing, and levels of indebtedness as well as inherited debt costs were well under control. All the figures seemed to add up to a major role for the bond market in the financing of the central city's rebirth.

In most cities, however, bond proposals had to be presented to the voters for their approval or rejection, and the electorate could balk at spending measures, even though borrowed funds were to pay the bills. Consequently, supporters of capital improvement programs had to mobilize their forces, and most notable among these advocates of borrowing were metropolitan newspapers, downtown business boosters, chambers of commerce, and mayors dedicated to urban revitalization. This coalition was especially active in Saint Louis, where it rallied behind the corporate chieftains in Civic Progress and lent strong support to bond issue campaigns in 1953 and 1955. In 1953 supporters of rejuvenation backed a $1.5 million bond issue for downtown slum clearance and redevelopment, a proposal that Mayor Joseph Darst regarded as "the key to all future progress in St. Louis."[73] All of the city's elite boosted the issue, including the Roman Catholic auxiliary bishop who announced, "Plans for rehabilitation of the downtown section are long overdue," and a leading rabbi, who warned, "The future of Greater St. Louis depends upon passage of the bond issue."[74] Claiming that the city was being "dismembered and disembowelled by decay," the *Post-Dispatch* also urged passage, and the editor of the leading black newspaper, the president of the Chamber of Commerce, and the chairmen of the Democratic and Republican city committees all did likewise.[75] Yet on election day in spring 1953 the issue failed by a small margin. Not until a second try in September 1953 did the proposal pass by a sufficient majority.[76]

Two years later Civic Progress activists were instrumental in placing on the ballot a $111 million bond proposal that appealed to a wider range of interests than had the downtown measure of 1953. It was to finance twenty-three capital improvement projects, including slum clearance, neighborhood rehabilitation, the construction of expressways, the building of hospitals and health centers, and the laying out of parks and playgrounds. Again every religious potentate, reputable business group, and major politician backed the proposal, and advocates paid for a television program proclaiming the merits of the scheme and organized a fifteen-mile parade to rally support.[77] On election day the publicity paid off, for the electorate voted overwhelmingly in favor of the mammoth borrowing plan.[78]

One problem facing Saint Louis and many other cities was that state law or the city charter required bond proposals to win approval by an extraordinary majority of 60 percent or more. In the Missouri metropolis bond issues had to receive the support of two-thirds of the voters, but in the spring of 1953 the downtown renewal measure had garnered a favorable vote from only 63 percent. Before 1950 Ohio required a 65 percent majority in favor of bond issues, and from 1950 onward supporters of bond packages in Cleveland and Cincinnati had to secure a 55 percent affirmative vote. Similarly, in Detroit a 60 percent majority was necessary, though in Chicago and Baltimore a simple 50 percent majority was sufficient. In cities requiring an extraordinary majority, sponsors of borrowing measures had to build a community consensus in favor of capital improvements, for any opposition by a major voting bloc would likely spell defeat for the proposal.

Despite this obstacle, supporters of bond issues could claim numerous victories in the late 1940s and the 1950s. From 1946 through 1961 Cleveland's electorate approved $239 million in bond issues, or 69 percent of the total of $345 million submitted. Voter support varied over the years, ranging from the approval of all $54 million submitted in 1952 to the defeat of all $20 million in 1958.[79] During the twelve years from 1952 through 1963, bond proposals appeared on the Philadelphia ballot annually, yet only once, in the 1953 primary, did Philadelphians reject a borrowing measure.[80] Between 1947 and 1957 Detroit's property owners and their spouses voted on four bond proposals to finance a massive sewer project and sanctioned borrowing in three of the four contests.[81] In the municipal elections of 1947, 1951, and 1955, Baltimore's electorate approved $108.5 million of the $129.5 million in proposed borrowing measures, and in the latter two years every one of the fourteen loan questions sponsored by the builder-mayor Thomas D'Alesandro won voter endorsement.[82]

Measures that seemed to burden the taxpayers with future debt for the benefit of only one segment of the city had a more difficult time than balanced bond packages offering something for everybody. Thus the 1953 downtown redevelopment scheme in Saint Louis originally failed to receive the requisite two-thirds approval, and in 1957 a $15 million Cleveland bond proposal intended to trigger construction of a new convention hall and adjoining hotel suffered defeat. Like the Saint Louis measure, the convention hall scheme was designed to revitalize a faltering central business district, and residents in outlying neighborhoods seemed to resent largesse lavished on the downtown. Opponents of this pet project of Mayor Anthony Celebrezze claimed that "the $15,000,000 issue would fall only on Cleveland taxpayers, who needed new sewers more than a hall."[83] Backers of bond issues could not, then, expect automatic approval from the electorate, but in most of the major central cities voters were generally favorable to borrowing for capital improvements that might truly benefit them.

The willingness of both officials and voters to exploit the bond market is evident from the statistics on long-term municipal debt. As seen in table 6, in each of the twelve major central cities of the Northeast and Midwest long-term municipal indebtedness increased between 1945 and 1958. But the rate of increase varied markedly among the aging urban hubs. Chicago, Cincinnati, Cleveland, Baltimore, and Philadelphia embarked on a policy of large-scale borrowing soon after World War II and

Table 6. Net Long-Term Municipal Debt, 1945–1958 (in Thousands of Dollars)

City	1945	1949	1954	1958	% Increase 1945–58
New York	2,285,233	2,134,401	3,273,347	4,157,034	81.9
Chicago	90,266	156,337	248,120	467,683	418.2
Philadelphia	316,423	388,083	504,823	609,834	92.7
Detroit	284,742	262,217	292,000	331,497	16.4
Baltimore	131,300	148,304	236,183	292,856	123.0
Cleveland	82,227	106,145	192,831	218,982	166.3
Saint Louis	48,005	36,903	29,839	51,885	8.1
Boston	95,044	75,321	63,585	111,915	17.8
Pittsburgh	49,789	46,796	54,697	82,354	65.4
Buffalo	66,582	39,685	77,196	99,480	49.4
Minneapolis	60,793	61,496	55,676	62,565	2.9
Cincinnati	42,523	53,243	108,501	147,777	247.5

Sources: U.S. Bureau of the Census, *City Finances, 1945, Compendium of City Government Finances in 1949, Compendium of City Government Finances in 1954, and Compendium of City Government Finances in 1958* (Washington, D.C.: U.S. Government Printing Office, 1947, 1950, 1955, and 1959).

continued to build up their debt throughout the 1950s. Thus in Chicago indebtedness soared more than 400 percent whereas in Cincinnati it rose almost 250 percent, and in both Baltimore and Cleveland the increase topped 100 percent.

Because of tax policy, however, in some cities the borrowing splurge began later and proceeded at a slower pace. Interest rates and levels of indebtedness may have been low, but voters and officials deemed the postwar tax rates too burdensome to warrant further borrowing with the accompanying rise in debt service expenditures. This was true, for example, in Boston, Buffalo, Minneapolis, and Saint Louis. In each of these cities fears of higher property taxes and general fiscal stringency kept municipal authorities from incurring new debts during the late 1940s and the early 1950s. Interest and principal payments had to come from the city's tax revenues, and if there was no revenue to spare it seemed best to postpone capital spending.

Minneapolis was trapped in a perpetual fiscal crisis throughout the late 1940s and the 1950s as local property owners rebelled against further tax hikes. Consequently, it could spend no additional money for debt payments, and by 1959 it had the lowest ratio of net debt to full value of property of any of the nation's seventeen largest cities.[84]

Saint Louis also was fighting to balance its budget and resorted to the practice of diverting revenues traditionally earmarked for its debt fund to its operating fund.[85] By 1950 the Missouri city had sold only $5 million of the $43.5 million of bonds authorized in the election of 1944, and not until the mid-1950s did it begin to borrow large sums for the rebuilding of its infrastructure.[86]

Fearful that any additional debt charges would add to its already high tax rate, until 1957 Boston likewise pursued the frugal practice of retiring more debt each year than it incurred.[87] Thrift was the watchword as well in postwar Buffalo, where Mayor Bernard Dowd's financial report of 1946–47 characterized debt reduction as "the most constructive fiscal reform in Buffalo's municipal history."[88] In 1949 Dowd further expressed his abhorrence for additional borrowing in his annual message to the city council, condemning roundly "the life-sapping fiscal poison of heavy debt."[89] By eschewing this financial venom, Buffalo could supposedly achieve the mayor's dream, a 30 percent drop in the property tax rate. Only after Dowd's departure from city hall at the end of 1949 did Buffalo begin to take advantage of its ample debt margin for the funding of capital improvements.

Though fears of higher taxes prevented borrowing in only a minority of the older central cities, in each of the aging hubs there was growing concern for the revenue base. Borrowing might fund much of the city's rejuvenation, but ultimately local taxes had to pay rising debt charges as well as mounting operating expenditures. Thus any postwar urban renaissance rested not only on a good credit rating but also on a sound tax structure. A steadily increasing flow of money from local taxpayers was just as necessary as access to the bond market.

Traditionally, property taxes had been the mainstay of local finances, yet in the postwar era this fiscal foundation seemed increasingly shaky. Without population or economic growth the rate of increase in the central city's property valuations remained sluggish and could even lag behind the rate of inflation. In fact, property taxation was ill-suited to an inflationary era such as the late 1940s and early 1950s, for property taxes were not as responsive to economic cycles as income or sales taxes. Owing in part to taxpayer resistance to higher valuations, reassessments of property often failed to keep up with changes in market values, and thus local governments could not take full advantage of the rise in real estate prices. The result was a property tax base that proved less than adequate to meet the rising expenses of day-to-day municipal services and long-term improvements.

In light of recent history the property tax seemed an especially unreliable source for increased revenues. From the early 1930s through the mid-1940s property valuations plummeted in each of the major central cities, markedly reducing municipal income. Assessed valuations began to head upward in the late 1940s, but not until the early 1950s did they reach the level of the early 1930s. As late as 1951–52 the assessed value of taxable real estate in New York City was only $18.8 billion as compared with the 1932 peak of $19.6 billion. Between 1946 and 1950 the city's property valuations did climb 14 percent, but the consumer price index rose 25 percent.[90] Cleveland's valuation did not surpass its 1930 level until 1953, Saint Louis's property base did not exceed the prewar peak until 1951, and real estate values in Philadelphia did not bound back to the 1931 high until 1953.[91] Moreover, in Philadelphia, Saint Louis, Chicago, Pittsburgh, and Buffalo as in New York City, assessed values rose during the late 1940s at a slower pace than consumer prices.

No city's tax base was as depressed, however, as that of Boston. In 1930 Boston's real estate valuation totaled $1,980 million, but that figure fell to $1,490 million by 1945, climbed slowly to $1,631 million in 1955, and then dipped again to $1,503 million in 1960, never having matched its predepression peak.[92] A gradual postwar rise in tax valuations in the other older central cities did relieve some stress on municipal treasuries, but unless there was massive redevelopment resulting in sharp increases in real estate values, it did not seem that the property tax base offered any lucrative windfalls for the city coffers in the near future.

Moreover, in most of the older central cities it was politically dangerous to attempt to enhance municipal fortunes through a marked increase in the property tax rate. Downtown business interests already felt overburdened by high taxes, and central-city homeowners were equally critical of increased levies. Concerned parents might accede to levy increases for school districts, which depended even more heavily on the property tax than the city governments. But wise mayors shied away from such burdensome taxes. In 1945 Baltimore's Mayor Theodore McKeldin expressed a typical view when he warned, "Further increases in real estate taxes may retard anticipated postwar building operations to the detriment of the taxable basis and loss of employment opportunities," and his budget director seconded the mayor's position, arguing, "The measured conviction [is] that real estate is already bearing more than its just share of the cost of maintaining the City Government."[93]

Thus during the late 1940s and early 1950s, city officials successfully sought to keep the tax rate in check and thereby win laurels from the electorate. In Baltimore the rate dropped from $29.90 per $1,000 value in

1946 to $26.20 in 1951; in Buffalo it fell from $33.39 in 1945–46 to $29.22 in 1952–53; and by 1953 Philadelphia's rate had been fixed at $17.00 for fourteen consecutive years.[94] Similarly, from 1948–49 to 1956–57 Detroit's city tax levy remained stable, fluctuating between a high of $21.882 and a low of $21.478, whereas from 1947 through 1955 the rate for Saint Louis only inched up from $17.70 to $18.10.[95] Fiscal stringency in the late 1950s forced more notable increases, but it was clear that property tax hikes were not a politically feasible means for funding the rejuvenation of the city. Poll-conscious politicians only backed sizeable increases in the property tax rate when red ink filled the municipal ledgers and they faced no other alternative.

The property tax was an especially sensitive issue in Boston and Minneapolis. Boston held the dubious honor of imposing the nation's highest property levy, and despite the economizing efforts of Mayor John Hynes, the tax rate continued to rise from $42.00 per $1000 valuation in 1945 to $78.70 in 1956. In 1955 the chairman of the board of Sears, Roebuck told a Boston department store executive that Sears would not consider any additional branches in the New England metropolis because of the exorbitant property tax, and many other business chiefs claimed to cross Boston off their list of possible sites for the same reason.[96] In Minneapolis the problem was different. Property taxes were not necessarily high; instead they were quite low for homeowners. By 1959 only three of the forty-nine cities, villages, and townships in Minneapolis's Hennepin County had a lower effective tax rate on residential property, though owing to inequities in the central city's assessment practices all had lower rates on industrial property.[97] The burden on residences was, then, inordinately light, and homeowners wanted to retain this advantage. Keeping a check on property taxes became a local obsession, limiting the leeway of public officials dedicated to improved and expanded services.

Yet throughout the postwar era rising municipal expenditures increased the pressure on local property tax rates, making it more and more difficult for mayors and city councils to keep the lid on taxes. The inflated cost of needed goods and materials forced expenditures upward, but of even greater significance were the higher wages and more generous benefits granted municipal employees. With its thousands of police officers, fire fighters, and garbage collectors, city government was labor-intensive and devoted the bulk of its income to personnel costs. Inflation necessitated periodic pay raises, and new pension programs and an expanded work force also took their toll on the municipal treasury.

For example, in 1954 Philadelphia began the practice of contributing to health and welfare plans on behalf of its employees, and two years later it adopted a municipally financed group life insurance program for city workers. Together these initiatives forced municipal spending for employee welfare up 1,629 percent between 1954 and 1959.[98] Meanwhile, from 1952 to 1958 the number of full-time city employees rose 20 percent, though Philadelphia's population actually decreased during the 1950s.[99] Moreover, Philadelphia was not the only city battling rising personnel costs. Elsewhere city councils were also acceding to generous pension proposals, and city agencies were expanding their work forces. Even though political and business leaders attempted to impose a ceiling on tax rates, the pressure to increase municipal spending was unremitting.

The answer to municipal fiscal problems seemed to be new sources of revenue. Rather than continue their heavy reliance on the property tax, most city officials felt it was necessary to exploit new forms of taxation that might better respond to the inflationary trend of the postwar era and that might seem less burdensome to the electorate. As seen in table 7, during the late 1940s and the 1950s, many of the older central cities gradually freed themselves from their financial bondage to the property tax, drawing an increasing share of their revenues from nonproperty levies. Whereas in 1945 ten of the twelve older central cities in the Northeast and Midwest reaped more than 60 percent of their income from the property levy, by

Table 7. Sources of General Revenue, 1945, 1950, and 1958

City	Property Taxes (%)			Nonproperty Taxes (%)			Intergovernmental Aid (%)		
	1945	1950	1958	1945	1950	1958	1945	1950	1958
New York	63.9	47.3	42.8	10.2	21.5	21.5	21.9	27.1	22.7
Chicago	63.9	48.6	42.6	21.8	25.1	32.7	7.7	19.3	14.9
Philadelphia	56.2	44.0	34.3	32.7	37.4	39.1	3.7	5.2	7.3
Detroit	66.5	61.6	58.8	0.9	1.6	1.9	19.2	18.7	26.4
Baltimore	67.5	51.9	50.4	4.3	7.8	8.2	20.6	33.2	33.0
Cleveland	64.2	56.5	57.1	1.4	2.9	2.9	17.7	22.2	20.3
Saint Louis	60.9	47.5	40.0	26.9	39.3	38.9	1.2	2.7	4.6
Boston	70.0	69.7	66.6	2.6	2.4	1.8	23.0	23.2	25.5
Pittsburgh	82.2	70.3	54.1	2.3	16.0	23.4	4.4	6.1	13.2
Buffalo	70.8	59.7	54.7	2.3	3.5	5.7	20.3	32.3	28.9
Minneapolis	72.4	69.5	60.0	3.7	4.1	6.8	11.9	14.2	12.1
Cincinnati	50.2	42.8	26.1	1.3	5.2	22.5	27.1	14.5	16.0

Sources: U.S. Bureau of the Census, *City Finances, 1945, Compendium of City Government Finances in 1950, Compendium of City Government Finances in 1958* (Washington, D.C.: U.S. Government Printing Office, 1947, 1951, and 1959).

1958 only one did so. In the late 1950s Boston still depended on property taxes for two-thirds of its funding, but in such cities as New York, Chicago, Philadelphia, Saint Louis, and Cincinnati, a majority of municipal receipts came from other sources.

Philadelphia was in the vanguard of the effort to liberate municipalities from dependence on the property levy. In 1939 Philadelphia imposed the first municipal income tax in the United States. It levied a 1.5 percent tax on the salaries and wages of all residents of Philadelphia, no matter their place of employment, and on all nonresidents employed within the city. Thus suburban commuters to central-city offices and factories henceforth had to pay a share of the expenses for governing the urban hub. The income tax immediately became the city's second largest revenue producer, surpassed only by the real estate levy. Moreover, its share of the city's general revenue fund climbed steadily from 20.2 percent in 1940 to 31.1 percent in 1952 whereas the property tax accounted for 72.1 percent in 1939, before imposition of the new levy, but fell to only 40 percent in 1952.[100] The income tax not only offered city officials a lucrative alternative to the property levy but also a means of raising money that might prove more palatable to the city's electorate. By 1954 an estimated 15 percent of the income tax revenues came from nonresidents ineligible to vote in city elections.[101] Philadelphia voters were no longer shouldering the full burden of municipal expenses but were able to pass on part of the cost to commuters who could not express their dissatisfaction at the polls.

Following Philadelphia's example, other major central cities also turned to income taxes. For example, in 1948 the Missouri legislature authorized Saint Louis to impose a 0.5 percent tax on the earnings of individuals employed in the city, no matter whether resident or nonresident, and on the income derived by corporations from doing business within the city. The authorization was for only two years, lapsing in 1950, but in 1952 Saint Louis secured permission to levy an earnings tax for an additional two years. On assuming office, Mayor Raymond Tucker dedicated himself to winning permanent authorization for the levy and toured the state to sell his proposal to Missouri's legislators and their constituents. According to the *Post-Dispatch*, "The mayor had to spend more of his first year in office as a legislative lobbyist than as a man in the mayor's chair."[102] Seeking to exempt their constituents from the city impost, suburban legislators countered Tucker's efforts, but in 1954 the legislature agreed to sanction a permanent income tax if Saint Louis amended its charter before 1957 to provide for such a levy. Downtown business interests, the metropolitan newspapers, and Mayor Tucker conducted a hard-sell campaign in favor of the requisite charter provision, emphasizing that the earnings levy would shift some of the tax burden from city dwellers to suburbanites. In September 1954 the city's voters responded favorably to this argument, approving the charter amendment by a sweeping six-to-one majority.

That same year Cincinnati also adopted an income tax that encountered little opposition from within the city but roused vocal protests from nonresident commuters. In recent tax referenda Cincinnati voters had defeated proposals for increased property levies, leaving the city in a fiscal bind. An income tax that soaked suburbanites ineligible to vote seemed the best solution to the financial stress.[103] Moreover, in the mid-1950s Pittsburgh city officials also opted for an earnings tax with an estimated 10 percent of the revenue coming from nonresidents working in the steel capital.[104] By the late 1950s the earnings or income tax was, then, beginning to transform central-city finances. It was more responsive to inflationary pressures than the real estate tax, and because it imposed some of the tax burden on nonvoters, elected officials in the central city viewed it more favorably than property tax hikes.

Though politically feasible from the standpoint of central-city voters and officials, the earnings tax might prove highly unfeasible if state authorization was necessary and suburban lawmakers could block approval of the levy. Thus for the present many of the older central cities had to adopt other new levies or rely more heavily on existing nonproperty taxes. Even before it adopted an earnings tax, Saint Louis was drawing less of its receipts from property levies and more from an assortment of business license and franchise taxes. In 1937 this category of imposts accounted for 14 percent of the city's revenues as compared with 70 percent from property levies; by 1945 the share of income derived from these business taxes rose to 27 percent, and the property tax produced only 61 percent.[105] Included in this growing category were a tax of two cents per package on cigarettes and a gasoline tax of one cent per gallon. Moreover, public utilities had to pay 5 percent of their gross receipts to the city, and all merchants and manufacturers paid a tax of $1.25 per $1,000 of gross sales. By 1958 these assorted taxes still provided 26 percent of Saint Louis's revenues whereas the earnings tax accounted for 13 percent of the total, and the property levy produced only 40 percent.[106]

Following the Saint Louis example, in 1953 Philadelphia imposed a mercantile license tax requiring most business establishments within the city to pay $3.00 per $1,000 of annual gross receipts, and by 1960 it accounted for 7 percent of the municipal revenues. In 1953 Philadelphia's city fathers also introduced a real estate transfer tax requiring payment to the city of 1 percent of the sale price of real property.[107]

New York City, however, was especially devoted to the creation or increase of minor taxes that drew cash from a wide variety of sources. Between 1946 and 1951 the city sales tax rose from 1 percent to 3 percent, and from 1946 to 1955 the city raised the rate of the financial business tax four times, producing an overall tenfold increase from one-tenth of 1 percent to 1 percent. Meanwhile, during the first ten years after World War II, New York adopted a new 5 percent tax on hotel rooms, a 15 percent levy on racetrack admissions, a cigarette tax, and a 5 percent amusement tax.[108] Rather than increase the financial burden on real estate, Saint Louis, Philadelphia, New York City, and other older municipalities were applying their ingenuity to the discovery of new levies that the electorate would tolerate and that would help fund mounting expenditures.

The dream of most mayors and city councils, however, was increased funding from the state capital and Washington. Money from the state and federal governments would allow cities to spend more while taxing less. Municipal officials would be able to realize their pet projects for the rejuvenation of the central city without having to face the political consequences of higher taxes. Following World War II many urban leaders believed that the central cities richly deserved this intergovernmental funding, which seemed so necessary to the salvation of the metropolis. In 1947 the Mayor of Chicago's *Report to the People* repeatedly complained about the "pitifully inadequate" state funds allotted to the city, claiming that Chicago received back from the state only one dollar out of ten that it paid in state taxes. "Although the City of Chicago supplies the bulk of all tax revenues collected by the State of Illinois," the report argued, "it receives back only a tiny fraction of these millions—a situation unparalleled among other large cities in the land."[109]

Minneapolis politicians did not think this was unparalleled, for they too portrayed the state as a freebooter robbing the city and offering little in return. In 1947 the *Minneapolis Tribune* asked candidates for the city council for "the best solution to the Minneapolis financial problem," and repeatedly the prospective council members mentioned "larger sharing in state funds," "more money from the state," and "a fair share of the revenue which the city now pays to the state." One candidate expressed the view of many when he claimed that Minneapolis was entitled to state funds "and the majority in the legislature are unfair when they do not allot more money to the city."[110]

During the first thirteen years after World War II, mayors and city councils were not very successful in correcting this supposed injustice, for intergovernmental funding did not increase any more rapidly than local tax receipts. Between 1945 and 1958 the percentage of municipal revenues derived from state and federal treasuries (table 7) generally remained stable, though it differed considerably from city to city. Throughout the postwar period Baltimore, Boston, and the cities in New York State received approximately one-fifth to one-third of their revenues from the state and federal sources whereas the two Pennsylvania metropolises and Saint Louis generally received less than 10 percent of their income from the higher levels of government.

Most of this intergovernmental funding came from the states and was earmarked for schools, welfare, and highway construction. State governments had traditionally subsidized local school districts, and many returned a portion of the state gasoline taxes to cities for the laying out of major thoroughfares. Between 1945 and 1958 federal aid remained minor. Washington helped finance the construction of municipal airports, and the passage of the Hill-Burton Act in 1946 released federal funds for the building of municipal hospitals and health centers. In 1949 Congress created a federal urban redevelopment program that was intended to subsidize slum clearance projects, but delays in implementation meant that little redevelopment money reached the cities before the late 1950s. In 1950 federal grants accounted for a mere 4.2 percent of New York City's total revenues, and this figure only inched up to 4.8 percent by 1957–58.[111] Of the $53 million in Cleveland's capital improvements fund in 1958, only $3 million were from federal government grants for airport construction or urban redevelopment.[112] Mayors viewed Washington as a potential benefactor in the struggle to revive the city, but during the late 1940s and the early 1950s the cajoling of members of Congress reaped relatively little additional cash.

Thus during the first decade following World War II, the fiscal relationship between the city and the state and nation generally remained unchanged. City officials continued to express their oft-heard complaints about the hostility, intransigence, or indifference of lawmakers in Abany, Harrisburg, Springfield, and Jefferson City. Moreover, they continued the practice begun in the 1930s of lobbying in Washington. But as yet national and state legislators had refused to open the floodgates of intergovernmental funding and channel vast new revenues to the central cities.

Though a new era of intergovernmental spending had not yet dawned, the older central cities were making some headway in their efforts to reform their revenue bases. Income and sales taxes were assuming new significance, so that municipal fortunes no longer depended so heavily on property levies. Moreover, the central cities were taking advantage of the favorable postwar bond market and funding capital improvements necessary to create a better way of life in urban America. There was no revolution in municipal financing, but the aging central cities were adapting to the fiscal realities of the postwar world.

A Foundation for Change

During the late 1940s and the 1950s, the elements necessary for revitalization seemed to fall into place. Business leaders organized to mobilize money on behalf of urban renaissance. Citizens' groups dedicated to selling the message of modern planning and revitalization assumed the task of bringing the general populace into line. Moreover, a new breed of leaders occupied city hall, public officials who could work with corporate moguls and planners to get the cities off dead center. The emphasis was on cooperation to overcome urban ills. In Saint Louis, Sidney Baer cooperated with Morton May, setting aside past retailing rivalries. In Pittsburgh, Democrat David Lawrence of Irish, Roman Catholic, working-class origin joined hands with Republican Richard King Mellon, a plutocratic Protestant, thereby creating a union of the public and private sectors for the benefit of the city. And in Philadelphia, neighborhood organizations worked with the Citizens' Council on City Planning to achieve a supposedly better city for all. The city was foundering, and only the concerted effort of all urban dwellers could again make it a viable vessel.

Meanwhile, many of the older central cities were effectively confronting past fiscal problems. The twin banes plaguing the prewar municipal treasuries had been a heavy debt burden and an overreliance on the property tax. During the decade following World War II, however, cities appeared to manage their debt capably, aided by highly favorable interest rates. At the same time, most of the aging hubs were finding new sources of revenue, freeing themselves to some degree from their dependence on property values.

Thus both the private and public sectors seemed ready for action, and the fiscal foundations of the city were firmer than at any time since the 1920s. The climate for change was favorable, and the forecast for success was optimistic.

CHAPTER THREE ○ Progress or Decay

In March 1950 the *St. Louis Post-Dispatch* initiated a series of articles entitled "Progress or Decay? St. Louis Must Choose." In the first installment the newspaper observed that the aging Missouri city could "keep a date with destiny in the second half of the twentieth century" and create "a great metropolitan community of healthy, satisfied people, pleasant homes, thriving industry and attractive landscape." But if it remained "content to jog along without aggressive action—there lurk[ed] decay, squalor, the threat of steady decline," and the prospect that "St. Louis would take a back seat among American cities."[1] The answer to the question of "Progress or Decay?" was obvious. Saint Louis had to choose progress and embark on the long list of improvements that the *Post-Dispatch* suggested. It had to clear slums, improve the waterfront, build new traffic arteries, construct parking facilities, and ensure its prominence in the air age by maintaining the most up-to-date airport. It had to keep that date with destiny, for it could not take a back seat to any city.

Moreover, business and political leaders in the other older cities believed the same imperative that faced Saint Louis confronted their communities. They too had to launch costly schemes of public works if they were to thwart decay and achieve progress. They had to cleanse their environment, provide the most modern and convenient transportation systems, build new housing, and create revitalized downtowns. To the leaders of the Allegheny Conference, Philadelphia mayors Clark and Dilworth, and the editors of the *St. Louis Post-Dispatch* there was no real choice. The aging hubs had to begin rebuilding.

Responding to this imperative, most of the older central cities did embark on extensive improvement programs during the decade after World War II. With the public and private sectors joining in an effort to create a new city, reconstruction finally began. Aging urban centers throughout the Northeast and Midwest were choosing progress over decay, and miles of asphalt, bulldozed slums, and cleaner skies and rivers were the visible evidence of their commitment. During the late 1940s and the 1950s, urban leaders were not able to attain every goal in their struggle to remake the aging central cities. In a few cities they were stymied early in their efforts. But by the late 1950s the portrait of the older urban centers bore many bold new strokes missing from the picture in 1945.

Reforming the Urban Environment

If the older central cities were to prove successful in their competition with suburbia, one of their first tasks had to be the cleansing of their environment and the whitewashing of their image. Since the mid-nineteenth century, the popular mind had conceived of suburbia as a clean, healthy environment characterized by fresh air and green trees. In contrast, the city seemed a filthy place, its buildings blanketed with smoke, its waterways awash with refuse, and its streets devoid of natural beauty. Fashionable suburbs clustered along the "heights" above the smoke pall of the city and advertised their wholesome, natural setting by incorporating "garden," "woods," "forest," "park," or "lawn" in their names. This is where Americans were migrating in the new automobile age, escaping from the bleak, polluted core.

Recognizing this, urban business and political leaders embarked on a postwar campaign to renew the urban environment. This entailed antismoke crusades and tougher ordinances aimed at ridding the atmosphere of soot and ash. It also required massive investment in sewage and water treatment plants to guarantee ample supplies of clean water. Though politicians and publicists of the 1950s devoted much rhetoric, many news columns, and a mass of glossy brochures to proposals for urban redevelopment, downtown revitalization, and superhighway construction, the largest portion of locally derived capital improvement funds actually financed sewer and water schemes. This is where the city was investing its own revenues, and throughout the 1950s public investment in the much-ballyhooed federal urban renewal schemes was minor by comparison. The goal of this massive enterprise was to create an urban center that no longer conformed to the traditional stereotype of grit, grime, and foul pollution but that offered a decent environment in which to live and work.

Perhaps the most glaring deficiency in the central-city environment was the soot and smoke that soiled the clothes of urbanites, irritated their eyes and lungs, and reduced their visibility. In an age when homes, factories, and railroad locomotives burned sooty bituminous coal, the pall of smoke hanging over the nation's cities had a serious blighting influence. No city suffered from this plague of pollution more than Pittsburgh. Commenting in 1946 on the "multiple scuttles of soot one must devour per annum as a part of the price of living in Pittsburgh," a national magazine claimed conditions were "hellish, tormenting, disease-abetting and spirit-wilting." According to this periodical, if one knew Pittsburgh well, "the very name [would] granulate in your mouth and your nostrils sting from the memory of the somehow acid quality in its air." In a movie of the period Groucho Marx eyed the rings of cigar smoke that he was belching and remarked, "This is like living in Pittsburgh—if you can call that living."[2] At the close of World War II the steel capital was, then, a national joke and could claim the dubious distinction of being the nation's dirtiest metropolis. When asked about the renewal of Pittsburgh, the acerbic architect Frank Lloyd Wright replied bluntly, "It'd be cheaper to abandon it!"[3]

Following the example of Saint Louis, in 1941 Pittsburgh's city council had enacted a tough antismoke ordinance but owing to World War II had postponed enforcement. In 1945, however, the United Smoke Council, consisting of a broad range of civic leaders, embarked on a campaign to ensure prompt application of the ordinance. The recently organized Allegheny Conference on Community Development, representing the monied might of the city's chief business executives, also threw its support behind the fight against pollution, and the council soon affiliated with the powerful conference, winning valuable financial and administrative assistance. Responding to the pressure for action, Mayor David Lawrence and the city council set October 1, 1946, as the deadline for industrial and commercial structures to comply with the restrictions and October 1, 1947, as the date of enforcement for private residences. The coal industry offered some protests, but as a principal stockholder of the giant Consolidation Coal Company, Richard King Mellon could dampen resistance to the ordinance.

Likewise, when the Pennsylvania Railroad opposed state legislation authorizing the county to restrict the emissions of locomotives, Mellon, who again was a leading shareholder and a member of the railroad's board of directors, threatened to divert the freight business of other corporations under his control from the Pennsylvania lines unless the company yielded. Partially owing to Mellon's influence and that of other Pittsburgh business moguls, the legislation passed, closing a major loophole in the stringent regulatory powers of the city and county. In 1949 a comprehensive county smoke ordinance covering railroads, industries, and residences became operative, complementing the city measure in full effect for the previous two years.[4]

Pittsburgh's antismoke campaign won even greater acclaim than that of Saint Louis, and soon local residents and observers from throughout the nation were lauding its success. In 1950 the chairman of the United Smoke Council claimed that during the first winter the smoke ordinance was effective "the city received 39 per cent more available sunshine than the previous winter" and after three years of experience "visibility [was] up by almost 70 percent, laundry and painting bills [had] gone down, buildings [had] been cleaned, and the whole aspect of the community [was] more cheerful and bright."[5] As early as 1949 *Newsweek* reported on the many proposed improvements in the steel city, the "greatest so far and the most visible" being the "victory over smoke." *Newsweek* claimed that Pittsburgh was "no longer the smoky city or the tired milltown, but an industrial metropolis with a new bounce, with clear skies above it and a brand-new spirit below."[6] That same year *Architectural Forum* likewise wrote of "Pittsburgh Renascent," where "smoke [was] becoming a thing of the past."[7] The *Christian Science Monitor* waxed especially enthusiastic when it observed: "Pittsburgh is the test of industrialism everywhere to rebuild upon the gritty ruins of the past a society more equitable, more spacious, more in the human scale."[8]

Less publicized but also significant was Cincinnati's battle against smoke. In 1946 the *Saturday Evening Post* reported that the Ohio city was "smeared with soot," and "the blinding smoke on many a winter day brown[ed] out the whole basin."[9] Responding to this problem, the Cincinnati city council law committee considered five hundred pages of testimony on the pall hanging over the metropolis, and both the leading newspapers printed indictments of the smoke nuisance.[10] A coal industry journal observed, "Cincinnati citizens cannot get together on many public improvements but on this smoke question, practically all citizens agree that the town must be cleaned up."[11] The result was a new ordinance modeled on that of Saint Louis. In 1948, the first full year under the tougher controls, observed smoke violations were down 44 percent from 1946, and by 1950 the number of infractions had fallen 77 percent from four years earlier.[12]

The praise heaped on both Pittsburgh and Saint Louis inspired still other cities to attempt to clear their murky skies and atone for their gritty pasts. In 1946 Chicago amended its pollution ordinance to prohibit the emission of dense smoke; previously, the city had permitted smoke of any density for period of six minutes per hour, thereby allowing unlimited emissions when new fires were being built or fires were being cleaned.[13] Meanwhile, Minneapolis's Mayor Hubert Humphrey invited a smoke control expert to his city and appointed a committee to study the air pollution problem.[14]

In 1947 a leading good-government organization in Philadelphia, the Bureau of Municipal Research, observed, "There is little question that the constant bombardment by smoke and other air pollutants had been a major contributor to the blight of many areas in the city." According to the bureau's newsletter, the "cost of redevelopment to overcome blight and costs incident to avoiding it, such as commuting expenses, are attributable in a great measure to blight-producing smoke and fumes."[15] The following year Philadelphia's city council responded to these complaints, adopting a tougher "air pollution control" ordinance to supplant the ineffective legislation dating from 1904, and in 1950 the Bureau of Municipal Research admitted, "There appears to have been real progress toward smoke elimination."[16]

In 1948 the *New York Times* observed that there was a great deal of "indignation against the smoke and soot nuisance in New York City," and the newspaper predicted that the city might be "on the threshold of really doing something against smoke."[17] Led by the reform-minded Citizens Union, the pressure for tougher restrictions mounted in New York City, resulting in 1949 in the creation of a Bureau of Smoke Control and a Smoke Control Commission to draft a code of rules to curb emissions.[18]

Throughout the country urban skies were clearing of soot and ashes during the late 1940s and the 1950s. For example, in industrial Cleveland, with its numerous steel mills and traditionally "dirty" industries, the city division of air pollution recorded a drop in the settled dust average per square mile from 48.8 tons in 1947 to 32.4 tons in 1951 and to 21.6 tons in 1958.[19] Much of this reduction was owing to the switch from steam to diesel locomotives and the replacement of coal furnaces with oil or natural gas heating units. This change may well have occurred even without the adoption of restrictive ordinances in the central cities. But no matter the cause, the marked increase in visibility and improvement in air quality in such cities as Pittsburgh offered new hope to urban leaders that the older industrial cities could eliminate the sources of blight and create a better environment in which to live and transact business.

To create such an environment, however, many cities also would have to tame and cleanse their waterways. River cities like Pittsburgh and Cincinnati suffered from frequent floods; for example, in 1936 the Allegheny and Monongahela crested at twenty-one feet above flood level and trans-formed the steel capital's downtown into the Venice of western Pennsyl-vania. The following year the swollen Ohio inundated one-sixth of Cincin-nati. Moreover, since many major cities had no sewage treatment plants, the rivers carried tons of raw wastes, threatening urban health and dis-couraging waterfront development. In 1946 a national magazine reported that Cincinnati's untreated sewage was dumped into the Ohio River only a few hundred yards below the intakes for the city's water supply so that on occasion "Cincinnati's water [came] from its own septic tank." "No matter how thoroughly or adequately purified the water may be," the magazine observed, "each time that they drink it, Cincinnatians have difficulty in keeping out of their minds the fact that it is, after all, secondhand."[20]

According to one commentator writing in 1947, Philadelphia's water-ways were not "even fit for ships. Acids and gases generated by decaying sewage eat the paint off their hulls, corrode their metal work, and, if they linger long enough, eventually eat holes in their bottoms." Naval men and merchant mariners visiting the City of Brotherly Love complained "that river fumes turn green their gold watches and rings and tarnish their small change."[21]

Likewise, by 1948 water conditions were so bad along New York's shoreline that health authorities were threatening to close all of the city's beaches. The health commissioner could not "recommend too strongly" that the municipal leaders face the water pollution issue and appropriate money "immediately for the construction and maintenance of sewage treatment plants in order to make certain that [New York's] remaining beaches [were] safe."[22]

The federal government accepted responsibility for checking the flood waters threatening Pittsburgh, with the Army Corps of Engineers spending $114 million in the twenty years following the 1936 deluge to construct ten major flood-control reservoirs in the Upper Ohio Valley. Similarly, in 1947 the corps completed an $11 million barrier dam and flood wall to protect Cincinnati's chief industrial zone, the Mill Creek Val-ley.[23] But during the late 1940s and early 1950s, the cities themselves would have to tackle the equally troublesome problem of sewage pollu-tion, investing unprecedented sums in the construction of treatment plants. Lakefront cities like Chicago and Cleveland had already built such plants before World War II to protect their drinking water supplies drawn from the Great Lakes. But river cities had traditionally expected the flowing waters of the Mississippi or Ohio to carry their raw sewage out of sight and smell, and cities on the Atlantic had regarded the ocean as a bottomless receptacle for all of their wastes. After World War II these river and seaport cities realized that such convenient arrangements blighted their waterfronts and threatened the recreational use of their waterways. To eliminate the cesspools at their front door, they launched one of the greatest programs of environmental reform in the nation's history.

Cincinnati led the movement to clean the waterways of the Ohio River Valley. In 1934 a member of the "Clean-up and Beautify Week" Committee of the Cincinnati Chamber of Commerce began the campaign for sewage treatment when he complained: "Citizens of Cincinnati don't want to be reminded every time asparagus is served for supper in Pittsburgh or some other upstream community. The time is at hand . . . to provide a rallying point for control of water pollution in our valley."[24] The Chamber of Commerce soon created a stream pollution committee that fought for over a decade for congressional approval of an interstate compact among the states of the Ohio River that would require construction of sewage treatment plants. In 1948 Congress acceded to the demands of Cincinnati's business leaders, and the Ohio metropolis proceeded to implement a treatment program that others in the valley could emulate. As early as 1938 Cincinnati voters had approved a $1 million bond issue for sewage treatment after supporters of the measure publicized the fact that the area's sewage load was equivalent to the daily dumping of 720 dead horses in the Ohio River, or one floating by the city every two minutes.[25] This funding, however, was hardly sufficient for the task, and in 1948 the city council decided to finance the project through issuance of revenue bonds with the debt costs defrayed by sewer service charges imposed on householders. Not until 1951 was construction begun on the first treatment plant, and work on additional facilities continued throughout the 1950s.[26]

Cincinnati's efforts forced upstream Pittsburgh also to take action. At the close of World War II Pittsburgh's waterways were at least as filthy as its air, but in 1946 the city joined with its suburbs to create the Allegheny County Sanitary Authority. After negotiating to borrow $100 million from Pittsburgh banks, in 1956 the authority finally broke ground for a giant treatment plant.[27] Meanwhile, in 1954 Saint Louis and its suburbs had likewise created a metropolitan sewer district to confront drainage and pollution problems, and in 1957 Detroit initiated a $33 million program to upgrade its existing treatment facilities and expand their area of service.[28] This was minor, however, compared to the $125 million spent between 1947 and 1957 for the first phase of New York City's pollution-control program. Five new sewage treatment plants opened between 1952 and 1956; whereas in 1950 the city treated only about 410 million gallons of the daily sewage flow of one billion gallons, by 1960, 803 million gallons were treated each day.[29]

Yet of all the aging central cities Philadelphia initiated the most notable campaign to cleanse its water. At the close of World War II polluted water was for Philadelphia what smoke was for Pittsburgh. It was a symbol of the city's decadence, and no account of the venerable metropolis was complete without an attack on its foul, sewage-laden water. The waters of the Schuylkill and Delaware were an oft-cited example of the city's lethargy, its lack of civic spirit, and its failure to revive itself. Even before World War II city leaders had determined to do something about this most obvious blot on the city's reputation, but not until the postwar era were good intentions translated into action.

The initiative began under the city's Republican administration during the late 1940s, but the reorganization of the water department under reform mayor Joseph Clark accelerated the pace of improvement. Between 1947 and 1955 Philadelphia placed in operation three new sewage treatment works that transformed local waterways.[30] In 1947 only 20 percent of the city's sewage received any treatment, causing the Bureau of Municipal Research to observe that "it is little wonder that huge sludge banks are formed [in the Schuylkill and Delaware], that foul river odors develop and that fish die."[31] By 1960, however, city plants treated 96 percent of the sewage.[32] Moreover, to rid the water supply of its vile tastes and odors, the city renovated and reconstructed its water treatment facilities. In December 1948, according to a local water engineer, tastes and odors in the "oily-aromatic" waters drawn from the Delaware had begun "to increase about the middle of the month, and continued until Christmas Day, when the produced complete unpalatability at taps."[33] A decade later such crises were only a memory.

These projects, however, required a massive financial commitment. From 1945 through 1955 Philadelphia invested $202 million in sewerage and water improvements, or 35 percent of all the public money spent on capital improvements within the city during that period. By comparison, the city and state expended only $133 million within the city for highways, streets, and bridges, or 23 percent of the total invested in public improvement projects.[34] Though public officials were responding to the demands of the automotive public for wide, unencumbered highways, the first priority was to battle stream pollution, provide adequate sewers, and guarantee a palatable supply of drinking water.

Elsewhere older central cities were also launching major programs for the improvement of water systems. In the late 1940s Baltimore invested $19 million in the construction of the seventeen-mile-long Patapsco-Montebello Water Tunnel to enhance that city's water supply and eliminate the threat of shortages during summer droughts. Whereas Cleveland

had invested $60 million in its water system up to 1946, during the ten
years from 1947 through 1956 it committed an additional $76 million to
maintain and expand its service.[35] Similarly, from 1953 though 1958 Chicago spent $104 million for capital improvements in its water system.[36]
Throughout the nation, then, city governments were allocating a giant
share of postwar capital improvement funds to their departments of water
and sewerage.

Facilitating this massive investment was the advantageous financial
position of the water and sewer departments. Water agencies and many
sewer authorities traditionally depended on user charges to cover all their
expenditures. Moreover, revenue bonds with debt charges defrayed by de-
partmental income generally funded capital improvements in the water
and sewer networks. Thus expansion of these systems would not trigger
increases in the city tax rate, and fears of higher taxes would not thwart
capital improvement plans. Necessary increases in water and sewer
charges to pay for expansion rarely aroused as much hostility as hikes in
the tax rate. Even if there were some complaints, opponents might not
prove an obstacle to capital investment, for in some states, such as Ohio,
revenue bonds did not require voter approval whereas tax-supported municipal bonds did. In other words, the citizenry and public officials looked
more favorably on revenue bonds because they were not linked to the sensitive issue of higher taxes, and the electoral barriers to issuance of revenue bonds were lower than for the issuance of bonds with debt charges
defrayed from tax receipts.

A combination of advantageous financial arrangements and public
demand thus produced a boom in municipal investment in water and
sewer projects. By the late 1950s the aging central cities enjoyed not only
clearer air but purer and more abundant water. With justifiable pride
mayors and city engineers could point to bigger and better facilities and
tougher restrictions that were relieving Pittsburgh and Philadelphia of
their past stigmas. Hundreds of millions of dollars of postwar improvement funds were paying for these environmental reforms, but many who
had suffered from stinging eyes in the steel capital, had gagged on Philadelphia's water, and had been barred from New York City's polluted
beaches no doubt felt the expense was merited.

Yet massive investment in these capital improvements did not necessarily narrow the environmental gap between the aging central city and its
suburbs. Most of the leading central cities either contracted to sell water
and to provide sewage treatment services to suburban municipalities or
combined forces with the suburbs to supply water and sewer services
through a metropolitan authority. Consequently, investment in water-

works and treatment plants not only ensured the central city a cleaner, more abundant water supply but also offered these advantages to the suburbs.

For example, Cincinnati's sewage disposal plants were designed to serve the needs of virtually all of Hamilton County with both central-city and suburban householders paying sewer fees for the support of the city's project. Likewise, the city waterworks pumped water to many suburbs, supplying an overwhelming proportion of the county's residents. Maryland statute required the city of Baltimore to supply water to surrounding Baltimore County, and by 1960 the Detroit Department of Water Supply provided water for a suburban population of 1,400,000 and sewage treatment for almost 1,000,000 suburbanites as well as 1,670,000 central-city inhabitants.[37] Moreover, when Pittsburgh agreed to join the Allegheny County Sanitary Authority and Saint Louis helped found the Saint Louis Metropolitan Sewer District, these central cities were committing themselves to combat pollution and drainage problems not only within their boundaries but also throughout the sprawling suburban zone.

In fact, in some cases the central city's postwar investment in water and sewage facilities was almost wholly owing to rising suburban demands. By 1958 the Chicago water system serviced fifty-seven outlying communities, and during the previous eight years the population of its suburban supply area had soared from 522,000 to 805,000. It was largely for these thousands of new suburbanites that the Chicago Department of Water and Sewers was constructing over $100 million in capital improvements.[38] According to the city's chief water engineer: "The philosophy adopted by Mayor Richard J. Daley and the present administrators of the Chicago water system is, in effect: What is good for the Chicago metropolitan area is good for Chicago." Consequently, the city of Chicago was "attempting to provide not only for its own needs and for the needs of suburbs it now serves, but also for the needs of suburbs that may be added to the metropolitan area during the next 25 years."[39] In 1957 Cleveland's commissioner of sewage disposal expressed a similar attitude when he wrote: "It is with considerable pride that the City of Cleveland has accepted the task of supplying water and sewerage service for so much of Greater Cleveland."[40] By the mid-1950s this task encompassed servicing 500,000 suburbanites as well as 900,000 Clevelanders and required millions of dollars of capital improvements each year. But it was a responsibility the central city readily assumed.

In the short run the central cities generally did not suffer financially from supplying the burgeoning suburbs. Though state statute forbid Baltimore to profit from suburban water sales and Chicago sold its water to the suburbs at the same rate as to central-city consumers, in Cleveland and Cincinnati the city councils imposed considerably higher water rates on the suburbs than on city residents.[41] Because of the ample suburban receipts, Cleveland and Cincinnati leaders were able to keep central-city rates low while still guaranteeing adequate income for the water department. Moreover, in Detroit more suburban customers also meant more revenue for the waterworks and consequently welcome savings for central-city users. The general manager of the Motor City's water supply claimed, "If we had not developed the additional revenue [from the suburbs], the rates in Detroit would have had to be at least 41 percent higher."[42] Therefore, expansion of the water and sewerage systems to outlying communities seemed to make good business sense.

Yet in the long run the creation of a water and sewer infrastructure for suburbia simply accelerated the decentralization of America's population and permitted taxpayers to escape the central city without losing the benefits of essential water and sewer services. Cincinnati did attempt to blackmail suburban residents into accepting annexation to the central city by threatening to refuse them water. But this added only 2.8 square miles to the city during the period 1946 to 1953, and by the late 1950s city leaders recognized that the policy was a failure.[43] Moreover, some administrators of water and sewer departments resented this "political" use of their utilities. The general manager of the Detroit Department of Water Supply told a gathering of fellow water engineers: "Annexation cannot be forced by creating a great thirst in the suburbs. This procedure only establishes that water supply is not functioning as a true utility, but rather is entangled with other governmental functions." According to this administrator, "A water utility should be concerned only with water supply and the protection of water supply."[44]

Thus in many metropolitan areas water and sewer networks expanded markedly with little regard for the long-range consequences for the older central city. Though air pollution controls may have reduced the environmental gap between the inner-city bottoms and the suburban heights, massive investments in water and sewer facilities often benefited both the hub and the periphery and opened new outlying territory for development. Costly public improvements and stiffer regulations had lifted a pall from the reputations of Pittsburgh and Philadelphia, but postwar construction projects sponsored by departments of water and sewerage did not dam the flow of population and wealth to suburbia.

Adapting to the Automobile and Airplane

Just as the sewer and water programs were on a monumental scale so were the construction plans for updating the urban transportation system. With the passing of the streetcar and railroad era, older central cities were suffering from a serious case of transportation obsolescence. At the beginning of the twentieth century the trolley tracks and rail lines converging on downtown and the inner-city depot had ensured that the central cities were, in fact, central to American life. In the rail age no place was more accessible than the central business district, and nowhere did more people congregate each day. Now in the automobile and air age the older cities faced the necessity of preserving their preeminence by adapting to new modes of transport. In the last years before World War II urban leaders like Boston's Mayor Maurice Tobin and New York's Fiorello La Guardia had recognized the threat facing the central cities and the need to respond to the transportation revolution. During the decade following the war, however, the aging urban hubs reacted with even greater urgency, striving boldly to retain their central importance in American commerce and life.

Helping the cities respond to the imperatives of the new age were the state and federal governments. Whereas the water supply and sewerage schemes of the late 1940s and early 1950s depended almost wholly on local funds, the massive urban highway projects drew heavily on the treasuries in Washington, Harrisburg, Lansing, and Springfield. State highway departments assumed responsibility for urban extensions of state highway systems, and throughout the 1940s and 1950s the mileage of urban thoroughfares within the state systems increased markedly. In 1934 these urban extensions totaled 16,000 miles nationwide; by 1954 this figure had risen to 41,000 miles. Expenditures for state highways within municipal boundaries likewise soared from $31.5 million in 1940 to $653 million in 1954. Moreover, during this same period, state grants to municipal street departments for the construction and maintenance of local thoroughfares mounted from $52.8 million to $254.4 million.

Some of this new funding actually came from Washington through the state highway departments. In 1944 Congress enacted legislation that earmarked 25 percent of all federal highway funds for road construction in urban areas, and Washington agreed to pay up to 50 percent of the cost of the new urban thoroughfares. From 1946 through 1955 this urban share of federal highway funds totaled $1.09 billion. Such largesse seemed minor when compared with the funding authorized by the Federal-Aid Highway Act of 1956. In this measure Congress empowered the federal government to pay 90 percent of the construction costs of an interstate highway system that was to include 5,300 miles of expressways in urban areas. By 1960 the states were receiving more than $1 billion annually for the building of urban superhighways, a sum sufficient to transform the map of metropolitan America.[45]

Meanwhile, the federal government was also subsidizing municipal efforts to meet the demands of the air age. In 1946 Congress had adopted the Federal Airport Aid Act, which established a program of matching grants for construction of local airfields, and by 1959 Washington had awarded $500 million in such grants. Moreover, during the early postwar era, the federal government transfered $1.6 billion in military aviation facilities to the civil authorities, providing the land, runways, and hangars for many municipal airfields.[46] Though millions of dollars derived from municipal bonds and local tax receipts also funded the postwar highway and airport schemes, state and federal aid was invaluable in realizing the transportation dreams of city planning departments, chambers of commerce, and ambitious mayors eager to refashion their urban domains in conformity with the transportation technology of the postwar world.

Heading the list of desired transportation projects in every major city was the construction of highways to relieve the worsening traffic snarls. Owing to gasoline and tire rationing during World War II, urban Americans had enjoyed a brief respite from traffic congestion from 1942 through 1945. But with the return of peace, automobiles again jammed the streets in ever-increasing numbers to the consternation of public officials, business leaders, the local press, and millions of swearing motorists. According to Baltimore's Master Transportation Plan of 1949: "The improvement and rebuilding of our cities to meet the demands of the automobile . . . is the greatest single challenge confronting civic leaders and planners today, [for] the present cost in time, money, human injury, death and property damage as a result of traffic congestion is appalling." Not only were the delays and accidents a serious urban problem, so was the blighting effect of automobiles and trucks clogging formerly tranquil residential streets. The city's planners noted, "The peace, quiet and safety of most of Baltimore's in-town residential areas have been destroyed by a blanket of traffic [so that] decent family living has become impossible [and] large sections have been blighted."[47]

Elsewhere the complaints were similar. Cleveland's General Plan of 1949 observed that the Ohio metropolis was "choked with more cars than it [could] handle," and the consequent delays in truck deliveries, the idling motors wasting fuel, and the mounting number of accidents added up "to several millions of real dollars that . . . Clevelanders [paid] yearly for traffic congestion."[48] In 1954 Buffalo's Chamber of Commerce complained, "Our traffic arteries are tragically out-of-date[,] . . . hampering economic progress to a dangerous extent." And like the Baltimore and Cleveland planners, the Buffalo businessmen noted, "[The] lack of adequate . . . arteries in Buffalo is costing our citizens more than $35 million annually in lost time, wasted fuel, wear and tear on vehicles, lowered property values and in accidents."[49] Finally, in 1956 Philadelphia's Urban Traffic and Transportation Board warned that the metropolitan area was "becoming mired in a traffic problem so intense that the region's livability, its efficient functioning and its competitive power to attract population and industry [were] all seriously impaired." By 1980, the Philadelphia traffic planners prophesized, "Unless drastic steps are taken to reverse the trend, the Central Business District quite literally will have reached the point of traffic saturation and will have lost its ability to function at a profitable level."[50]

Delays, accidents, blighted neighborhoods, central business districts choking on an overdose of automobiles, all these dire symptoms of the omnipresent traffic malady seemed to point to debility and possible death for the aging central city. Highway improvements to remedy traffic woes were, then, viewed as a necessary means for preserving the urban core. In 1947 the federal commissioner of public roads expressed the prevailing attitude of postwar America when he wrote that new highways, "developed with vision, will do much to stop the decay of our cities and prevent the attendant decrease in property values."[51] Two years later Detroit's leading highway booster, Mayor Albert Cobo, reiterated this view when he predicted that "highways would lure residents of neighboring areas to shop [in Detroit]" and would "retard the decentralization of business into suburban areas which pay no Detroit taxes."[52] Improved thoroughfares would not simply facilitate the movement of vehicles but ensure the continued vitality of the traditional business center and free residential neighborhoods of the stream of cars and trucks so threatening to their quality of life. According to Cleveland's planners, the goal of the local highway program was "not only fast and safe traffic but, equally important, quiet and safe neighborhoods."[53]

Yet the widening of existing thoroughfares or the construction of a single expressway was not sufficient to preserve the prosperity and well-being of downtown and the neighborhoods. Instead, planners believed that the public authorities had to build a comprehensive system of limited-access highways designed to solve the existing traffic problems. With six to eight lanes and no traffic lights or intersections, these highways would accommodate more vehicles at higher speeds and thus reduce congestion and delays. Moreover, by diverting through traffic from downtown arteries and numerous cars and trucks from residential streets, the new highways would loosen the automotive stranglehold on the central business district and eliminate one of the causes of neighborhood blight. To achieve its ends, however, the urban expressway system had to be properly designed, and during the postwar era, highway planners agreed on a scheme that theoretically would produce the desired ends.

According to the highway plans adopted in one city after another, freeways were to radiate from the central business district like spokes from a hub, thereby supposedly ensuring that the downtown would remain the single dominant center of the metropolis in the automobile age as in the streetcar era. But the radial freeways were not to penetrate the downtown; instead, they were to terminate at an inner-belt freeway ringing the central business district that was to distribute the centripetal flow of traffic to various downtown exits. At the suburban edge of the metropolis an outer-belt expressway would carry intercity traffic around the urban area, thus freeing city streets of one source of congestion.

During the late 1940s and the early 1950s, a number of these urban expressway schemes moved from the planning to the construction stage. As early as 1946 the Detroit city council authorized the state highway department and the county road commission to acquire the rights-of-way for the John Lodge and Edsel Ford radial expressways, and by 1953, $105 million had been spent or committed for the Motor City's freeway program.[54] In 1947 the Philadelphia city council ordered the city's planning commission and director of public works to draft preliminary plans and negotiate with the state highway department for construction of the Schuylkill Expressway, the first of the proposed superhighway spokes to emanate from the downtown hub. Six years later the state awarded the initial contracts for the Schuylkill artery, and actual building of the highway began.[55]

In 1953 the first sections of Pittsburgh's Penn-Lincoln Parkway opened to traffic, channeling automobiles from the city's east side to the Golden Triangle.[56] In 1955 construction started on the Cincinnati expressway network proposed in the city's master plan of 1948.[57] Also in 1955 the Major Deegan Expressway opened, carrying automobiles and trucks southward through the Bronx toward Manhattan and Long Island, and the building of the controversial Cross-Bronx Expressway proceeded slowly but surely.[58] Moreover, by 1957 the Congress Expressway, the first leg of Chicago's superhighway scheme, was completed from the Loop to the city's western edge.

At the beginning of 1956, 184 miles of expressways already carried traffic through the older central cities of the northeastern quadrant of the United States, and 94 miles were under construction.[59] Thus even before passage of the landmark Federal-Aid Highway Act of 1956, municipal authorities in cooperation with state highway departments were cutting costly traffic arteries through the body of the metropolis to draw the life blood of commerce to the city's faltering heart. After 1956 the pace of construction quickened, but by the mid-1950s the rights-of-way had been purchased and the ground had been broken in older central cities from Boston to Saint Louis.

Even in the initial years of freeway building, some critics voiced complaints about the construction schemes, but the overwhelming sentiment favored the new traffic arteries. In the early 1940s Baltimore's municipal legislators had expressed doubts, and when Chicago's council first reviewed that city's superhighway plans, individual neighborhoods rallied against any facet of the proposal that seemed to threaten their well-being. In words to be repeated in one city after another, a South Side alderman argued that the proposed superhighway trespassing on his bailiwick "would destroy the homes, churches, and schools of people who lived there 40 and 50 years."[60]

Likewise, during the 1950s, some homeowners and neighborhood associations attacked the specific routing of the expressways or the elements of design. In 1955 the Walnut Park Improvement Association of Saint Louis denounced a bond issue to finance the Mark Twain Expressway because it disliked the selected route of the superhighway. The head of the Walnut Park organization announced quite definitely: "[Our group] is opposed to this bond issue and I personally am opposed to it."[61] But very few Americans were against the construction of freeways per se, and thus critics could rally opposition only among the small minority directly displaced or inconvenienced by highway plans. On election day 1955, 84 percent of Saint Louis voters backed the expressway bond issue, and such returns were not unusual.[62] Across America, superhighway proposals won broad popular support, for they seemed to promise greater mobility and a new boost for the central cities burdened by a horse-and-buggy street system.

A network of expressways, however, would be of little benefit if there was no place to park at the motorist's destination. In each of the older central cities business leaders and planners complained that parking problems spelled doom for the downtown. For example, in 1951 Cleveland's planning commission reported a simple fact of life in the automobile age: "When people find it too much trouble to park downtown, they stop coming downtown." Consequently, "bad parking makes poor cities. Literally poor."[63] Similarly, a parking survey of Saint Louis soberly stated the consensus of opinion when it observed, "If decentralization of the Central Business District is to be avoided and the rehabilitation of the area accomplished . . . , the demand for suitable and adequate motor vehicle parking . . . must be met."[64]

Thus construction of freeways was not sufficient; a municipal program to provide parking facilities was also necessary. In fact, the realization of freeway proposals would increase the need for additional parking. As early as 1945 the *Cincinnati Enquirer* editorialized that construction of parking garages and lots was "a necessary corollary to the development of super highways which funnel traffic from a wide area into the downtown sectors."[65] Two years later Detroit's planning director reiterated this view when he noted, "Storage garages, . . . surface lots, and perhaps mechanical parking gadgets still uninvented, all must be mustered in a concerted attack on [parking] problems before the expressway swamps the area it is supposed to save.[66] That same year a Philadelphia business leader expressed the sentiment most simply: "We can no more think of building a freeway without terminal facilities, that is parking, than to build a railroad without a station."[67]

Responding to the perceived need, older central cities embarked on a variety of parking programs during the late 1940s and early 1950s. In 1947 the Pittsburgh city council created a parking authority that by the close of 1953 had completed two garages accommodating almost 1,500 cars plus two lots for more than 300 vehicles. Moreover, the authority had begun excavation for an underground parking facility for almost 900 additional automobiles.[68] Pittsburgh's widely acclaimed efforts inspired the founding of similar parking authorities throughout the nation, all intended to encourage motorists to shop and transact business downtown. In 1948 Detroit created its Municipal Parking Authority, which mobilized for action more slowly than the Pittsburgh counterpart, but by 1953 it could claim four city-owned parking lots.[69] Also in 1948 Baltimore established an Off-Street Parking Commission, which offered long-term loans to private parties who wanted to construct and operate parking facilities.[70] Two years later Philadelphia copied the example of its sister cities and organized a parking authority that soon broke ground for 500-car garages at Rittenhouse Square and in the heart of the retail district on Chestnut Street.[71] In 1952 Buffalo followed suit with a Board of Parking and the next year authorized a $4 million bond issue to finance the building of three downtown garages.[72]

Meanwhile, Chicago was drafting a financial plan that dwarfed that of

Buffalo. In December 1952 the Windy City issued $22.6 million of revenue bonds, the principal and interest to be paid from the income from the proposed municipal garages and lots. This scheme was intended to provide seven thousand parking spaces, and the Chicago Park District's two garages beneath lakefront Grant Park were to have an additional capacity of 4,000 cars.[73]

The central cities had, then, initiated schemes of major proportions. Yet the demand for spaces seemed to grow faster than the city could pour concrete for the ever larger parking decks. In 1956 Philadelphia's Urban Traffic and Transportation Board reported, "If automobile traffic increases at current rates, as many as 20,000 additional off-street parking spaces may be needed in the Central Business District by 1980."[74] The following year Pittsburgh's parking authority reported that parking demands in the Golden Triangle would increase 10 percent by 1960 and an additional 8 percent between 1960 and 1965. To handle this rising burden, the authority recommended the provision of seven hundred new spaces per annum.[75] The central cities seemed trapped on a treadmill, building ever larger garages but unable to reach the goal of convenient parking for all. In 1958 a Buffalo Chamber of Commerce booster could write, "As a result of the recent expansion of downtown parking facilities it is often possible for a shopper to park nearer a store in the downtown area than in some [suburban] plazas."[76] But few auto-borne customers seemed to believe this claim. Suburbia still had an advantage over downtown in terms of parking, even though the central cities tried desperately to close the gap.

Not only did the older central cities have to accommodate the ever-increasing wave of auto traffic, they also had to confront America's new-found devotion to flight. Between 1946 and 1957 the number of airline passengers in the United States more than quadrupled, soaring from thirteen million to fifty-three million.[77] Airplanes were fast supplanting trains as the most popular mode of intercity passenger transportation, and none of the central cities felt it could ignore this fact. Economic decline seemed the sure penalty for a city that failed to provide sufficient air facilities. In 1946 Cleveland planners advised that the municipal airport "if properly developed" could "prove to be the deciding factor influencing [the city's] future growth and prosperity."[78] Two years later Philadelphia's Bureau of Municipal Research expressed a typical sentiment when it warned that "Philadelphia cannot afford to be left behind in the highly competitive field of air commerce."[79] In 1950 the *St. Louis Post-Dispatch* offered similar advice, noting, "It is of high importance that St. Louis does not become an aviation flag stop through inadequate facilities, civic indifference, . . . and beyond all, through . . . indecision."[80]

Each city, then, had to try to beat the others in the competition for aviation supremacy and the resulting economic preeminence. The consequence of this battle for first rank was an epidemic of airport construction during the 1940s and the 1950s, with each metropolis claiming a better, more modern facility than that of its rivals. In June 1950 Baltimore finished construction of its new $15 million Friendship International Airport. The mayor's report for that year announced enthusiastically, "Every Baltimorean can be proud of owning the finest airport in the world," a facility that "aviation experts have acclaimed . . . as being the only really modern airport in existence.[81] In 1953 Philadelphia opened its International Airport Terminal Building, which an official of the city planning commission claimed was "generally conceded to be among the world's finest structures of its type."[82] Between 1951 and 1956 Saint Louis erected a $6 million terminal widely applauded not only for its contribution to air travel but also for its architectural distinction.[83] Meanwhile, in the early 1950s Cleveland was planning a new $4 million terminal building, which according to the city's annual report was designed to be "as nearly perfect as could be attainable."[84]

Chicago, however, was to win the battle for the skies. In 1947 the mayor's *Report to the People* stated clearly, "Ever since aviation was first recognized as an essential mode of travel and transport, Chicago has been determined to have the world's greatest airport."[85] Ten years later the Windy City proudly referred to its Midway Field as the "World's Busiest Airport," and eleven million people arrived and departed annually at the city's three municipal airports.[86] Moreover, with admirable foresight the city Department of Aviation had a new jetport at O'Hare Field waiting in the wings ready to supersede Midway in the early 1960s. As early as August 1945 the mayor had appointed an Airport Selection Board to choose the site for an airfield of a much larger scale than Midway. The board was instructed to select a site for "the best airport—the safest, the most convenient and with the most capacity of any airport on this continent."[87] A discarded World War II proving ground won the board's favor, and over the next decade the city would gradually improve the field, which in 1949 acquired the name of O'Hare. Finally, in 1958 the city council demonstrated its commitment to retaining Chicago's aviation supremacy in the jet age when it approved the sale of $120 million of revenue bonds for the improvement and extension of O'Hare Airport.[88] The resulting facility would dwarf the previously acclaimed efforts of Baltimore, Philadelphia, Saint Louis, and Cleveland.

In each of the aforementioned cities airport development remained in the hands of municipal officials and was just as much a function of city government as street paving or sewer construction. But in both New York City and Boston postwar city officials surrendered responsibility for the building and maintenance of airports to independent authorities headed by gubernatorial appointees. In 1939 New York City's ambitious Mayor Fiorello La Guardia dedicated his namesake airfield built on landfill along Long Island's north shore, and two years later he began development of present-day Kennedy Airport along the south shore. La Guardia's aviation dreams, however, proved monumentally expensive, and in 1946, when William O'Dwyer succeeded to the mayor's chair, La Guardia Field was losing almost $1 million annually, and its runways were sinking six inches a year back into Flushing Bay. Moreover, completion of the new south shore giant was estimated to cost $171 million. Unable to shoulder such a burden, in 1949 New York City transferred both airports to the independent New York Port Authority, an agency created in 1921 to govern harbor facilities along both the New York and New Jersey shores. Henceforth, authority commissioners chosen by the governors of New York and New Jersey controlled the aviation destinies of the nation's largest metropolitan area.[89]

In 1948 Boston ceded control over Logan Airport to a State Airport Management Board, and eight years later the legislature authorized creation of the Massachusetts Port Authority to supersede the board. At the close of World War II former Boston mayor, and now Massachusetts governor, Maurice Tobin had told the state legislature that Boston needed modern air facilities "to keep pace with progress" and urged the state to intervene if the city faltered.[90] Thus when the city proved unable to answer the needs of the new transportation era, Logan Airport shifted to the control of the state.

Whether through agencies of municipal government or independent authorities, each of the major central cities did come to terms with changing transportation technology. Using federal grants and general obligation bonds with interest and principal defrayed from tax revenues, the central cities financed the first stages of airport expansion in the 1940s. By the late 1950s, however, the profitability of airport operations had produced increasing reliance on revenue bonds with debt charges paid from airport income. During the decade and a half after World War II, the central cities had, then, created the giant airports needed to keep pace with the demands of the new age, and they no longer expected the taxpayer to foot the bill. Reviewing its history of airport development, a city like Chicago could justifiably boast and speak with pride.

Though older central cities devoted much time and money to servicing new modes of transportation, they did not ignore the older forms of public transit. Later critics have lambasted the postwar preoccupation with the automobile and the resultant neglect of electric rail and bus lines. Public officials and business leaders in New York City, Chicago, Philadelphia, and Detroit certainly felt the imperative of adapting to autos and aircraft more strongly then the necessity of expanding public transit systems. The transit networks were already in place whereas the expressways and airports were virtually nonexistent and had to be built if the central cities were not to become museum pieces representative of a bygone era. But the focus on cars and planes did not mean that transit lines throughout the nation were left to rust into oblivion. There was public investment in mass transit, and in most cities this was an integral part of the transportation plan.

Especially noteworthy was the growing sense of public responsibility for mass transit. Private corporations had traditionally owned and operated the streetcars, subject to the franchise provisions imposed by city governments and to the regulations of state public utility commissions. In the 1940s, however, an increasing number of cities purchased streetcar and subway lines, making transit a municipal function. For example, in 1940 New York City bought the principal subway and surface lines within its boundaries; two years later the city of Cleveland acquired the local transit system; and in 1947 a public transit authority paid $87 million for the transportation properties of the Chicago Surface Lines and the Chicago Rapid Transit Company. Moreover, in 1947 the Massachusetts legislature authorized the newly created Metropolitan Transit Authority (MTA) to purchase the stock of the Boston Elevated Company and assume full control of the transit network.[91] In 1955 the Mayor's Committee on Mass Transportation in Baltimore recommended the creation of a metropolitan authority to acquire and operate the Baltimore Transit Company lines, but the recommendation was not implemented until the 1960s.[92]

With many transit companies facing imminent bankruptcy or cutting service to ensure profits, public ownership seemed necessary to guarantee adequate transportation for urban residents and to keep buses and streetcars moving. To most postwar urban leaders the automobile represented the wave of the future, but mass transit lines also had to remain in operation. Consequently, in the largest cities the public sector entered into the breach and shouldered responsibility for perpetuating rail and bus transportation.

In some cities the municipal authorities went further and invested millions of dollars in the expansion and improvement of the transit network. Philadelphia was especially dedicated to building and equipping new lines, and from 1950 to 1955 the public sector completed $42.9 million in transit improvements within the city as compared to $34.7 million spent for bridges and highways and $29.7 million for airports.[93] The principal transit project was the extension of the Market Street subway from Twentieth to Forty-sixth streets, permitting the destruction of an ugly elevated line along that route. Philadelphia's Department of City Transit also purchased the equipment necessary for operation of the Locust Street subway, which had been constructed in the 1930s but which had stood empty for almost two decades.[94]

Moreover, in Cleveland the capital improvements program for 1951–56 allocated more money for transit than for any other single category, recommending $39.6 million for public transportation as compared with $36.1 million for freeways.[95] Most of this transit funding was for the completion of the city's first rapid transit line, which opened in 1955.[96] Meanwhile, the Chicago Department of Subways and Superhighways was expanding its new underground system, which began operation in 1943. In 1958 Chicago won national attention when it opened the West Side Subway along the median strip of the Congress Expressway, the first rapid transit line to share a right-of-way with a freeway.[97] Boston's MTA moved more slowly in the 1950s, though downtown interests urged subway expansion as a means of refocusing commerce on the central business district. From 1952 to 1954 the MTA added four miles to the East Boston line, and in 1959 it completed a nine-mile extension through the western suburbs of Brookline and Newton.[98]

Though the late 1940s and the 1950s would never rank as a golden age in the history of New York City's subways and surface lines, from 1946 to 1959 the local transit authority did authorize $809 million in capital funds for improvement of the system, whereas from 1900 to 1945 capital investment had totaled $1,357 million.[99] New York's powerful czar of highway construction, Robert Moses, denigrated the significance of public transit and seemed an ever-present obstacle to increased transit spending. But even Moses could not stop the public sector from pouring hundreds of millions of dollars into new rolling stock, line extensions, and station improvements.

The most notable development in transit during the postwar era, however, was the replacement of streetcars with buses. Buses were more compatible with automobiles and thus better suited to the auto age. Streetcars, for example, required mid-street loading areas where passengers could board or alight, but these loading zones occupied valuable street space necessary for auto traffic. To gain access to the mid-street loading area, transit passengers had to dart between automobiles and trucks, a maneuver that endangered the passengers and slowed the flow of vehicles.

Streetcar tracks also broke the smooth surface of the street to the irritation of motorists. In contrast, gasoline-powered buses loaded at the curb and required no tracks nor any unsightly overhead wires. Moreover, since they did not operate on tracks or wires, buses were more flexible in their movement, thus facilitating the speedier flow of auto traffic. In recommending the elimination of trolleys, a 1949 transportation study sponsored by Pittsburgh's Allegheny Conference repeatedly complained of "the inflexible path of street cars" and their inability "to pass even minor obstructions in the path of travel." When blocked by "automobiles and trucks that [were] backing into or pulling out of curb parking spaces," the streetcar could not dodge the obstacle but had to come to a standstill, halting all auto traffic behind it.[100]

More flexible buses could also take advantage of the new postwar freeways, and transit authorities would be able to route express buses along the superhighways linking the suburbs and city center. In fact, buses could operate wherever cars could, so that bus lines could potentially exploit the highways of the auto age whereas the streetcar could not. In 1946 Detroit's Department of Street Railways recognized this when its transportation plan observed, "The ultimate form of rapid transit will be by modern motor buses operating over the expressway highway network."[101] Inexpensive gasoline and the faster ride supposedly offered by buses were other factors dooming the once ubiquitous streetcar.

Throughout the nation transit authorities were sounding the death knell for the old-fashioned trolley. From 1945 to 1949 New York City's Board of Transportation spent $30 million to purchase 1,725 new buses while reducing its inventory of trolley cars from 1,228 to 606.[102] In 1947 Chicago was boasting, "Comfortable, easy-riding buses are being substituted for rattletrap streetcars that should have been derailed at the scrap heap years ago."[103] By the middle of 1954 only four streetcar lines remained in the Windy City, and in June 1958 the Chicago Transit Authority retired its last trolley.[104] Likewise, the Detroit Department of Street Railways eliminated its last streetcar line in April 1956.[105]

By adapting mass transit to the automobile, urban leaders were accepting that henceforth the private car would be the primary means of transportation and buses and rail the secondary mode. Figures indicating a marked drop in transit use reinforced this type of thinking. From 1945 to 1958 the total number of transit passengers in the United States plummeted from thirty-five billion to twelve billion, and in each of the major central cities buses, streetcars, and subways lost customers at an alarming rate.[106] Between 1945 and 1958 the number of revenue passengers riding the Detroit transit system dropped 66 percent, and patronage of the

Philadelphia Transportation Company declined 51 percent. Even in transit-dependent New York City with the most extensive subway system in the world, the number of transit users fell 34 percent from a high of 2,620 million in 1947 to 1,733 million in 1958.[107] Though cities like Cleveland and Philadelphia were investing in major transit improvements, no one could deny that American workers and shoppers were opting for the automobile.

Thus the miles of new freeways as well as the acres of new airports seemed justified. The era of public transit was waning, and government officials had few qualms about spending for the automobile and the airplane rather than for the streetcar or locomotive. Centripetal expressway radials would supposedly draw customers to the central-city core just as the streetcar lines had in earlier decades, and airfields would ensure that Chicago remained the transportation capital of America in the air age as in the rail era. The older central cities were staving off transportation obsolescence with billions of dollars of capital improvements, and during the decade following World War II few persons questioned the wisdom of the investment.

At the close of the 1950s, however, it was becoming clear that the chief beneficiaries of the freeways and airports would be the suburbs rather than the central cities. Outer belts designed to bypass the commercial hub were themselves to become magnets for manufacturers, retailers, and office developers. The freeway systems would not dam the flow of capital and jobs from the central city to the suburbs; instead, they would channel the decentralization of population and commerce along outlying highway corridors. Likewise, airports located beyond the central-city boundaries or at the edge of the central city would become hubs of commerce adding millions of dollars of tax revenues to suburban tills. During the late 1940s and the 1950s, urban leaders were attempting to perpetuate central-city supremacy through massive transportation schemes. Later decades would prove the futility of their efforts.

Attacking the Slums

Clearing the air, cleaning the streams, bulldozing rights-of-way, and paving runways were all vital elements of the postwar physical renewal campaign in America's central cities, but the ultimate dream of planners, public officials, and civic leaders was the eradication of slums. Acres of housing deemed uninhabitable by middle-class observers and blocks of little-used, soot-begrimed warehouses and factory lofts formed a dingy ring around the downtown, and these gray areas seemed to be creeping outward, undermining property values and carrying with them the social problems of crime, delinquency, and welfare dependency. Moreover, pockets of decay in the central business district were threatening the city's prime source of property taxes. Only through the elimination of this dilapidated housing and these sundry commercial eyesores could the city halt the engulfing wave of blight and attract the favorable attention of households and businesses contemplating a shift of their tax dollars to suburbia. Thus during the late 1940s and the 1950s, the older central cities launched an attack on the slums, seeking to replace or rehabilitate these visual reminders of urban decay.

In the 1940s one state after another empowered its cities to initiate slum redevelopment programs. On the eve of World War II, New York, Illinois, and Michigan had already authorized municipalities to use the power of eminent domain to assemble slum properties for private redevelopment. In 1943 Maryland's legislature passed a similar measure for Baltimore, and two years later lawmakers in Minnesota and Pennsylvania followed suit, enabling Minneapolis, Philadelphia, and Pittsburgh to take slum property and sell it to private developers. By 1946 Massachusetts had authorized the Boston Housing Authority to act as that city's redevelopment agency, and after failing to enact redevelopment legislation in two previous sessions, in 1949 Ohio's solons gave Cleveland and Cincinnati the power to assemble blighted properties for clearance and reuse. Missouri's lawmakers adopted a different approach, authorizing private redevelopment corporations, subject to the city's approval, to exercise the power of eminent domain and force slumlords to part with their property. Moreover, in Missouri, as in New York, Michigan, and Massachusetts, the state legislature granted a tax abatement to the redevelopers, requiring them to pay property taxes on only the assessed valuation of their raw land, exclusive of buildings and improvements, during the first ten years after purchase.[108]

Most of the older central cities acted promptly to implement the state laws. By 1948 Baltimore, Chicago, Minneapolis, and Pittsburgh had created redevelopment authorities guided by leaders from the business community with a heavy representation from the real estate and building industries. Moreover, in November 1947 Chicago voters approved a $15 million bond issue for urban redevelopment, and one year later Baltimore's electorate endorsed a $5 million bond proposal for the same purpose. In 1949 Minneapolis levied a special property tax of one mill to finance the survey, planning, and acquisition of land for redevelopment. Meanwhile, Detroit's city council had appropriated $1 million from general tax revenues for land purchases.[109] Responding to this flurry of activity at the state and local level, as early as 1947 the proceedings of the American Society of Planning Officials included a report optimistically entitled "Urban Redevelopment Is Under Way."[110]

Much of this optimism, however, was predicated on the expectation of federal aid. In 1945 Senators Robert Taft, Robert Wagner, and Allen Ellender introduced a federal housing bill that included an urban redevelopment provision to aid local agencies to purchase and clear slum properties and then sell the cleared land to private developers. After four years of debate Congress finally approved the Wagner-Ellender-Taft Housing Act of 1949 with the urban development provision incorporated in Title I of the measure. Under Title I the federal government would pay two-thirds of the net cost incurred by the local authorities in purchasing and clearing blighted sites. The locality had to shoulder the remaining third. But Title I authorized federal capital grants only for projects that cleared "predominantly residential" slum tracts or prepared land for "predominantly residential" developments.[111] In other words, the measure emphasized that federal redevelopment was primarily to serve the housing needs of the nation's cities. It was not a subsidy for the wholesale rebuilding of the aging urban core.

Though this legislation seemed to open the floodgates of federal aid, prior to the late 1950s the flow of funds from Washington was not that ample. As seen in table 8, the amount of federal urban renewal capital grants disbursed from 1949 to 1958 varied from $34 million awarded New York City to nothing for Buffalo. But in none of the cities could the outlays rival the amounts spent for highways, airports, or water and sewerage facilities. Local planning of the projects consumed many months, and bureaucratic roadblocks in Washington also delayed massive implementation of the federal program. In some cases private developers were re-

Table 8. Urban Renewal Capital Grants Disbursed by 31 March 1958

City	Amount ($)	City	Amount ($)
New York	34,064,229	Cleveland	2,314,165
Chicago	13,723,422	Cincinnati	1,895,000
Baltimore	4,825,456	Boston	1,808,294
Philadelphia	3,468,032	Minneapolis	1,516,337
Detroit	2,809,302	Saint Louis	999,190
Pittsburgh	2,704,438	Buffalo	0

Source: Urban Renewal Project Directory, March 31, 1958 (Washington, D.C.: Housing and Home Finance Agency, 1958), pp. 4, 6–7, 9, 11–12, 17–21, 23.

luctant to invest in proposed projects, again slowing the renewal process. Moreover, the housing act's emphasis on predominantly residential redevelopment discouraged some private entrepreneurs who might have readily invested in commercial structures. For whatever reasons, however, the federal redevelopment law did not spark an immediate wave of rebuilding in the central cities.

Actually, the most highly publicized and widely admired redevelopment schemes of the late 1940s and the 1950s were the product of cooperation between local authorities and private enterprise with the federal government playing no role. This was most notably true in Pittsburgh, the greatest exemplar of urban renaissance during the first decade following World War II. Federal urban renewal funds subsidized only one of the ten redevelopment projects certified by the Pittsburgh City Planning Commission prior to 1958. In the other nine cases the Pittsburgh Redevelopment Authority assembled the requisite land for the developer through exercising its power of eminent domain, but Washington did not enhance the deal with a cash contribution. For example, the redevelopment authority took residential properties along both the north and south sides of the Monongahela and sold them to Jones and Laughlin Steel Company to enable the expansion of existing mills and the construction of new open hearth furnaces. Similarly, the authority acquired parcels in residential areas surrounding the University of Pittsburgh, thereby freeing the institution of some undesirable neighbors and providing it with space to expand its health center and build a new gymnasium.[112]

The greatest achievement of the postwar Pittsburgh renaissance, however, was the redevelopment of the downtown Point at the juncture of the Allegheny, Monongahela, and Ohio rivers. This, too, relied heavily on the local redevelopment authority's power to take property, but the state was also a vital actor in the massive project. Once the site of pre-Revolutionary forts Duquesne and Pitt, at the close of World War II the Point was a gray area of railroad yards and shabby warehouses. Before the war Pittsburgh boosters had attempted to interest the National Park Service in the construction of a national historic site at the meeting of the rivers. But having failed to attract federal dollars, in 1945 the Allegheny Conference on Community Development convinced Pennsylvania's governor to endorse the creation of a state park covering thirty-six of the fifty-nine acres in the redevelopment area. The redevelopment authority was to assemble the remaining twenty-three acres for the Equitable Life Assurance Society, which was to construct a complex of office buildings known as Gateway Center. By 1949 demolition for the Point Park had begun, and in 1952 and 1953 three 20- to 24-story stainless steel office towers in Gateway

Center welcomed their first tenants. Moreover, in 1956 the Hilton chain announced plans to construct a hotel overlooking Point Park, a year later a new state office building opened nearby, and in 1958 the Bell Telephone Company completed a new office tower in the redevelopment area.[113]

The Gateway Center project quickly won national acclaim. As early as 1949 *Architectural Forum* labeled the aging steel capital "the biggest real estate and building story in the U.S. today."[114] Five years later the assistant director of the Allegheny Conference boasted in a national magazine: "Have you seen Pittsburgh, Pennsylvania lately? You would hardly know the town . . . In downtown Pittsburgh . . . the change has been so dramatic that only the picturesque hills and rivers . . . remained unaltered."[115] And in 1959 a travel magazine published an article entitled "Pittsburgh: The City That Quick-Changed from Unbelievable Ugliness to Shining Beauty in Less Than Half a Generation."[116] The perennial ugly duckling of urban America seemingly had turned into a swan, demonstrating that cities could conquer blight and apply a new face to their aging downtowns. All this, however, was a cooperative effort of the city, the state, and private enterprise. The much-awaited federal urban renewal program had played no part in the transformation.

Philadelphia's almost equally acclaimed Penn Center project likewise owed nothing to Washington. For decades a Pennsylvania Railroad viaduct known locally as the "Chinese Wall" had loomed over Philadelphia's West Market Street, depressing property values and grimly blighting the western entrance to the central business district. Finally in 1952 the railroad began demolition of the hated elevated tracks, and the city moved quickly to influence the railroad corporation's plans for the twenty-two-acre cleared site. Philadelphia's city planning commission guided by planner Edmund Bacon unveiled a widely publicized model showing how the land should be redeveloped, and in 1953 Mayor Joseph Clark appointed an Advisory Committee on the Penn Center Plan to express the city's views on the proposed project. Though the private developers did not necessarily heed the advice of the committee or the planning commission, the resulting complex of high-rise office buildings, known collectively as Penn Center, was not a product of unbridled private enterprise.[117] But neither was it the child of federal largesse.

Elsewhere the showpieces of supposed urban renaissance also were monuments to local initiative rather than to federal money. The pride of Detroit was its locally financed civic center along the previously dingy riverfront. In 1947 the City Plan Commission engaged the prestigious architectural firm of Eliel and Eero Saarinen to develop a plan for the civic center, and by 1950 a Veterans Memorial Hall was completed, followed in

1955 by the nineteen-story City-County Building and the Henry and Edsel Ford Auditorium, funded in part by the city and in part by the Ford family and Ford dealers. By the late 1950s work was also under way on the giant Cobo Hall and Convention Arena, billed as the world's largest facility of its kind.[118]

In 1957 the Prudential Insurance Company purchased thirty-two acres of railroad yards in Boston's Back Bay to construct what one local journalist called "the world's largest integrated commercial development."[119] Aided by a local tax abatement but without any federal funding, Prudential was to implement its scheme in the late 1950s and early 1960s, creating one more symbol of resurgent urban America.

In Baltimore early plans for that city's redevelopment masterpiece, Charles Center, included no provision for federal involvement. A joint creation of the Committee for Downtown and the Greater Baltimore Committee, Charles Center was to include offices, stores, apartments, a hotel, and a theater. Originally, the private sector and the city of Baltimore were to pay the entire bill for all of this, and one of the scheme's early planners claimed that Baltimore boosters "took a great deal of pride" in this independence from federal aid.[120] The general citizenry also was ready to assume the expense, and in 1958 Baltimore's voters approved a $25 million bond issue to help finance the assembly of land for the project. Not until 1960 did Charles Center promoters turn to Washington for funds, choosing to spare the city the debt charges incurred through the issuance of municipal bonds. But they decided to rely on Washington not because the project needed federal money but because a change in the federal urban renewal law meant that money was now available that could be used to lighten the burden on Baltimore taxpayers.[121]

Compared to the much-publicized redevelopment schemes sponsored by local agencies and private enterprise, the federally funded urban renewal projects of the early and mid-1950s were hardly inspiring monuments of urban rebirth. Because of the "predominantly residential" requirement of the 1949 act, the first federal projects consisted primarily of moderate-income housing. For example, Cleveland's earliest redevelopment project under the 1949 act, Longwood, was designed to replace "hundreds of unsanitary, sagging condemned homes" with modern garden apartments for moderate-income blacks.[122] The city's second project, Garden Valley, included both moderately priced private apartments and low-rent public housing, again intended to serve the city's expanding black population.[123] When the first tenants moved into these projects in 1957, some acclaimed the city's efforts to supplant slums with decent, modest dwellings, but the change was not as dramatic or as widely reported as the metamorphosis of Pittsburgh's Point or the construction of Penn Center on the site of the detested Chinese Wall. Both Longwood and Garden Valley were financed in part by the Cleveland Development Foundation, yet that group's investment never reaped public relations rewards equal to those of the Allegheny Conference.

Similarly, Minneapolis's first federal renewal development, Glenwood, contained moderately priced private residences, low-rent public housing, and peripheral industrial sites. For an area described by one local planner as "the worst slum in the city," this renewal plan represented a marked improvement over previous conditions and would supposedly realize the Minneapolis Housing and Redevelopment Authority's objective of "replacing blighted neighborhoods with healthy neighborhoods."[124] Yet the renewed Glenwood would not thrust Minneapolis into competition with Pittsburgh for the title of renaissance city.

Philadelphia's early Title I projects also were low- or middle-income housing schemes that were dull but characterized by good intentions. The city's first project was the East Poplar scheme, where the Redevelopment Authority sought to create racially integrated housing for both middle- and low-income Philadelphians in new and rehabilitated structures. For example, Penn Towne in the East Poplar district was the first Title I project in the nation to be completed, and it offered 138 new and 36 rehabilitated low-rise units for middle-class blacks and whites. Handsomely designed and not so bleak as later projects, this housing attracted some attention but Philadelphia's national reputation as a renaissance city rested much more on Penn Center than Penn Towne. Across the street from Penn Towne was Spring Garden Homes, completed in 1957, the first project where Title I funds were used to clear a site for public housing. Though described by the Redevelopment Authority as "garden-type apartments," Spring Gardens was actually a collection of grim brick boxes intended to "provide decent, safe and sanitary living for low-income families."[125]

Nearby in West Poplar the Redevelopment Authority cleared land for two 18-story public housing giants that opened in early 1958, offering again supposedly decent, safe, and sanitary shelter. Meanwhile, in the Southwest Temple area on the north side, the Redevelopment Authority was also cooperating with the Housing Authority to build drab public housing projects as well as constructing Jefferson Manor, a complex of moderate-income, private rental row houses, each with "a modest front lawn, . . . ample landscaping and grassy plots in the rear." According to the Redevelopment Authority, this greenery gave "the development the aura of a 'garden-suburb in center-city.' "[126] In fact, the modest front yards and few saplings were not enough to relieve the stultifying dullness of the unadorned brick rows that attracted black occupants largely because they had few other options given the city's residential segregation. Undistinguished Jefferson Manor certainly would not win recognition as a prominent landmark on the road to renaissance.

Even the better-designed Penn Towne scheme appeared to be a failure by the mid-1950s. Though the first dozen families moving to Penn Towne were divided evenly between blacks and whites, after that an overwhelming proportion of applicants for apartments were black. Moreover, the occupancy rate remained low, with middle-income families of both races refusing to move into a complex across the street from public housing.[127] The Redevelopment Authority's efforts to create a community of racial harmony and mixed-class living in the City of Brotherly Love had foundered.

No city took greater advantage of Title I than New York, but there, as elsewhere, federally aided redevelopment primarily produced necessary but uninspiring middle-income apartment blocks. Under the dictatorial command of the ubiquitous Robert Moses, the city's Committee on Slum Clearance had completed 7,800 Title I dwelling units by the close of 1959, and 7,400 more were under construction. The first four projects approved for construction in 1950 were typical of the early efforts of the New York committee. One was sponsored by the International Ladies Garment Workers' Union, and union members were expected to occupy one-third of the apartments; according to the *New York Times*, the units quickly attracted "families who had given up hope of finding a good apartment renting under $100."[128] Two other projects were in Harlem and designed to house middle-income blacks, and the fourth was near the Columbia University campus and was intended for employees of that institution.[129] Each supplanted deteriorating neighborhoods and displaced lower-income residents, but none offered the dramatic rags-to-riches transformation of Gateway Center.

Some of New York City's Title I projects constructed later in the 1950s included higher-priced apartments and nonresidential structures. For example, the Columbus Circle project comprised an office tower, exposition hall, and high-rent apartments. Yet in the first years of the Title I program Moses seemed dedicated to realizing the original intent of the law as he perceived it. According to New York's master builder, federal urban renewal was to provide "housing for the middle-income group which [was] ineligible for low-rent housing yet [could not] afford the higher speculative rentals."[130] New York's original projects did just this.

Though Moses's massive apartment complexes were at best dull and at worst depressing, a few early Title I projects stirred the imagination. For example, the renowned architect Mies van der Rohe designed the initial buildings in Detroit's first Title I scheme, Lafayette Park. In 1959 his twenty-story Pavilion Apartments opened on the former slum site, providing luxury residences within walking distance of downtown. But this first stage of redevelopment was the product of thirteen years of trial and error that was more discouraging than encouraging. Even though plans for the site were formulated as early as 1946, it required years of cajoling and negotiation before a private developer would agree to invest in Lafayette Park.[131] Detroit's premier project may have revealed the architectural possibilities of federal redevelopment, but it also exposed the lack of investor interest in downtown housing.

Meanwhile, many city leaders believed that rehabilitation of buildings and conservation of neighborhoods were just as necessary to achieve urban rebirth as were clearance projects like Lafayette Park or Gateway Center. Though later commentators have generally labeled the 1950s as an age of bulldozer redevelopment dedicated to clearance rather than conservation, a number of cities during this period experimented with rehabilitation of existing structures and preservation of established neighborhoods. Repair was as much a part of the revitalization effort as redevelopment, and clean-up crusades were on the municipal agenda as well as clearance projects. The Housing Act of 1954 formally recognized the growing interest in rehabilitation and conservation by authorizing federal financing of intensive building code enforcement campaigns, fix-up programs, and such minor improvements as new curbs, paving, playgrounds, and street lights that might upgrade declining neighborhoods. Henceforth, slum clearance and neighborhood conservation were the dual goals of the federal urban renewal program.

Prior to 1954 no city had pursued the rehabilitation option as vigorously as Baltimore. In 1945 Baltimore's Mayor Theodore McKeldin had called together representatives of various city departments to initiate a joint effort to upgrade housing standards through concerted enforcement of the housing, electrical, fire, zoning, and building codes. Moreover, the cooperating agencies were to focus on certain blighted neighborhoods, systematically investigating every residence block by block rather than responding only to specific complaints. And committees composed of neighborhood residents were to mobilize local support for the rehabilitation program. To aid in enforcement, in 1947 the city created a housing court charged with handling only those cases arising from code violations in dwellings. This concerted program of code enforcement soon became known as the Baltimore Plan and was heralded as a means for eradicating slums.[132] Supposedly, by enforcing the codes and requiring repairs and rehabilitation, the cancer of blight could be forced into remission without the drastic surgery of slum clearance and redevelopment.

During the 1950s, the Baltimore Plan was applied in various Baltimore neighborhoods and in other cities as well. The showcase of the plan was East Baltimore, where from 1951 to 1953 the city conducted a pilot demonstration project with a privately financed "Fight-Blight" fund to help homeowners who were too poor to finance rehabilitation.[133] To help guide and implement the code enforcement program, Baltimore's mayor created the Housing Bureau Advisory Council, consisting of seventeen civic leaders headed by James Rouse, later chair of the Greater Baltimore Committee's urban renewal effort.

In 1953 Detroit initiated a neighborhood conservation program, choosing the Mack-Concord area three miles east of downtown for the pilot project. By 1955 the City Plan Commission was drafting a ten-year conservation program for fifty-five neighborhoods housing one-third of the city's population. Included were the standard proposals for coordinated, intensive code enforcement and organization of neighborhood councils, but the city also intended to use federal urban renewal funds for removal of the most dilapidated structures, for creation of new playgrounds, and for street and alley improvements.[134]

By the mid-1950s Saint Louis was also organizing pilot rehabilitation projects in the inner-city neighborhoods of Hyde Park and Cherokee. In 1957 a Saint Louis city planner reported that "slum clearance could not keep up with the spread of slums" and thus "was not the answer." Instead, "the solution to the problem of decaying areas was . . . a program of slum prevention or permanent neighborhood improvement—in a word: *rehabilitation*."[135] From 1955 to 1958 the city of Saint Louis spent about $434,000 in improvements for parks, playgrounds, and other community facilities in the targeted areas whereas the residents responded to notices for more than twelve thousand code violations with $1.3 million in repairs.[136]

Elsewhere there was also growing interest in community conservation and rehabilitation of existing structures. In 1953 Boston's Mayor John Hynes appointed an Advisory Committee on Rehabilitation and Conservation together with fifteen subcommittees of neighborhood leaders, each subcommittee representing one of the city's health and welfare districts. The subcommittees surveyed community conditions and, according to the City Planning Board, sought "to develop between the various neighborhood associations and the city a cooperative effort to correct defects."[137] The particularly active South Boston subcommittee arranged for the

planting of trees and improved street lighting and convinced some property owners to take part in a "fix-up, paint-up" project.[138]

In Chicago as well local organizations were focusing greater attention
on conservation. In 1953 the Metropolitan Housing and Planning Council
reported that its "present major activity [was] in conservation," and that
year it sponsored a three-volume study of the subject that led to the passage of Illinois's Urban Community Conservation Act. Though it believed
that an emphasis on slum clearance was proper, the council complained
that "little or no attention [had] been given to the equally important job of
'slum prevention.' "[139]

At the same time, the Chicago Urban League maintained a Community Organization Department serving eighty-seven block clubs by 1953.
These clubs in predominantly black South Side and West Side neighborhoods organized clean-up campaigns and encouraged such cosmetic
changes as new coats of paint and replanted lawns. To reward these
efforts, the Urban League conducted an annual "Block Beautiful" contest. The Urban League block clubs had a special reason to push for conservation, for according to a study of the Metropolitan Housing and
Planning Council: "Fear of displacement in order for redevelopment to
proceed appears to be a basic one in this section of the Negro community."[140] In other words, for many blacks it seemed like a question of clean
up or clear out, and considering the tight housing market, conservation
appeared preferable to clearance.

The most varied attempts at rehabilitation and conservation occurred
in Philadelphia. From the beginning of its renewal program the Philadelphia Redevelopment Authority was willing to use every conceivable
means to restore its city. In its first projects—Penn Towne and an adjacent scheme sponsored by the Society of Friends—the authority experimented with the extensive rehabilitation of existing brick houses, but the
renewal agency and the Friends found rehabilitation more costly than
expected. The Redevelopment Authority concluded that the Friends'
"dwellings units, averaging about four and a half rooms each, cost as
much as a three-bedroom new home . . . in a new area.[141]

Meanwhile, the authority launched "Operation Fix-Up" to encourage
the removal of backyard trash, the repair of roofs, and the replacement of
doors and windows. According to the authority's executive director, his
organization "offered groups representing a block of neighbors rather
complete aid in making their homes and surroundings attractive."[142] In
1949 Operation Fix-Up included the creation of an experimental backyard
common for the use of all the houses on the block; the renewal agency with
the cooperation of the residents removed unslightly sheds and fences and

cleared an open expanse for the mutual enjoyment of the neighbors. The next year the enthusiastic authority sought to repeat this throughout the city, campaigning for "50 in '50." In fact, it completed only three more commons.[143]

Demolition and new construction proceeded as well during the 1950s, but by 1956–57 the Philadelphia Redevelopment Authority was dissatisfied with the bulldozer approach and decided to shift its emphasis from slum clearance and focus even more fully on conservation. Explaining the change, the authority's annual report observed, "It was originally hoped that the creation of an 'island of gold' would favorably affect the 'swamp of bad' immediately surrounding it." But the reverse proved true; people "did not rush to move into the new middle-income accommodations because of neighboring slum conditions," and "families displaced by demolition often moved to the fringe of the cleared area, further overcrowding the houses there," turning "what was sometimes only somewhat bad into totally bad sections."[144] Thus the city drafted a more balanced program of conservation and redevelopment that Philadelphia's Development Coordinator characterized as "a showdown test between an old and sprawling but determined city and 'the demon blight.' "[145] Henceforth, the authority planned to concentrate "a substantial proportion of available resources" in "neighborhoods beginning to show the first signs of blight" rather than "clearing the very heart of Philadelphia's slums."[146] Instead of pursuing a futile offense against slums, Philadelphia was now opting for a defensive strategy, a containment of blight.

Even before this announced shift in policy, Philadelphia had begun to experiment with conservation projects that rested heavily on the development of concerned community leaders. With a demonstration grant from the federal government, in 1954 the city launched its Leadership Program to stimulate the interest of residents in the rehabilitation of their neighborhoods. The city was to support the grass-roots leaders with intensive code enforcement and through demolition of the most dilapidated structures. But the chief aim of the program was to encourage residents to organize community councils and block clubs and to stir demands for a cleaner, safer neighborhood.[147]

In Philadelphia as in Saint Louis, Detroit, and Baltimore, a blitzkrieg attack by city inspectors and an aroused grass-roots leadership were intended to galvanize blighted communities and rid them of their worst features. Yet in one city after another the community organization and rehabilitation campaigns produced disappointing results. In too many cases effective community organizations did not perpetuate rehabilitation projects; instead, city officials or settlement house workers propped up the programs. Without these external supports the programs generally collapsed.

A study of Baltimore's pilot project noted a "lack of real neighborhood organization and lasting morale" and concluded that the "ability to 'take over' . . . never materialized on a neighborhood scale."[148] After only two years the Philadelphia Redevelopment Authority abandoned Operation Fix-Up, and among the reasons given by the authority's executive director was that "neighborhood organization was difficult" and "the sustained will to maintain the improvement . . . seemed to fail without continued pressure, which seems to require sustained effort by paid personnel."[149] Similarly, an evaluation of the Leadership Program in Philadelphia's East Poplar area claimed that "virtually nothing tangible [had been] accomplished," and though the community included more than five hundred households, attendance at the open meetings of the committee guiding the neighborhood effort averaged about six during the project's early years and three or four later.[150] In the Hawthorne Leadership Area the results were "fairly bleak" and attempts at block organization failed.[151]

In the other two Philadelphia leadership areas, both of which were of higher economic status, community interest was greater and positive signs of rehabilitation were evident. But the city's Office of Development coordinator concluded from the leadership experiment that a community-based program was "unlikely to produce the desired rehabilitation in a seriously blighted area."[152] By 1962 the Detroit City Plan Commission had also found in the Mack-Concord district that "the lack of interest in home upkeep among tenants and some owners" was among the "formidable obstacles to the conservation of the area."[153]

Combined with this community apathy were other factors at odds with the rehabilitation programs. Poor homeowners often could not afford the needed repairs, and unless financial institutions eased their lending requirements or private philanthropists or government agencies created something comparable to Baltimore's Fight-Blight Fund, improvements in housing standards might remain impossible. Moreover, the positive consequences of rehabilitation proved fleeting, for despite a new coat of paint and mended window screens, the deterioration of aging structures continued.

In 1951 Baltimore's Planning Commission pointed out that the disadvantage of the Baltimore Plan "is that relief can be only partial and somewhat temporary in nature."[154] Two years later Chicago's Metropolitan Housing and Planning Council reported that areas in Baltimore "which were inspected have begun to go down again" and referred to the Baltimore Plan as "merely a temporary palliative."[155] In early 1955 the chief of the Philadelphia Redevelopment Authority observed that less than five years after the creation of the four backyard commons only two of them were "still attractive."[156] Similarly, a Saint Louis city planner warned, "Rehabilitation can never stop, because blight never stops."[157] Because of the creeping threat of blight, neighborhood vigilance seemed to be a prerequisite of revitalization. Conversely, grass-roots apathy, such as that found in East Baltimore, East Poplar, Hawthorne, and Mack-Concord, was the Achilles' heel of rehabilitation efforts.

In middle-class areas conservation efforts, however, seemed more promising. Middle-class property owners were more easily recruited to campaigns of civic activism than poor tenants, and they were also better able to finance improvements. Thus in the more affluent confines of Chicago's Hyde Park–Kenwood district the neighborhood conservation movement would achieve its greatest success. Troubled by the illegal conversion of single-family dwellings into apartments and the threat of white flight as blacks moved into the area, in 1949 Hyde Park–Kenwood residents organized the Hyde Park–Kenwood Community Conference. It launched a successful effort to organize block clubs throughout the area, to report zoning and housing code violations, to encourage higher levels of property maintenance, and to create racial harmony in an integrated neighborhood.

At first the area's dominant institution, the University of Chicago, refused to cooperate with the conference, but by 1952 worsening neighborhood conditions were causing a loss of faculty and students, thus requiring the university to intervene. A community activist reported that the trustees and administrators were "forced to admit that if they didn't engage in community action, they might end up with a $200,000,000 investment in a slum, without anybody to do research or any students to educate."[158] Responding to the problem, the university was instrumental in organizing and funding the South East Chicago Commission headed by the university's president. The commission stepped up pressure on the city to halt illegal conversions, and the university's private police force patrolled Hyde Park, supplementing the inadequate municipal protection. Beyond this the commission drafted a plan for renewal of the area that included spot clearance of the most blighted properties and conservation of the remaining district. Demolition began in 1955, and in 1956 the federal urban renewal commissioner approved $26 million in capital grant funds for the project.[159] During the remainder of the decade, Hyde Park–Kenwood attracted national attention as a model of community conservation.

Yet elsewhere even middle-class neighborhoods were finding the conservation crusade a tough battle to win. For example, in Saint Louis the West End Community Conference was attempting to preserve a district that had once housed the city's elite. According to the conference's first annual report, in 1955 West End residents "after hearing of the Block Units in the Hyde Park–Kenwood Area of Chicago felt a similar structure was necessary for [their] area."[160] The conference's stated goal was to "provide safer streets, adequate schools, better shopping facilities, higher property values, less crime, and high neighborhood pride and morale."[161] Moreover, like the Hyde Park–Kenwood Conference the West End group favored a racially integrated neighborhood, seeking to retain white residents while welcoming black newcomers, so long as they were of the right social class. Conservation in both areas meant preservation of a middle-class population.

To achieve this goal, the West End Conference organized the standard efforts to clean up vacant lots, to ensure strict enforcement of building and zoning codes, and to obtain better police protection. In 1957 after two years of organizing, lobbying, and cajoling, the group's chairman reported optimistically, "The Conference is clicking[;] every day it is producing concrete improvements."[162] Yet by the close of the 1950s the West End was only clinging tenuously to middle-class status, and the perceived threat of blight was not at bay. Lacking a powerful institution like the University of Chicago to supply added artillery, the Saint Louis conference seemed to be losing its battle.

In fact, by 1958 the struggle for urban renewal had produced few victories, but it had taught certain lessons. First, code enforcement and clean-up campaigns were only temporary solutions that momentarily slowed blight but did not create a permanently renewed city. Second, the Philadelphia Leadership Program as well as the pilot projects in Baltimore and Detroit had demonstrated that stirring community participation among the poor was not an easy task. Cultivating the grass-roots of America's urban slums did not necessarily produce a bumper crop of poor but concerned citizens. Middle-class residents were more amenable to neighborhood activism, but even they could find the task daunting. Third, Gateway Center, Penn Center, and the Detroit Civic Center proved that urban revitalization could proceed without federal funding. Cities were able to progress along the road to renaissance relying only on their powers of eminent domain and the dollars of private developers. Fourth, the Pittsburgh renaissance showed that if mayors and boosters wanted to attract maximum attention to their cities, they needed to push for dramatic, large-scale projects transforming dingy rail yards into gleaming steel and glass towers. Drab, moderate-income housing while practical would never earn a mayor national acclaim nor would it win a decaying metropolis a reputation as a comeback city. To obtain the biggest boost for the buck, older central cities needed to invest in glittering downtown showpieces.

The 1960s would demonstrate that city leaders did not necessarily heed the second and third of these lessons. But the fourth would nurture downtown developments in one city after another. During the late 1940s and the early 1950s, America's aging cities may not have eradicated their slums or achieved their dreams of renewal, but they had experimented with redevelopment and rehabilitation and prepared the ground for more massive projects in the future.

An Era of Achievement

By 1958 urban Americans could look back on a dozen years of achievement that demonstrated the possibility of reawakening dormant central cities. During the postwar era, one aging metropolis after another had discarded the seedy politicos of the past and opted for a new breed of mayors who promised more dynamic rule. A number of cities were also experimenting with new sources of revenue to supplement the traditional reliance on property taxes. Moreover, the proceeds from municipal bond issues were financing sewer and water plants, scores of airports, and miles of highways, and through their power of eminent domain cities were taking land for much-publicized monuments to urban renewal. Throughout America there were enough signs of change in previously dismal cities like Pittsburgh and Philadelphia to warrant a belief that a better age was beckoning.

This agenda of achievements was the product of local initiatives. Not until 1956 did Congress authorize funds to battle pollution of the skies or waterways, and that same year witnessed the adoption of the federal interstate highway act. Until then the state and localities had to provide at least half of the dollars for urban expressways, and the impetus for the great traffic arteries constructed during the late 1940s and early 1950s came from city hall and not Washington. Moreover, at the beginning of 1958 central cities looked forward to receiving promised federal urban renewal funds, but as yet they had cashed relatively few checks from the national treasury. Private funds and state aid had fueled the most notable revitalization projects; federal funds remained trapped in the bureaucratic pipeline. Thus during the first dozen years after World War II, local decision makers dominated the physical renovation of America's central cities. Washington played only a supporting role.

The boasted local achievements of the late 1940s and early 1950s, however, produced some side effects that could prove harmful in the future. The new politics of postwar America undermined the role of political parties as brokers, leaving future mayors and other public officials exposed to the pressures and attacks of the multitudinous interest groups operating within the older central cities. No longer would a party boss or organization buffer the mayor by making deals, forging alliances, and building support for policy initiatives. By 1958 urban Republicans were dead or fast fading, and most city Democratic organizations were hobbled objects of contempt. A no-party system was developing with candidates running on their own.

Meanwhile, the environmental achievements and enhanced transportation facilities of postwar urban America benefited the suburban competition as much as the central-city boosters. Massive water and sewer schemes ensured that suburbanites would enjoy the amenities of urban life. Moreover, expressway networks did not produce a recentralization of population and commerce but sped the outward flow of persons and dollars. Likewise, the city-financed airports were to make suburbia the hub of intercity transportation and to spell doom for the downtown rail depots. Though urban officials boasted of the billions of dollars invested in the public infrastructure during the late 1940s and early 1950s, the central cities were, in fact, weaving a golden noose that choked the core rather than resuscitated it.

Finally, the advent of urban renewal also presented ominous possibilities. Gleaming new towers might supplant dingy slums, but the price paid was a new dependence on federal mandates. The Housing Act of 1949 together with the Federal-Aid Highway and Water Pollution acts of 1956 meant that Washington was getting its foot further in the door of local government. During the late 1940s and early 1950s, the federal role was as yet limited, and the physical rehabilitation of the cities depended primarily on state and local resources. By the second half of the 1950s the promise of federal funds offered hope of even greater achievements, but it also meant that a new cast of players was moving toward center stage.

CHAPTER FOUR ○ Bad News and Good

When in 1961 critic Jane Jacobs published her landmark volume, *The Death and Life of Great American Cities,* her title summed up the prevailing attitude of urban observers toward the aging central cities. Though many urban experts disagreed with Jacobs's diagnosis of the causes of the urban malady and took exception to her prescribed cure, throughout the nation commentators recognized signs of impending death in the great American cities while also confidently proposing nostrums of renewed life and vitality. During the late 1950s and early 1960s, Americans confronted the harsh realities of accelerating urban decline and responded with an accelerating output of plans, proposals, and federally subsidized schemes. The central city seemed to be dying, but the situation was far from hopeless. By the early 1960s the discouraging facts of economic, social, and political life in the older central cities had cast shadows over the bright hopes of the 1950s. The new breed of reform mayors was not ushering in an urban renaissance throughout the nation; even in the showcase city of Pittsburgh the gleaming towers of Gateway Center could not blind the observer to the city's gradual eclipse. Yet massive renewal and highway projects were being implemented, more plans for revitalization were on the drawing boards, and strategies for change filled the pages of books and journals.

Thus urban boosters faced both bad news and good in the late 1950s and early 1960s. The census data, sales figures, and employment and income statistics conveyed the bad news: the central city continued to lose ground in competition with the suburbs, and the twin threats of decentralization and blight were taking an increasingly heavy toll. Similarly, the news from the city controller's office was often grim, and reports from city hall seemed to indicate a resurgence of mediocrity among the municipal chieftains. For many central-city business and political leaders, however, accounts of grandiose urban renewal proposals brought encouragement and new hope, and a fresh crop of office towers downtown seemed to mark the beginning of a better era.

To most commentators the urban prospect was not bright. "Death" preceded "Life" in the title of Jacobs's book, and by the mid-1960s library shelves would display such gloomy titles as *Sick Cities* and *The Twilight of Cities*.[1] But the morbid metaphors of urban jeremiahs were producing heightened cries for programs of revitalization and renewal. Renaissance might still be just around the corner.

Signs of Decline

Especially troubling to the business leaders and politicians watching for an urban upturn were the unavoidable statistics pointing to decline. Dropping population figures and income and sales data offered numerical proof of the decay evident to all urban observers. By the early 1960s there were fewer residents in the older central cities, and the remaining population was of lower economic status than the central-city citizenry of a decade earlier. Downtown retailing was slowly withering, and suburbia was siphoning off an increasing share of the shopping dollars. As early as 1940 the real estate community and municipal officials had recognized signs of decline in the city, and by the early 1960s these signals were even more blatant and alarming.

The 1960 census offered the most heralded indicators of decadence. In that head count the list of older cities losing population was lengthy. The populations of Boston, Saint Louis, and Pittsburgh all fell by more than 10 percent; the number of residents in Detroit, Buffalo, and Minneapolis declined 7 percent to 10 percent; and Cleveland, Philadelphia, Chicago, New York City, Baltimore, and Cincinnati lost less than 5 percent of their inhabitants (see table 9). By comparison, the suburbs were booming, soaring in population by 60 percent to 70 percent in a single decade. Though the news was worse for some cities than for others, negative growth rates in each of the aging urban hubs brought only gloom to the chambers of commerce and mayors' offices. Moreover, the stark contrast between the suburban and central-city figures only heightened perceptions of the stagnation of the urban core. By 1960 the central-city limits seemed to mark the boundary between growth and decline.

Table 9. Population Change in Central Cities and Their Suburbs, 1950–1960

City	% Change in Central City	% Change in Suburbs
New York	− 1.4	+ 75.0
Chicago	− 1.9	+ 71.5
Philadelphia	− 3.3	+ 46.3
Detroit	− 9.7	+ 79.3
Baltimore	− 1.1	+ 72.9
Cleveland	− 4.2	+ 67.2
Saint Louis	− 12.5	+ 51.9
Boston	− 13.0	+ 17.6
Pittsburgh	− 10.7	+ 17.2
Buffalo	− 8.2	+ 52.1
Minneapolis	− 7.4	+ 115.7
Cincinnati	− 0.3	+ 42.1

Sources: U.S. Bureau of the Census, U.S. censuses of 1950 and 1960 (Washington, D.C.: U.S. Government Printing Office, 1952 and 1961).

Even more discouraging was the obvious failure of central cities to retain or attract middle-class residents. Before World War II many commentators had complained of the migration of the middle class to suburban havens beyond the central-city boundaries, and in the postwar era thousands more joined the outward trek, taking their tax dollars with them. In fact, the 1960 census showed that the central city was becoming the poor relation of the metropolitan community, increasingly shunned by the more affluent. Already in 1950 the median income figures for each of the twelve older central cities of the Northeast and Midwest were below the median income figures for its metropolitan area as a whole (see table 10). But by 1960 the disparity between the central-city income figures and the metropolitan figures had widened in ten of the twelve metropolises. Whereas in 1950 Detroit's median income was only 3 percent lower than the metropolitan area income, by 1960 it was 9 percent lower. In 1950 the median income of residents in the city of Buffalo was only 4 percent below the metropolitan area as a whole, but ten years later the gap had grown to 12 percent. Pittsburgh with such central-city middle-class strongholds as Squirrel Hill and Shadyside and with a ring of depressed industrial suburbs improved relative to its metropolitan area. Similarly, affluent neighborhoods like Hyde Park, Mount Lookout, and Clifton kept Cincinnati from dropping relative to its suburbs, some of which rivaled the grimness

Table 10. Median Central-City Income as Percentage of Median Metropolitan Area Income, 1950 and 1960

City	1950 (%)	1960 (%)
New York	94.8	91.3
Chicago	96.4	91.9
Philadelphia	94.1	90.5
Detroit	97.2	90.9
Baltimore	96.3	92.4
Cleveland	91.2	86.5
Saint Louis	91.6	86.3
Boston	86.9	85.4
Pittsburgh	93.2	94.5
Buffalo	95.7	88.1
Minneapolis	95.6	94.7
Cincinnati	90.9	92.3

Sources: U.S. Bureau of the Census, U.S. censuses of 1950 and 1960 (Washington, D.C.: U.S. Government Printing Office, 1952 and 1961).

of the Pittsburgh satellites. Yet overall the central cities were slipping behind in the race for riches.

Not only were many of the middle class departing, there was a concurrent influx of poor newcomers, people who were tax consumers but not very lucrative sources of tax revenue. The most notable migrants to the city were southern blacks, millions of whom moved to northern industrial centers during the 1940s and 1950s. As a consequence the percentage of the central-city population that was nonwhite soared, and in 1960 more than a quarter of all residents in Baltimore, Detroit, Cleveland, Saint Louis, and Philadelphia were black (see table 11). Whole neighborhoods changed from virtually all white to all black in a single decade as Afro-Americans broke through the traditional boundaries of the racial ghetto. By 1960 Bedford-Stuyvesant and Brownsville in Brooklyn rivaled Harlem as the center of black life in New York City, whereas in Chicago the black belt encompassed large new tracts of the South and West sides, and in Cincinnati the focus of the black community shifted from the West End to Avondale and Evanston.

This influx of blacks not only heightened the problem of poverty in the central cities, it also threatened to aggravate racial animosities endemic to American society. Given the American tradition of racism, the thousands of blacks encroaching on white neighborhoods, schools, and

Table 11. Percentage of Nonwhite Residents, 1950 and 1960

City	1950	1960
New York	9.8	14.7
Chicago	14.1	23.6
Philadelphia	18.3	26.7
Detroit	16.4	29.2
Baltimore	23.8	35.0
Cleveland	16.3	28.9
Saint Louis	18.0	28.8
Boston	5.3	9.8
Pittsburgh	12.3	16.8
Buffalo	6.5	13.8
Minneapolis	1.6	3.2
Cincinnati	15.6	21.8

Sources: U.S. Bureau of the Census, U.S. censuses of 1950 and 1960 (Washington, D.C.: U.S. Government Printing Office, 1952 and 1961).

jobs were bound to stir old fears and hatreds. Race riots had erupted in New York City and Detroit during World War II, and in response cities across the Northeast and Midwest had created human relations commissions to handle racial grievances and stamp out grass-roots brushfires before they developed into full-fledged rioting. Throughout the late 1940s and the 1950s these local commissions tried to keep racial peace and lower the barriers of racial discrimination. But by 1960 only the most optimistic pollyanna could assume that the racial shift in the central cities no longer posed a threat to social harmony. The migration of blacks together with long-standing racism offered a volatile mix that might well derail the city on its journey toward renaissance.

Also moving northward to the older urban hubs were thousands of poor whites and Hispanics. Midwestern cities attracted especially large numbers of white migrants from Appalachia, and by the late 1950s Cincinnati's Over-the-Rhine neighborhood, Chicago's Uptown, and Cleveland's near west side had won local reputations as "hillbilly ghettoes." Meanwhile, Puerto Ricans poured into New York City so that by the beginning of the 1960s they constituted about 8 percent of the population.[2] Though the cultural heritage of white Appalachians, Puerto Ricans, and blacks differed markedly, they shared one common trait—they were disproportionately poor. Downtown merchants seeking big-spending customers and municipal officials anxious to attract taxpayers who could pay their share of the city's bills could hardly rejoice at the arrival of these newcomers. Rather than swelling the forces of renaissance, the Appalachians, blacks, and Hispanics seemed likely recruits in the onward march of decay.

Not only were the migration patterns of the 1950s and early 1960s draining the central city of residential wealth, the changing age distribution of the population also offered little reassurance for government budget makers. People between the ages of twenty and sixty who contributed the most in tax revenues and demanded the least in services constituted a declining proportion of the central cities' residents whereas the dependent young and old were growing in numbers. In each of the twelve older central cities of the northeastern quadrant of the United States, the percentage of the population sixty-five years and older increased during the 1950s. In 1950 this category represented at least 10 percent of the population in only Cincinnati; by 1960 in eight of the twelve cities more than one-tenth of the inhabitants were senior citizens. Yet older residents were most likely to require treatment in municipal hospitals and demanded greater police protection owing to their special vulnerability to crime. Moreover, because they generally were retired, they paid little or no municipal wage taxes.

But the base of the age pyramid was broadening as well, causing problems for hard-pressed urban school boards and inadequate city recreation and park facilities. Though the population of New York City dropped 1 percent between 1950 and 1960, public school enrollments rose 13 percent. Likewise, in Philadelphia there was a 17 percent increase in school enrollments while the number of inhabitants fell 3 percent.[3] The pattern was the same everywhere. America's postwar baby boom was crowding the public schools and recreation centers even in areas where the ranks of the adult taxpayers were thinning. In addition, many of those filling the central-city classrooms were black migrants, whose presence heightened the attraction of lily-white suburban school districts for many white parents. Already before the 1950s suburban schools catering to college-bound children were luring the white middle class beyond the central-city boundaries. Now the city schools were becoming even less competitive in the battle for middle-class offspring. Thus the baby boom forced central cities to invest in costly new schools and playgrounds as well as additional teachers despite an overall decline in their population. Yet this investment did not promise to even the score between the increasingly black city and the white suburbs.

Though most urban commentators emphasized the new burdens confronting local governments and dwelled on the signals of headlong descent, the 1950s was not an era of unqualified economic, social, and demographic decline in the older central cities. In only two of the twelve aging cities of the northeastern quadrant did the number of households actually decline between 1950 and 1960. Except for Boston and Pittsburgh, the older central cities were adding to their housing inventory, and by 1960 more than 10 percent of the existing housing units in New York City, Chicago, Philadelphia, Detroit, Baltimore, and Cincinnati had been constructed within the last decade. Generally, the loss of population in central cities was owing to smaller households and less doubling up of families in overcrowded units. In eleven of the twelve cities the percentage of dwelling units that were overcrowded dropped markedly during the 1950s, and in the twelfth, Cleveland, the degree of crowding was almost the same in 1960 as ten years earlier. The population decline thus may have been indicative of an improvement in central-city housing conditions. In fact, the largest drops in population were often in the decayed inner-city lodging-house and flophouse districts, areas that added little luster to the reputation of the aging metropolises.

Also encouraging to those who sought to reinforce the central-city tax base was the continued construction of thousands of new middle-income dwellings in many of the older urban hubs. Though "white flight" was much publicized and much evident during the 1950s, in one city after another the fringe areas within the municipal limits filled with new homes for middle-class white families and skilled blue-collar workers. In Philadelphia the population of the Far Northeast area soared 152 percent between 1950 and 1960, rising from twenty-six thousand to sixty-six thousand, and most of the newcomers had incomes that at least equaled the suburban median. On Chicago's southwest side the population of the Garfield Ridge community tripled, and the Ashburn area more than quintupled in number of residents, increasing from seven thousand to almost thirty-nine thousand.[4] Likewise, in New York City, formerly vacant expanses on Staten Island and in the Queens were the sites of thousands of new houses and apartments. In northwest Detroit and the far south side of Minneapolis as well as in northeast Philadelphia, southwest Chicago, and Staten Island, housing construction was as common a feature as in the burgeoning suburban municipalities.

But thousands of new homes on the urban fringe were little consolation to central-city officials and business leaders. For the bottom line read that the central cities had lost population, and in the minds of growth-oriented Americans this meant decline and all the opprobrium associated with that word. Moreover, by 1960 there were few unbuilt tracts left in Chicago, Minneapolis, or Detroit, so the next decade seemingly promised worse news. The central city was losing the contest with suburbia for population and residential wealth, and the losses would continue. That blacks, Puerto Ricans, and Appalachian whites might have a bit more living space mattered little, for these residents were not going to pay the city's bills or boost the fortunes of Marshall Field's and Macy's.

The decline of downtown retailing simply added to the fears of leaders in both the public and private sectors. As middle-class consumers moved farther from the urban core and deposited their dollars in the cash registers of auto-oriented suburban shopping malls, downtown business districts felt the dire financial consequences. Testifying to the truth of such promotional slogans as "There's more of everything downtown," women shoppers consistently preferred the central business district to suburban shopping centers when surveyed about range of merchandise available. But when questions focused on accessibility, traffic, and parking, downtown received low marks.[5] The downtown stores had the goods, but their location along narrow streets far from the shopper's home and with little or no parking made them just too inconvenient. This was especially true for middle-class shoppers who had formerly been the mainstay of the big downtown department stores. In 1959 a Cincinnati survey showed that 43 percent of downtown shoppers had an income of less than $4,000 whereas only 21 percent of shopping center patrons were in that category.[6] Moreover, as lower-income persons, often black, came to dominate the downtown sidewalks, the appeal of the central business district stores for white middle-class consumers diminished even further. Baltimore's Planning Council summed up the dilemma when it reported, "Greater numbers of low-income, Negro shoppers in Central Business District stores, coming at the same time as middle and upper income white shoppers are given alternatives in . . . segregated suburban centers, has had unfortunate implications [for downtown merchants]".[7]

Throughout the nation these unfortunate implications were readily apparent as a number of downtown retailing landmarks closed their doors. Between 1952 and 1957 eight major stores in New York City went out of business. In 1953 James McCreery and Company abandoned its Thirty-fourth Street store after 116 years of retailing, and the next year a lower Manhattan institution, the big John Wanamaker outlet, followed suit. After 122 years of business, in 1956 Lewis and Conger moved its store from midtown Manhattan to suburban Manhasset whereas in 1957 the Namm-Loeser Company closed its downtown Brooklyn establishment while keeping its two modern Long Island branches.[8]

In Pittsburgh two leading downtown department stores, Frank and Seder and Rosenbaums, folded, and in 1957 the 104-year-old R. H. White department store closed its block-long, five-story emporium on

Boston's main retailing street after unsuccessfully seeking a 50 percent tax reduction from the city.[9] Between December 1961 and March 1962 downtown Cleveland suffered a double blow when two of its six department stores made their last sales. According to the *Cleveland Plain Dealer*, Bailey's, like its counterparts in many central cities, closed "because of a decline in downtown business and the population growth in the suburbs."[10] Responding to the suburban trend, Bailey's management promised to expand the company's branch outlets once its downtown white elephant was discarded.

Throughout the 1950s downtown sales figures dropped despite inflation and the nation's generally favorable economic climate. Especially discouraging was the continued decline during the late 1950s and early 1960s. As seen in table 12, in eleven of the twelve aging central cities, downtown retail sales dropped between 1958 and 1963, and in the twelfth, Boston, the increase was less than 1 percent. In six of the cities sales were off more than 10 percent, and in beleaguered downtown Buffalo there were almost one-fourth fewer dollars spent in 1963 than in 1958. In the early 1950s a Buffalo City Planning Commission proposal warned, "Unless some dramatic program to recapture Downtown's past appeal is initiated, economic collapse may well face the Central Business District with similar ramifications upon the tax base of the entire city."[11] The gloomy

Table 12. Change in Retail Sales, 1958–1963 (in Current Dollars)

City	% Change in Central Business District	% Change in City as a Whole	% Change in Metropolitan Area
New York	− 2.2	+ 6.1	+ 15.2
Chicago	− 3.3	+ 0.5	+ 17.0
Philadelphia	− 6.7	+ 2.5	+ 18.8
Detroit	− 13.3	+ 0.9	+ 20.9
Baltimore	− 18.6	− 3.9	+ 17.9
Cleveland	− 14.6	− 9.6	+ 16.7
Saint Louis	− 17.7	− 8.0	+ 17.4
Boston	+ 0.9	− 4.0	+ 17.6
Pittsburgh	− 9.7	− 1.1	+ 8.9
Buffalo	− 23.5	− 15.6	+ 10.2
Minneapolis	− 9.6	+ 0.7	+ 20.5
Cincinnati	− 17.1	− 0.2	+ 18.8

Sources: U.S. Bureau of the Census, U.S. censuses of retail trade for 1958 and 1963 (Washington, D.C.: U.S. Government Printing Office, 1961 and 1966).

sales figures of 1963 seemed to indicate a realization of the commission's worst fears.

Most central-city neighborhood shopping districts did not suffer as severe a decline as the downtown, but the sales figures for the city as a whole were far from encouraging. In seven of the twelve cities, sales were down for the entire city, and in three of the remaining five the increase was less than 1 percent. If the figures were adjusted for inflation and translated into constant dollars, all of the cities would record a drop.

In contrast, the figures for the metropolitan area as a whole were all positive with suburbia making up for the sluggish performance of the urban core. Downtown department stores were energetically establishing branches in suburban shopping malls in an attempt to keep their traditional middle-class customers who no longer would make the trek to the city center. In 1958 Pittsburgh's downtown department stores contained 844,000 square feet more than all other department stores in the metropolitan region. At the close of 1963, however, suburban department store space totaled almost 171,000 square feet more than the big outlets in the Golden Triangle.[12] And this phenomenon was repeated in metropolitan areas throughout the nation. Downtown was gradually losing its long-standing dominance in urban retailing, and the consequences were empty storefronts on Main Street and declining profits for the massive emporiums that continued to compete for a share of the diminishing corps of downtown shoppers.

Whereas the news from central-city retailers was dismal, reports from the managers, owners, and builders of office space were much more encouraging. By the mid-1950s an office boom was beginning to sweep the nation, and it continued unabated through the early 1960s. After a construction lull of more than two decades new office towers arose in the urban core, yet despite the upsurge in building, vacancy rates remained inordinately low. In many older metropolises the demand for office space seemed insatiable. Fueling this demand was a sharp rise in the number of white-collar workers as the financial, insurance, and business service sectors of the economy outpaced manufacturing and retailing. Moreover, a desire for better accommodations and the need for more space to house new office equipment meant that the square footage per office worker rose approximately 20 percent between the late 1940 and early 1960s.[13] In other words, there were more office employees and a demand for more space per employee. The consequence was good times for the downtown real estate interests who had long campaigned for the revitalization of the central city.

The national media were well aware of this heartening sign of vitality in the aging urban hubs. In 1955 *Business Week* reported that office towers were "building fast, [and] filling fast." The following year it printed an article entitled "Offices: They Can't Catch Up" that announced, "a few cities are taking a breather, but most see no easing of [the] demand for more office space."[14] By 1960 this popular business journal exclaimed, "The postwar mushrooming of downtown office buildings has completely changed city silhouettes."[15] Similarly, in 1960 *Fortune* wrote of the "$2 Billion Building Boom" in Manhattan, happily observing that the borough's "real estate in the last six years, to the surprise of almost everyone, [had] returned to life and financial glamour in a terrific visible demonstration of the vitality of purely private enterprise."[16]

Even more encouraging to urban boosters and friends of private enterprise were the hard figures that supported such journalistic claims. In New York City the building boom started earlier than in other cities, and between 1947 and 1961, 137 new office buildings were completed in Manhattan with almost 46 million square feet of rentable area, about half as much as all the borough's existing office space at the close of World War II. Yet throughout this period the vacancy rate never rose above 3 percent.[17] In 1958 the net area of office space in downtown Chicago rose by more than one million square feet for the first time since 1930, and in 1961 and 1963 the million mark was likewise exceeded. Overall, between 1946 and 1963 the square footage in Chicago's central business district increased 26 percent.[18]

Elsewhere the signs were also positive. In 1958 the twenty-two-story Illuminating Building opened in downtown Cleveland, the first major addition to that city's office inventory since 1934, and in 1959 a twenty-one-story glass-and-aluminum-curtained structure was dedicated a few blocks away.[19] That same year a twenty-eight-story bank building opened in downtown Minneapolis, the first office tower constructed in the central business district since the Depression. Similarly, in 1962 Baltimore boosters cheered the opening of the soaring One Charles Center, designed by the famed Mies van der Rohe, and doubly encouraging was the concurrent completion of the thirty-story Blaustein Building across the street. Though some feared that the two new structures would produce excess office capacity in the Maryland metropolis, by spring of 1964 both buildings were more than 90 percent leased.[20] As in New York City and Chicago, new construction did not produce unwanted glut. Instead, the market for office space was growing, and the fully occupied towers were ample testimony to the expansion of white-collar employment.

In some cities the news was not so good. For example, in the late 1950s the developer of Buffalo's only major postwar office building had trouble attracting tenants. Downtown Saint Louis witnessed no new office construction before the mid-1960s, earning that city a reputation for unequaled sluggishness.[21] But after the long construction drought stretching from the 1930s to the mid-1950s, the reports from New York City, Chicago, Cleveland, and Baltimore aroused unexpected new hope that downtown was not inevitably doomed.

Not only were new office buildings accentuating the central-city skyline, a fresh crop of hotels also was finally offering new accommodations for travelers. Overbuilding during the hotel construction boom of the 1920s had resulted in a wave of bankruptcies in the 1930s that in turn nurtured a postwar reluctance to invest again in hotels. In 1961, however, the first major hotel completed in Manhattan since 1931, the Summit, welcomed its initial guests, who, according to the *New York Times,* could drive "into a five-story, 250-car sub-basement garage and then be whisked up to a huge modernistic lobby in a high-speed elevator."[22] One observer claimed that "the Summit's two-color terrazzo sidewalk, marble, glazed brick, and ceramic tile exterior give it all the quiet elegance of a Main Street brass band on the Fourth of July."[23] Yet despite its gaudiness, it was a welcome sight to New York boosters, who had waited thirty years for the debut of new accommodations. By early 1962 twelve additional hotels with 8,000 rooms were rising in midtown Manhattan, including the world's tallest hostelry, the fifty-story Americana, and the 2,153-room New York Hilton.[24] Much of this construction was in anticipation of an expected flood of visitors to the New York World's Fair of 1964.

But in other central cities as well new hotels supposedly signaled a downtown revival. In the late 1950s the construction of the thirty-nine-story Executive House seemed to prove that there was still considerable life in the lodging industry in Chicago's central business district. Meanwhile, by 1961 downtown Minneapolis was experiencing a hotel construction boom with the groundbreaking of a new Sheraton, a 200-room addition to the Radisson, and the building of two other fifteen-story hostelries. Not a single new hotel had opened in Minneapolis since 1924, but now fortunes finally seemed to be changing in that city's downtown.[25]

This wave of new hotels, however, was deceptive, for it actually masked a continuing decline in the central-city lodging trade. By 1963 the national occupancy rate for hotels had fallen to 61 percent from a high of 93 percent in 1946.[26] Despite a healthy economy, the rate was the worst since the depression-stricken 1930s. In some cities the decline during the 1950s and early 1960s was even more serious. By 1961 Buffalo's hotels were operating at only 48 percent of capacity.[27] That same year the occupancy rate in Cleveland was a dismal 55 percent, worse than the 56 percent recorded in the depression year of 1933.[28] Even in Minneapolis the occupancy rate dropped from 87 percent in 1951 to 70 percent in 1960, causing many to doubt the wisdom of those investors who were breaking ground for new hotels.[29] And in New York City older hotels, faced with fresh competition, were converting their former guest rooms and leasing them as office space.[30] In fact, the flurry of new construction in Manhattan mystified some experts. "The whole situation doesn't make sense," said one manager of a large midtown hotel. "I can't understand how financial institutions can invest their customers' money in hotel mortgages when there is not enough demand for hotel rooms."[31]

Underlying the troubles confronting downtown hotels were changing patterns of transportation. More air travel resulted in the construction of airport hotels, which drew customers from the downtown establishments. Moreover, mounting reliance on the automobile made the outlying motel with its ample and convenient parking a desirable alternative to the downtown hotel. These automobile-oriented hostelries could claim occupancy rates 10 percent to 12 percent higher than those for the hotels, graphically demonstrating the disadvantages of the older accommodations constructed during the railroad era.[32] But the general lethargy of downtown also undermined the demand for hotel rooms in the urban core. One Cleveland hotel manager summed up the attitude of many of his colleagues when he claimed that the central business district's hostelries would continue to suffer "as long as there's nothing to do downtown."[33] As the center of metropolitan life moved outward from the increasingly dormant cores of Cleveland and Buffalo, the reasons for staying downtown gradually diminished.

By the early 1960s, then, the reports from downtown were mixed. Retail sales were falling and major department stores as well as long-established specialty shops were closing. Going-out-of-business sales with prices slashed 25 percent to 50 percent were commonplace as stores sought to get rid of their inventories and find a new home in the suburbs. Likewise, older hotels were finding it difficult to make a profit and were losing the competitive edge to suburban motels. Yet downtown office space remained in high demand and wrecking crews were clearing away derelict hotels and obsolete department stores to make room for new office towers.

The function of downtown was narrowing; it was becoming primarily a center for corporate offices, banks, and business services. Responding to the announced closing of Bailey's, a *Cleveland Plain Dealer* columnist realistically observed: "The character of downtown . . . has changed and no amount of exhorting, wishful thinking or promoting of 'urban renewal' projects will change it back. It will remain what it long has been, a business center, mainly office buildings and financial institutions."[34] Likewise, in 1962 the Pittsburgh Regional Planning Association noted, "The Triangle's breadwinner is its office buildings." Henceforth, these office structures would be a "major reason for the existence of a downtown."[35] Perceptive observers throughout the nation were recognizing the prevailing trend in the central business district. Downtown remained the dominant financial district, but in retailing and the hospitality industry it was losing its preeminence.

Meanwhile, the older cities were also losing ground as centers of manufacturing. In the postwar world manufacturers needed expansive tracts of cheap land to accommodate employee parking lots, truck loading areas, and single-story plants adapted to the latest horizontal assembly-line techniques. Yet large plots of empty land were just what the older central cities lacked. Moreover, as trucking became a more significant mode of freight transport, the traffic congestion of the central city became a serious obstacle to industrial growth in such urban hubs as Chicago, Philadelphia, Baltimore, and Boston. Tracts along broad and uncongested suburban highways were the preferred sites.

The consequence was declining manufacturing employment in the central cities accompanied by an increase in factory jobs in suburbia. For example, between 1958 and 1963, manufacturing employment dropped 6 percent in New York City but rose 14 percent in its suburban counties, plummeted 11 percent in Philadelphia but climbed 19 percent in that city's surrounding communities, declined 8 percent in Baltimore while increasing 3 percent in its environs, and fell 9 percent in Saint Louis but rose 9 percent in adjacent suburbia.[36] The figures were the same in older central cities throughout the northeastern quadrant of the United States. Older multistory mill buildings in the central cities were losing tenants to new single-story plants stretching along outlying freeways. By the early 1960s obsolete factories were a common feature of the urban landscape, and figures for central-city manufacturing paralleled the downward trend of retail sales statistics.

Thus after two decades of much talk, considerable planning, and some implementation of schemes to revitalize the aging central cities, the hard facts were hardly encouraging. Central-city business leaders and mayors could find few heartening signals in the data on population, retailing, hotel occupancy, or manufacturing. Only the beginnings of a resurgence in office construction seemed to point to happier days ahead. Before World War II, real estate interests, planners, and journalists warned that the central cities were skidding downward inexorably, and they called for strong action. Now twenty years later their prophecies seemed to be coming true. As yet there were few signs of renaissance and little cause for rejoicing.

Mixed Reports from City Hall

By the late 1950s and early 1960s signs of economic decline were not the only bad news troubling the older central cities. Voters, journalists, and business leaders also were witnessing an apparent resurgence of mediocrity in the highest municipal offices, and no one was able to ignore the mounting problems with city finances. In the mid-1950s, national publications had praised the new breed of mayors, the Clarks, Dilworths, Tuckers, and Wagners who inspired the much-ballyhooed dreams of renaissance and seemed capable of realizing them. Moreover, tax reforms had broadened the sources of municipal revenue and had reduced the city's traditional dependence on real estate levies. At the beginning of the 1960s, however, the new breed was disappearing or growing a bit stale. Few of the central-city mayors seemed exciting harbingers of a new era. And the municipal ledgers did not seem to signal a golden age ahead. Fiscal crises occurred at an increasing rate as city leaders tried to piece together a municipal budget that would somehow balance. Though the rhetoric of renewal survived in the speeches of every mayor from Boston to Saint Louis and the older central cities did maintain a precarious solvency, the reports from city hall offered less hope of impending renaissance than they had a few years earlier.

Perhaps most discouraging to urban boosters was the drab corps of lackluster figures who assumed the mayor's office in one city after another. In September 1957 Detroit's builder-mayor Albert Cobo died of a heart attack and city council president Louis Miriani succeeded him, serving as chief executive until 1962. A short, plump cherubic figure, Miriani was described by friends and foes alike as a "whiskerless Santa Claus with eyeglasses." While mayor he was most conscientious about his grooming, never appearing without a perfect crease in his trousers, but he could claim few other distinctions.[37] Time magazine offered a fair assessment of him when it labeled Miriani a "competent but complacent bureaucrat."[38] The federal authorities disturbed this complacency in the late 1960s when they jailed Miriani for evading taxes on $259,000 acquired during his last three years as mayor.

In 1959, following Mayor David Lawrence's election as governor of Pennsylvania, Joseph Barr began a ten-year stint as Pittsburgh's chief executive, continuing Lawrence's policies but without the national publicity that his much-acclaimed predecessor was able to engender. A goose-stepping, unimaginative devotee of the Democratic party machine, Barr expressed his priorities when after Lawrence's death he eulogized the molder of Pittsburgh's renaissance as "a great mayor, governor, public official, and above all, politician."[39]

In 1959 Baltimore's reform-minded but forgettable J. Harold Grady replaced the dynamic three-term builder of public improvements, Tommy D'Alesandro, Jr. Throughout his three years as mayor, Grady futilely attempted to steer the rudderless vessel of Baltimore government and after running aground a few too many times retired to a safe judgeship.

During the first years of the 1960s, equally ineffectual or uninspiring figures moved into city hall in Philadelphia, Cleveland, and Buffalo. The change in command in Philadelphia's city hall was especially dramatic, for in February 1962 Mayor Richardson Dilworth stepped down to run for governor of Pennsylvania, ending ten years of rule by patrician reformers who had won for Philadelphia a reputation for renewal and revival second only to that of Pittsburgh. Dilworth's successor was city council president James Tate, a longtime ward politico who appropriately entitled his memoirs "In Praise of Politicians." Tate was the type of old-fashioned politician who boasted at the end of his career of having "attended perhaps a thousand wakes and funerals," going to three or four a week while mayor.[40]

Though such solace may have won him votes in the city's working-class wards, it failed to earn Philadelphia a continuing place among the front ranks of comeback cities. In the recurring articles about urban revival, Philadelphia's name appeared less frequently than in the halcyon days of Tate's well-bred predecessors, and by 1963 the *Philadelphia Evening Bulletin* was editorializing, "The feeling is inescapable and widespread that the momentum picked up under Clark and Dilworth is grinding to a halt."[41]

In Cleveland five-term mayor Anthony Celebrezze yielded to bespectacled Ralph Locher, the soporific longtime city law director. Honest but inordinately dull, Locher hardly added flair to the image of his declining lakeside city. In Buffalo the local tradition of corruption and incompetence continued unbroken under Mayor Chester Kowal, who conveniently died awaiting trial for his role in a municipal garbage dump scandal.[42]

Even in cities where the new breed of mayors survived through the early 1960s, these once-acclaimed figures no longer seemed to exercise as much control or offer as much promise. During the last years of his administration, Philadelphia's Mayor Dilworth had to make more concessions to Democratic ward politicians than did his less flexible predecessor Joseph Clark. In Saint Louis the engineer-reformer Raymond Tucker remained in office and continued to work for rejuvenation of his sluggish city. Yet his days of unprecedented popularity were over, and in the 1961 Democratic primary he captured the party nomination for a third term by fewer than 1,300 votes out of almost 80,000 cast.[43]

Similarly, in New York City the high hopes that had accompanied Mayor Robert Wagner's early years in office were waning by the close of the 1950s, and the once-lauded executive was winning an unenviable reputation for inaction and indecision. In 1957 *Fortune* had acclaimed Wagner one of the bright stars appearing in city halls across the country, but only three years later it ran an article on New York City government entitled "The Vacuum at City Hall" that characterized the mayor as "an amiable, well-informed, and hardworking (if somewhat disorganized) executive whose principal flaw appears to be his reluctance to make hard decisions or to fight for his programs."[44] In 1961 Wagner broke with the regular Democratic organization and won the party primary and a third-term victory without its backing. Yet the *New York Times,* which had endorsed Wagner in the 1957 election, was not impressed by his new independence and in 1961 urged his defeat. Citing the mayor's "general air of indecisiveness and timidity" and his "government by fits and starts," the *Times* argued that reelection would mean "the near-certainty of continued mediocrity."[45] Throughout Wagner's third term this bad press continued with an increasing number of New Yorkers claiming that the mayor commanded a stalled government that was doing little to advance the troubled city.

Two mayors, however, contrasted sharply with their uninspiring colleagues of the late 1950s and early 1960s and fueled heightened hopes of revival in their older central cities. Both Chicago's Mayor Richard Daley and Boston's Mayor John Collins seemed cut from the same pattern as dynamic postwar builder-mayors like Cobo, D'Alesandro, and Lawrence. In 1955 Daley's ouster of reform Mayor Kennelly at first offered little encouragement to business and civic leaders who wanted a new Chicago. The rule of parochial ward politicians had seemingly returned. Yet Daley soon proved that he could speak the language of urban revivalism as ably as he could operate the levers of machine politics, and his devotion to such artifacts of renewal as the McCormick Convention Center, the Chicago Circle campus of the University of Illinois, and O'Hare Airport won him a following among many business moguls who felt little love for the old-fashioned machine.

John Collins also was a traditional Irish Catholic politician who had served his apprenticeship in the Boston city council and Massachusetts legislature. But his 1959 election as mayor of Boston marked the beginning of an urban renewal blitz that was to transform the core of New England's metropolis.[46] Together with his dynamic redevelopment director, Edward Logue, Collins tried to sell his city and the nation an image of the "New Boston," a revived hub in marked contrast to the languishing backwater of his predecessor John Hynes or the corrupt cesspool of the earlier James Curley. Largely successful in revamping the city's reputation, during the early 1960s Collins was what Clark and Lawrence had been a decade earlier, a model of a renaissance mayor.

Yet Collins's success in the early 1960s was little consolation to other cities where postwar hopes of executive dynamism had yielded to political doldrums. The political changes of the late 1940s and 1950s may have seriously weakened party organizations and traditional partisan politics. But they did not necessarily usher in an era of high-minded dynamos that would lead the central cities to new heights of achievement. By 1960 it was evident that the new politics of urban America could nurture mediocrity just as readily as the old system.

Moreover, the advent of Tate and Miriani and the decline of Tucker and Wagner did not mean a revival of party rule with strong party organizations acting as brokers to ensure viable governing coalitions. Instead, the role of the parties continued to diminish in every city but Chicago and Pittsburgh, where Democratic machines remained powerful throughout the 1960s. Tate, for example, was a machine politician without a machine, campaigning for reelection in 1967 without the backing of the Democratic party organization.[47] Running as an independent "reformer" in 1961, Wagner likewise leveled a fatal blow at New York City's Tammany organization, and party "boss" Carmine DeSapio fell from power that same year. In one city after another, relatively weak figures assumed authority without the support of powerful party organizations that in earlier times had propped up spineless stooges in the mayor's office. Now the Tates, Mirianis, and Wagners had to take the helm by themselves, and the course they charted did not inspire confidence among those seeking to reach the shores of renaissance.

Hampering the efforts of these mayors were the mounting fiscal problems in many cities. Even more popular and capable leaders might have achieved little when faced with the growing dilemma of too little revenue and too much expenditure. In the past mayors had faced budget crises, and the leaders of the late 1940s and early 1950s had been forced to create new levies to stave off financial debacle. By the late 1950s and early 1960s, however, the problem seemed to be worsening. Every year produced austerity budgets, and calls for state and federal aid became increasingly common. City officials continued to find means for paying municipal bills, but a note of desperation was heard in the budget messages of a growing number of central cities.

Especially troublesome to budget makers was the economic recession of the late 1950s, a downturn that in a number of older industrial cities lingered into the early 1960s. Inordinately sensitive to drops in consumer demand, the automobile capital of Detroit suffered a four-year fiscal crisis from 1958 to 1962. No major American city, other than Boston and Minneapolis, still relied so heavily on the property levy, and yet in the late 1950s Detroit's assessed valuation was actually declining even though inflation was forcing prices upward. Moreover, Detroit was the only Michigan city to finance a municipal welfare program, and this sorely taxed the city treasury in 1958, when 20 percent of the local workforce was unemployed. That year Mayor Miriani took the drastic action of slashing the budget by 5 percent, laying off seven hundred city employees. Yet deficit spending continued, and the city resorted to borrowing for operations like street resurfacing that previously had been financed from current revenues. In addition, in 1959 and 1960 the mayor refused to allocate sufficient funds to meet the actuarial requirements of the city's pension system. Despite this belt tightening, at the end of the fiscal year 1961–62 the operating fund deficit reached $19.5 million, and a court had ordered the city to appropriate an additional $15 million for the pension fund to compensate for past neglect.[48]

The nation's steel capital did not fare much better than the hub of the automobile industry. In November 1958 outgoing Mayor Lawrence blamed "the head-on collision of recession and inflation" for proposed reductions in city services and raises in taxes. The resulting budget for 1959 was, according to Lawrence, "the most difficult . . . ever submitted" in his tenure as chief executive of Pittsburgh.[49] Two years later Mayor Barr complained that the city was still "going through a prolonged period of economic hardship," and to close a $3.8 million budget gap he recommended doubling the municipal earned income tax rate.[50] The following year Barr fashioned a budget "balanced in every respect, that impose[d] no new tax load upon our citizens," but he also warned that Pittsburgh was "rapidly running into a fiscal dead-end."[51]

At the close of 1962 the mayor still characterized his city as "in the throes of economic readjustment" and cited a 12 percent unemployment rate as evidence of local hardship. Confronted by this "prolonged period of transition," Barr parroted the words of his predecessor four years earlier and presented "the most difficult budget" in his "tenure as chief executive." This troublesome budget cut more than 175 positions from the municipal payrolls and eliminated all the traditional grants to such cultural institutions as the symphony, the art and natural history museum, and the educational television station.[52] Though the mayor promised that the city's much-vaunted renaissance would eventually liberate it from the economic deadweight of the sluggish steel industry, as yet Gateway Center and the other new office towers in the Golden Triangle were not paying enough into city coffers to relieve the problems of municipal budget makers.

Meanwhile, the nation's largest and wealthiest central city seemed trapped in a perpetual fiscal crisis that made the woes of Pittsburgh appear trivial. Like so many of his colleagues in city halls across the country, Mayor Wagner had to present a "budget of austerity" for New York City that reduced the appropriations of 46 of the city's 115 departments and agencies and eliminated 2,700 positions from the payroll to keep total expenditures under $2 billion.[53] The *New York Times* characterized this 1958–59 budget as the "first pause in expansion of program and services in recent years" and observed that this was "the first year in which Mr. Wagner [was] running scared on money."[54] The economy-minded Citizens Budget Commission did nothing to allay Wagner's fears when it published essays with such foreboding titles as "Does Crisis Lie Ahead?" and issued warnings of a $100 million budget gap for 1959–60.[55]

Such dreary prognostications were not without merit, and in 1959 Wagner presented what he described as another "austere" budget based on "an inadequate revenue program," though some questioned the austerity of a budget that promised $178 million in additional expenditures.[56] Protesting reduced pay raises, thousands of city employees picketed city hall on the day Wagner introduced the budget, but their modest job action was only a precursor of dire days ahead.[57] For by 1963 the city was in the midst of an even more serious fiscal crisis. That year Wagner submitted the city's first $3 billion budget with a revenue gap of a quarter of a billion dollars that could be closed only by stiff tax hikes.[58] Dissatisfied city teachers promised to conduct an all-night vigil outside of city hall on the eve of the budget hearings to dramatize "the plight of the schools" that were to suffer from the "completely unacceptable" proposed appropriations.[59]

Despite mounting expenditures, the city appeared unable to catch up with needs, and always the problem seemed to be too little money. "This budget represents a day of reckoning," the *New York Times* editorialized. "All the deceptive expedients, all the financial gimmicks were already used up. The city has been spending money it didn't have . . . Now the collector is at the door."[60] A commission on city finances appointed in 1963 to study the fiscal dilemma repeated the warning of the *Times* when it concluded, "The City has exhausted most of the easy solutions in its efforts to balance the expense budget in recent years." This commission representing business, labor, and academia grimly pronounced, "For both the immediate future and the decade ahead, the City must find difficult answers and face hard choices."[61]

Among the difficult answers that Wagner and his fellow mayors proposed for the immediate future were a long list of new taxes together with increases in old levies. A city income tax seemed at least a temporary solution to Detroit's problems, and in 1962 adoption of a 1 percent levy brought an end to four years of fiscal woes in the Motor City.[62] Pittsburgh not only doubled its earned income tax rate, but Mayor Barr also proposed a 10 percent tax on the gross receipts of parking operators and an occupation privilege tax of $10 levied on all persons working in the city.[63] Philadelphia's real estate tax rate remained unchanged from 1936 until 1957, but it increased that year and once again in 1961, forced upward by mounting costs. Moreover, in 1957 Philadelphia's city income tax rate rose from $1\frac{1}{4}$ percent to $1\frac{1}{2}$ percent and then jumped to $1\frac{5}{8}$ percent in 1961.[64]

In response to what Mayor Tucker described as a "critical financial situation," in 1959 Saint Louis voters approved a charter amendment permitting an increase in the earnings tax rate from $\frac{1}{2}$ percent to 1 percent.[65] That ensured solvency for the next two budgets, but by 1963 Mayor Tucker was again estimating a $4.7 million gap between income and proposed expenditure and suggesting a rise in the property tax rate, an extension of the business license taxes to establishments previously not covered, a hike in liquor license and building inspection fees, and an increase in the city cigarette tax from three cents to four cents a pack.[66]

The city property tax rate in Chicago soared 41 percent between 1958 and 1962, when it finally leveled off. In 1959 Chicago's economy-conscious Civic Federation warned its members that "the stampede for more money from taxpayers [was] on."[67]

But perhaps no city invented taxes more readily or raised them more quickly than did Mayor Wagner's New York. Though faced with financial crisis, Wagner opposed increasing the burden on real estate and kept the property levy relatively stable. To fill the revenue gap, in 1959 New York City thus resorted to increases in the cigarette tax, the sales tax on meals and liquor, the general business tax, and the financial business tax. Moreover, the city created a new real property transfer levy and a new tax on coin-operated amusement devices, charging $25 per jukebox. Then in 1960 the city doubled its gross receipts tax on utilities and invented a levy on commercial motor vehicles. A new annual vault charge followed in

1962, and the financial problems of 1963 produced an increase in the city sales tax from 3 percent to 4 percent, a doubling of the cigarette tax, and a new commercial rent or occupancy tax.[68] The 1963 raises aroused the opposition of the Citizens Budget Commission and the New York Chamber of Commerce and led to the organization of the Anti–4 Per Cent Sales Tax Committee. Moreover, within two days after the release of Wagner's budget message, city hall had received 230,000 signatures on form letters and petitions protesting the mayor's tax package.[69]

Wagner and his fellow mayors did not prefer to face such fury. Instead, the hope of city officials across the country was for a reprieve from the state and federal treasuries, and throughout the late 1950s and early 1960s, calls for increased intergovernmental funding mounted as city officials argued that it was time for Albany, Harrisburg, Lansing, and Washington to shoulder greater urban responsibilities. Mayor Miriani persistently contended that the state of Michigan should relieve Detroit's fiscal problems, especially by funding city welfare costs. "That's where we need help," said Miriani, "at the state level."[70] Speaking of the long-term solution to Pittsburgh's financial woes, in 1960 Mayor Barr told the city council, "There must be a reassignment of public functions between the City, the County, the State, and yes, the Federal Government."[71]

No one, however, was as dogged in his pursuit of intergovernmental aid as Mayor Wagner. Each year the Democratic mayor petitioned for greater state aid from Republican Governor Nelson Rockefeller and the Republican-controlled legislature in Albany, and each year state leaders pared his bloated request, granting considerably less than demanded. Then when budgetary problems arose, Wagner invariably blamed them on his partisan foes upstate, claiming that he and the city suffered only because of hostile lawmakers at the state level. In 1959 the *New York Times* noted that "a drearily peevish tone of complaint against the state" pervaded the mayor's budget message, and that tone was to become familiar to city hall observers by the mid-1960s.[72] Albany did hike its appropriations to the city but never enough for Mayor Wagner. Moreover, Wagner urged greater federal help, writing in 1960 that urban problems "must be attacked by national policies meshed with local needs, policies developed with the full and ungrudging cooperation of the national government working with state and local governments."[73]

During the late 1950s and early 1960s, however, the trends in municipal financing did not change markedly. The declining reliance on the property tax continued, and by 1963 in eleven of the twelve older central cities a lower percentage of general fund revenues derived from property taxes than in 1958 (tables 7 and 13). Whereas in the 1945 all twelve of the

Table 13. Sources of General Revenue, 1963

City	Property Taxes (%)	Nonproperty Taxes (%)	Intergovernmental Aid (%)
New York	37.8	22.4	25.3
Chicago	47.9	24.7	12.7
Philadelphia	32.5	37.6	10.6
Detroit	45.1	13.9	26.9
Baltimore	42.7	5.4	42.2
Cleveland	53.3	2.9	19.2
Saint Louis	32.2	44.5	6.3
Boston	61.0	1.2	30.5
Pittsburgh	49.1	24.0	22.8
Buffalo	53.6	4.5	30.5
Cincinnati	21.5	18.5	20.9
Minneapolis	57.7	4.7	14.0

Source: U.S. Bureau of the Census, *Compendium of City Government Finances in 1963* (Washington, D.C.: U.S. Government Printing Office, 1964).

cities had acquired a majority of their general revenues from property taxes and as late as 1958 seven did so, by 1963 only four were that dependent on property levies. Mayors were able to win some increments in intergovernmental aid, with that category contributing a higher percentage of revenues in ten of the twelve cities. In addition, reliance on user fees and charges continued to increase gradually. In Detroit the adoption of the municipal income tax produced a sharp rise in the proportion of revenue derived from nonproperty taxes. But in most of the older central cities of the northeastern quadrant of the United States, the gradual shifts of the late 1940s and early 1950s continued without a dramatic break with the financial pattern of a decade earlier.

Thus the federal and state governments were not handing over the treasury keys to America's discontented mayors and permitting an unprecedented bounty of intergovernmental aid. But during the late 1950s and early 1960s, many urban leaders believed that much more state and federal help soon would be necessary. A number of the aging hubs had not rebounded from the 1958 recession as rapidly as the rest of the nation, and a return to prosperity had not bailed out many of those municipalities. The underlying problem, however, was greater than a single recession and was not simply related to the economic cycle. Instead, the combined emigration of wealth to suburbia and immigration of poverty to the urban core meant a shrinking tax base and a relative reduction in the sources of future revenue. In the long run this was what threatened the central city, and Mayors Wagner, Barr, Tate, and Miriani were all aware of this grim fact. The fiscal consequences of decentralization and blight that had worried business leaders and public officials as early as 1940 were becoming painfully evident in a growing number of cities by the early 1960s.

The news from city hall was, then, at best mixed. In Boston and Chicago there was dynamic leadership and unprecedented strength in the mayor's office. Yet elsewhere the new breed of postwar executives was yielding to figures less likely to win national plaudits or inspire hopes of renaissance. Cities like Minneapolis, Cincinnati, and Cleveland were still keeping taxes down and balancing budgets, though Detroit and New York City limped along in apparently endless fiscal misery. Overall, however, the leadership and ledgers of the aging urban hubs did not seem as encouraging as they had five or ten years earlier. By the early 1960s prudent observers perceived that the path to revival was longer and less direct than optimistic boosters had formerly hoped.

Dreamers and Detractors

Even though the mayors and municipal budgets of the late 1950s and early 1960s may have inspired little confidence, the plans and models for rebuilding the older central cities did lift the spirits of urban boosters and win enthusiastic praise from the metropolitan dailies. During the period 1958–63, the federal urban renewal program finally began to have a major impact on American cities after a slow start in the early 1950s, and at this time optimistic planners unveiled some of the grandest, most ambitious schemes for renovating the decaying urban hubs. With big plans and federal backing, the central cities seemed poised to embark on a true revival. Yet also during this period, Americans heard the first major outcry against plans for physical renewal, the initial complaints and protests about the untoward consequences of the highly vaunted projects. It was, then, a time of both dreamers and detractors, when many central cities set out on the road to the much-sought renaissance and when some urbanites began to doubt the wisdom of the journey or at least the merits of the means of travel.

In one city after another renewal schemes proliferated on the drafting boards of planners. Moreover, money was finally flowing from Washington for projects, and ground-breaking ceremonies were becoming increasingly frequent. As seen in table 14, by the middle of 1962 the federal government had disbursed millions of dollars in urban renewal grants in each of the older central cities of the northeastern quadrant of the United

Table 14. Urban Renewal Capital Grants Disbursed by 30 June 1962

City	Amount ($)	City	Amount ($)
New York	74,987,499	Saint Louis	18,036,249
Chicago	51,814,696	Boston	10,847,382
Philadelphia	35,387,136	Pittsburgh	11,077,073
Detroit	16,100,872	Buffalo	8,308,416
Baltimore	18,388,694	Cincinnati	8,385,051
Cleveland	7,828,204	Minneapolis	11,171,406

Source: *Urban Renewal Directory, June 30, 1962* (Washington, D.C.: Housing and Home Finance Agency, 1962).

States. Whereas just four years earlier (see table 8) only New York City had received more than $10 million in grants, now nine of the twelve aging cities topped that mark. In 1958 Buffalo had not yet obtained one dollar in urban renewal grants; by 1962 it had garnered over $8 million. The financial data seemed to indicate that the federal program created by the Housing Act of 1949 had finally taken off.

Moreover, by the late 1950s the federally funded urban renewal program was changing direction. Whereas the earliest projects had provided moderate- or middle-income housing, now local planners sought to apply federal dollars to more glamorous schemes that emulated such successful privately funded projects as Pittsburgh's Gateway Center or Philadelphia's Penn Center. Commercial or luxury apartment developments seemed to promise more dramatic results than the comparatively modest and pedestrian housing schemes of the early 1950s. Amendments to the federal urban renewal law in 1959 and 1961 gave cities greater leeway in spending renewal funds for commercial projects, and many localities readily responded to this new opportunity.

The proliferation of federal urban renewal projects and the planning of increasingly ambitious schemes were characteristic of older central cities throughout the United States. New York City pioneered the use of federal renewal funds for high-rise luxury housing in its Kips Bay and Washington Square projects, and the Lincoln Center development constructed during the early 1960s included not only high-rent housing but a complex of theaters and concert halls.[74] Pittsburgh continued its earlier projects but made greater use of federal funds, most notably employing money from Washington to clear ninety-five acres of slums in the Lower Hill district adjacent to the Golden Triangle. In place of 1,300 dilapidated structures the city erected the eighteen-thousand-seat Civic Arena completed in 1961, a 396-unit apartment building, and a 2,200-car parking garage while also planning the construction of Chatham Center, which was supposed to include a hotel, offices, and apartments.[75] At the same time, Baltimore was implementing its Charles Center project of offices, stores, apartments, and theaters, relying now on federal funds rather than depending solely on local government and private initiative.[76]

Other cities that had previously been less active also were making big plans and implementing some old ones. For example, between 1959 and 1962 contracts for construction of Saint Louis's 630-foot Gateway Arch were finally let, though clearance of the land had been completed as early as 1942 and President Truman had dedicated the site in 1950. Officially the Jefferson National Expansion Memorial, the project depended not on urban renewal funding but on special appropriations granted by a sometimes reluctant Congress that questioned the wisdom of paying so much for an ornament to uplift the spirits of Saint Louis.[77] Meanwhile, in 1961 the city's first federal renewal project, Plaza Square Apartments, opened to tenants, offering middle-class housing in the central business district, and plans for the luxury Mansion House apartments and for a downtown sports stadium were also on the drawing boards.

Upriver in Minneapolis the urban renewal authority was planning its own waterfront facelift known as Gateway Center. Described by the city planning commission as "a run-down, skid-row type of area lying between the present Central Business District and the Mississippi River," the compact district known originally as the Lower Loop was home to three thousand transient men, forty-three bars, and fifteen liquor stores. In December 1958 the renewal authorities began demolishing the Lower Loop structures, and during the next decade, high-rise apartments, bank buildings, and the Sheraton-Ritz Hotel were to provide a new "respectable" front door for the Minnesota metropolis.[78] Even in lethargic Buffalo the Greater Buffalo Development Foundation was drawing up plans for the downtown waterfront, an area that the foundation described as "a public eyesore and an economic waste." Yet it also presented "the greatest opportunity for regeneration" and was in the eyes of the foundation boosters "a jewel waiting to be cut and polished and set in the crown of a reviving metropolis."[79]

Perhaps no cities were as ambitious in their schemes for physical regeneration, however, as Cleveland and Boston. During the 1950s, both had ranked among the least dynamic of the older central cities, but by the 1960s each was drafting impressive plans for the future. The keystone of Cleveland's revival was to be Erieview, a 163-acre scheme that planners described as "undoubtedly the most ambitious project so far undertaken under the Federal Urban Redevelopment Program."[80] With a master plan designed by the distinguished planning and architectural firm of I. M. Pei and Associates, Mayor Anthony Celebrezze enthusiastically presented the scheme in November 1960, announcing his belief "that history [would] record the 1960s as the decade of the rebirth of the American city."[81]

According to Pei's grandiose proposal, soaring skyscrapers of thirty and forty stories flanked by sprawling six-story blocks interspersed with malls and parks were to replace the dilapidated warehouses, light industrial workshops, and makeshift parking lots that cluttered the site adjacent to downtown Cleveland.[82] These new structures would house offices, apartments, hotels, stores, and entertainment facilities, nurturing a full-range of activities that would restore vitality to the urban core. Moreover, Cleveland's redevelopment officials expected Erieview "to spread its rejuvenating influence—like ripples from a stone dropped in a pool—to neighboring blocks."[83]

Simultaneously, Pei's busy firm was designing a similar plan of skyscrapers, open spaces, and sprawling low-rise structures for Boston's 61-acre Government Center on the site of Scollay Square, the city's skid row and longtime "amusement" center for seamen in search of burlesque houses, honky-tonk bars, tattoo parlors, and prostitutes. To include a new city hall as well as state and federal office buildings, when completed the $185 million project was expected to draw some fifty thousand people to the area daily, bringing new vitality to Boston's core.[84] In order to house some of the downtown employees and attract the middle class back to city living, Boston's redevelopers were meanwhile constructing the 48-acre West End project, which cleared a rundown Italian neighborhood flanking Boston's central business district and replaced it with 2,400 swank high-rise apartment units. In December 1959 the *Boston Globe* said of the ambitious development, "If the West End can be switched from dilapidation to delight as was New York's East Side, it may be the trail-blazing spark which could revitalize Boston."[85]

Certain common denominators characterized the "trailblazing" renewal projects of the late 1950s and early 1960s that were intended to rejuvenate the heart of America's older cities. Each of these projects cleared gray areas adjacent to the established central business district, thus eliminating blight that might threaten the city's prime real estate. Moreover, they leveled shabby structures that cluttered the entrance to downtown and that further tarnished the image of the already dingy central cities. Aging waterfronts were frequent targets of redevelopers, and tawdry skid rows also fell under the wrecker's ball in Minneapolis,

Boston, Philadelphia, and Detroit. Dilapidated warehouse and light industrial zones were likely renewal victims as well.

In place of these drab blocks, generally described as economic wastelands, one city after another proposed multiuse projects with retailing, hotels, entertainment, offices, and housing. Charles Center, Erieview, Minneapolis's Gateway Center, and Chatham Center all were supposed to provide a diversity of functions, for developers were dedicated to maintaining the city core as the center of all activities. Ideally, the downtown fringes were not to be redeveloped as simply a complex of offices with thousands of nine-to-five white-collar workers. Especially important to redevelopers was the provision of luxury housing downtown. From Boston to Buffalo to Saint Louis central-city boosters confidently predicted a return to the city by upper-middle- and upper-income childless people who were tired of commuting and eager for the convenience of downtown living. If only apartments were provided for them, they would supposedly flock to the urban centers and patronize the new stores, restaurants, and theaters of the renewal projects.

Across the country these common beliefs were producing slick plans of gleaming towers and sunny plazas. But the much-vaunted downtown projects were not the only renewal efforts initiated in the late 1950s and early 1960s. Also on the drafting boards were plans for new industrial parks on the site of former residential slums. These industrial renewal projects would not only markedly enhance the real estate tax base of the city and provide new jobs and new sources of earnings tax revenue, they would as well eliminate some of the nation's worst housing. Factories were departing for suburbia at an unprecedented rate, taking employment and tax dollars with them. One of the chief reasons for this exodus was lack of space in the central city for expansion or for the construction of single-story plants adapted to assembly-line production. Industrial clearance seemed an admirable solution, especially since federal renewal funds would pay two-thirds of the bill.

One of the largest of the industrial developments was Cincinnati's Kenyon-Barr project. In the late 1950s twenty-five thousand people (98 percent nonwhite) inhabited the 400-acre site, but dilapidation was widespread, and according to the city planning commission only 4 of the 2,800 buildings were without code violations. Enveloped on two sides by railroad tracks and switching yards and in the path of the proposed Mill Creek Expressway, the derelict area seemed to planners a natural location for industry, and in March 1959 the federal Housing and Home Finance Agency approved Cincinnati's proposal for industrial redevelopment. Lauded by *Architectural Forum* as "the most carefully thought-out industrial renewal scheme" in the nation, the Kenyon-Barr plan provided for thirteen superblocks each with a parking lot of eight to ten acres surrounded by fifteen to twenty light industrial concerns. And the superblocks would also contain banks, restaurants, and shops to serve the workers. Expected to provide fifteen thousand jobs and increase tax revenues from the tract three- or fourfold, in the early 1960s Kenyon-Barr seemed a heady tonic for the slipping economy of Ohio's Queen City.[86]

Kenyon-Barr may have received greater plaudits than other industrial projects, but it was hardly unique. The nation's largest urban renewal scheme was Philadelphia's 2,500-acre Eastwick, which was intended to be a "city-within-a-city" with moderate-income housing, shopping centers, and the remainder of the land set aside for industrial development. It was a low-lying, oft-flooded expanse of dilapidated housing, junkyards, and abandoned automobiles, but with ten million cubic yards of hydraulic fill and a modern sewer system Eastwick was expected to attract new manufacturing plants and provide jobs for twenty thousand Philadelphians.[87]

In 1958 the Saint Louis renewal authority embarked on the Mill Creek Valley project, clearing 454 acres of the city's worst slum for redevelopment. Nineteen percent of the land was devoted to housing, but the remainder was for industrial, commercial, institutional, and highway use. As in the case of Kenyon-Barr the Mill Creek project was conveniently located in the path of a new freeway, and Saint Louis leaders hoped the transportation assets of the area would attract light manufacturing that would boost city revenues without generating undesirable industrial pollution.[88]

Similarly, Buffalo was planning the 1,200-acre Thruway Industrial Park, and on a smaller scale Cleveland was developing 97-acre Gladstone, described by the Cleveland Development Foundation as an "island of opportunity" in the slums that would supposedly lure more than $33 million in new plant facilities to the aging manufacturing city.[89]

The office-apartment-shopping complexes like Erieview or Gateway Center and the industrial schemes like Kenyon-Barr and Mill Creek Valley were massive clearance projects dedicated to obliterating existing buildings, and the redevelopment authorities even rerouted streets and utilities to adapt these large land tracts to a new and supposedly higher economic use. During the late 1950s and early 1960s, such bulldozer renewal seemed to dominate accounts of urban revitalization and appeared to offer the best means of achieving the drastic remedy that central cities needed as quickly as possible. Yet at the same time, city leaders were initiating federally funded rehabilitation projects, and as in the mid-1950s these remained significant in the multipronged attack on blight and decentralization. While the bulldozers were clearing Erieview and the dredges were pumping fill into swampy Eastwick, renewal authorities were also subsidizing investments in paint, sandblasting, and refinished woodwork in an effort to upgrade the building inventory that already existed. During the late 1950s and early 1960s, the rehabilitation crusade was very much alive in the older central cities.

In fact, during this period, federal renewal funds were pouring into what would become one of the nation's most famous restored districts, Philadelphia's Society Hill. First developed in the eighteenth century, this neighborhood adjacent to Independence Hall could boast of scores of houses from the colonial and early national periods, but by 1957, 83 percent of the residences were classified as substandard. Having designated Society Hill an urban renewal project, in 1959 Philadelphia's redevelopment authority condemned all the existing properties. If the previous owners agreed to rehabilitate their buildings, the redevelopment authority would sell back the holdings.

A nonprofit organization of prominent Philadelphians, the Old Philadelphia Development Corporation, had the responsibility of finding redevelopers for the other buildings. The object of the Old Philadelphia Development Corporation was to create a neighborhood of owner-occupied, single-family dwellings restored to their original appearance. In its planning report from 1958, the redevelopment authority summed up the philosophy of the Society Hill rehabilitation project when it announced that "every effort should be made to preserve all that remains of the past in this unique area to avoid contemporary 'projectitis' "[90] One of the earliest of the affluent migrants to the upgraded area was Mayor Richardson Dilworth, who enthusiastically promoted rehabilitation, and by 1959 the *Philadelphia Bulletin* was already writing of the "flowering of Society Hill" and reporting, "On weekdays, Society Hill is overrun with workmen—carpenters, plasterers, painters, bricklayers."[91]

Meanwhile, New York City was experimenting with federally funded conservation of neighborhoods, opting for moderate rehabilitation that did not displace existing residents rather than the radical upgrading practiced in Society Hill. In 1959 the mayor's office launched the Neighborhood Conservation Program, and in June 1960 the federal Housing and Home Finance Agency granted the city $136,000 for a two-year project intended to develop and test "techniques for the prevention of blight in neighborhoods that [were] not appropriate for either slum clearance or complete remodeling." Focusing on seven Manhattan neighborhoods, the city sought to improve the physical and social environment by strictly enforcing municipal codes, by assisting property owners to obtain financing for moderate rehabilitation, and by helping families to relocate in order to relieve overcrowding. Moreover, the city attempted to organize tenants; arrange clean-up campaigns; identify the health, welfare, education, and public safety needs of the community; and build a community organization that would ensure the continuing participation of local residents in the improvement of their neighborhood.[92] Resembling the earlier Fight-Blight project of Baltimore and the Mack-Concord experiment in Detroit, the New York City scheme offered yet another means for staving off the forces of urban disintegration. By requiring landlords to patch roofs and repair plumbing in accord with building, health, and sanitation codes and by making sure local residents kept up the good work, the city could supposedly guarantee that "gray" neighborhoods would not slip into decay just as the more expensive downtown projects would brake the downhill slide of the central business district.

Elsewhere rehabilitation and conservation of neighborhoods were also continuing. In Chicago the Hyde Park–Kenwood project was gaining national attention, and the city was designating additional conservation areas. Pittsburgh was moving beyond its previous reliance on bulldozer clearance and sponsoring its first conservation program in the East Liberty district. Likewise, Minneapolis launched its initial rehabilitation project in the Harrison neighborhood adjacent to the Glenwood renewal area.[93]

Saint Louis remained committed to its neighborhood rehabilitation program begun in 1954 in the Hyde Park and Cherokee districts. In fact, in 1962 Saint Louis voters approved a $2 million bond issue to pay for reconditioned streets and alleys, new sidewalks and streetlights, and parks and playgrounds in the areas targeted for upgrading. The *St. Louis Post-Dispatch* stated "This is the most prudent form of urban renewal since it prevents blight—or stamps out the first signs of it[,] . . . enhances the attractiveness of a neighborhood instead of letting values slip until the wreckers come[, and] . . . enables people to continue to live where they want to live."[94] But the *Post-Dispatch* recognized the shortcomings of the program when it observed, "Every house in St. Louis could be spruced up—as a good many are being rehabilitated—without many persons elsewhere knowing about it." Expressing the view of many central-city boosters, the newspaper contended, "It is the dramatic touch that brings out the full value of urban redevelopment, that catches the attention which brings people and enterprises to a city."[95] Rehabilitation was not enough. Soaring arches and new stadiums were necessary to establish a reputation as a comeback city.

By the early 1960s, however, the aging central cities were clearly trying everything to combat decline. Glittering downtown showpieces, sprawling industrial parks, upgraded historical districts, and cleaned-up neighborhoods all were elements in the broad-based attack on physical blight. Moreover, by the early 1960s cities were taking full advantage of federal funding to realize the innovative programs and ambitious projects that planners were inventing. City budgets may have been discouraging and municipal politics may not have lifted the collective spirits of the cities, but the plans and proposals of the period stirred excitement among even the most pessimistic. During the late 1950s and early 1960s, the older central cities were not idly observing their decline. Instead, they were taking the initiative and fighting for a much-needed revival. Despite the disheartening census returns and the obvious signs of decay, this was an age of heady expectations and big dreams. The blueprints for renaissance were complete, and only implementation was necessary.

While cheering announcements of imminent revival dominated the late 1950s and early 1960s, in the background could be heard an emerging chorus of complaints and doubts. At the national level Jane Jacobs's *The Death and Life of Great American Cities* published in 1961 offered the most biting commentary on contemporary efforts to reconstruct the older central cities. She wrote of the "wistful myth that if only we had enough money to spend . . . we could wipe out all our slums in ten years, reverse decay in the great, dull, gray belts . . . , anchor the wandering middle class and its wandering tax money, and perhaps even solve the traffic problem." She castigated "the luxury housing projects that mitigate their inanity, or try to, with a vapid vulgarity" and the "expressways that eviscerate great cities." According to Jacobs: "This is not the rebuilding of cities. This is the sacking of cities." Moreover, she argued that "the economic rationale of current city rebuilding [was] a hoax," claiming that the increased tax revenues from renewal sites did not compensate for the ruthless destruction of established communities and small businesses that resulted from the wholesale clearance of urban tracts.[96]

Leveling her blows at the much-publicized bulldozer projects, she largely ignored the rehabilitation and conservation efforts of the previous two decades. In fact, she endorsed upgrading on a small scale, emphasizing the preservation of existing neighborhoods and structures. Had she not indiscriminately dismissed all efforts of the recent past with withering disdain, she might well have perceived some merit in the neighborhood rehabilitation programs of such cities as Saint Louis and Baltimore.

But by 1961 one did not have to read Jane Jacobs to discover criticisms of the renewal process. In one city after another, individuals less articulate than Jacobs but just as outraged were expressing complaints and raising questions about the justice and economic feasibility of urban renewal. Virtually everyone seemed to believe that the older central cities needed to take action to halt decay. Yet when they began to take action some did not like what was happening.

Especially bitter were those who expected to be displaced from renewal sites. Throughout the late 1950s and early 1960s irate residents expressed their vehement opposition at public hearings on proposed projects. As early as the summer of 1957 a hearing on Philadelphia's Eastwick proposal attracted more than 1,500 of the site's 6,500 residents, who organized a protest motorcade of 250 cars to transport opponents of the scheme. According to the *Philadelphia Evening Bulletin*, the residents "sometimes booed officials and frequently stated their objection in bitter terms"; moreover, some of the women "were in tears as they listened to officials patiently explaining the project." A spokesperson for Eastwick Workers against Redevelopment expressed the views of opponents when she announced: "I'm here to protest our homes being taken under condemnation and given to a group of real estate people in league with the Redevelopment Authority."[97] The following spring Society Hill's residents likewise stated their complaints in a hearing on the city planning commission's plan for redevelopment of their neighborhood. Critical of the lack of moderate-rent housing in the proposal, one resident argued, "What we have here is a plan for an area of wealthy poodled people," and a local delicatessen operator reiterated this when she complained, "All we'd have here are bluebloods and executives."[98]

The uproar accompanying the clearance of Boston's West End reached a decibel level far higher than the comparatively gentle protests in the City of Brotherly Love. Like their Eastwick compatriots the West Enders believed interests eager for a profit were conspiring with public officials to steal their homes, specifically charging in a brief submitted to the federal housing commissioner that "ill-advised elements in the City Council, in league with Federal bureaucrats" were "threatening to buy the prime residential part of Boston." At a 1957 hearing on the project in Massachusetts' state house, six hundred angry West Enders turned out. According to the *Boston Globe*, "mingled boos and applause, sharp verbal exchanges and partisan arguments were the order of the day," and "the commotion at one point" was "so violent that Capitol Police were called to restore order."[99]

Demolition began in 1958, and during the next five years, the displaced West Enders won a sympathetic hearing from a number of academic observers. Sociologist Herbert Gans wrote of the emotional attachments of the working-class Italian-Americans to their neighborhood, and clinical psychologist Marc Fried supported Gans's argument by reporting that 46 percent of West End women and 38 percent of the community's men gave "evidence of a fairly severe grief reaction or worse" when questioned about their displacement from the close-knit ethnic neighborhood. Housing expert Chester Hartman also found that the median monthly rent of the displaced soared an average of 73 percent owing to their relocation in more expensive housing.[100] By 1963 to many commentators the West End was a symbol of all that was wrong with urban renewal.

Between 1958 and 1963 complaints about displacement and the upheaval resulting from renewal were to become increasingly common in other cities as well. Especially troublesome was the problem of relocating the many low-income blacks displaced by projects. For example, Cincinnati whites resisted the migration of Kenyon-Barr's evicted blacks into their neighborhoods, and even moderate-income blacks sought to exclude the refugees. According to a Cincinnati journalist, when a small public housing project in a hilltop neighborhood for a few of the displaced was announced, "Negroes of the neighborhood hired a lawyer and hurried down to City Hall to protest[;] they wanted no public housing in their respectable neighborhood, and no trashy characters from the . . . Basin."[101]

Residents of Chicago's Near West Side were mobilizing in opposition to the proposal to replace their homes with a new campus of the University of Illinois. In February 1961 more than one hundred of the area's predominantly Italian and Mexican residents marched on city hall to protest the project; their leader, Florence Scala, told reporters, "Mayor Daley and others think it is easy to run roughshod over us, [but] we aren't going to take this lying down."[102] In New York City the reaction of site residents to renewal projects was equally negative. Led by Jane Jacobs herself, in 1961 West Village homeowners and tenants fought an urban renewal plan encompassing both rehabilitation and redevelopment of their community. According to the *Village Voice*, at one meeting held to sell the plan to the community, "the audience response in the form of catcalls, boos, and indignant speeches proved the attempt to be conspicuously unsuccessful."[103] Meanwhile, on the Upper West Side the West Side Renewal Plan was facing similar resistance, which delayed implementation of that scheme of redevelopment and rehabilitation.[104]

Projects that sought to clear gray commercial areas often evicted relatively few residents but aroused the ire of businesses threatened with relocation. For example, in 1962 firms on the southern edge of downtown Saint Louis opposed a bond issue to fund clearance of their area in preparation for a new sports stadium. Organizing the Stadium Relocation Association, the owners of the threatened businesses proposed placement of the stadium in the already cleared Mill Creek Valley tract. City hall rejected this as unfeasible with Mayor Tucker labeling opponents of clearance a "small, self-serving group," but the angry proprietors claimed that they were only trying to protect themselves from the undue financial burden imposed upon them by renewal plans.[105] A leader of the group argued, "The businesses which will be displaced by the stadium are being asked to assume a greatly disproportionate share of the load—a sacrifice which far exceeds that of any other group."[106] At the same time, the Tandy Businessmen's Association was attacking a redevelopment and rehabilitation plan for the Tandy neighborhood on the North Side of Saint Louis. The neighborhood business people, like their colleagues on the southern edge of downtown, feared that they were to become the victims rather than the beneficiaries of civic progress.[107]

Some of those affected by renewal projects across the country passively accepted their fate, recognizing the need for sacrifice. In 1958 a young Society Hill resident said, "I'd hate to have to move. But urban renewal is a good thing," and two years later a tailor with a shop on the site of Cleveland's Erieview agreed philosophically: "We want Erieview, but we know we are going to be eliminated."[108] Yet in Saint Louis, Philadelphia, and Cleveland many felt that loss of home and business was too much to expect.

Exacerbating the bitterness of opponents was the failure of redevelopment authorities to produce results as quickly as promised. Throughout the country, wrecking crews leveled the homes and businesses of urban Americans, who then watched their former properties sprout weeds and remain fallow for years. Endorsed by the city council as early as 1954, Buffalo's Ellicott project was a model of delay, procrastination, and inaction. It displaced 2,200 black families, and as late as 1964 the 161-acre tract only contained six new single-family homes intended for middle-income blacks, who proved reluctant to buy real estate adjacent to a "near slum." A staff member of the Buffalo Area Chamber of Commerce observed that the Ellicott clearance "left a 29-block scar on the face of the city that could lead naive lightplane pilots to assume the city was constructing a landing strip for them next to its busiest retail area."[109]

The manufacturers and retailers located on the site of Buffalo's proposed waterfront project also suffered the consequences of procrastination; their problem was not premature clearance as in the Ellicott project but delayed demolition that left them in economic limbo. Though the project was presented to the city council in 1954, it still had not received federal approval ten years later. Living in perpetual expectation of demolition, firms dropped expansion plans, put off maintenance, and found few buyers for properties whose future was so unclear.[110] Thus the dilapidated area grew more dilapidated as no one knew what was happening.

In Saint Louis the snail-paced redevelopment of the Mill Creek Valley similarly embarrassed city officials and fueled the doubts of skeptics. By 1963 the cleared but largely undeveloped tract was known locally as "Hiroshima Flats," and the *New York Times* reported that "frustrated St. Louisans [had] had to become accustomed to seeing a vast weedpatch in the heart of their city."[111] A year later, *Times* architecture critic Ada Louise Huxtable contended that the Mill Creek project presented "the questionable spectacle of one of the country's most unsuccessful re-development programs." "It is now dotted by desultory building," Huxtable observed, including "a few apartments and town house groups of bravely cheerful design which seem to be whistling in the wilderness, and some spotty commercial and industrial enterprises."[112] Moreover, re-newal advocates recognized that local residents were just as disenchanted as the New York critic. When city officials, the metropolitan dailies, and business leaders sought voter approval in 1962 of a bond issue to help finance renewal plans combining both redevelopment and rehabilitation, they repeatedly emphasized that the proposed projects represented "a new approach in St. Louis's fight against decay" unlike the previous Mill Creek clearance.[113]

Even Point Park, Pittsburgh's symbol of expected urban renaissance, still remained under construction in the mid-1960s, twenty years after the state had approved its creation and fifteen years after demolition had be-gun at the site. According to the chronicler of the project's history, from 1954 through 1963, "Point State Park seemed to move sluggishly, almost in slow motion."[114] The first towers of adjacent Gateway Center were com-pleted by the close of 1953, but not until 1974 would Pittsburgh celebrate the park's dedication. Proving more implacable battlers than the French and British two centuries before, the Daughters of the American Revolu-tion successfully fought with the Allegheny Conference and state au-thorities to retain ownership of the Fort Pitt blockhouse, thereby delaying development. But the Daughters' hard-line stance was only one obstacle, and no one seemed very committed to rapid completion of this renais-sance centerpiece.

Not all renewal projects were stalled or crawling slowly toward com-pletion, and a number of mayors had the pleasure of cutting ribbons at opening ceremonies in the late 1950s and early 1960s. Yet even when completed, a renewal project could prove an embarrassment and under-mine hopes for revival. For example, when Pittsburgh's Civic Arena opened in 1961, it aroused more criticism than praise. It was the keystone of the Lower Hill renewal scheme that had cleared 100 acres occupied by eight thousand residents, most of them black. This wholesale destruction seemed to lend credence to the argument that urban renewal was simply Negro removal, a means of clearing unwanted blacks from areas adjacent to downtown and resegregating them in more distant neighborhoods where they would be out of sight and out of mind. Moreover, the Civic Arena itself and its retractable stainless-steel dome spawned numerous critics. With a 415-foot diameter the dome was an engineering marvel, the largest of its kind in the world at the time of its construction. But technical ingenuity seemed to be its only merit. One commentator wrote that the dome "added enormously to the expense and [was] hardly ever practical to open because of weather, wind, or noise." Nor did it "improve an acoustics problem that [made] musical entertainment at the Civic Arena a painful experience for all concerned."[115]

Some of the other elements of the Lower Hill project also did not fall perfectly into place. Because of the bankruptcy of one of the private developers, only one of the three projected towers in the Washington Plaza Apartments complex was ever completed, and much of the rest of the renewal site was a sea of parking lots. Twenty-five years after the opening of the arena an adjacent 9.2-acre tract remained a vacant lot where, in the words of a local newspaper, "the men of the Renaissance [had] been unable to produce anything but a crop of weeds."[116]

Other projects fell equally short of the promoters' goals. Except in New York City, demand for middle-class downtown apartments lagged behind expectations, leading some to question the success of such vaunted schemes as Detroit's Lafayette Park. In 1961 Saint Louis's Plaza Square Apartments opened to middle-class tenants, but occupancy lagged and in 1965 *Business Week* reported that the complex had been "in technical default to FHA since the first payment was due."[117] That same year Bethesda General Hospital purchased one of the six Plaza Square towers and converted it into a home for the aged, thus relieving the previous owners of some empty units but hardly adding youthful vitality to the city core.[118]

In Philadelphia as well the middle class did not necessarily flock to inner-city renewal areas. By the late 1950s Penn Towne was clearly a disappointment, failing to attract whites or retain blacks. In 1959 one observer reported, "A Negro family with increased income and a desire for better housing moves to Penn Towne and almost immediately begins searching for a home in mixed and middle-income areas in other parts of Philadelphia." "The family wants to own a home," this critic claimed, "but not in a project surrounded by some of the worst housing in the city."[119] Neither Penn Towne nor Plaza Square offered much competition for suburbia. Most of those who could afford to leave the city continued to do so, and few persons of any race sought to populate middle-class oases in the slums.

In Cleveland the story was even grimmer. Reviewing the fate of the Longwood and Garden Valley renewal projects, in 1961 the *Cleveland Plain Dealer* concluded: "The high hopes that once were held for . . . urban renewal housing units here have been deflated."[120] The intended project tenants, moderate- and middle-income blacks, avoided slum-ringed Longwood and Garden Valley just as their counterparts in Philadelphia departed from Penn Towne as quickly as possible. One builder who was losing $6,000 a year on a Garden Valley complex explained: "People don't want to be confined to ghettos. The tenants we want, those with steady incomes, are buying homes or renting in better areas."[121]

Lower rents could have ensured full occupancy, but they also would have guaranteed no profit. Thus developers found themselves in a financial bind with a number failing to meet mortgage or tax payments. In 1962 two nonprofit organizations formed by the Cleveland Development Foundation assumed ownership of the 1,219 apartment units in Longwood and Garden Valley, bailing out the developers and the development foundation that had $1.3 million in loans invested in the projects.[122] Yet in November 1963 the president of the development foundation announced that the Garden Valley apartments, with only about a 50 percent occupancy rate, would have to be vacated and boarded up because of a broken sanitary sewer. Mayor Locher, however, promised action, and in early 1964 the city replaced the sewer. By May 1964 still only 53 percent of the units were occupied and tenants were complaining about the lack of maintenance and the need to rehabilitate the project opened only seven years earlier.[123]

With such problems plaguing the city's first renewal projects, it was natural that many Clevelanders doubted the feasibility of the more ambitious redevelopment schemes proposed in the late 1950s and early 1960s. Referring to the Saint Vincent clearance and redevelopment project on the southern edge of downtown, a Longwood developer observed, "The city is clearing land prodigiously and has wonderful plans but is not doing enough to assure its development." "Just clearing areas is living in a dream world," the builder argued. "A day of reckoning is coming."[124] Such skepticism did not faze the city's urban renewal director, who responded: "Even if we don't find ready builders for St. Vincent housing, just clearing the land to get rid of those slums justifies what we are doing."[125] When Mayor Celebrezze presented the grandiose Erieview plan, the executive vice president of the Apartment and Home Owners Association replied to the mayor's optimism with a remark that struck at the heart of the renewal faith. This heretic proclaimed, "Market analysts to the contrary, people who know the city are very skeptical that you're going to reverse the trend and bring the people back to live downtown."[126] The owner of an art store on the Erieview site was similarly doubtful, admitting, "It's fine to tear out eyesores," but questioning, "Who's coming down here to be tenants?" And a neighboring barber added, "I don't think it will work but they are the ones investing the money."[127]

Yet some taxpayers when asked to invest public dollars in such projects took a less equivocal view. Though the models of soaring ultramodern towers, landscaped plazas, and pristine shopping concourses still entranced most urban Americans, by the early 1960s the doubts expressed in Cleveland and elsewhere were undermining voter support for urban renewal bond issues. For example, in 1962 Saint Louis voters twice failed to approve an urban renewal bond issue by the requisite two-thirds majority, even though eight of the eleven issues for other purposes passed. Following the second defeat, the director of the city's Land Clearance and Housing Authority conceded that the proposed renewal projects were dead.[128]

In 1963 an $8 million slum clearance bond issue in Cleveland won the approval of less than 50 percent of the voters, causing Mayor Locher to postpone action on the second stage of Erieview and to close five of the city's neighborhood rehabilitation centers.[129] Opposition from a number of downtown merchants critical of certain details in the Erieview scheme was enough to jettison the mayor's bond proposal and send planners back to their drafting boards.

In 1964 Baltimore's electorate likewise rejected a loan measure to fund the first stage of an Inner Harbor renewal plan proposed by the Greater Baltimore Committee. Six years earlier the committee had won acceptance of a municipal loan issue for Charles Center, but now the voters were less compliant. A representative of the Chamber of Commerce claimed that the 1964 loans had not been "well understood by many voters," yet the defeat may have reflected new misgivings among many of the citizenry.[130]

Voter resistance, skepticism, and opposition, however, were as yet the exception rather than the rule. The euphoria of the 1950s, when Pittsburgh seemed to have opened the door to urban nirvana, was waning, but in older central cities throughout the nation renewal advocates could marshal a long list of figures and point to some handsome structures that proved the wisdom of their cause. Once rebuilding began, the assessed valuations of renewal sites rose dramatically, realizing one goal of the happy city officials. Moreover, cities profited from renewal projects even when developers were losing. A financial debacle from the private standpoint, Cleveland's Longwood yielded $200,000 in city real estate taxes after redevelopment compared with only $49,000 before.[131] Once the initial ten-year abatement on the Plaza Square apartments expired, Saint Louis was expected to receive $146,000 annually in taxes on the property in contrast to the $61,000 collected prior to clearance. Even with the tax abatement the estimated gain in property tax revenues during the first twenty-five years would be about $1 million.[132]

In addition, renewal advocates could argue convincingly that much of the new was aesthetically and socially superior to the old. Famed architect Mies van der Rohe was designing landmark buildings for Baltimore's Charles Center and Detroit's Lafayette Park. Then-fashionable Minoru Yamasaki was creating the lacy, columned Northwestern National Life Insurance Building in Minneapolis's Gateway Center, I. M. Pei had drawn the plans for Philadelphia's Society Hill Towers, and internationally renowned Eero Saarinen was architect for the gleaming Gateway Arch in Saint Louis. In the early 1960s few mourned the loss of those seedy skid rows and dilapidated commercial slums that were yielding to monuments by such acclaimed figures. Instead, clearance and renewal seemed a viable means not only for enriching city coffers but for applying a fresh and more reputable face on America's aging urban hubs.

Yet detractors were taking their toll by the early 1960s, and dreams of renewal were vulnerable. Underlying the gradual loss of faith were the exaggerated expectations engendered by renewal advocates. To sell the projects and arouse civic enthusiasm, mayors, redevelopment directors, business leaders, and planners had to promise a great deal. According to the grand plans, glittering glass-and-steel skyscrapers would rise on the sites of slums, and upper-middle-class Americans would flock back to downtown luxury apartments creating a Park Avenue lifestyle in Cleveland, Detroit, and Buffalo. Drab downtowns would come to life, and the doldrums of past decades would disappear. Moreover, the proposed timetable for change was unrealistically short; throughout the nation the evangelists of urban revival gave the impression that the gestation period for rebirth would be short and without difficulties. Unfortunately, reality never equaled the pie-in-the-sky expectations. Problems invariably arose, and the process of land condemnation, demolition, sale, and rebuilding could never proceed according to the planners' tight schedules. Given the magnitude of urban renewal dreams, disappointment was virtually inevitable.

A more serious problem was that the renewal programs were defying the social, cultural, and economic trends of the period and attempting to impose on American society a new way of life that few actually wanted. Throughout the renewal process, redevelopment authorities sought to force change and either failed or faced debilitating resistance. In Boston's West End and Chicago's Near West Side the Italians did not think that their neighborhoods were slums and did not want to leave their inner-city ghettos. With the power of eminent domain, the city could force their removal but only at the cost of unfavorable publicity and time-consuming strife. In Buffalo and Cleveland middle-income blacks would not conform to plans and inhabit the slum-rimmed ghettos of Ellicott or Longwood. Whereas the Italians would not move, the blacks would not stay. And the upper-middle-class whites would not come back. Despite prophecies to the contrary, affluent suburbanites did not vie for new downtown apartments but largely remained in suburbia. No power existed comparable to eminent domain that would enable redevelopment authorities to force the middle class into new central-city homes. Instead, the long-standing trend of decentralization continued while the older urban hubs fought futilely for a reversal.

Thus too often the big dreams of the aging central cities were predicated on social fantasies. There was a real need for new downtown office space, but efforts to reestablish the central business district as the focus of diverse functions would not yet succeed. Moreover, any change for the better would take more time than planners wished to admit. By the early 1960s, however, many city leaders preferred fantasy over reality. Reality was too grim.

New Directions in Transportation

Accompanying the urban renewal boom of the late 1950s and early 1960s was an acceleration of highway building in the central cities. Passage of the Federal-Aid Highway Act in 1956 unloosed a new wave of money from Washington to finance the freeway schemes drafted by city planners in the 1940s and early 1950s. From 1956 to 1960 the federal aid authorizations for interstate highways in urban areas soared from $79 million to $1,125 million.[133] Finally, the swaths of asphalt and concrete were cutting through the city, slashing vital minutes from the travel time of hurried urban residents. By the early 1960s hundreds of miles of additional limited-access highways had opened to traffic in the older central cities, seemingly realizing the dreams of earlier transportation planners, who had sought to adapt such aging hubs as Boston and Buffalo to the world of twentieth-century transportation.

Yet in the wake of construction new doubts arose about the wisdom of highway policy. Just as criticism of urban renewal was becoming increasingly common so were attacks on superhighways. Moreover, these doubts led many to look in another direction for a solution to the urban transportation dilemma and to reconsider the merits of mass transit. By the early 1960s some were questioning whether expressways were vital elements in the rebirth of the central city. Possibly subways, commuter trains, and buses were instead the vehicles of revitalization.

Everywhere the earlier faith in freeways was diminishing. Some doubted whether they were enhancing traffic safety, and Philadelphia's poorly designed Schuylkill Expressway was the scene of so many accidents that it soon won the nickname "sure-kill." Others deplored the aesthetic damage wreaked by the new arteries. For example, in 1959 *Architectural Forum* published an article entitled "Expressway Blight" that described how Boston's John F. Fitzgerald Expressway "cut a rude gash" through downtown Boston, creating a "tangled web of old streets, ramps, and parking lots shadowed in gloom below the elevated structure."[134] Following paths that would require the least displacement and minimize costly acquisition and demolition of buildings, freeways frequently passed through urban parks, thereby further raising the ire of those concerned about preserving the city's amenities. Boston's Fens, Buffalo's Delaware Park, Philadelphia's Fairmount Park, and Saint Louis's Forest Park all were to lose land to the new expressways, and by 1961 highways had already robbed New York City of more than four hundred acres of parkland.[135] But in 1963 when preliminary plans for Philadelphia's Delaware Expressway called for the sacrifice of about thirty acres of Roosevelt Park, the local Citizens' Council on City Planning protested. The council expressed the views of many park defenders throughout the nation when it told city administrators: "Freeways should not encroach upon park land. They should add to rather than subtract from the city's open spaces."[136]

The new superhighways not only paved over much-needed open spaces and destroyed urban greenery, they also blighted the city's air. Postwar cities had upgraded their environments and reputations by eliminating smoke, but now the federal government was subsidizing the creation of less visible but still troublesome pollution through its urban freeway program. By 1962, Cincinnati's Bureau of Air Pollution Control, for example, could boast of "a 90% reduction in visible smoke emission" since 1947 and "the elimination of 14,000 tons a year of airborne grit and grime." But the bureau also reported, "Today automotive vehicles discharge to the atmosphere more than 800 tons of contaminating gases or an increase of 115% over the 1947 figure."[137] Carbon monoxide had supplanted soot as the air pollution enemy of America's cities, and just as coal-burning railroads had blackened skies in the past, now highways created to revive the urban core were corrupting the urban environment with noxious gases.

Displacement of residents and businesses, however, was the crux of the most serious controversies over freeway construction. In 1942 planners had first proposed an East-West Expressway to relieve Baltimore's streets of through traffic. Yet in the early 1960s the highway was no closer to realization than twenty years earlier because of debate over various suggested routes. In its annual report for 1962 the Greater Baltimore Committee promised that it would "spend every effort to obtain official City, State and Federal approval of a route for the East-West Expressway," for "a firm decision [had to] be reached early in 1963."[138] A year later, though, the route was still not defined. A spokesman for the Chamber of Commerce described the general attitude as "build your expressway but don't let it affect me or my business."[139] Though the superhighway was deemed necessary, very few wanted it to pass through their living rooms or shops. If someone needed to be displaced, it should be the other guy.

Opposition to uprooting existing households and firms also stymied construction of New York City's Lower Manhattan Expressway. As early as 1941 the City Planning Commission first endorsed the idea of a superhighway across lower Manhattan, and in September 1960 the city's governing Board of Estimate approved the expressway route linking the Holland Tunnel under the Hudson River with the Manhattan and Williamsburg bridges over the East River. But 1,972 families and 804 commercial tenants lived and worked in the proposed pathway, and many of them were determined to remain there. Fearing voter reprisals, Mayor Wagner and the Board of Estimate delayed approval of condemnation of properties along the route, and at a series of stormy Board of Estimate hearings in 1962 opponents berated city leaders for even considering the scheme. At one eleven-hour hearing an irate resident concluded his remarks by threatening the Manhattan borough president: "Don't approve this road if you want to remain in office." The area's assemblyman called the highway "a mad visionary's dream" and "a pork-barrel grab," and he urged the board to "kill this silly proposal to cut the city's throat." Moreover, Eleanor Roosevelt added her distinguished imprimatur to the protesters' cause in a letter read at the hearing that urged abandonment of the project.[140] Residents picketed city hall, and the hearings continued with the Board of Estimate always deferring action. By the close of 1963 still no property had been taken for the expressway, and construction seemed a distant dream, or nightmare.

Public officials in most of the older metropolises were growing more skeptical about the efficacy of superhighway programs in bolstering central-city fortunes. Central cities would never be able to adapt to the automobile as completely as their suburban competitors. Short of wholesale demolition of the entire building stock and street system, there was no way to make central-city thoroughfares as suitable for automobile traffic as suburban highways nor would parking in the urban core ever be as convenient, abundant, or cheap as in suburbia. If the central city based its hopes on the automobile, it was sure to lose to the forces of decentralization. Freeways simply funneled more cars into cities that could not handle them. As such they hardly seemed as promising a solution to the central-city dilemma in 1963 as they had in 1953.

Faced with such facts, by the late 1950s and early 1960s an increasing number of city leaders were advocating a "balanced" approach to urban transportation problems that would emphasize not only freeway construction but improvements in mass transportation as well. Recognizing "the headaches which [came] from the ever-increasing avalanche of automobiles," in 1960 Saint Louis Mayor Tucker told the Board of Aldermen, "It is more economical to provide good mass transit than it is to constantly [build] more and more highways and more and more parking facilities." Tucker argued that to attract more riders to mass transit and minimize traffic, buses and streetcars would have to offer "better service at the least possible fares," and to achieve this goal, he proposed public ownership of the local transit companies.[141] Only through government ownership could the city supposedly provide an adequate solution to the problem of debilitating traffic congestion. When in 1963 a metropolitan authority finally assumed control of the fifteen formerly private transit companies in the Saint Louis region, Tucker went one step further, urging "development of adequate mass *rapid* transit."[142] Buses were no longer sufficient; instead the mayor now was envisioning a high-speed rail system for the beleaguered city of Saint Louis.

Elsewhere public officials were expressing similar sentiments with increasing frequency. As early as 1957, at a national conference on metropolitan transportation, Philadelphia's Mayor Dilworth had proposed that the federal government "make it possible to include in the financing of the highway system provisions for improving . . . mass transportation."[143] Throughout his remaining years as Philadelphia's chief executive, Dilworth would continue to lobby for mass transit, establishing himself as one of the most vigorous champions of revived rapid rail service.

In 1958 Detroit's Rapid Transit Commission presented a report to the mayor and city council urging construction of a monorail system in the Motor City. The commission stressed the importance of rapid transit to the revitalization of Detroit, arguing that the monorail would contribute to the "preservation and expansion of existing commercial, industrial, and residential values for the economic, social and tax well-being of Detroit's citizens and taxpayers." Moreover, it would "help develop concentrated business and industrial areas to their greatest economic extent by bringing in more patrons and employees with great facility."[144] In other words, a monorail would bolster the economic position of the aging downtown much more effectively than the city's developing freeway system.

In 1961 Baltimore's Traffic and Transit Commissioner Henry Barnes told an interviewer, "The ultimate answer to our metropolitan area transportation problems lies in mass transportation," for "we never can build enough highways and parking facilities and, even if we could, it wouldn't be economically sound to do so." According to Barnes, "mass transit holds the key to the future."[145] That same year the general manager of Cleveland's transit system also advocated a "balanced approach" and contended that "greater effort must be made to improve mass transit so people will want to use it."[146]

The mayors, traffic commissioners, and transit managers all agreed that the older central cities had to temper their policy of adaptation to the automobile with new efforts to rehabilitate mass transit. Cities had to make mass transit competitive with automobile travel, thereby encouraging people to leave their cars at home rather than joining in the traffic jams that clogged urban thoroughfares. Moreover, if mass transit could be made popular, central cities and central business districts would regain their competitive advantage over suburbia. Although suburbia had the upper hand in an automobile-dominated world, the existing web of transit lines converging on the hearts of New York City, Chicago, and Philadelphia gave the older hubs the edge in a society dependent on mass transportation. New freeways radiating from the central business district no longer seemed the transportation answer to decline in the central cities. Like Baltimore's Commissioner Barnes, an increasing number of urban boosters now saw the subway, train, and bus as the hope of the future.

The problem confronting converts to mass transit was how to fund its revival. In 1961 *Fortune* summed up the views of many observers when it concluded: "The American consumer, in deciding between private and mass transportation, has for years and years been presented with a market heavily rigged in favor of using his own car in city traffic."[147] While the federal and state governments were spending billions of dollars to ease the flow of automobile traffic and enhance the comfort and safety of the driver, no such funds were benefiting city subways, streetcars, and buses. The result supposedly was a decline in the quality of mass transit and a government-subsidized boost in the advantages of automobile travel. If the cities were to achieve their balanced approach, balanced funding seemed necessary. And fiscally distressed mayors looked to Washington to even the financial scales between mass transit and the automobile.

The assault on the federal treasury began in the late 1950s as big-city mayors responded to an emerging commuter-rail crisis. The federal Transportation Act of 1958 broadened the power of railroads to discontinue unprofitable passenger service, and in the winter of 1958–59 New York City's commuter lines responded by cutting service. At the same time, Philadelphia's Mayor Dilworth prevented cuts in commuter-rail schedules in his city only by offering the railroads a municipal subsidy of from six to nine cents a ride.[148] But New York's Mayor Wagner insisted that "the burden of commuter railroad deficits" could not "be borne by the local communities alone."[149] At a conference in January 1959 representatives of twelve major cities, including Chicago, Philadelphia, New York, Cleveland, Boston, Saint Louis, Detroit, and Baltimore, all agreed federal aid was necessary.[150]

The product of this consensus was the mass transit provision of the federal Housing Act of 1961. This law authorized the federal government to loan $50 million for the purchase and rehabilitation of urban mass transportation facilities and provided as well for $25 million in transit demonstration grants, seed money that could not be used for "major long-term capital improvements."[151] Also Washington was to offer planning assistance for transportation surveys and studies of the traffic-clogged cities. Though the sums committed to mass transit were petty cash compared to the federal appropriations for urban freeways, the law meant that transit advocates now had their foot in the door of the federal treasury. *The New York Times* spoke for the big-city mayors when it characterized the law as "particularly welcome, albeit rather pale, beginnings."[152]

Thus the older central cities began embarking on a new transportation strategy in their long-term march toward renaissance. Miles of expressways had proved inadequate. Perhaps a return to mass transit would produce the much-awaited return to the city.

CHAPTER FIVE ○ **Rebellion and Reaction**

In 1966 New York's Mayor John Lindsay warned, "All across the nation, the ills of urban living are prompting a growing demand for sweeping changes in big-city government."[1] Crime rates were soaring, riots were erupting in black neighborhoods, city treasuries were empty, city streets were clogged with traffic, and signs of continued decline were pervasive. To Lindsay and many others an urban crisis was at hand; the day of reckoning had arrived.

New York's dynamic mayor called for sweeping changes, and by the mid-1960s a growing chorus of voices agreed that drastic action was necessary. If the nation's older central cities were again to become decent places in which to live and work, more needed to be done, including a possible shake-up of established power structures. Since the late 1930s, politicians, business leaders, and journalists had been calling for new initiatives to revive the central city. Now the demand was for accelerated action and additional programs. The city needed human renewal programs that would enhance the social and economic opportunities of poor blacks as well as physical renewal schemes to upgrade the building stock and public infrastructure. There had to be heightened concern about the dire signals of social as well as physical disintegration. A new shrillness pervaded the rhetoric of urban revitalization; a new urgency produced unprecedented initiatives for change.

These new initiatives and this enflamed rhetoric, however, also aroused new opposition to government-sponsored programs. Within city governments many entrenched, and often underpaid, civil servants resented any invasion of their professional prerogatives, even though political leaders deemed violations of bureaucratic turf necessary in achieving racial equality. Like those displaced by physical renewal projects, the city employees felt they were bearing an undue burden so that politicians could implement farfetched schemes of dubious merit. Similarly, working-class whites saw few benefits for them in proposals to rebuild the physical and social structures of the city. In their minds physical renewal meant money for downtown business people who lived in the suburbs, and human renewal meant money for blacks. In the journey to social and physical renaissance they were being left behind, paying the bills but getting little in return other than unwelcome disruption of their lifestyles by advocates of busing and racial mixing.

Thus the late 1960s was an era of rebellion and reaction, a period when many were calling for sharp change and rejection of established social and political structures while others were building roadblocks to disruptive reform. Both seemed to recognize a crisis in urban life, a crisis characterized by crime and violence, riots and demonstrations, insufficient municipal funds, and inadequate federal or state concern. But the responses to these problems differed, leading to divisive conflict that did not speed the central cities toward their goal of renaissance. In fact, conflict and bitterness were joining blight and decentralization as prime enemies of central-city revival and prosperity. Rioting, mugging, and angry confrontation were becoming as much a part of the tarnished image of the older central cities as were grime, dilapidation, and obsolescence.

Rebellion

Among those rebelling against the established order was a new wave of central-city mayors. Campaigning as foes of the stale past, these newcomers promised a new era not only of physical rebuilding but of social justice. They expressed an unprecedented concern for the status of racial minorities, believing that enrichment of the central city was possible only if the growing number of black urbanites won their fair share of the economic pie. At the same time, they challenged entrenched politicians and tried to evoke an upbeat spirit of dynamism and action in sharp contrast to the drab, mediocre leaders of the early 1960s. Moreover, they cultivated ties with Washington and placed great faith in the ameliorating effects of federal dollars. With the Democratic administrations of the 1960s promising unprecedented federal aid, these leaders saw an opportunity for achieving greater goals than their predecessors. Not only would slums disappear and tax-rich structures rise in their place, city government would become more responsive to the needs of the least advantaged urban dwellers and contribute to the national crusade to eliminate poverty and racial inequality.

The most notable and best publicized of this new generation of city executives was New York's Mayor John Lindsay. Tall, young, and handsome with impeccable breeding and a prep school and Yale education appropriate to a thoroughbred, Lindsay won volumes of publicity from the national media, which were eager to cover the brightest new star on the political horizon. Moreover, after the seeming lethargy and indecision of Wagner's final years in office, the almost blinding dynamism of the city's fresh white knight naturally drew the attention of the nation and aroused renewed optimism among many New Yorkers. His lean, athletic appearance as well as his combative rhetoric seemed to promise a vigorous, activist approach to city government.

In his inaugural address in January 1966 he set the tone of his early years in office when he summoned the citizenry "to enlist in the fight for a better New York" and then listed the specific "fights" against poverty, pollution, and ignorance that New Yorkers had to engage in.[2] In an article on the mayor's personality the *New York Times* noted that his favorite words were "tough," "nitty-gritty," and "guts," and during his first months in office, he told an interviewer, "We have to have *doers*."[3] Whereas Wagner had stood for mediation, procrastination, and evasion, the new mayor seemed ready to tackle forthrightly and vigorously the problems confronting his troubled city. He was ready to lead New York on a crusade for renewed life.

But it was not to be a grim battle for revival, for an aura of glamor and a sense of flair pervaded the early Lindsay years. The mayor labeled his beleaguered metropolis "Fun City," and he continually attempted to make reality coincide with the nickname. Lindsay's ebullient parks and recreation commissioner sponsored kite-flying happenings in city parks and organized rock concerts and traveling theater. The vibrant mayor walked the streets of Harlem exuding a charisma that charmed even those boiling with racial resentment. New York City's leader had embarked on a crusade that was both noble and chic.

Yet Lindsay's crusading spirit was also flawed. During his early years in office, the principled young mayor offended many New Yorkers with his moral arrogance and his rigid abhorrence for compromise. One critical reporter claimed, "Lindsay only knows one way to deal with people— challenge them." "As the resident knight-in-shining armor," the journalist complained, "Lindsay would rather throw down the gauntlet than talk things over." An insider at city hall likewise criticized Lindsay and his staff for their "self-righteousness, arrogance, [and] claims to omni-science," declaring "[Lindsay] comes on as if he's bearing the white man's burden." "He can play Batman all he wants," commented one state as-semblyman, "but that doesn't accomplish anything. You've got to play politics to get things done."[4]

"Playing politics," however, was one of the traditional practices Lindsay sought to purge from New York City's government. Lindsay was elected the nominee of the Republican and Liberal parties, but he cam-paigned as a nonpartisan contender appealing to reform Democrats who could not stomach the Democratic organization's candidate. During the mayoral contest of 1965, he promised, "If elected mayor, I will not rest until reform is brought to both political parties."[5]

On assuming office, he continued this theme, rejecting the past poli-tics of deals, bargains, and partisan maneuvering. In his inaugural ad-dress he attacked the "irrelevant dictates of party politics" and told New Yorkers, "The question now before us [is] whether men of conscience and conviction can reject ignoble partisan intrigue and join a massive effort to make real our dreams for New York."[6] During his first year in office, he reiterated this point when he wrote, "The condition of most cities today should leave little room for partisan divisions," and "The very complexity of modern urban life argues most eloquently for the abandonment of tradi-tional partisanship in municipal government."[7]

Moreover, he was true to his words, refusing to toe the party line or link himself too closely to either of the major party organizations. Though a registered Republican, he soon cultivated the hatred of the state's Re-publican leader, Governor Nelson Rockefeller, and since the city was heavily Democratic and the other major municipal officeholders were Democrats, he recognized the practical wisdom of keeping a distance from the GOP hierarchy. He was, then, a man without a party who repeat-edly castigated the old politics of Wagner and his predecessors.

Rather than rely on politicians to usher in the new era, Lindsay placed his faith in a corps of experts whom he labeled "urbanists." Ac-cording to the mayor, "An 'urbanist' is a modern man who is probably more finely trained in the complicated business of present and future do-mestic government than any other public servant in history." He "brings in a whole new world, a world of Washington, of large and complicated programs, of science, design, and planning[,] . . . a world almost wholly foreign to the precinct power dealer."[8] In other words, superadministra-tors attracted from all over the country would create the brave new world of Fun City, individuals with imagination, toughness, and an ability to get federal dollars. They would displace the ward heelers of the past. After a year in office Mayor Lindsay said confidently, "We are getting urbanists who are real professionals and only need the money to do the job."[9]

Not only was Mayor Lindsay ready to reject the traditional politician, he was equally dedicated to pruning the power of what he regarded as an intransigent and unresponsive city bureaucracy. Lindsay complained to an interviewer of "the colossal depth of the bureaucracy and the way it [had] of digging in even deeper into old habits—its tendency to say, 'You can't do that, it's never been done this way before.' " After a year in office the exasperated mayor observed, "The machinery is still so slow . . . The goddam bureaucracy can drive you crazy."[10] For a mayor dedicated to vigorous action and change, the red tape, delays, and cumbersome standard operating procedures were infuriating. To expedite the delivery of services and streamline a bureaucracy that Lindsay characterized as "bigger and slower and clumsier than [he] thought it would be," the mayor pushed through a reorganization of the city's bureaus, establishing ten administrations to oversee the functions of almost fifty separate departments and agencies.[11] Supposedly by reducing the administrative divisions in city government and by placing the ten new superagencies under the control of acclaimed "urbanists," Lindsay would cut through "the bureaucracy's maddening maze of dams and baffles."[12]

To further ensure that the bureaucracy served rather than exasperated the public, Lindsay proposed the establishment of little city halls scattered throughout the metropolis. In his inaugural address he told New Yorkers, "We can open direct lines of communication between the people and their government [through] Little City Halls in the neighborhoods of our city, manned by the people in those neighborhoods."[13] Though he favored "centralization of the decision-making process" in his ten superagencies, at the same time he urged "decentralization of the process by which the results of those decisions are delivered to the neighborhoods." In other words, the urbanists downtown would "decide which streets [were] to be repaved," but the storefront city halls in the neighborhoods would give "the people in [the] various communities a fuller voice in designating which streets [had] the highest priority."[14] According to the activist mayor, "The city must create new relationships between government and the community—relationships by which the disbursement of city services may be coordinated at the community level and guided by community need."[15] Thus new leaders both at city hall and in the neighborhoods would tame the unresponsive bureaucracy. Urbanists recruited from out of town and community representatives in little city halls would supposedly prod the entrenched civil service into unprecedented action and make sure that it served the needs of the people.

But to fuel the newly activated engine of city government, Lindsay needed ample funding. When he assumed office, the mayor found his city virtually bankrupt, caught in the worst fiscal bind since the early 1930s. Lindsay was able to impose new city income and commuter taxes that momentarily closed the yawning revenue gap. In the long run, however, he looked to Washington for the money to finance the central city's rebirth. Along with criticism of the traditional political order and the sluggish bureaucracy, his demand for additional federal aid formed the foundation of Lindsay's program for New York City.

The dynamic young mayor soon put pressure on Washington for help. Fulfilling a campaign promise, during his first year as mayor, Lindsay opened an office in Washington to lobby for appropriations and legislation favorable to the city. In 1966 he told a congressional committee that New York City would need an additional $50 billion of federal aid during the next ten years. Justifying this plea for such an extraordinary sum, he explained, "We're in a fiscal crisis, and so are the other big cities . . . We've got to wake up Congress."[16] Without massive federal investment the older cities were simply going to continue their slide to oblivion, and the activist Lindsay was not prepared to stand by and witness that dismal fate. According to the new mayor, the nation had to seek "the renascence of the city that serves as the nucleus of the metropolis, a reconstruction in which the Federal government should be the major architect."[17] Though Lindsay did not win everything he desired from Washington, New York City's dependency on federal dollars did increase markedly during the late 1960s. Whereas in 1965–66 the federal government paid only 6.8 percent of New York City's expense budget, by 1972–73 Washington's share had risen to 20.6 percent. By the latter year intergovernmental aid from Washington and Albany together totaled 44.3 percent of the municipal budget, and local revenues were paying only 55.7 percent of New York City's bills.[18]

Underlying Lindsay's petitions for more money and his criticisms of the political and bureaucratic establishment was a sincere concern about the city's poor and especially its poor blacks. Basic to the new activism of the Lindsay administration was a dedication to ensuring racial equality and to opening new social and economic opportunities to the victims of racial discrimination. In the 1965 election Lindsay had won the active support of such black celebrities as baseball great Jackie Robinson, comedian Dick Gregory, entertainer Sammy Davis, Jr., and boxer Sugar Ray Robinson, and his Harlem rallies drew record crowds.[19] Though he failed to beat the Democratic candidate in the black neighborhoods, he garnered 40 percent to 45 percent of the black vote in November, a remarkably favorable showing for a Republican candidate. In gratitude, the mayor-elect's first act on the day after the election was to visit the black districts of Bedford-Stuyvesant and Harlem to express his thanks. That day he announced to a Harlem crowd, "My friends I told you if I were elected Mayor, I would come back. Now I'm back. And I'll come back again and again."[20]

He did come back, his walks through black districts soon becoming a well-known part of his executive repertoire. Moreover, his concern was genuine; an aide noted, "One thing I always admired about John was that he could really get angry when he saw some poor black guy stuck in a lousy ghetto. He never got hardened to it."[21] To Lindsay the political system had to change, and the bureaucracy had to get moving largely to allow that poor black guy to rise out of the lousy ghetto. Lindsay's dream of rebirth for New York City was not simply a dream of new buildings and enhanced tax rolls but a vision of human renewal and rehabilitated lives. He would not be satisfied until he achieved a social as well as a physical restructuring of the city.

Heightened concern for the poor, especially poor blacks, rebellion against old party politics, attacks on bureaucratic intransigency and self-ishness, and demands for ever-increasing federal aid were, then, the hall-marks of the Lindsay era. The urban renewal, antipollution, and transportation programs of the 1950s and early 1960s would not alone transform the central city into a truly decent place in which to live and work. According to the young rebels of the Lindsay administration, more action was needed, action that attacked the roots of city politics, the civil service, and racial prejudice. A physical facelift of the city would not create renaissance; a conversion of the urban soul was necessary.

Throughout the country during the second half of the 1960s, the glamorous and dynamic Lindsay and his activist ideas received newspaper and television coverage, influencing other urban leaders and public officials. A city leader often described as "Lindsayesque," who shared many of the concerns of the New York mayor, was Jerome Cavanagh of Detroit. Elected as the Motor City's chief executive in November 1961, Cavanagh served the next eight years as mayor, bringing the same spirit of youth and dynamism to city government as was his New York colleague. Only thirty-three years old when he assumed office, Cavanagh was described by one admirer as "handsome" with "charm enough to reduce a cobra to a lap pet and a wit sharp enough to hone a rusty blade for a television commercial."[22] Reporters adored him, and local newspapers and national magazines lavished applause on the young dynamo. Just as Lindsay seemed a supercharged opposite to sluggish Mayor Wagner, so the vigor and zest of Cavanagh's administration contrasted markedly with the doldrums presided over by his predecessor Mayor Miriani. The *Detroit Free Press* commented, "Only under Cavanagh does a city hall take on the appearance of a launching pad," and a *Free Press* reporter later reminisced that during Cavanagh's first term "for the first time in years—perhaps in Detroit's entire history—the city seemed vibrant and on the move."[23]

Moreover, Cavanagh like Lindsay promised more for the city's disadvantaged and especially its black population. He defeated his predecessor largely by appealing to black voters, whom Miriani had offended when a crackdown on crime he had ordered resulted in the police manhandling of blacks. Cavanagh also attacked past emphasis on downtown development and the consequent neglect of low-income neighborhoods. According to the *Free Press*, when campaigning, Cavanagh "talked about people and the problems they face[d] in their every day life . . . He sympathized with the unemployed and he talked to the men who [were] considered the real leaders in the Negro community by the Negroes themselves."[24] His solicitude paid off, for blacks cast an estimated 72 percent of the votes Cavanagh won in 1961.[25]

On assuming office, Cavanagh appointed a black as controller, the most important city post next to that of mayor. His new police commissioner was a flaming liberal with no police experience but a long history as a staunch civil libertarian and civil rights advocate. This new chief of law enforcement in Detroit observed, "My first job was to teach the police they didn't have a constitutional right to automatically beat up Negroes on arrest."[26]

Like Lindsay, Cavanagh saw the federal government as a necessary partner in the human renewal of the central city. He asked the city council for a $50,000 annual appropriation to fund an office in Washington, and in 1965 he told an interviewer: "Crime, delinquency, dropouts, you name it—these are city problems, and the cities are expected to cope with them. Well they can't do it alone." Cities were "the real unfinished domestic business of this country," and only federal dollars could complete the job of urban revival.[27]

In Cleveland another new face was shaking up the old political establishment dominated by officeholders of Eastern and Southern European ancestry and bringing a momentary boost to the spirit of the grim Ohio city. In 1965 a thirty-eight-year-old black, Carl Stokes, came within 2,200 votes of defeating the dreary incumbent, Ralph Locher, and two years later this challenger won the mayor's office by an equally narrow margin. Young and personable with a dynamic speaking manner, Stokes entered office with the enthusiastic support of blacks and the solid backing of white downtown business leaders, who believed that he might be able to placate black agitators and move the city off dead center. Moreover, Stokes himself was dedicated to invigorating a city government that he viewed as long dormant. He wrote, "Cleveland has been a city in which 'caretaker' mayors . . . could respond mainly to public relations and ignore the gut issues."[28] In contrast, Stokes hoped to confront those issues and bring about change. As the *Cleveland Plain Dealer* observed, on assuming office, Stokes was "the Great Black Hope and the Great White Hope." Both blacks and the downtown white elite "hoped that the decay of the last 25 years would be washed away with something new and exciting replacing it."[29] In the mid-1970s the *Plain Dealer's* editor reminisced that Stokes's election had "looked like the dawn of a new day in volatile Cleveland, . . . after five years of floundering under Mayor Locher."[30] The city's white ethnics did not succumb to Stokes's charms, but business leaders vowed to raise $4 million for the new mayor's "Cleveland: NOW!"—a booster project intended to aid community activities not eligible for federal funds. In early 1968 some believed that perhaps Cleveland was finally turning the corner and headed for revival.

Lindsay, Cavanagh, and Stokes all exemplified what one journalist called the "new glamour-boy breed of big-city mayors."[31] They exuded confidence, youth, and dynamism in sharp contrast to the Wagners, Mirianis, and Lochers that had preceded them. Yet they also seemed to have a genuine sensitivity to the problems of the poor and to conceive of urban renewal as improved health care, better education, and racial justice as well as the traditional brick-and-mortar projects.

During the few years that their stars shown brightly, they spawned a number of other fresh candidates that fit the concerned, committed, glamor-boy mold. In 1967 thirty-eight-year-old Kevin White won Boston's highest office, projecting a Lindsayesque image of vigor, youth, and activism. Reiterating the New York mayor's concern about an unresponsive bureaucracy, White said that Boston's fundamental problem was "communications between government and the people" and proposed a neighborhood services department, neighborhood city halls to bring "municipal government closer to the people, and the people closer to their government," and the "physical presence" of the mayor and leading officials on the city streets.[32]

At the same time, thirty-eight-year-old Thomas D'Alesandro III, son of the former mayor, had won the chief executive's office in Baltimore. In December 1967 the *Baltimore Sun* observed optimistically, "Seldom if ever in city history has a new mayor been installed with less political bitterness, or with more popular unanimity, or with a faster running start on his job." "This man," the newspaper claimed, "has a rendezvous with destiny." In his inaugural address "Young Tommy" called Baltimore "the city of our hope," and he expressed his special concern for blacks when he promised that his first priority would be "to root out every cause or vestige of discrimination." Moreover, he was true to his words, seeking "to rebuild [Baltimore] in both physical and human terms" and showing an unprecedented concern for the city's poor during his years in office.[33]

Older and more pedestrian leaders remained in charge in many of the aging central cities, but even they recognized the need for rebuilding in human as well as in physical terms. And every city official was joining the chorus of demands for more federal money. As early as 1964 Pittsburgh's Mayor Joseph Barr, hardly a young glamor boy, boasted, "We are bringing a new dimension of human renewal into our total rebuilding effort," describing this proudly as "the Pittsburgh way."[34] Three years later in his annual message to the city council, he repeated his "oft-stated belief that welcome and beneficial as the present rate of Federal assistance [had] been, it [had to] be drastically expanded." In words that Lindsay, Cavanagh, and Stokes would readily second, Pittsburgh's executive proclaimed, "We need a massive re-ordering of priorities at the national level."[35]

Philadelphia's Tate and Chicago's Daley remained in office throughout the late 1960s, but they too would have endorsed Barr's views. Even Cincinnati's Mayor Eugene Ruehlmann, an organization Republican, in the late 1960s began to take walks through ghetto neighborhoods and attended black churches on Sunday mornings to stimulate communication with the black community.[36] In each of the older central cities politicians, the bureaucracy, and the federal government had to pay more attention to the poor and the blacks.

This new concern was a response not only to the growing number of black voters but also to the emerging militance of black leaders. Civil rights crusaders in the South had demonstrated the potential of black activism, and now the movement for a stronger voice was shifting northward. By the second half of the 1960s a growing number of Afro-Americans wanted their fair share of the government of the city and were not willing to accept further excuses for delay. The Lindsays, Cavanaghs, and D'Alesandros did not simply want to take action. They had to do so, for their black constituents demanded it.

Black militance was a marked departure from the traditional pattern of urban politics in northern cities. Since World War II, blacks had been the bulwark of the urban political establishment, casting their ballots loyally and predictably for Democratic candidates. In the 1963 election Philadelphia's Democratic Mayor Tate failed to carry a majority of his city's white voters and only remained in power because of his overwhelming success in black wards.[37] That same year Chicago's Mayor Daley also won reelection in an unusually tight race only because of solid black support. If white voters alone had decided the fate of Chicago's political boss, he would have been out of a job.

Moreover, in the 1950s and early 1960s some blacks had acquired considerable political clout by working within the white Democratic organization. Chicago's black Congressman William Dawson bossed the South Side wards and ranked among the kingmakers of Chicago politics. He was as much a creator of the powerful Democratic organization as its creation. In New York City, Hulan Jack, a black of West Indian ancestry, won the borough presidency of Manhattan in both the 1953 and 1957 elections, thus securing one of the eight seats on the city's chief governing body, the Board of Estimate.[38] In 1964 J. Raymond Jones, a black Harlem city councilman, became Manhattan's Democratic party leader, though the Tammany organization he inherited was much weakened by internecine battling.[39] By 1960 black politician Chester Carr had become Democratic majority leader of the Cleveland city council and served as chairman of the council's all-important finance committee. Even in the border-state metropolis of Saint Louis, Jordan Chambers held a seat on the Democratic City Committee from 1938 until his death in 1962, controlled the nineteenth ward, and among politicians was known as the "Negro mayor of St. Louis."[40] Believing that greatly outnumbered blacks could win political advantage only by joining the establishment rather than challenging it, these older leaders remained dedicated to ensuring that their followers turned out on election day and voted a straight Democratic ticket. Rather than being troublemakers, black urban politicians had long ranked among the most faithful supporters of the powers that be.

In the late 1940s and the 1950s blacks also had not posed serious obstacles to the white-dominated urban revitalization crusade. Protesting the clearance of a predominantly black district for the construction of Chicago's Lake Meadows project, area residents in the early 1950s distributed handbills warning, "This is the zero-hour for Negroes . . . "Land-grabbers [want] to herd you like Indians or Jews to reservations or concentration camps."[41] But Chicago's black community was not united in opposition to the middle-income, racially integrated Lake Meadows apartments, and as in the case of all urban renewal schemes, those displaced by the new construction howled the loudest.

Some blacks defended revitalization efforts. For example, the chairman of the board of the National Association for the Advancement of Colored People (NAACP) favored even more slum clearance and renewal in New York City's Harlem, claiming that such efforts would attract whites and further integration. In 1957 he explained: "The white groups doing business on 125th Street must find Harlem so wholesome that they will not go to the suburbs to live but will be willing to make their homes in Harlem."[42] Such black defenders of renewal were as amenable to the schemes of planners and business moguls as William Dawson was to Mayor Daley's Democratic machine. They were not rebels against prevailing white opinion but were accommodating themselves to the system.

By the mid-1960s, however, many young Turks were no longer willing to accept the accommodationist stance of leaders they viewed at best as too moderate or at worst as Uncle Toms interested only in lining their pockets with white money. Burrowing from within the political establishment no longer seemed acceptable. Blacks had to defy the traditional political leadership and demand power. With that power blacks had to secure policies aimed at ameliorating their social and economic conditions. The Dawsons and Chambers were to this new wave of black leaders what Miriani was to Cavanagh and Wagner to Lindsay. The dead wood of the past had to be cleared and a new age of activism initiated.

This attitude, for example, was evident in normally quiescent Philadelphia. The militant president of the local NAACP chapter, Cecil Moore, launched the challenge to Philadelphia's Democratic organization, sponsoring five insurgent candidates in the 1964 party primary. At the behest of Moore, each of the challengers ran as blacks, appealing overtly to the racial loyalty of fellow blacks and attacking black candidates allied with the white-dominated party organization as "so-called Negroes" and "tools of the white power structure."[43] By 1967 Moore was running unsuccessfully for mayor as the candidate of the militant Political Freedom Rights Party. Casting aspersions on the intelligence of incumbent Mayor Tate, candidate Moore told Philadelphians, "It's about time you voted for a smart black man because you've been voting for a dumb white man in the last four years."[44] Moreover, the Congress of Racial Equality (CORE) initiated a direct protest in April 1963; seven of its members picketed Mayor Tate's home for two hours, carrying signs criticizing racial discrimination by building trade unions whose members were employed on municipal construction projects. Between that date and June 1965, black groups in Philadelphia organized at least seventy-eight boycotts, demonstrations, and picketing campaigns and threatened an additional forty-two protests. Indicative of the new spirit of independence, one of the protests was against the Democratic City Committee.[45]

Meanwhile, in Saint Louis, CORE and a young black alderman, William Clay, were taking on John J. Dwyer, the chairman of the city's Democratic Central Committee, and Mayor Raymond Tucker. In 1963 CORE organized a picketing campaign against the Jefferson Bank and Trust Company, claiming that the bank refused to hire blacks for positions of responsibility. Alderman Clay was among the nineteen civil rights leaders arrested for demonstrating against the bank in violation of a court order. Following the conviction of Clay and his colleagues, CORE stepped up its efforts, demanding that Dwyer, who was city treasurer as well as party leader, withdraw municipal funds from the bank. As a loyal friend of the bank president, Dwyer refused, and thirty CORE members proceeded to picket the treasurer's apartment while 119 demonstrators moved on city hall and demanded action from Mayor Tucker. Tucker also rejected the protesters' petitions and earned the enmity of Clay and his allies.[46]

The battle between the young Turks and the Democratic establishment continued to simmer for the next two years and would contribute to Tucker's defeat for a fourth term in the Democratic primary of 1965. Not only had Tucker backed Dwyer in the Jefferson Bank controversy but he had also seemed to favor closing the city's black hospital, an institution that for many years had trained black physicians and nurses and provided trusted health care as well as needed jobs for the ghetto community. In early 1965 a local black newspaper editorialized, "An accurate slogan for the incoming Mayoral campaign might be 'Mayor Tucker versus the Negro community.'" When Tucker suffered defeat in part owing to a drop in black support, this same newspaper proclaimed, "In a magnificent display of raw political power Bill Clay . . . emerged from last Tuesday's primary election as the number one delivery politician in the city of St. Louis." He had overcome "tremendous odds in an effort to unseat an entrenched political machine run by Tucker [and] Dwyer." Though the black journal may have mislabeled Tucker's supporters as a machine, it correctly identified the young civil rights leader as a real force in local politics, a person who was creating his own racially based organization that would not serve white politicians like Dwyer and Tucker. Clay was succeeding to Jordan Chambers's title as "Negro mayor of St. Louis," but white politicians would find him less tractable than his cooperative predecessor.[47]

By the late 1960s, however, the insurgency of leaders like William Clay and Cecil Moore seemed mild compared to the civil disorders erupting in black neighborhoods across the nation. First Harlem was the scene of rioting in 1964, then the Watts district of Los Angeles erupted in 1965, followed by riots in Cleveland's Hough neighborhood in the following year and Jerome Cavanagh's Detroit in 1967. Snipers and arsonists were conveying the message of upheaval and rebellion to millions of television viewers watching the evening news. And their actions expressed the desperation of the older cities much more forcefully than did the rhetoric of Lindsay and D'Alesandro or the picketing of Clay and Moore. In the streets, at CORE headquarters, and in the mayors' offices, the signs of impatience were clear. The old order no longer sufficed; change was imperative.

Moreover, federal policy during the mid- and late 1960s was nurturing the expression of grass-roots discontent and mobilizing the forces calling for change. Community action councils represented a basic component of Lyndon Johnson's War on Poverty launched in 1964. According to the Economic Opportunity Act, these councils were to develop, conduct, and administer antipoverty programs "with the maximum feasible participation of residents of the areas and members of the groups served."[48] On the basis of this provision the federal Office of Economic Opportunity stressed the need for the poor themselves to serve on the councils and help make policy regarding the health, education, and welfare services provided. In other words, the community action councils would strengthen the political muscle of the poor, enabling the disadvantaged to express their own needs and concerns rather than serving as pawns in a game played by college-educated welfare workers and city planners. Enhanced services alone supposedly would not defeat poverty. If the poor were to rise from their abject condition, they needed political power.

Elections to select community action council members soon proved that many of the poor were not ready to be mobilized. In one city after another the poor failed to cast votes for council members and demonstrated an apathy reminiscent of the neighborhood organization experiments in Baltimore, Philadelphia, and Detroit in the 1950s. During the 1960s, as in the previous decade, the vast majority of low-income city dwellers seemed to have little interest in town meetings, poverty councils, or community mobilization. In 1965 only 13,493 of almost 500,000 eligible Philadelphians participated in that city's well-publicized community action council election.[49] The turnout for New York City's neighborhood council contests ranged from 1 percent to 7.7 percent of the eligible voters, whereas in Boston 2.4 percent of the poor cast ballots and in Cleveland 4.2 percent.[50] A survey of antipoverty staff workers in Pittsburgh found that 80 percent expressed dissatisfaction with the results of citizen participation; most were troubled "by the quantitative paucity of low-income participants."[51]

Poor whites showed especially little interest in a program that many perceived as being designed for blacks only. In 1965, 55 percent of the impoverished in Philadelphia were white compared with approximately 30 percent of those attending the antipoverty town meetings.[52] Two years later in Pittsburgh 62 percent of the neighborhood action council members were blacks, but blacks constituted only 34 percent of the population of the city's poverty areas.[53] In 1969 an observer of Detroit's program faulted the local antipoverty organization for "its almost complete failure to establish rapport with or provide services for a sizeable poor white population in Detroit."[54]

Even though the Community Action Program did not inspire an outpouring of civic enthusiasm among America's slum dwellers, it did allow self-styled spokespersons for the poor to spend federal dollars and loudly express their disenchantment with the political establishment. By the late 1960s the action councils in a number of cities were focusing less attention on providing services and more on political activism and pressuring city hall. In New York City the guidelines for the 1967–68 Community Action Program gave the highest funding priority to educational services such as the Head Start program for preschoolers. The 1969–70 guideline, however, awarded first priority to programs involving "advocacy planning and action" that had "the common aims of inducing local citizens to exert pressure on institutions to alter their policies and services in response to articulated community goals."[55]

In simple language, antipoverty funds were to subsidize protests against the establishment. By 1968 Baltimore's Community Action Agency was dedicated to development of political power bases in the black ghettos, curtailing the funding of library and child care services at neighborhood centers to appropriate more money for political mobilization. In the spring of that year it delivered eight hundred people to the local Poor People's Rally, and it organized a demonstration of six hundred to seven hundred angry citizens at city hall to protest municipal housing policy. On the agency payroll were twelve "activists" dedicated to radicalizing tenant councils in public housing.[56] In 1969 a student of Detroit's community action organization found spokespersons for slum neighborhoods equally rebellious, describing poverty program meetings as "a constant and embittered dialogue between those who are alleged to represent the establishment . . . and those who claim to represent the poor."[57] Chicago's Mayor Daley and Philadelphia's Mayor Tate kept a tighter rein on their community action councils, ensuring that the poverty program did minimal damage to the authorities in city hall. But elsewhere community action seemed to produce as much acrimony as services, and in New York

City, Baltimore, and Detroit local officials of the late 1960s witnessed the unusual spectacle of government-sponsored rebellion.

Thus during the second half of the 1960s, the so-called establishment took a drubbing from all sides. Mayors like Lindsay, Cavanagh, and Stokes claimed that they intended to discard the lethargic politics of the past and invigorate physical and social renewal programs. This was their prescription for central-city rebirth. Increasingly militant blacks like Moore and Clay argued that they had to overthrow accommodationist ghetto politicians and create new black power organizations. And anti-poverty activists raged against establishment oppression and even lambasted self-proclaimed dynamos like Lindsay and Cavanagh as too conservative and too reluctant to take action. By the late 1960s last year's reform panacea was this year's example of reactionary, establishment thinking as the rhetoric of discontent heightened and proposals for change grew ever more radical. If harmony and good will were characteristics of the renaissance city, then the goal of rebirth seemed to be receding rather than approaching.

Revolt of the Bureaucracy

To initiate his reign as king of Fun City, Mayor Lindsay had planned an inaugural fete complete with five borough receptions; in the words of the *New York Times* the inauguration was to be "the showiest since George Washington was sworn in here as the first President in 1789."[58] Yet on inauguration day, January 1, 1966, Lindsay had to cancel the borough celebrations, for on that day New York City's transit system went on strike creating fears of traffic jams that the borough events would only exacerbate. The sad fate of Lindsay's inaugural plans was representative of his entire administration; lavish schemes repeatedly foundered on difficult realities. And prominent among the troubling realities was labor unrest. The transit strike was only the first of a long list of labor actions plaguing Lindsay. Moreover, the mounting unrest among municipal employees reinforced New York's image as an ungovernable, unlivable metropolis in rapid decline.

Though New York City's labor plight was more widely publicized than that of other cities, the revolt of the municipal bureaucracy was a widespread phenomenon of the late 1960s. Throughout the nation civil servants engaged in a growing number of work stoppages and slowdowns, and pickets were an increasingly common sight before city halls from Boston to Minneapolis. Whereas in 1958 the United States experienced only fifteen strikes by government workers involving 1,720 employees and 7,520 worker-days, by 1968 the number of stoppages in the public sector had soared to 254 with 202,000 employees walking off the job and 2.5 million lost worker-days.[59] Police officers, firefighters, garbage collectors, and bus drivers were adding their voices to the dissonant outcry of the late 1960s, and their angry attacks on mayors and commissioners rivaled those of the increasingly militant blacks.

Moreover, in the labor-management battle of the late 1960s, the bureaucracy could claim more victories than defeats. Wages increased, pensions grew more generous, and unions acquired greater control over public personnel policy. Though Lindsay and others had sought to check the autonomy of the civil service and assume firm command of the municipal bureaucracy, by 1970 elected officials had less control over city employees rather than more. In fact, with public employees unions being increasingly involved in municipal election campaigns, they proved able to determine who were the elected officials. Instead of capturing the bureaucracy and taking charge, at the close of the decade many mayors found themselves hostages of government employee unions. They now were forced to serve the city's public servants.

The powerful civil service unions did not appear overnight but actually had been gaining strength throughout the 1950s and early 1960s. In 1956 Philadelphia's District Council 33 of the American Federation of State, County, and Municipal Employees (AFSCME) won exclusive bargaining rights for city departments in which a majority of the workers were AFSCME members. Two years later the Dilworth administration strengthened the position of District Council 33 even further, making it exclusive bargaining agent for all city workers with the exception of supervisory personnel and uniformed employees in the fire and police departments.[60]

As early as 1951 Cincinnati's city council in effect established a system of collective bargaining for civil servants, and by 1958, 2,200 of the city's 3,800 nonuniformed employees were dues-paying members of the AFSCME. That same year Cincinnati's lawmakers bolstered the financial position of that union by authorizing union dues deductions from city paychecks.[61] Meanwhile, in New York City, Mayor Wagner was currying the favor of municipal employee unions. His most notable concession was Executive Order 49 in which he granted the privilege of collective bargaining to city workers.[62] Thus as early as the 1950s union leaders in a number of major cities were in a favorable position to influence personnel policy and force pay hikes.

Not until the second half of the 1960s, however, did labor-management relations in the older central cities become critical. This was in part owing to the inflationary pressures that squeezed the wallets of city employees and also forced municipalities to attempt economies. In 1964 the consumer price index rose only 1.2 percent, but by 1966 it was increasing at an annual rate of 3.4 percent, and in 1969 the index climbed a startling 6.1 percent. During the first half of the decade, from 1961 through 1965, the annual price rise averaged only 1.3 percent, but the average for the period 1966 through 1970 was 4.5 percent. Though hardly runaway inflation, the climbing prices did mean that frequent pay raises were a necessity. With some justification municipal employees had long claimed that they were not paid on a comparable scale with workers in the private sector. Now further relative slippage threatened unless cities granted generous pay hikes in each new wage contract.

But inflation was not the only factor exacerbating labor-management woes. Souring relations even further were the mounting racial and social tensions of the late 1960s that made city employees suspicious of every initiative from city hall. Under barrage from black militants and their white liberal sympathizers, white police officers, for example, feared any moves that might undercut their professional prerogatives. They did not intend to become the scapegoats for racial unrest in the nation or sacrificial victims for white liberals seeking to atone for past sins and simultaneously quiet threatening blacks. White public employees negotiating for pay raises from intransigent city officials also were not mollified when they heard television reports of antipoverty funds pouring into black neighborhoods to enhance the fortunes of unwed mothers on welfare.

Moreover, the rhetoric of the activist glamor boys in city hall hardly soothed the angry feelings of hostile sanitation workers and firefighters trying to survive on modest salaries. With his criticism of the bureaucracy as selfish and sluggish, Mayor Lindsay seemed especially offensive and unsympathetic to the problems of employees, who day after day provided the municipal services. The well-heeled WASP Yale graduate who sent his children to private schools outside the city appeared to be placing the blame and burden for municipal ills on Italian-American high school dropouts working on garbage trucks whose children had to walk the dangerous city streets to dreary P.S. 149. According to one labor official, "There wasn't a union leader in town who didn't want to get even with Lindsay," and the overwhelming desire was "to put Lindsay in his place."[63] The mayor had declared war on the entrenched bureaucracy, and the bureaucracy responded with counterrevolution.

This antagonism was evident in Lindsay's clash with the police force over the issue of a civilian review board. One of the chief complaints of the black community was of police brutality and the reluctance of the police department to take action against officers who mistreated black suspects. In his mayoralty campaign of 1965, Lindsay pledged that if elected he would add four civilians to the existing panel of three deputy police commissioners that judged charges of undue force. Representing 25,000 of the city's 28,000 policemen, the Patrolmen's Benevolent Association (PBA) opposed this "political interference" in the operation of the police department, and its president said that the group was prepared to spend its entire treasury of $1.5 million to fight the reform. The newly elected Mayor Lindsay, however, denied "that the Police Department [was] a law unto itself" and proceeded to create the reformed board by executive order.[64]

In response, the PBA successfully petitioned for a citywide referendum on the question of the board, and in November 1966 the police won a decisive victory over Lindsay when 63 percent of the electorate voted to abolish the mayor's panel. This was just the beginning of a rocky relationship between the city's police and its mayor. Fearful that the activist executive was ready to violate the professional standards of the department to win the votes of racial minorities, the police were ever on their guard against Lindsay. Moreover, since the voters supported the police, the mayor usually found himself on the losing side.

In 1968 the mayor and his activist allies again became embroiled in a battle with public employees that had ominous racial overtones. Responding to proposals by the mayor and his liberal supporters as well as to the demands of black militants, in 1967 the New York City Board of Education launched a program of decentralization, creating three experimental districts with governing boards elected by district residents. Rather than allowing white administrators in downtown offices to determine all policy for ghetto schools, blacks from the neighborhood were to assume a stronger role in the conduct of their children's education.

One of the three experimental districts was the deteriorating black community of Ocean Hill–Brownsville in Brooklyn. By the spring of 1968, however, the Ocean Hill board was showing greater independence than the city's board of education or even the United Federation of Teachers (UFT) had expected. Finally, on May 8 the black local board ordered the involuntary transfer of nineteen white teachers and administrators, an act the predominantly white UFT interpreted as racially inspired and in violation of the educators' guarantees of job security. In retaliation the UFT struck the Ocean Hill schools, and the following fall the dispute escalated, producing a succession of three citywide teacher strikes that kept most of the city's public schools closed from early September to mid-November.

By the end of 1968 the decentralization experiment was in shambles, and the UFT had demonstrated that city leaders could not act in defiance of the professional interests of the well-organized school teachers. Replying angrily to the report of the Mayor's Advisory Panel on Decentralization, the UFT complained that the panel's plan had ignored "the new power and integrity of the professional teacher who [would] not continue to teach in any school or district where professional decisions [were] made by laymen."[65] In the Ocean Hill struggle as in the review board controversy, civil servants were defining their professional prerogatives and telling Mayor Lindsay and his ilk to keep hands off.

Not only did the transit workers, police officers, and teachers do battle with the Lindsay administration, so did a number of other civil servants. In December 1966 the city's park workers threatened to strike and two thousand of them expressed their anger by disrupting the Christmas tree lighting ceremony at City Hall, tearing up the wires leading to the tree.[66] In February 1968 sanitation workers called a nine-day strike, leaving heaps of garbage in the city streets, and in November municipal incinerator stokers walked off the job, closing all eleven city incinerators and again delaying garbage collection.[67] Meanwhile, in October, the city's firefighters had conducted a slowdown, refusing to perform nonemergency duties.[68]

Though New York City's employees were angrier, more militant, and more disruptive than were municipal workers elsewhere, in other central cities mayors and commissioners were also experiencing an unprecedented rebellion among their civil servants. In 1967 the Detroit Police Officers Association (POA) demanded a 20 percent pay raise and backed up its demand with a month-long slowdown in the writing of traffic tickets and a "sick-in," during which one-third of the force called in ill. "This is nothing more than a shakedown," protested Mayor Cavanagh, "and, if I give in to the police, I would be helping those who have acted most irresponsibly." But this "blue-flu" epidemic left the department so shorthanded that the city had to negotiate a settlement that included not only pay increases but a new grievance procedure with POA representatives sitting in on disciplinary proceedings.[69] That same year the Minneapolis city council refused to approve police pay raises, and the local Police Officers Federation retaliated with work slowdowns and protest parades through downtown.[70]

In 1968 the president of Buffalo's police organization, the Erie Club, described his members as "fighting mad" over the city's refusal to grant a 20 percent salary increase and threatened that the police would take "militant action" unless the city yielded. In fact, negotiators only narrowly averted a strike by Buffalo's law enforcement personnel. [71] Meanwhile, in May 1968 Cleveland's garbage truck drivers went on strike, leaving refuse to pile up at a rate of tons a day. [72] The following year 1,850 nonuniformed AFSCME members in Cincinnati walked off their jobs. Claiming that the city's overwhelmingly white police officers and firefighters had won generous settlements, the AFSCME members, about 50 percent of whom were black, demanded equal treatment. One expressed the racial overtones of the strike when he told the press: "Most of the uniformed men are Caucasian and most of the non-uniformed men are Negro. I feel this is the reason we are not getting the raise."[73]

Threats of civilian review of police conduct also stirred union activism not only in New York City but throughout the nation. In 1968 the Boston patrolmen's union cooperated with city council members to block implementation of Mayor White's proposal for a civilian complaint board. Buffalo's police lobbied successfully against a measure that would have strengthened the authority of the city's Commission on Human Relations in investigating police behavior, and in 1970 Baltimore's police unions thwarted adoption of a proposal for a civilian review board. Likewise, Philadelphia's Fraternal Order of Police convinced the pliable Mayor Tate to scrap an existing civilian panel charged with hearing complaints of misconduct. In December 1969 before a cheering police audience, Tate offered the board's abolition as a "Christmas present" to his public safety personnel. [74]

Throughout the nation the story was the same. Inflation, racial tensions, and fears of "political interference" fueled the discontent of municipal employees and caused them to bolster their defenses through militant unionization. Each year mayors faced tougher negotiating sessions as city employees demanded more and proved less willing to compromise. Though police officers deplored the "lawlessness" of civil rights demonstrators and Vietnam War peace protesters, by the late 1960s they too were taking to the streets with placards and threatening to strike in violation of state statute. Not only was the underclass erupting in the ghetto, the government itself was in revolt as public employees shed past restraints and donned the prevailing belligerence of the age.

A serious liability of many big-city mayors who attempted to deal with this revolt was their lack of a solid political base. With the decline of partisan politics in the 1950s, a number of city executives were left without the support of a reliable party organization that could broker the conflicts between city hall and civil servants, between whites and blacks, between downtown and the neighborhoods. Moreover, having no solid party base, mayors had to piece together electoral coalitions if they

wished to remain in office. In most cities the party organizations could no longer confidently deliver the votes of certain wards to mayoral candidates. By the late 1960s not even black wards produced sure majorities for Democratic standard-bearers. To win, one had to cater to a variety of blocs and somehow fashion a victorious combination. Among the most important groups that candidates wooed were the public employee unions, for when mobilized, these organizations could deliver votes like old-fashioned political machines. Thus the unions occupied the vacuum left by the decline of party politics and wielded unprecedented clout. When not up for reelection, mayors could fuss and fume in defiance of union demands, but in election years an increasing number of candidates were docilely buying union votes with generous wage settlements.

This phenomenon was evident, for example, in Philadelphia. By late 1966 the chairman of Philadelphia's Democratic City Committee had made it clear to Mayor Tate that the party organization would not support him for reelection in 1967. Not willing to retire without a fight, the vote-hungry Tate embarked on a courtship of labor that would cost the city millions of dollars. He sponsored a very handsome pension proposal, which the Pennsylvania Economy League described as a "bonanza" that would "pay liberal benefits, higher than almost any other civilian system, public or private."[75] Moreover, the insecure mayor sweetened the labor package with substantial pay increases for municipal employees.

In gratitude, the unions, which usually remained neutral in Philadelphia's primary contests, sided strongly with Tate, contributing more than $100,000 to pay poll watchers and vote canvassers in those wards where the regular Democratic organization was working against the mayor. In fact, labor created a parallel organization for Tate to rival the regular organization of the city committee. Labor's endeavors proved successful in both the primary and general elections, retaining the mayor's office for the generous Tate. In his memoirs Tate gratefully recognized, "Labor's tremendous effort in my behalf—unequalled even in presidential campaigns in my memory—was one of the decisive factors in my victory."[76] No longer could the Democratic party chieftains or ward leaders determine who would preside over the City of Brotherly Love. Instead, the support of District Council 33 of the AFSCME was more decisive, and that support could be bought with taxpayers' dollars.

Even New York City's Mayor Lindsay temporarily cast aside his anti-bureaucracy bluster and bought union backing for his reelection campaign. In 1969 Lindsay like Tate was a man virtually without a party, a political independent who had to create a coalition if he was to stay in office for another four years. Even the Republican party denied him the

nomination for reelection, leaving Lindsay with the support of only the minor Liberal party. Recognizing his political weakness, in 1969 Lindsay finally reached an accommodation with labor after three years of strife. Each of the municipal unions obtained generous settlements, and strikes were avoided. In return, the unions either backed the mayor or remained neutral. After winning its best contract ever, the formerly hostile Transit Workers Union endorsed Lindsay's reelection and while negotiating its new contract made a large financial contribution to the mayor's campaign fund. The sanitation workers union that only a year earlier had struck the city now backed the mayor, and even the UFT did not oppose its old enemy but adopted a neutral stance. The *New York Times* noted, "A liberal outlay of public money has taken some long steps . . . to establish peace on the municipal labor front."[77] Perhaps the head of the sanitation union summed up the situation best. Explaining his switch from foe to friend, he candidly admitted, "The Mayor has more than evened the score."[78]

Only in Chicago did the traditional political organization and its boss retain enough clout to keep the unions subservient. In contrast to the politically vulnerable Mayor Lindsay, Chicago's Mayor Daley remained firmly in control of a political organization that was powerful enough to elicit the cooperation of labor rather than its opposition. Under the weak regime of John Lindsay, New York City employee organizations were able to fight city hall and profit handsomely from the battle. In Daley's Chicago one could win more by working with the city administration than against it. Thus the Daley administration ensured its employees were well paid, but it did so without the pageant of threats, diatribes, and counterthreats that was giving New York its damaging reputation as an ungovernable city. By the close of the 1960s, however, Chicago was an anomaly. In most of the aging central cities the executive was posturing or pandering for power rather than exercising it.

Further undermining the position of elected municipal leaders in checking labor demands was the advent of compulsory arbitration procedures in some major cities. In November 1967 Pennsylvania's voters approved by an almost four-to-one margin a state constitutional amendment authorizing compulsory and binding arbitration of disputes between municipalities and police and firefighters over pay and working conditions. Labor rallied behind the proposal, and the state president of the Fraternal Order of Police said the amendment was "a shot-in-the-arm for police and fire personnel across the state," for "it elevate[d] the status of the policeman to that of a professional."[79] During the next few years, the new procedure greatly rewarded public safety employees; Philadelphia firefighters and police officers won more substantial pay increases from a

mandatory arbitration panel in 1970 than they had in any previous year with the exception of 1966–67, when Mayor Tate was purchasing votes.[80]

But some city officials fumed at the heavy financial burden mandated by third-party arbitrators, who did not have to worry about raising the revenue to pay salary hikes. Pittsburgh's Mayor Barr opposed adoption of compulsory arbitration, and in 1968 his worst fears were realized. That year arbitrators settled the impasse between the city and its public safety employees by awarding police officers a 19 percent raise and firefighters a 25 percent pay hike. Barr claimed, "These extraordinary increases . . . have shaken the foundation of the City budget," and attacked the state for granting "a blank check for outsiders to resolve [Pittsburgh's] wage negotiations."[81]

In 1969 Michigan also adopted a compulsory arbitration law for police and firefighters, and it too was to arouse the ire of city officials. During the decade following enactment of the law, wages for Detroit public safety workers increased 40 percent faster than did the wages for the other municipal personnel who were not covered by the arbitration legislation. At the close of the 1970s, Detroit Mayor Coleman Young contended, "Slowly, inexorably, compulsory arbitration destroys sensible financial management." "The arbitrators seem to believe there is no limit to how much of our money they should spend," the Detroit executive complained, and he insisted that the compulsory arbitration awards had "caused more damage to the public service in Detroit than the strikes they were designed to prevent."[82]

Yet by the late 1960s an increasing number of states were adopting compulsory arbitration procedures, especially for public safety personnel. In one city after another such arbitration may have staved off disruptive strikes, but it also seriously compromised the authority of local officials. Arbitrators who were not responsible to the voters fixed the level of expenditures in Pittsburgh, Philadelphia, and Detroit, not the duly elected mayors and council members. Moreover, once again the bureaucracy gained while the authority of public officials diminished.

One notable consequence of the emerging ascendancy of city employees was soaring labor costs. From 1966 to 1969 the consumer price index rose 13 percent, yet the median maximum salary for police officers in cities having more than 500,000 people soared 29 percent, and the median maximum pay for firefighters climbed 27 percent.[83] Municipal appropriations to retirement pension funds likewise rose sharply, draining large sums from city treasuries. For example, by 1969 in New York City, appropriations to the firefighters' pension fund amounted to 30 percent of total fire department personnel costs.[84] In other words, almost a third of the money New York City was paying for public safety employees was actually for persons no longer fighting fires or capturing criminals. For older central cities with stagnant tax bases and recurring fiscal problems, such figures were hardly encouraging nor did they bode well for the financial future.

By the close of the 1960s, however, many city officials had no alternative but to grant ever higher salaries and commit the municipal treasury to mounting expenditures. Despite the well-meaning intentions of Mayor Lindsay and his colleagues in city hall, the power of the civil servants was not checked. Instead, municipal bureaucrats grew more independent and more powerful, demanding new respect for their professional prerogatives and more money in their pay envelopes. Moreover, they were willing to organize, demonstrate, and even strike in defense of their interests. Yet the work stoppages, slowdowns, and acrimonious labor negotiations did little good for the reputations of the older central cities. Already bearing the burden of extensive blight, racial unrest, narrow streets, and inadequate parking, New York City, Detroit, Cleveland, and Cincinnati now could claim the added problem of an unbridled bureaucracy threatening to cut off such basic services as police and fire protection, schooling, and garbage collection if it did not obtain its demands. In 1969 the forces ganging up on the older central cities seemed insuperable.

Backlash

In the mid-1960s the young glamor boys in city hall had promised to shake up the municipal structure and bring new life to the faltering old metropolises. With high ideals and big promises, they had won votes and lavish media coverage. By the late 1960s, however, the promises seemed like so much hot air as the media now reported on riots in the cities rather than on renewal. Crime was rampant with the murder rate nationwide climbing 61 percent between 1965 and 1970 and the robbery rate soaring 153 percent. During the last half of the 1960s, the violent crime rate in New York City quadrupled, and in Detroit and Baltimore it tripled. Though some claimed this rise was in part owing to more accurate reporting of crimes, most urban Americans were not interested in quibbling over statistics. They knew the streets were becoming more dangerous, and they were mad about it. Lindsay, Cavanagh, and the others had not unleashed a new era of urban vitality but an age in which violence and unrest were the watchwords.

Reacting to the unwelcome upheaval of urban life was a wave of new figures in municipal politics who promised a return to the old days when one could walk the streets at night, when blacks remained quietly in their ghettos, and when meddlers from city hall or the federal government were not trying to destroy neighborhood schools or impose racial mixing. Representing what the media called white backlash, these figures challenged highfalutin notions of human renewal that seemed only to mean public money for blacks but not for whites. Moreover, they supported their local police rather than criticized them. What the cities needed was a reassertion of traditional authority on the streets and in the classroom. Government needed to promote law and order rather than encourage militance and discontent.

Among the new defenders of authority were some police officers who had shed their holsters in order to seek the mayor's office. Fed up with liberal restraints on police authority during a period of rising crime, these figures campaigned strongly on the law-and-order issue. With their police backgrounds, they could convincingly claim an expertise in how to restore peace to the city. Their assurances of renewed safety and calm struck a responsive nerve in beleaguered working-class white voters.

Charles Stenvig of Minneapolis was representative of this new breed of police politicians, building a political career on the law-and-order issue. Blacks constituted only 4 percent of the population of Scandinavian-dominated Minneapolis, but the city was not immune from the racial discontent of the late 1960s. In the summer of 1966 about fifty youths, mostly black, smashed the windows of twenty-five businesses on the Near North Side, and during the following summer, the National Guard was called out to deal with sporadic outbreaks of violence. Though petty compared to disorders in Detroit or Newark, the Minneapolis "riots" aroused a storm of controversy among whites. In the eyes of many whites, including police officers, liberal Mayor Arthur Naftalin, an old friend and ally of Hubert Humphrey, seemed too sympathetic to black militants, and his weak stance appeared to fuel the unrest rather than squelch it.

During this period, the president of the Minneapolis Police Officers' Federation was Charles Stenvig, who not only complained about Naftalin's law-and-order policies but also organized militant protests to secure pay raises for the police. Traditionally more highly politicized than other police forces, Minneapolis's law enforcement officers under Stenvig's guidance adopted a political role unprecedented even in the Minnesota metropolis. In late 1966 they turned out en masse for the Democratic precinct caucuses and together with other municipal employees elected enough delegates to control the 1967 Democratic city convention, to secure backing for their wage demands, and to win endorsement for three aldermanic candidates friendly to police interests.[85]

Two years later, however, Stenvig went one step further and declared his candidacy for mayor, claiming that he could restore order to the city. In his campaign Stenvig repeatedly emphasized his devotion to "strong, fair, impartial law enforcement for everybody."[86] Replying to criticism of this stance, the police officer said: "The only one who has to fear the word 'strong' is someone who intentionally breaks the law. There won't be a police state, just a return to law and order in Minneapolis."[87] Attacking the outgoing Mayor Naftalin's moderate stance toward window-smashing youth, Stenvig told the people of Minneapolis at rallies, in interviews, and on the radio, "You cannot appease hoodlums."[88] Though he generally avoided other issues, Stenvig also stated his support for the spread of public housing into all neighborhoods as long as the city did not use eminent domain and as long as the housing was in the same economic class as the existing housing."[89] Stenvig thus promised that blacks as well as whites would be forced to obey the law and guaranteed that the city would not impose schemes of class or racial integration on neighborhoods. A Stenvig administration would crack down on crime and not threaten the property values or tranquility of white homeowners.

This was an appealing platform in 1969, and on election day Stenvig defeated his Republican opponent, winning 62 percent of the vote. In his victory speech he reaffirmed his devotion to traditional values when he told jubilant followers: "I'm going to make my first appointment now. My chief advisor is going to be God, and don't you forget it."[90] God seemed to be on Stenvig's side that day in 1969, for the police officer carried eleven of the city's thirteen wards, losing only the two most affluent and Republican wards. He ran strongest among white working-class voters who had no more than a high school education, and they were to remain his staunchest supporters. Stenvig was to win two additional mayoral elections, serving as Minneapolis's chief executive from 1969 to 1973 and from 1975 to 1977. One author has described Stenvig's stance during these six years in office as "conservative populism," for the mayor remained dedicated to "law and order" and to the preservation of neighborhoods and neighborhood schools and maintained a cool relationship with downtown business interests, which were especially angered by his veto of a downtown domed stadium proposal.[91]

At the same time Stenvig was capturing the mayor's office in Minneapolis, another "tough cop" was rising to political prominence in Philadelphia. An Italian-American raised on Philadelphia's south side, Frank Rizzo joined the police force in 1943 and had risen to the position of police commissioner by 1967. A dedicated attention-getter, Police Commissioner Rizzo carried a pair of pearl-handled revolvers, was not reluctant to express his views on law and order, and cultivated the favor of the press, inviting reporters from the three major daily newspapers to his office for conversation and coffee each morning. By 1970 he was receiving more press coverage than was the lackluster Mayor Tate, and there was no question that he and not the mayor controlled police policy in the city. Popular among white ethnics, Rizzo became an obvious choice for the Democratic nomination for mayor in a city increasingly troubled by street crime. Thus in January 1971 the outgoing Mayor Tate asked his charismatic police chief to run as the Democratic standard-bearer and Rizzo promptly accepted the offer.[92]

In the ensuing Democratic primary and general election, Rizzo adopted much the same stance as Stenvig. He attacked "lenient judges" who turned "wild animals back on the street," and when speaking of lawlessness in the City of Brotherly Love, he warned: "Let me tell you this, we'd better all wake up. We're going to have to soon."[93] Like Stenvig, Rizzo defended traditional values and neighborhood schools, bitterly attacking Philadelphia's liberal school superintendent. "I'm not an educator," the tough cop admitted, "but maybe we'd better go back to the old way—remember, you wrote As for a week, Bs for a week, Cs for a week."[94] In fact, Rizzo had little sympathy for any of the liberal social-engineering schemes of the late 1960s or early 1970s. Explaining why he was running for mayor, he said, "I couldn't let this city fall into the hands of the lefties."[95] Though black heavyweight champion Joe Frazier endorsed Rizzo, the police commissioner did little campaigning in black wards. Moreover, his opponents claimed that Rizzo's law-and-order platform was simply a veiled appeal to white racism. Former mayor Richardson Dilworth, who bolted his party in 1971, contended, "The Democratic campaign slogan, 'Rizzo Means Business,' means that Rizzo will keep the blacks in their place."[96]

In both the primary and general elections Rizzo, like Stenvig, won chiefly because of support from the white working and lower-middle classes. He captured 66 percent of the white vote in his primary contest against an Irish Catholic liberal and a black militant and virtually the same proportion in the general election against a patrician Republican. Meanwhile, he lost overwhelmingly black wards by seven or eight to one in the primary and as the Democratic standard-bearer ran behind his Republican foe in the black divisions by about three to one.[97] As in Minneapolis, most blacks deviated from their traditional Democratic allegiance and cast their ballots for the more palatable Republican.

Police officers, however, were not the only figures to articulate and exploit the fears and anxieties of white ethnics in the working and lower-middle classes. In Boston, Buffalo, and Detroit women candidates dedicated to defending the family, neighborhood, and traditional schooling also preached what the press labeled the "white backlash" message. Though no woman had ever held the office of mayor in a major American city, now the perceived threat from liberal social planners and militant blacks drew some females into the fight for executive power. "Law and order" was part of their message, but compared with Rizzo and Stenvig they focused more heavily on the traditional "motherly" concerns of neighborhood environment and schooling. What aroused the Boston and Buffalo candidates most were not the rioting and crime in the streets but the plans for busing white children to black neighborhoods to achieve racial balance in the schools.

No one gained greater publicity as an opponent of busing than Boston's Louise Day Hicks. A mother and attorney from staunchly Irish South Boston, Hicks was chairing the Boston School Committee when in 1965 the Massachusetts legislature adopted a statute requiring all school committees in the state to "adopt as educational objectives the promotion of racial balance and the correction of existing racial imbalances in the public schools."[98] What this meant to Hicks and her supporters was that white Irish children from South Boston would be bused to black Roxbury and black children from Roxbury would be traveling to South Boston each school day. Stirred to action, Hicks embarked on an antibusing crusade that won nationwide press coverage and attracted a devoted following among many of Boston's whites.

Capitalizing on this popularity and dedicated to cleansing Boston of programs that endangered the family, the home, or the white neighborhood, in 1967 Hicks entered the race for mayor, challenging Kevin White in the general election. Throughout her campaign she attacked busing and the racial-imbalance law, arguing that the prevailing attitude "among mothers" was that "they [did] not want their little children bused."[99] Moreover, she warned Bostonians who did not send their offspring to the public schools, "Busing is going to cost the taxpayers of Boston millions of dollars," and "This is where your pocketbook will be affected, whether your children go to Boston schools or not."[100]

Preservation of neighborhood schools was the chief plank in her platform, but she also addressed other issues. She told a group of senior citizens, "Today we must declare . . . war on lawlessness in the city of Boston," and she opposed legislation outlawing racial discrimination in the sale or rental of property, insisting that an owner "has the absolute right to choose who is going to live on their property . . . or who is going to buy it."[101] And when asked about "homosexual bars" in downtown

Boston, Hicks replied: "I certainly do not believe they should be toler-ated. They should be suppressed in the best interests of all the people of Boston."[102] Campaigning as the "candidate of the people," Hicks won no support from downtown business interests but like other "backlash" fig-ures preached a conservative populism, lashing out at "the Establish-ment" and the "suburban power brokers."[103] Defense of the neighborhood school, the white homeowners' rights, law and order, and traditional moral values—these were the basis of Hicks's appeal.

On election day this was not enough, for she lost to Kevin White, carrying only 47 percent of the vote. Like Stenvig and Rizzo, she did her best among moderate- and middle-income whites, especially those of Irish ancestry, and lost the largely black Ward 12 by a vote of 5,404 to 317. Mayor-elect White summed up the voting pattern when he told an aide: "The rich love me and the poor. But everyone in the middle hates me."[104]

Louise Day Hicks, however, was not the only woman to challenge the liberal establishment and defend home, family, and the neighborhood school. In Buffalo a forty-year-old mother of two, Alfreda Slominski, took up the Hicks cause, running for mayor on the Republican ticket. Like Hicks, Slominski was a former member of the local board of education who had parlayed her outspoken views on schooling into a political career. Having already been elected member-at-large of the city council, in 1969 she tried to unseat incumbent Mayor Frank A. Sedita in a campaign that combined antagonism to busing with a strong law-and-order appeal. Ac-cording to the *Buffalo Evening News*, Slominski "called education the most important issue and accused the Sedita administration of failing to provide adequately for school children."[105] Not only did she attack im-posed racial balancing in Buffalo schools but she also lashed out at sex education and other newfangled educational ideas thrust on the city by so-called experts. "We must return the public schools to the people," Slominski said. "Schools are not private playthings of professional educa-tors."[106] But she also emphasized, "Crime in the streets is killing our community," and promised to restore order.[107]

Mayor Sedita castigated her "extremism and appeal to fear and big-otry," and a leading businessman summed up the feeling of the downtown elite when he admitted: "I'm not interested in the racial issues. I simply think that the lady would be bad for business."[108] On election day, Slominski suffered the same fate as Hicks, losing to the moderate Demo-cratic candidate by a vote of 87,300 to 67,900. With a Polish name and a platform that appealed to working- and lower-middle-class white ethnics, Slominski carried the predominantly Polish but usually Democratic Lovejoy and Fillmore districts. Mayor Sedita won the more affluent and normally Republican Delaware and University districts and garnered handsome majorities in black neighborhoods as well.[109]

Detroit's spokeswoman for the so-called "white backlash" was a twenty-year veteran of the city council, Mary Beck. A vehement foe of Jerome Cavanagh and leader of an attempt to recall the young mayor, Beck was dedicated to old-fashioned discipline and scornful of the new permissiveness. Busing was not an issue in Detroit, so in her 1969 campaign for mayor, Beck emphasized law and order, though her rhetoric had a stronger moralistic tone than that of her male counterparts in Minneapolis and Philadelphia. "It shall be my primary goal, if elected mayor, to sweep this city clean of crime and corruption and every form of pollution," Beck told the voters, "and to make our streets, our homes, and our business places safe and wholesome once again."[110] Though a favorite of many white homeowners, Beck joined Slominski and Hicks in the losers' column, winning only 71,000 votes compared with the frontrunner's 125,000. Beck explained her defeat by remarking, "There was much more discrimination than I thought against a woman holding an executive position as opposed to a legislative position."[111] Comparing the failures of Hicks, Slominski, and Beck with the victories of Stenvig and Rizzo, perhaps one can perceive some truth to the observation.

Besides the female defenders of morality, home, and neighborhood, and the tough-cop politicians ready to crack down on criminals, there were a number of other candidates during the late 1960s who challenged liberal programs and urged a return to order and discipline in the aging central cities. In 1967 Cincinnati Republicans retained control of their city's government by running on a strong law-and-order platform. According to the *Cincinnati Enquirer*, one successful council candidate explained, "[Rioters] must realize that rioting is a one-way ticket to the Workhouse," and contended, "Law and order is an American way of life."[112]

Two years later in Cleveland, Robert Kelly, former services director under Ralph Locher, unsuccessfully challenged incumbent Mayor Carl Stokes for the Democratic mayoral nomination, relying heavily on law-and-order rhetoric and charges that Stokes was soft on crime. Kelly described Cleveland as a "jungle," and his supporters argued, "There has been a complete breakdown in the protection of life and property that has shocked the nation."[113]

In 1969 New Yorkers also witnessed a law-and-order campaign with both the Democratic mayoral candidate Mario Procaccino and the Republican John Marchi identifying crime and lax law enforcement as the chief issues in their struggle to unseat incumbent Mayor John Lindsay. Contending that the overriding problem facing New York was "safety in the streets and security in the home," Procaccino defeated former Mayor Wagner in the Democratic primary.[114] Similarly, Marchi denied Lindsay the Republican nomination by campaigning in that party's primary as "very, very hawkish" toward crime and civil disorder.[115] Referring to Stenvig's recent triumph in Minnesota, the liberal *New York Times* criticized those voting in the New York mayoral primary for succumbing "to the same ugly sentiments that [had] recently swept . . . Minneapolis."[116] But with the law-and-order vote split between Procaccino and Marchi, Lindsay, running on the Liberal party ticket, squeaked through to victory in the general election, winning with only 42 percent of the vote.[117]

Though Lindsay remained in office and "backlash" candidates across the country enjoyed only mixed success, the new uprising among formerly quiescent white ethnics and the working- and lower-middle classes simply added to the tumult of the older central cities in the late 1960s. In the 1950s it had appeared that these aging hubs were dying with a whimper; now they were going out with a bang. Dynamic young mayors had proved false messiahs, producing more promises than results. Meanwhile, blacks had grown increasingly militant, and the federal government's community action program had financed their anger. Municipal employees were also taking to the streets, striking, and forcing mayors to kowtow to their wage demands. Police officers, however, were not only picketing; they were running for office, conducting campaigns that polarized whites and blacks. Moreover, for the first time angry women were seeking the city's highest office in order to protect the home, morality, and traditional schooling. By 1970 Fun City had grown frantic, and in the other major metropolises as well the prognosis for peaceful, harmonious revival was not good.

Hitting Bottom

On taking office in 1966, Mayor John Lindsay warned New Yorkers that if his reform crusade failed "the implications of [New York's] defeat" would be "assessed throughout the nation, to be proclaimed by the cynics as proof that great cities" were "no longer governable."[1] Eleven years later a former member of the Lindsay administration published a book entitled *The Ungovernable City* in which he argued, "Only a compulsive optimist could overlook the distress signals emanating from city hall, which strongly suggest that the city has become the sick man of American government."[2] By the mid-1970s it was clear that the Lindsay offensive had floundered; the problems of the aging central city had proven too intractable for the shining white knight of American politics. In 1966 the incoming Mayor Lindsay had found New York near bankruptcy; in 1974 the outgoing Mayor Lindsay left it virtually bankrupt. At the beginning of his eight-year stint, the crime rate was spiraling upward, blight was spreading, and municipal employees were restive. When he left office, New York City was renowned as the mugging capital of the world, vast tracts of urban real estate were abandoned and in ruins, and public employee unions had seriously compromised the prerogatives of elected officials. To many observers New York City had simply gone from bad to worse.

But Lindsay's fate was not unique. By the early 1970s older central cities throughout the nation seemed to be descending to new depths, and the bright young mayors of the 1960s were among the casualties of the unremitting but unsuccessful battle against blight and decentralization. Disheartened by Detroit's race riot of 1967 and the accelerating physical and social deterioration of his city, the once-handsome young Mayor Jerome Cavanagh grew fat and depressed. In late 1968 a reporter for the *Detroit Free Press* observed: "The world of Mayor Jerome P. Cavanagh has come down like an old pair of socks. Even a friend says: 'He's just like Job; the only thing he hasn't got are those sores.' "[3] At the beginning of 1970 he moved out of the mayor's office, never again to hold a public position.

In Cleveland, Carl Stokes hung on as mayor for four years, but the early euphoria of his administration soon soured when it was found that some of the booster funds from the "Cleveland, NOW!" project had ended up paying for the rifles of police-sniping black militants. In 1971 Stokes chose not to run for reelection, leaving Cleveland to become a television news anchorman in New York City. By the mid-1970s he seemingly even had doubts that black was beautiful, divorcing his second wife and marrying a Nordic beauty who had reigned as Miss Finland for 1969. In 1971 Baltimore's Mayor Thomas D'Alesandro III, likewise, chose not to run for another term. According to the *New York Times*, D'Alesandro quit because he realized "the increasing powerlessness of the big city Mayor . . . to close the pandora's box of urban troubles," and the exasperated executive complained, "I've exhausted every avenue of taxation available to me."[4] Among the glamor-boy dynamos of the 1960s only Boston's Mayor Kevin White remained in office, in 1971 again defeating Louise Day Hicks. Yet in 1970 White also stumbled, losing the Massachusetts gubernatorial race to a Republican, who even carried the overwhelmingly Democratic city of Boston. Moreover, by the mid-1970s White was changing his political style, discarding the outmoded Lindsayesque image of the late 1960s and refashioning himself into a more traditional politician.[5]

Everywhere the high hopes of the 1960s seemed naive by the mid-1970s. The urban electorate had given a mandate for action to its most dynamic young leaders, and these activists had proved no more effective than the tired Mirianis, Lochers, and Wagners of the past. In fact, the signs of decline were proliferating. No longer did mayors or candidates speak confidently of eradicating poverty and achieving human renewal. Now the struggle was for survival rather than revival. The aging urban hubs had to stave off bankruptcy, dam the outward flow of population, and stanch the wave of building abandonment. Their very lives seemed at stake.

After 1968, race riots did cease, but the crime rate continued to rise and public employees seemed to grow more militant. Between 1970 and 1974 the nation's murder rate climbed 30 percent, and the robbery rate was up 26 percent. Winning the nickname of "Murder City," Detroit's homicide rate was more than twice the national average, and its incidence of robbery also was more than double that of the nation. Even in Philadelphia, where tough-cop Mayor Frank Rizzo had promised, "I will make Attila the Hun look like a faggot," the rate of violent crime rose by almost one-third during the early 1970s.[6]

Meanwhile, municipal employees were calling strikes and disrupting governmental services. In January 1970 Cincinnati's nonuniformed employees struck, remaining idle for four weeks. Claiming that "a state of war exist[ed] between organized labor and the wielders of power," the executive secretary of Cincinnati's Labor Council pledged a "massive civil disobedience campaign" unless the city responded to the workers' demands.[7] In February 1972 Cleveland garbage collectors and water department employees both went on strike, leveling the city a double blow.[8] The following year three thousand Saint Louis school teachers walked off the job for four weeks.[9] Equally serious was the 1974 work stoppage or slowdown by more than four thousand Baltimore police officers, garbage collectors, park workers, dog pound employees, and water and sewer maintenance laborers.[10] Across the country each of the major central cities attempted to cope with the rebellion among municipal employees. Again the issue was survival. During the 1970 strike, Cincinnati's waterworks superintendent admitted, "We're sitting on a powder keg insofar as repairs to any water main break are concerned."[11] Other municipal supervisors echoed the remark; the perpetuation of services vital to civilized urban existence seemed precarious.

By fall 1971 the prospect for the aging hubs was so serious that the journal *Public Interest* asked two distinguished urban scholars, "Is the Inner City Doomed?" Neither admitted that it was absolutely defunct, but both assigned the older central cities a humiliating new function in American life. George Sternlieb described the function of the central cities in the 1970s as that of a sandbox where the poor and the socially maladjusted were dumped to amuse themselves and keep out of the way of the more affluent and productive mainstream of society.[12] The other commentator, Norton Long, conceived of the existing city as "an Indian reservation made up of inmates and keepers, economically dependent on transfer payments from the outside society made in consideration of custodial services rendered."[13] Both foresaw the older central city as no longer the heart of American civilization but as a foster parent for the nation's human undesirables, dependent on constant federal financial transfusions for retaining any semblance of life.

Five years later the diagnosis was even worse. In the pages of *Public Interest*, William Baer now actually explored the idea of "the city as cemetery" and forthrightly wrote of "urban thanatopsis." According to Baer:

"Urban death—or at least neighborhood death—in the nation's cities is coming to pass. It may be hindered by expertise, detoured by cajolry, impeded by charismatic leadership, and delayed by simple faith; but it will come."[14] Meanwhile, others were expounding a triage theory of urban policy, urging the public sector to write off inevitably dying sections of the central city as beyond hope. Better to save limited public dollars for neighborhoods that still could be redeemed.[15]

Overall, a morbid tone pervaded the analysis of cities like Buffalo, Cleveland, Detroit, and Saint Louis. They appeared to be hitting bottom, largely unaffected by attempts to buoy their fortunes. The Lindsays and Cavanaghs had failed as had the earlier exponents of renewal, and gloomy commentators were already composing postmortems. By the mid-1970s the road to renaissance had seemingly reached a dead end.

The Gloomy Urban Scene

Reinforcing the gloomy prognostications of urban death were the data collected in the 1970 census. According to this enumeration, eleven of the twelve older central cities in the nation's northeastern quadrant again lost population, with only New York City inching upward in number of inhabitants (see table 15). Moreover, in eight of the eleven cities the percentage of population loss was greater in the 1960s than in the 1950s. In fact, six of the cities dropped in population by more than 10 percent, and Saint Louis won the dubious distinction of declining most rapidly, with a 17 percent loss. Even more discouraging was the loss of housing units. No longer were households simply shrinking as in the 1950s; now they were disappearing. Whereas during the 1950s, only two of the twelve central cities had suffered a decline in the number of households, in the 1960s nine did so. Thus urban boosters could not dismiss population decline as the result of smaller family size. Instead, for the first time in the history of most of the older cities, demolition and abandonment of dwelling units were producing an actual loss of households.

Though overall population was declining, the number of blacks was growing as were the ranks of the aged. As seen in table 15, the percentage of population that was nonwhite increased in each of the cities, and by 1970 more than 40 percent of the residents of Baltimore, Detroit, and Saint Louis were black. Yet the influx of poor migrants from the South had slowed during the 1960s. Between 1965 and 1970 Saint Louis even suffered a net out-migration of eight thousand blacks as middle-class Afro-Americans began to follow their white counterparts to suburbia. Many of the aged, however, could not afford to move to outlying areas nor did they

Table 15. Demographic Changes, 1960–1970

City	% Change Total Population	% Change No. of Households	% Nonwhite 1960	% Nonwhite 1970	% over 65 1960	% over 65 1970
New York	+1.5	+6.9	14.7	23.4	10.5	12.0
Chicago	−5.2	−1.7	23.6	34.4	9.8	10.6
Philadelphia	−2.7	+4.3	26.7	34.4	10.4	11.7
Detroit	−9.5	−3.3	29.2	44.5	9.5	11.5
Baltimore	−3.5	+5.0	35.0	47.0	9.0	10.6
Cleveland	−14.3	−8.0	28.9	39.0	9.9	10.6
Saint Louis	−17.0	−13.3	28.8	41.3	12.3	14.7
Boston	−8.1	−3.0	9.8	18.2	12.3	12.8
Pittsburgh	−13.9	−5.5	16.8	20.7	11.2	13.5
Buffalo	−13.1	−6.6	13.8	21.3	11.6	13.3
Cincinnati	−10.0	−1.2	21.8	28.1	11.7	13.0
Minneapolis	−10.0	−2.8	3.2	6.4	13.4	15.0

Sources: U.S. Bureau of the Census, U.S. censuses of 1960 and 1970 (Washington, D.C.: U.S. Government Printing Office, 1961 and 1973).

want to abandon neighborhoods where they had lived for decades. Consequently, during the 1960s, the percentage of persons 65 or over rose in each of the older central cities, and each of the hubs had a larger proportion of senior citizens than did its metropolitan area as a whole. Unfortunately, muggers and street thugs found the aged especially easy targets. Thus just when the criminal ranks were expanding, the potential pool of ready victims was growing. In response, older residents demanded greater police protection, which cost the cities millions of dollars.

One bright sign in the population data was the decline in the number of the very young. During the 1950s and early 1960s, the central cities had suffered from a demographic imbalance. The number of residents was declining as were the city's economic resources, but the corps of school-age children was expanding, overcrowding schools in neighborhoods that were losing population. By 1970, however, the baby boom was over, and the number of children entering central-city schools was beginning to drop sharply. Hard-pressed school districts in New York, Philadelphia, and Chicago could enjoy some relief from enrollment pressures in coming decades.

Yet that was a minor consolation for urban leaders. All of the statistics indicated that the older central cities had not turned the corner, and throughout the early 1970s the population estimates and demographic data remained negative. Between 1970 and 1976 central-city populations dropped even more rapidly than before, the number of dwelling units declined steadily, and the inner-city neighborhoods that were not abandoned seemed destined to become little more than grim receptacles for permanent welfare recipients and the immobile aged. Especially disheartening was the continuing evidence of disparity in wealth between the urban core and its suburbs. The middle-class flight to suburbia was accelerating rather than slowing during the early 1970s, draining the older centers of the relatively few productive and affluent citizens that had not already joined the outward trek in earlier decades. As seen in table 16, by 1976 the per capita income of each of the twelve older central cities was less than that of its suburbs. With their stable middle-class neighborhoods and ring of blue-collar industrial suburbs, Cincinnati and Pittsburgh measured up best when compared with the outlying communities. But the per capita income of six of the central cities was no more than 80 percent of the per capita suburban income, and the average income of each Cleveland resident was only about two-thirds that of the outlying residents. These figures admirably summed up the story of the past thirty years. Just as government and business leaders had feared, as early as the late 1930s money had left the central city and settled in suburbia. This

Table 16. Per Capita Income, 1976

Metropolitan Area	Central-City Per Capita Income ($)	Suburban Per Capita Income ($)	Central-City Income as % of Suburban Income
Cincinnati	4,843	4,947	97
Pittsburgh	4,919	5,125	95
Minneapolis	5,439	5,760	94
New York City	5,222	6,182	84
Philadelphia	4,660	5,562	83
Boston	4,503	5,530	81
Detroit	4,661	5,812	80
Saint Louis	4,278	5,308	80
Chicago	4,984	6,270	79
Buffalo	4,234	5,329	79
Baltimore	4,577	5,806	78
Cleveland	4,084	5,987	68

Source: *Central City–Suburban Fiscal Disparity and City Distress* (Washington, D.C.: Advisory Commission on Intergovernmental Relations, 1980), p. 44.

was true in the 1940s, 1950s, and 1960s, and it was still the case in the first half of the 1970s. Decentralization was proceeding on its unrelenting course, leaving blight in its wake.

Though the figures on central-city income told an old story, it was evident to many urban leaders that the cities had entered a grim new chapter. The villain was no longer just shabbiness and dilapidation; now the foe was abandonment. One city after another faced the unprecedented problem of property owners simply abandoning apartment buildings and houses, tossing them away like trash. In fact, once stripped of fixtures and torched for insurance money, they were worth no more than trash. First a few houses were abandoned, then whole blocks. The charred ruins of apartment buildings stood next to weed-covered lots cleared by wrecking crews while down the street a few well-maintained homes still struggled to survive the wave of abandonment. This was an increasingly common scene in the central city during the early 1970s, and it was stark testimony to the accelerating decline of the older hubs.

Nowhere was abandonment more dramatic or better publicized than in New York City's South Bronx. Once the home of middle-income Jews, in the 1950s and 1960s poor Puerto Ricans and blacks moved into the district in increasing numbers. By the late 1960s drugs and crime were rampant, causing the flight of those who could afford to leave. And in the early 1970s an epidemic of arson was to force out many of the residents who had remained. Under city welfare policy, tenants burned out of their homes received top priority for admission to low-rent public housing as well as two to three thousand dollars from the welfare department to compensate for loss of personal property. This was ample incentive for some welfare recipients to set fire to their South Bronx abodes. Landlords also were willing to torch their apartment buildings to collect insurance money. Moreover, if fire cleared a building of residents, then scavengers, often in need of drug money, could descend on the structure and strip it of valuable brass and copper pipes and whatever fixtures and hardware might bring a price at the junkyard. In other words, many New Yorkers could profit from the burning of the South Bronx, and during the early 1970s, they did so. One news story told of two Bronx youths, one ten and the other fifteen years old, who admitted proudly that they had set forty to fifty fires, being paid as little as three dollars per fire by landlords and other profiteers of destruction.[16] In 1974 alone there were 12,300 blazes in the district, or an average of 34 a day. Observers repeatedly compared the devastated district to "Dresden after the bombing," though sometimes the comparison was to Berlin in 1945.[17] Overall, an estimated 104,000 dwelling units were abandoned in New York City between 1970 and 1975, and the South Bronx accounted for many of these.[18]

Though the South Bronx became almost synonymous with abandonment, other cities also faced the same problem. In 1970–71 a study sponsored by the federal Department of Housing and Urban Development found that "abandonment in the Montgomery neighborhood of St. Louis [had] reached a stage where it [was] highly concentrated and contagious; one-fifth of all standing units [were] abandoned" and "300 parcels of land [were] vacant, many as a result of the demolition of abandoned buildings." As in the South Bronx, the real estate market for properties in the Montgomery area had evaporated, and rental income from remaining tenants was not sufficient to cover maintenance. Rather than operate interminably at a loss, landlords opted for abandonment.

Moreover, abandonment was accelerating at a dangerous pace. The federal survey reported 2,072 "vacant and derelict residential structures" throughout the city of Saint Louis in July 1970; by November 1970 the total was up to 2,500; and in January 1971 the figure was 3,500.[19] Similarly, Cleveland's Hough area was reverting to vacant lots, as it proved to be one of the growing number of unprofitable and unlivable communities within America's central cities. After the riot of 1966 Hough rapidly declined, with its population falling from 59,000 in 1965 to 45,000 in 1970. In 1965 Hough could claim 919 stores, but by 1971 there were only 596, and according to the *Cleveland Plain Dealer*, "A high percentage of the merchants left behind were either unscrupulous credit dealers or inexperienced local businessmen who had once-viable enterprises palmed off on them."[20] Crime seemed to be the only growth industry in the district; in 1972 the *Plain Dealer* reported grimly, "The murderer, rapist, robber and burglar terrorize Hough, spreading a fear that dominates the lives of the community's people."[21]

The *Plain Dealer*'s words could apply to a number of "forbidden zones" that were emptying of residents in cities across the country. Unsafe and no longer a viable investment, black North Philadelphia, in the words of a local journalist, "became the South Bronx of Philadelphia—the bombed-out, burned-down wasteland of countless federal programs that failed."[22] By 1973 Chicago's Woodlawn was likewise being described as a "zone of destruction." Thirty years earlier it had been the site of one of the nation's earliest neighborhood rehabilitation projects, but now the city was demolishing abandoned buildings in the community at the rate of 500 dwelling units a year.[23] The core of Buffalo's black district also was rotting with almost 21 percent of its housing units and 30 percent of its commercial structures vacant by 1975. Largely because of demolition in this dying inner-city area, the number of dwelling units in Buffalo dropped from 166,000 in 1970 to 151,000 in 1975. If the clearing of Buffalo had continued at that rate, in fifty years there would not have been an apartment or home remaining in the city.[24]

Accompanying the economic decay and abandonment of urban neighborhoods was a continued decline in central-city retailing. Fewer affluent residents lived in the central cities, and downtown drew an ever-diminishing proportion of suburban shoppers. Just as crime was driving residents from the inner-city neighborhoods, it also had joined parking and traffic problems as one of the chief factors keeping customers from patronizing central business district establishments. According to a prominent Cleveland businessman interviewed in 1971, the "biggest problem" was that people were "afraid to come downtown," and the chairman of the board of Cleveland's Halle's Department Store complained that if newspapers would not play up crime so much "it would help bring the people back."[25] Cleveland's downtown restaurant owners also noted a dearth of dinner customers. One explained that this was partly because "after 7 P.M., a lot of people [were] just scared to death to be downtown," though others complained that "with the movies closing, little evening shopping and little other entertainment" downtown had nothing to offer after-dark patrons.[26]

But Cleveland was not the only city suffering. When adjusted for inflation, central business district retail sales between 1967 and 1977 dropped 48 percent in Baltimore, 44 percent in both Saint Louis and Cleveland, 38 percent in Boston, 36 percent in Minneapolis, and 29 percent in Pittsburgh.[27] Everywhere the downtown department stores were losing business to suburban branches. In 1967 branch sales amounted to 54 percent of the total department store business, but by 1976 this figure was up to nearly 78 percent.[28] In the fall of 1976 Baltimore's Hochschild Kohn Company closed the sixth floor at its downtown flagship store, thereby reducing sales space by 17 percent, and at the same time the nearby Hutzler Brothers Company eliminated 20 percent of the selling area at its downtown outlet. Hutzlers' president expressed the view of most central-city merchants when he said, "Downtown business is far from good, far from easy . . . I don't know who is really doing a job [of bringing back sales;] some sources are beginning to show a turnaround but I don't know if there's enough of it."[29]

Changing patterns of residence and heightened fears of crime also forced the closing of many grand downtown movie palaces. Traditionally, these theaters had a monopoly on first-run films, but by the 1970s movie distributors were introducing their wares at new suburban houses. White, middle-class customers thus eschewed the trip to the distant and dangerous downtown, leaving the older theaters in the core to concentrate on porno films and black "exploitation" pictures characterized by a heavy dose of violence. Writing in 1975 of the downtown theaters, a Chicago journalist complained, "These scummy joints draw the kind of negative people who make honest folk uneasy if not downright petrified." According to this bitter observer, the "mere presence" of "the mopes who patronize[d] . . . the skin flicks and the palaces of sadistic violence . . . suffice[d] to scare off people."[30] In Boston the proximity of the porno strip "Combat Zone" to the traditional theater district did little to encourage an influx of middle-class patrons. Prostitutes, muggers, and pickpockets gradually spread outward from the Combat Zone, working the theaters as well as the streets. In fact, one bold prostitute even solicited Mayor Kevin White in a theater lobby. Then the well-publicized stabbing of two Harvard football players in the Combat Zone leveled one more telling blow to downtown nightlife. By late 1976 the show business journal *Variety* was reporting, "Fear blitzes downtown Boston," resulting in "a particularly deserted city at night."[31]

In each of the older central cities, however, the porno and black exploitation films were just the last act in the gradual demise of the downtown movie theaters. Owners invested as little as possible in maintenance, waiting for office developers to relieve them of these white elephants. Meanwhile, city building inspectors harassed theater managers, and even die-hard fans of perversion and sadism grew less willing to make the trip downtown.[32] Between 1971 and 1977 the capacity of Chicago's downtown movie houses dropped 8,697 seats, or 36 percent.[33] When the 3,000-seat Oriental closed, *Chicago Tribune* movie critic Gene Siskel described a visit a year earlier to that theater's mezzanine, where he had "found foot-high trash from God knows when filling every row." Siskel also debated with the critic for the *Chicago Daily News* over whether a mouse or rat had crossed their path at the State Lake Theater.[34]

Movie houses were also disappearing from Detroit's downtown theater strip. The Family Theater had become the Follies, "a porno grind house," prior to its destruction by fire in 1973. One year later the last two theaters on the strip faced the wrecker's ball.[35] At the close of 1975 Minneapolis's 2,400-seat State Theater showed its last film, and the other establishments along Hennepin Avenue, the city's chief entertainment thoroughfare, switched to X-rated fare. Once described by a local newspaper as an "Italian Renaissance extravaganza," in 1978 the State Theater was sold to the fundamentalist Jesus People Church as an interim headquarters until the congregation could build a suitable structure in the suburbs.[36] In

1977 developers slated Cleveland's Embassy and Roxy theaters for razing, the Roxy having recently specialized in what *Variety* labeled "sexplicity" films. With their closing, downtown Cleveland could claim only one movie house offering matinees and a small-scale twin theater in a new apartment and shopping complex.[37]

Even more discouraging to downtown boosters was the decline in demand for new office space during the early 1970s. Both downtown retailing and the movie business had been skidding downward since World War II; thus the problems of Hochschild Kohn, Hutzlers', the Roxy, and the Oriental were nothing new. But the one bright spot in the downtown scene during the late 1950s and the 1960s had been the office building boom. Politicians, journalists, and business leaders had cited this as concrete evidence that the central business district was reviving and not dying. Now, however, even this vital sign of life was growing faint as the economic recessions of the early 1970s discouraged construction starts and the opening of new office behemoths begun in the 1960s produced a glut of office space. Moreover, suburban office parks were drawing an increasing number of tenants, and corporations were abandoning the congested, crime-ridden urban core and erecting new headquarters in sylvan campus-like settings convenient to the executives' homes along the metropolitan fringe. In cities throughout the nation, downtown was accounting for less of the metropolitan office space, and fewer steel skeletons of future office towers were appearing on the central-city horizon.

After two decades of booming office construction, the slowdown of the early 1970s hit New York City especially hard. By late 1973, the vacancy rate for Manhattan office buildings was estimated at 12 percent compared with less than 3 percent in the halcyon days of the late 1950s and early 1960s.[38] Moreover, the mammoth 110-story World Trade Center in lower Manhattan added nine million square feet of new office space during the mid-1970s so that by 1975 the vacancy rate for New York City was almost 21 percent, the worst figure since the depths of the 1930s depression.[39] The 44-story office tower at 1166 Avenue of the Americas was a monument to the debacle of Manhattan real estate. Completed in late 1974, it failed to attract tenants, and four years later it still stood empty. Dubbed the "towering fiasco" by one journalist, 1166 was a visible reminder throughout the mid-1970s that the once insatiable market for Manhattan office space could indeed be sated.[40]

Exacerbating the problems of New York landlords and office developers was the exodus of corporate headquarters during the late 1960s and early 1970s. In the late 1950s and early 1960s New York's share of Fortune 500 headquarters had remained relatively constant with the city claiming 140 of the 500 in 1956 and 139 in 1967. In 1967, however, the mass flight from Manhattan began, and by 1974 only 98 of the 500 largest industrial corporations still maintained their headquarters in the central city.[41] Within a ten-day period in February 1967 both American Can Company and Pepsi-Cola disclosed plans to transfer their international headquarters to the suburbs; Olin Mathieson announced that it would shift the offices of a large chemical group to Connecticut; and Bohn Business Machines revealed that it expected to move its headquarters to the metropolitan fringe as soon as it could locate adequate office space.[42] Moreover, that same month the chairman of the board of the world's largest location consultant reported that 14 corporations employing a total of about 11,500 persons were considering a transfer of their headquarters from New York City.[43]

Similar reports were commonplace during the late 1960s and early 1970s as corporations abandoned New York City for a variety of reasons. Some cited high taxes, the need for more space, or the desirability of an office site closer to the homes of middle-class office personnel. Others complained of the dearth of adequate clerical workers among the increasingly poor, unskilled, and unreliable population of the central city. But underlying the decision of many corporations to move was what the *New York Times* referred to as "the general socio-economic problems of the city."[44] In 1967 a leading expert on corporate location reiterated this view, citing "the commutation problem, the rising crime rate, swollen welfare rolls and the subway strike" as factors in the flight of headquarters from New York. "They all add up to the same thing," the expert observed. "New York is not a happy place to be."[45] Thus corporate executives were coming to the same conclusion as the middle-class resident, the shopper, and the retailer. Fun City was no fun; it was not a desirable place to live or work, and it was getting worse rather than better.

Though the departure of corporations was more dramatic in New York City than elsewhere, it was a phenomenon common to other declining central cities as well. Between 1956 and 1974 the number of Fortune 500 headquarters in Chicago dropped from 47 to 33, in Pittsburgh the figure fell from 22 to 15, in Detroit from 18 to 6, and in Philadelphia from 14 to 8.[46] Some of the change was owing to the new importance of corporations headquartered in southern and western cities, but as in the New York area, suburbia was also undermining the significance of the older urban hubs as corporate capitals. For example, in 1971 General Dynamics Corporation announced that it was moving its headquarters from New York City to the Saint Louis area, stirring new hopes in the oft-disappointed Missouri city. The Saint Louis municipal development commissioner found three possible downtown locations for the General Dynamics offices, and Mayor Cervantes personally interceded with the chairman of the board to woo the company to the central business district. Moreover, the private booster group Downtown St. Louis headed by the president of the city's largest department store, joined in the campaign to lure General Dynamics to the urban core. In the end, however, General Dynamics announced that it would locate its headquarters in suburban Clayton. According to the *St. Louis Post-Dispatch*, "Clayton, seemingly without even trying, had won."[47] This was a scenario replayed in one city after another. Mayor Lindsay exhorted and Mayor Cervantes pleaded, but corporate trophies fell into the lap of suburban communities that sometimes did not even want office complexes.

Not only could other central cities empathize with New York City's distress over corporate flight, they were also experiencing the same slowdown in office demand that was forcing Manhattan landlords and developers into bankruptcy. New York's plight was the worst, but Chicago's vacancy rate rose from 4 percent in 1970 to 12 percent in 1974 to almost 17 percent in 1975.[48] Just as construction of the World Trade Center added to the office inventory of New York at exactly the wrong moment, so the completion in 1973 of the world's tallest office building, the Sears Tower, created excessive space that depressed the Chicago market through the mid-1970s. In February 1975 a real estate analyst concluded, "It seems clear that we face a period of reduced construction activity in the office market in Chicago." Expressing the uncertainty of the period, she observed, "Whether this slackening turns out to be a deep sleep, as in the 1930s, or merely a pause for breath before a new era of rapid expansion, only time will tell."[49]

Builders were heeding her words, for in 1975, for the first time in seven years, no new office space opened in downtown Chicago, and the same was true in 1977. Only 4.1 million square feet of new space opened from 1974 through 1977 compared with 18.9 million square feet for 1970 through 1973.[50] In Boston a similar pattern prevailed, though the New England metropolis's building drought struck slightly later. After the completion of a record amount of office space in 1975, little new activity followed, with no space added in 1978 and 1979. Whereas from 1972 through 1975 Boston witnessed the opening of 6.7 million square feet, from 1976 through 1979 the figure dropped to 1.4 million.[51] Similarly, in Minneapolis, downtown office construction was sluggish after completion of the giant IDS Tower in 1973 with only one new office site in 1974 and none in 1975 and 1976.[52] In 1974 the city planning director claimed that a "wait-and-see attitude" prevailed among Minneapolis developers.[53] As in

Chicago and the other older cities, caution rather than optimism seemed to be the watchword of the Minnesota metropolis.

Caution yielded to abject pessimism when urban observers turned their attention to the fortunes of central-city manufacturing. As is evident from table 17, between 1967 and 1977 the long decline in manufacturing was not abating; if anything, it was accelerating. From 1947 to 1967 New York City had lost 175,000 manufacturing jobs, but during the next ten years it lost almost 286,000. Between 1950 and 1967 manufacturing employment in Boston dropped 21 percent; from 1967 to 1977 it fell 36 percent.[54] Each of the older central cities lost thousands of factory jobs in the late 1960s and early 1970s with Philadelphia suffering the sharpest decline and Cincinnati recording the best retention rate. Yet even the Queen City of Ohio had almost one-quarter fewer manufacturing jobs by 1977 than it had ten years earlier. Cincinnati's record was miserable; Philadelphia's was horrendous.

Moreover, this loss occurred despite central-city efforts to preserve local industry. Ironically, Philadelphia had organized one of the first and most highly acclaimed programs for retaining manufacturing concerns. The city sponsored a land bank that offered vacant tracts to existing establishments needing room for expansion and to new firms willing to make Philadelphia their home. In 1967 New York City also created a munici-

Table 17. Manufacturing Employment, 1967 and 1977

City	No. of Employees (1,000)		% Change 1967–1977
	1967	1977	
New York	895.3	609.7	−31.9
Chicago	546.9	366.0	−33.1
Philadelphia	263.9	157.5	−40.3
Detroit	209.7	153.3	−26.9
Baltimore	106.7	72.9	−31.7
Cleveland	171.3	120.8	−29.5
Saint Louis	131.9	92.6	−29.8
Boston	79.6	50.9	−36.1
Pittsburgh	85.6	55.3	−35.4
Buffalo	66.7	46.4	−30.4
Cincinnati	84.5	64.4	−23.8
Minneapolis	69.2	52.0	−24.9

Sources: U.S. Bureau of the Census, U.S. censuses of manufactures for 1967, 1972, and 1977 (Washington, D.C.: U.S. Government Printing Office, 1971, 1976, and 1981).

pally financed industrial renewal program that assembled land and made it available for development. According to enthusiastic city planners, during the first four-and-a-half years of its existence, the industrial renewal program was responsible for providing 10,000 new manufacturing jobs.[55] Overall, however, the city lost about 130,000 manufacturing positions during these initial years of the program. In other words, the city's initiative to halt the outward flow of factories and jobs hardly made a difference. New York was attempting to dam a flood with a handful of sand.

By the early 1970s the inadequacy of other urban renewal programs was also becoming painfully evident. With downtown stores languishing, the office market depressed, and central-city manufacturing disappearing, many of the big projects initiated in the early 1960s seemed to be frauds, and others appeared to have fallen far short of success. Urban renewal was supposed to buoy the city's fortunes, restore its vitality, and reverse the centrifugal flow of people and dollars. In the early 1970s the returns were in on the much-ballyhooed projects, and too often the urban renewal initiative seemed to have missed its objectives. Urban renewal had not halted decline or forced the cancer of blight into remission. Instead, many of the great federally funded projects had joined the list of central-city failures. They had not demonstrated the continuing strength of the central city; they had proved that even federal dollars and grandiose plans could not stay the powerful forces of decay.

Typical of the urban renewal doldrums of the early 1970s was the experience of Minneapolis. According to the original renewal contract, the redevelopment of thirty-three-acre Gateway Center was supposed to be completed by 1971. Instead, by that date only 60 percent of the land had been redeveloped with the other 40 percent devoted to unsightly parking lots. Moreover, only three buildings had been started in the previous five years, one of which was a parking ramp. The *Minneapolis Tribune* reminded its readers, "Not many years ago, the Minneapolis Gateway redevelopment project was being hailed nationally as an example of how a city could rebuild its blighted lower downtown business district." Yet the newspaper sadly observed, "Today, the project is nearly at a standstill."[56]

Newer projects were also bogged down. In 1975 the lack of any progress on the Nicollet Lake and Loring Park schemes became a campaign issue in the municipal election. The city had borrowed $29 million for investment in the two projects with increased tax revenues from the redeveloped districts expected to cover debt expenses. But there was no redevelopment or any additional revenues, so the city was left with a hefty bill for interest and principal payments.[57] Proposals for a new downtown domed stadium also were generating more talk than construction, and doomsayers were daily predicting the imminent departure of the Twins and Vikings.[58]

Meanwhile, the long-awaited Cedar-Riverside "new town-in town" was welcoming its first tenants. Expected to offer an exciting new experience in urban living with mixed-income high-rise housing, cultural and recreational facilities, community organizations, and retail establishments, during its planning stages, the Cedar-Riverside project attracted attention from admirers throughout the country. Its developers claimed that the project promised "a new dream[,] a new meaning" for the neighborhood, where "a new kind of urban life [was] emerging. A life filled with involvement. Filled with vitality that [could] only be measured by the depth and breadth of experience." Yet a survey of the initial residents in 1974 found that only 45 percent regarded the project as a distinct improvement over their previous housing, and 27 percent viewed it as a poorer housing environment. Moreover, that same year tenants organized a rent strike against the developer, and a lawsuit citing the adverse environmental impact of the giant high-rise project resulted in an injunction halting construction of its second stage. At the same time, the federal Department of Housing and Urban Development labeled the project as "clearly not viable," and foreclosure loomed over all plans for completion.[59] By 1975 the promise of nirvana in Minnesota had collapsed.

But Minneapolis was not the only city where projects were stalled or producing unexpected consequences. Planners had scheduled completion of the first stage of Cleveland's Erieview project for 1965, but, in fact, it was not officially closed out until 1973, and only in 1983 was construction actually finished. Developers of Erieview's largest apartment complex, with 990 luxury units, defaulted on mortgage payments soon after its opening in 1973, discouraging further investment in downtown housing for the upper middle class.[60] No developers were willing to carry out the original plan for housing construction in the Saint Vincent project south of downtown Cleveland, causing the city to reallocate the land to such tax-exempt institutions as a community college and a hospital. As a result, the assessed taxable valuation of the tract dropped from $2.4 million before redevelopment to $2.1 million afterward.[61]

By 1968 redevelopers had built only 16 percent of the expected new construction in Philadelphia's mammoth Eastwick project, and in the early 1970s city officials were proposing to use the empty expanses of the once-heralded "new town-in town" for a world's fair to commemorate the bicentennial of American independence. Yet even the plans for a fair failed, and Philadelphia neither cashed in on its historic significance in 1976 nor profited as expected from the Eastwick scheme.[62] Meanwhile, during the early 1970s, the city could not find a developer for the Market East project, a retail and office development proposed in 1961 for Philadelphia's main downtown thoroughfare. In early 1974 the city finance director said the delay was owing to a glut of office space and a lack of confidence among the business community. "Business abhors uncertainty," he noted, "and we all realize we are in a tremendously uncertain period."[63] In addition, court suits and investor reluctance had halted any work on the $100 million Penn's Landing scheme, which had been designed as a complex of apartments, offices, and stores on 22.5 acres of landfill along the Delaware River waterfront.[64]

Similar disappointments troubled Saint Louis. In 1972 Saint Louis's Mansion House luxury apartment project went into default, proving that in the Missouri metropolis as in Cleveland very few of those with money enough to escape would remain downtown after working hours.[65] By 1975 the *St. Louis Post-Dispatch* was reporting of the once-vaunted renewal project, "In Mansion House's nine years, there have been no payments on the principal to either the Government (which now holds the mortgage) [or] the previous note holders." The newspaper concluded that Mansion House had "become, for the Federal Government, a colossal throbbing headache—and perhaps even a monument to questionable planning."[66] Though the landmark Gateway Arch was finally open to tourists and the Cardinals were playing in the new downtown Busch Stadium, Saint Louis's revival efforts were especially jinxed. In 1969 Mayor Cervantes secured a full-scale replica of Columbus's flagship, the Santa Maria, as a tourist attraction to be moored along the Saint Louis riverfront adjacent to the Arch. The ship drew good crowds until one windy day it broke loose from its moorings and smashed into the Illinois shore.[67] The sunken hulk seemed to symbolize the fortunes of Saint Louis. By the early 1970s the city was sinking fast, and neither large sums of federal money nor bold luxury apartment schemes appeared able to keep it afloat.

Even the most highly acclaimed renaissance cities of past decades seemed to have lost whatever renewal momentum they had once built up. During the early 1970s, the renaissance showcase of the 1950s, Pittsburgh, had, according to one local journalist, "arrived at a period in which things were leveling off." The executive director of the Allegheny Conference blamed the stagnation on Mayor Peter Flaherty. "A few months after Mayor Flaherty took office in 1970 everything was over," the irate director claimed, "all progress came to a standstill." And, he continued, "A great and powerful city came under the power of a nitwit."[68] Obviously, the long-standing alliance between city hall and the business moguls sponsoring the Allegheny Conference had collapsed, and the euphoria of the past had vanished. Boston had shared Pittsburgh's renaissance laurels during the 1960s when Edward Logue had presided over the redevelopment authority. But in 1967 Logue resigned, and a string of less dynamic chiefs succeeded him. One planning expert wrote of "the degenerative process in which talent and fervor drained away following Logue's exodus, to be replaced, for the most part, by a pyramidal mass of mediocrities."[69] By the early 1970s Boston, like Pittsburgh, was no longer on the cutting edge of redevelopment.

As in earlier years there were some redevelopment success stories to brighten urban prospects. The favorable response to Minneapolis's construction of a landscaped mall open only to pedestrian and bus traffic along Nicollet Avenue compensated somewhat for the sluggish progress at Gateway Center and for the stadium stalemate. Philadelphia's Society Hill was attracting investment even if Eastwick was not. And Boston's Government Center was winning kudos from critics long after Logue's departure from the New England metropolis. Yet both developers and the general public had witnessed too many failures, and they were proceeding warily. Few persons were confident that a new and better future invariably lay ahead; instead, renewal seemed a hit-and-miss proposition that might yield rewards but also might prove a bust. All recognized that despite numerous redevelopment projects blight continued to spread and decentralization persisted.

Faced with the gloomy figures on abandonment, retail sales, construction starts, job loss, and redevelopment defaults, by the mid-1970s some commentators were already writing off certain aging cities. In late 1973 a Rand Corporation study advised Saint Louis to forget its past pretensions as the dominant regional hub and accept the realistic role of "one suburb among many in metropolitan St. Louis."[70] According to the experts at Rand, the city would "most likely continue to decline," and the option of becoming "one of many large suburban centers of economic and residential life [held] more promise than reviving the traditional central city functions."[71] In 1976 a former city administrator advised "planned shrinkage" of New York City's population, economy, and municipal services and argued for the desirability of this course because "the golden door to full participation in American life and the American economy [was] no longer to be found in New York."[72] Saint Louis was only a suburb, and New York should plan for a more humble position in the constellation of world cities. After more than three decades of efforts to revive the older central cities, defeatism rather than renewal was ascendant.

Fiscal Crisis

Not only was the 1970s a period of residential abandonment, retail decline, depressed demand for office space, and deflated dreams, it was also an era of fiscal crisis in the older central cities. Though the financial position of the aging hubs had been deteriorating in the 1960s, not since the Great Depression had the cities faced a money crunch as severe as that during the 1970s. Revenue sources were relatively stagnant, but the cost of municipal services was soaring. The consequence was bankruptcy for a few major cities, and many anxious moments for public officials in all of the older centers. Moreover, the headlines about possible default and proposed layoffs of municipal employees just added to the evidence that America's aging central cities were dying, not reviving.

Underlying the difficulties was the weakening tax base of the central cities. Though prices were rising sharply during the early 1970s, assessed valuations in the older cities were not. In part this was owing to a blight-induced decline in property values in many neighborhoods, but assessors also were failing to raise valuations sufficiently to keep up with the increasing market worth of land and buildings. Sharply increased assessments were politically unpopular, and consequently the property tax traditionally was not as responsive to inflationary trends as were the sales or income taxes. Between 1970 and 1975 the assessed valuations of Saint Louis, Cleveland, and Chicago actually fell, with the Windy City's tax base shrinking by $440 million. By 1975 the assessed value of property in Cleveland was $36 million less than it had been in 1959 and $70 million less than in 1969. The taxable worth of Saint Louis was likewise less in 1975 than it had been twenty years earlier, and it dropped every year from 1970 through 1977. Some cities benefited from a modest rise in assessed valuation. In Baltimore it inched up 1 percent between 1970 and 1975; Detroit's taxable worth increased 9 percent during the same period; and Pittsburgh's tax base expanded by 10 percent.[73] Yet this was hardly adequate during an era when the consumer price index climbed from 3 percent to 11 percent annually.

Exacerbating the problem was the pressure to increase municipal expenditures. For example, in response to the persistent rise in street crime, urban dwellers demanded more police protection, and this translated into more police officers and higher personnel costs. In 1974 Chicago's police force was 11 percent larger than in 1970; Baltimore's had 14 percent more personnel; and in the much-abused murder capital of Detroit, there were 17 percent more police employees. Perhaps no city was so security conscious as Cincinnati, which beefed up its police force by 26 percent between 1970 and 1975. Moreover, militant union action and inflation pushed the wages of public employees ever higher. Between 1970 and 1974 the mean maximum salary of city police in the United States rose almost 31 percent, and the maximum salary for firefighters climbed 29 percent.[74] With more personnel earning higher wages and a stagnant tax base, the older central cities were obviously headed for trouble.

Evidence of worsening financial conditions was readily apparent throughout the early 1970s. In 1969 Saint Louis's comptroller claimed that the budget proposal for the coming year revealed "the greatest fiscal crisis in the city's recent history."[75] To deal with the yawning revenue gap, the city imposed a 1 percent local sales tax that was expected to ensure financial solvency in the future. But in 1971 the *Saint Louis Post-Dispatch* was again reporting "City Hall talk of drastic budget cuts, stiff tax increases and a year-end deficit of several million dollars." The city budget director admitted, "It seems impossible that we could be in such a desperate financial situation within just a year."[76] Moreover, the problem would persist with Saint Louis running a deficit for three of the four years from 1971 through 1974, including a record $10.7 million shortfall in the latter year.[77]

Pessimists in Philadelphia perceived equally discouraging signals of fiscal distress. In 1971 the Federal Reserve Bank of Philadelphia published a study that predicted "greatly increased fiscal deficits for City and School government in Philadelphia—reaching a half billion dollars for the year 1975." "The deficits of all the years between now and 1975," the study argued, "could cumulate to over one-and-a-quarter-billion dollars."[78] In 1971 the city government of Philadelphia did record a deficit of $28.7 million, and the following year the school district ran $36.2 million in the red. Increased intergovernmental payments from Washington and Harrisburg staved off disaster during the next few years, but in April 1975 the Federal Reserve Bank published another report that claimed "the revenue/cost pinch appears to be as tight as ever."[79]

Meanwhile, the cities of Baltimore and Buffalo were facing even more dire financial straits. Confronted by a four-week-old teacher's strike, the likelihood of tough salary demands by other municipal employees in the near future, and revenues growing only 1 percent annually in recent years, by the spring of 1974 the Maryland metropolis had become, in the words of the city council president, a "textbook case of what the term 'urban crisis' is all about." "If our taxes go up much more," the council executive complained, "I know a number of businessmen who have a choice—either get out or go broke."[80] Already property taxes were far higher in Baltimore than in surrounding suburban counties. The city's northern border ran down the center of Willowglen Drive. Middle-class home-owners on the north, or county, side of the street paid about $900 each year in property taxes, but holders of similar houses on the south, or city side, were levied $1,200 annually.[81] Yet even the higher taxes imposed on city dwellers were not sufficient to balance the municipal books.

Matters were equally dismal in upstate New York. In 1974 Buffalo's Finance Commissioner was almost ready to give up, suggesting only partly in jest to one interviewer, "Perhaps we should just take the charter and the keys, send them to Albany, and say 'Okay, you solve it. We can't do any more.' "[82] The city's assessed valuation for 1973–74 was $6 million less than for 1964–65, and there was no sign that the figure was about to turn sharply upward.[83] Moreover, the Penn Central railroad's recent bankruptcy hit the city especially hard. "A lot of real estate in the city is owned by Penn Central," the finance commissioner noted, "but we can't touch it. [Instead,] we are in line with others waiting for bankruptcy proceedings against the railroad to be completed, [but] in the meantime we can't collect $6-million in unpaid taxes."[84] Thus insolvency in the private sector was drawing the public sector closer to the brink of bankruptcy.

During the early 1970s, city officials attempted to cope with the fiscal crunch in a number of ways. One temporary solution was the divestment of municipal assets and responsibilities. No city pursued this course so actively as Cleveland. From 1971 to 1977 Ralph Perk served as mayor of the Ohio metropolis after winning office with promises not to raise taxes. Through sale of certain municipal properties and transfer of functions, Perk was able to compensate, at least in part, for the lack of tax revenues. Cleveland had traditionally provided sewage treatment services for both suburban and city residents, but by 1970 the city's failure to adequately treat wastes forced the Ohio Water Pollution Control Board to impose a ban on additional sewer connections, thereby holding up construction projects in the suburbs. To resolve the problem, the city and suburbs agreed to the creation of a metropolitan sewer authority that henceforth would govern the disposal of wastes in Cleveland and thirty-nine other municipalities. The authority paid the central city $35 million for its existing sewage treatment facilities, a sum that Perk quickly applied to the general debt service payments and operating costs of his hard-pressed municipality.[85] Then in 1975 county voters approved the creation of the Regional Transit Authority, which purchased the city-owned Cleveland Transit System for $8.9 million.[86] Moreover, Perk secured city council approval for the sale of the municipally owned electric power plant, though this decision to divest was later reversed. Within a few years, however, Cleveland had transferred its control over sewerage and mass transportation to regional authorities in exchange for a much-needed $44 million.

Saint Louis was similarly seeking to shift some of the burden of government to suburban taxpayers. Traditionally, only the city had provided tax revenue for the local zoo and art museum, with central-city property owners annually paying four cents for every $100 of assessed value for the art museum alone. Suburban residents used the facilities but did not contribute to their tax support. Like virtually everything in the central city of Saint Louis, by 1971 the zoo and museum were in sad shape. The museum's director said, "We are not able to make a single purchase [of a work of art] out of the tax money we receive because our operating budget is pared to the bone."[87] Since the museum lacked air-conditioning or humidity control, any works that were obtained suffered from destructive fluctuations in climate. The former president of the zoo board warned, "The unvarnished truth is that sooner or later those institutions will die [without tax funding from suburbia]."[88]

To remedy the situation, supporters of the museum and zoo proposed transferring ownership of the institutions to a new metropolitan district that would levy taxes on both city and suburban residents. On election day voters in both city and suburbs approved the proposal, relieving Saint Louis of further responsibility for the zoo and museum. In the future the two institutions could draw not only on the city's shrinking tax base but on the expanding resources of suburbia.

Another solution to budgetary problems was simply cutting back on personnel and paring city payrolls. Most mayors avoided this obvious move until all other budgetary maneuvers had been exhausted. But Pittsburgh's Peter Flaherty made payroll slashing the hallmark of his mayoral career and was the most successful budget cutter of the early 1970s. On assuming office in 1970 Flaherty rated Pittsburgh's fiscal problems as his greatest challenge and told reporters, "We're going to watch the budget closely," and "Nobody should ever think he is guaranteed a permanent job."[89] By the end of his first term many realized the impermanence of municipal employment, for Flaherty had cut the city's payroll from 7,000 to 5,400.[90] At the close of 1970 the mayor frankly told the city council: "Let us be candid—hundreds of jobs on the payroll were political . . . in addition, hundreds of jobs were placed on the payroll because each year in the past certain favored labor leaders were permitted to add jobs into the budget as favors to their friends." Now the mayor promised to "weed out all unnecessary personnel," and he kept his promise.[91]

In contrast with many other older central cities the Flaherty administration even slashed the number of police officers, reducing the force from 1,797 in 1970 to 1,535 in 1974. Every year from 1971 through 1975 the property tax rate for Pittsburgh residents dropped, and each year from 1970 through 1974 the city closed its books with a surplus.[92] An appreciative electorate awarded Flaherty both the Democratic and Republican nomination for mayor in 1973, an unprecedented feat in the steel capital.

But not everyone was so enamored with the money-conscious mayor. His Democratic primary opponent had the support of the municipal employee organizations, and the business community was cool toward Flaherty because of his failure to back costly renewal projects. A leading critic of the mayor, the *Pittsburgh Post-Gazette* claimed, "The Flaherty Administration has piled up surpluses by deferring expenditures for major maintenance, a plague for future administrations." According to the newspaper, Flaherty had headed "a sort of caretaker government," and it urged him to change his attitude and "lead Pittsburgh to face the harder tasks necessary to beat the pressing urban problems of the 1970s and beyond."[93] Many taxpayers, however, were thankful for a mayor who provided present services at a low cost and did not invest tax money in expensive initiatives for future greatness.

Flaherty's dedication to fiscal restraint made him something of an anomaly among the big-city mayors of the early 1970s. But dire financial straits did force some other executives to cut back at least temporarily. Cleveland's Mayor Perk resorted to layoffs, and in 1972 he asked public safety employees to accept a 10 percent wage deferrment.[94] Faced with a cancer that "could be terminal unless the fiscal structure of [Boston] undergoes major surgery," in 1971 Mayor Kevin White told the city council that "no vacancies in nonessential positions will be filled" in the hope of reducing "the city's payroll by 500 employees."[95] Two years later in a statewide television address and in his annual message to the council, White announced, "The city work force will be cut by 10 percent," though he intended to achieve this goal through retirement incentives "as well as absolute cuts and discharges."[96] In Buffalo, Mayor Stanley Makowski eliminated more than eight hundred city jobs, but he did not share Mayor Flaherty's enthusiasm for budget slashing.[97] Prior to 1975 necessity might have required an unwelcome sacrifice of municipal employees, yet nowhere were economy and fiscal conservatism so highly touted as in thrifty Pittsburgh.

In fact, for all of Mayor White's bluster, Boston's complement of employees did not diminish during the early 1970s nor did the corps of municipal workers in eight other of the twelve older central cities. As seen in table 18, only in hard-pressed Cleveland and Buffalo as well as in Flaherty's Pittsburgh were there declines in the numbers of city em-

Table 18. Number of City Employees, 1970 and 1974

City	No. of Employees	
	1970	1974
New York	415,392	447,504
Chicago	45,333	45,376
Philadelphia	35,762	38,274
Detroit	26,681	27,574
Baltimore	37,944	39,924
Cleveland	16,159	13,460
Boston	24,871	27,288
Saint Louis	13,965	14,037
Pittsburgh	7,308	6,058
Buffalo	14,395	13,995
Cincinnati	16,041	18,065
Minneapolis	5,645	5,991

Sources: U.S. Bureau of the Census, *City Employment in 1970*, and *City Employment in 1974* (Washington, D.C.: U.S. Government Printing Office, 1971 and 1975).

ployees. Though the population was falling in each of these urban centers, city leaders were still attempting to maintain the full roster of civil servants.

Most city officials strongly preferred borrowing money to bitter clashes with well-organized municipal employees dedicated to keeping their jobs and winning pay raises. Especially in New York City, short-term borrowing was the most common device for covering budget deficits and keeping the municipal government seemingly solvent. From 1969 to 1970 New York City's outstanding short-term debt rose 72 percent, climbing from $747 million to $1,288 million. Then it soared 80 percent between 1970 and 1971, and by 1974 it was up to $3,416 million.[98] Borrowing was becoming an increasingly important crutch for the city's crippled finances. Whereas in 1970 short-term debt equaled 18.9 percent of the city's total revenue, by 1973 this figure was up to 24.4 percent.[99] Because of its heavy reliance on short-term paper to pay municipal bills, during the early 1970s, New York City consistently accounted for about one-quarter of all the outstanding short-term state and local indebtedness in the nation.

Most of the older municipalities were not becoming as addicted to the quick fix of borrowing as was New York City, but in some of the other urban hubs necessity also forced reliance on short-term loans. Boston's short-term debt amounted to $85 million in 1970 and $130 million in

1971; the city's total annual revenues during these years averaged only about $400 million.[100] Mayor Perk's administration in Cleveland was also relying on borrowed funds to pay operating expenses, issuing $45 million in bonds and notes in 1972 and $65 million in 1974.[101] By 1973 short-term debt amounted to 29 percent of total revenues in Cleveland, a figure even more ominous than that of New York City.[102] Meanwhile, Buffalo was another city unusually dependent on short-term borrowing, accumulating heavy debt obligations that had to be refunded or repaid at frequent intervals.

Rather than borrowing, an obvious solution to budget problems was raising taxes. Yet this was no more popular among city leaders than slashing payrolls. In some cities revenue shortfalls forced a hike in the property tax with Baltimore's rate rising 19 percent from 1969–70 to 1972–73 and Buffalo's soaring 44 percent over the same period.[103] Traditionally burdened with the highest property tax rate of all the older cities, Boston was in no danger of losing this dubious distinction as its levy increased by an extraordinary 115 percent over the decade from 1967 to 1977.[104] In some cities, such as Philadelphia, assessments lagged behind market values, meaning that the effective rate actually dropped.[105] Moreover, in Cleveland the restive citizenry voted a sharp reduction in the city's property levy.[106] If taxes had to be raised, most mayors preferred to avoid the property tax alternative and opt for a multitude of less offensive levies and charges. For example, in his 1972 budget Chicago's Richard Daley chose "to avoid increasing the burden on the property taxpayer" and instead proposed a new municipal cigarette tax of two cents per package and a levy on parking facilities of fifteen cents per automobile.[107] Likewise, in 1971, when the new 1 percent sales tax proved insufficient to solve the budget problems of Saint Louis, Mayor Cervantes recommended a hike in the public utility tax, an additional one cent per pack for the cigarette tax, and an increase in the charges for city permits.[108]

Divestment of assets and functions, payroll pruning, borrowing, and new taxes were all possible alternatives for momentarily piecing together a balanced budget, but the favorite solution for virtually all mayors and budget directors was increased intergovernmental aid. During the early 1970s as in the late 1960s, the cries for help from the state and federal levels were loud and persistent with one mayor after another testifying in Washington, Harrisburg, Columbus, and Albany in support of additional state and federal funding for the cities. Congressional approval of general revenue sharing in 1972 was a boon to the money-hungry central cities, and other windfalls from the federal and state treasuries also staved off bankruptcy in the first half of the 1970s.

As seen in table 19, by 1975–76 New York City, Baltimore, and Buffalo derived more than half of their general revenues from other levels of government, with the latter two obtaining almost two-thirds of their funds from intergovernmental sources. In each of the twelve older central cities, with the exception of Chicago and Boston, intergovernmental payments accounted for a larger share of general revenues than property tax receipts, and only in Saint Louis did nonproperty taxes outrank aid from other governmental units. In less than a decade the role of the federal and state governments in central-city finances had changed markedly. Now the fortunes of Detroit, Pittsburgh, and Cincinnati seemed to depend less on local tax assessments than on their clout in the halls of Congress and the lobbies of the state legislatures.

Despite the extraordinary boost in state and federal funding, mayors were still berating state and federal lawmakers for their failure to adequately aid the cities. In 1970 Saint Louis's Alfonso Cervantes complained of the financial neglect of the cities compared with the lavish expenditures on space exploration, claiming, "The equipment which was jettisoned by the astronauts prior to re-entry cost enough money to run our entire City government for two or more years."[109] Two years later Boston's Kevin White charged, "Our tax resources are robbed by the state and federal government," contending, "For every $25 Boston contributes to the state and federal governments we receive back in aid only $1."[110] In 1974 Buf-

Table 19. Sources of General Revenue, 1975–1976

City	Property Taxes (%)	Nonproperty Taxes (%)	Intergovernmental Aid (%)
New York	21.7	18.4	50.2
Chicago	29.8	28.7	29.0
Philadelphia	10.9	35.3	38.6
Detroit	20.9	17.9	45.3
Baltimore	17.3	8.2	65.3
Cleveland	15.8	22.4	26.7
Boston	45.7	0.4	42.2
Saint Louis	13.0	42.4	28.5
Pittsburgh	34.0	15.8	41.6
Buffalo	25.9	1.0	66.2
Cincinnati	5.7	15.4	43.3
Minneapolis	36.7	5.7	39.4

Source: U.S. Bureau of the Census, *City Government Finances in 1975–1976* (Washington, D.C.: U.S. Government Printing Office, 1977).

falo's Mayor Stanley Makowski asserted that "the last answer" to his city's fiscal problems had to be "found at the state level." According to Makowski: "We are creatures of the state—its children, if you will. If we cannot turn to our parent, where can we turn?"[111] Though Washington and Albany were paying more than 60 percent of the bills, that was not enough. The hard-pressed municipal offspring needed ever larger sums of parental aid to bridge the ever-widening revenue gaps.

One solution that state lawmakers could authorize was the creation of metropolitan tax-sharing districts. In 1971 Minnesota's legislature passed the Metropolitan Development Act providing for a sharing of the growth in the nonresidential tax base in the Twin Cities metropolitan area. Forty percent of the net increase in commercial-industrial valuations was to be placed in a regional pool, and then each governmental unit in the metropolitan area was allocated a share of the pooled valuation according to a formula based on population and per capita market value. Thus each governing unit shared in 40 percent of the rise in the nonresidential tax base no matter whether the growth occurred within its boundaries or not. For a central city like Minneapolis, where manufacturing establishments were moving out and tax values were rising slowly, the tax-base sharing plan was obviously a desirable reform. In 1977 an early proponent of the scheme wrote, "The growth which the city of Minneapolis has experienced in commercial-industrial evaluation since 1971 is almost solely due to the tax-base sharing law."[112] By 1978 Minneapolis was receiving about $40 million in valuation from the pool while contributing less than $500,000.[113]

The plan also attracted admirers outside of Minnesota. In 1973 Johns Hopkins University economists drafted a tax-base sharing plan for Baltimore that was proposed to an unsympathetic Maryland legislature.[114] Three years later Michigan's governor sponsored a similar scheme for the Detroit metropolitan area, but lawmakers in Lansing were no more enthusiastic about the plan than their counterparts in Annapolis.[115] During the 1970s, among the older central cities only Minneapolis benefited from tax-base sharing, but the scheme remained an alternative that other aging hubs could strive to achieve.

By 1975 a number of cities desperately needed some solutions to their fiscal problems, for local levies and existing state and federal payments would no longer suffice. Economic recession had once again slowed the nation's economy, increasing unemployment rates and cutting municipal revenues. One city after another faced unprecedented deficits, and the money market finally turned on the central cities, declaring them bad investments. In the 1960s and early 1970s older cities had found it increasingly difficult to match revenues and expenditures, and mayors and comptrollers had frequently told city councils and municipal employees that fiscal crisis loomed. But now debacle truly was at hand. The cities were going broke.

The collapse of New York City's finances in 1975 initiated the nationwide crisis. To cover revenue shortfalls, New York markedly increased its short-term borrowing in 1974; its outstanding short-term debt rose from $3.4 billion in June to $5.3 billion in November. As doubts about the city's financial soundness grew during the winter of 1974–75, banks and investment houses decided to forego further purchases of city notes. In February, Mayor Abraham Beame announced his proposed expense budget for 1975–76 with an estimated revenue gap of $1.68 billion, which he hoped to bridge with various financial maneuvers plus almost $900 million of hypothetical new federal and state aid. The *New York Times* responded by declaring, "This metropolis faces a fiscal crisis from which there can be no escape without drastic cuts in personnel and services and substantial increases in taxes."[116] No such cuts or increases were forthcoming from the Beame administration, and in the spring of 1975 the banks refused to refinance the city's maturing short-term debt, closing New York out of the financial markets. The nation's largest city was, in effect, bankrupt, a pariah to all lenders.

For the next four years New York City remained closed out of the money markets, and as a fiscal incompetent it became a ward of the state. The state legislature created the Municipal Assistance Corporation (MAC) to restructure the city's debt, and the Emergency Financial Control Board, dominated by state appointees, assumed control of the administration of city finances. MAC demanded heavy layoffs, a wage freeze, increased fares for public transportation, and an end to free tuition at City University, and the control board was likewise to insist on cutbacks in expenditures and increases in user fees. State intervention alone, however, was not sufficient, and in November 1975 the city also secured congressional approval for up to $2.3 billion of short-term loans from the federal government. At the close of 1975, economist Milton Friedman summed up the situation when he stated: "New York City is now being run by the caretakers appointed by the state of New York. At the moment New York doesn't have any self-government."[117]

Though beleaguered New York City grabbed the headlines in the mid-1970s, other cities were experiencing similar crises. At the close of 1976 Boston's Municipal Research Bureau was reporting on the "financial emergency" in the New England metropolis. The city had concluded its previous fiscal year with a $20.7 million deficit, and the bureau was predicting a $30 million shortfall for the current year.[118] Moreover, Boston's short-term borrowing to cover operating expenses increased markedly during 1976, and $30 million in notes remained unpaid at the close of the fiscal year.[119] With its heavy dependence on property tax levies, two consecutive years of declining real property valuation seemed especially ominous, and in 1976 overall valuation dropped for the first time since 1963.[120] To meet this emergency, the city raised property taxes 29 percent in 1977 and held the increase in general fund expenditures down to 2 percent. It also sold its water and sewer systems to a newly established independent commission, thereby relieving itself of the burden of funding water and sewer operating deficits and much-needed capital improvements.[121]

Financial matters were equally grim in Philadelphia. The City of Brotherly Love closed the 1975–76 fiscal year with a $73 million deficit, and the projected shortfall for the next year was $100 million. Responding to these figures, the city hiked local taxes an extraordinary 30 percent, raising the rate of both the wage and property levies. Despite this effort to ensure the city's financial integrity, the investment advisory firm of Moody's dropped Philadelphia's bond rating one notch, a decision that possibly meant the loss of millions of dollars because of added interest charges.[122] One journalist seriously discussed the merits of Philadelphia declaring bankruptcy. This observer was willing to relinquish rule to court-appointed administrators and like New York City temporarily abandon self-government.[123]

Throughout the country the house of cards of municipal financing seemed to be collapsing. According to Mayor Coleman Young, during the mid-1970s, Detroit had suffered "the worst budget crisis . . . since the 1930s."[124] With the city's unemployment rate averaging 20 percent, municipal income tax collections lagged, forcing Mayor Young to lay off about one-fifth of the city payroll in 1975. In his "state of the city" message in January 1976, Young predicted a revenue shortfall of $50 million and warned: "Sometime in March, just to meet the payroll, the city of Detroit will have to borrow $64 million. That's three times as much money as we've ever borrowed before."[125] To blunt the impact of the fiscal emergency, state aid to Detroit more than doubled between 1975 and 1978 with the state largely assuming the city's former share of the financing of the Detroit Institute of Arts and the main branch of the Detroit Public Library system.[126]

In May 1975 the *New York Times* correctly described Buffalo as "on everybody's list of cities in serious financial trouble."[127] Buffalo's budget director complained that delinquencies in property tax collections were "running higher now than at any time since the Great Depression and rising every month," and the result was a loss of sorely needed revenue.[128] In October 1975 the upstate New York metropolis narrowly avoided defaulting on its short-term debts when at the last minute local banks agreed to purchase the city's notes.[129]

Cincinnati was also beginning to experience unexpected financial woes. In November 1975 the Associated Press distributed a story that contrasted the fiscal soundness of Cincinnati with the debacle in New York City, claiming that Ohio's Queen City "savor[ed] a fifth year of budgetary surpluses."[130] Yet that same month the *Cincinnati Enquirer* was arguing that the city had not been "fiscally responsible for the past few years" and was warning about "the probability of a shortfall in 1976." "Though the financial picture of Cincinnati is far from critical in the New York sense," the *Enquirer* editorialized, "it is clearly reaching the point where [the] council will have to be more forthright in its appraisals of the city's fiscal outlook."[131] The newspaper was correct about impending deficits, and the city council responded with sharp budget cuts in 1976–77. In an effort to balance its books, Cincinnati eliminated 893 full-time positions from the city payroll and adopted a divestment policy that resulted in the transfer of responsibility for the city courts and the University of Cincinnati to the state.[132]

It was Cleveland, however, that suffered the most severe financial humiliation in the wake of New York City's collapse. In 1970 Mayor Carl Stokes had sponsored a proposal to raise the city income tax from 1 percent to 1.8 percent, but to induce voter support for the increase, he did not request renewal of a 5.8 mill property tax levy. On election day Stokes's ploy failed, for Cleveland's thrifty voters defeated both the income tax hike and the property tax renewal. As a result, property tax receipts fell from $41 million in 1970 to $23 million in 1971 and did not increase markedly during the remainder of the 1970s. Voters defeated two subsequent income tax raises during Stokes's mayoralty, and they remained adamantly opposed to tax increases throughout Ralph Perk's tenure in city hall.[133] In 1977 thirty-one-year-old Dennis Kucinich became mayor and pledged no new taxes while promising to hire two hundred more police officers within the next year and a half.[134] But the city's fiscal condition continued to worsen, and in spring 1978 the state auditor declared that the municipal accounts were unauditable and referred to "Cleveland's financial and bookkeeping chaos."[135] Moreover, in the summer of 1978 the accounting firm of Ernst and Ernst found that $52 million in bond receipts earmarked for capital improvements had been misspent for operating costs.[136] Meanwhile, the principal investment advisory firms in the municipal bond trade were shutting Cleveland out of the money market. Moody's down-graded the city's bond rating, and Standard and Poor's took the more drastic step of suspending Cleveland's rating. The chief of Moody's municipal division commented, "It looks to me like the people in charge of managing [Cleveland's finances] don't have the foggiest idea of what they are doing."[137] With the rating firms united against it, Cleveland would henceforth find no buyers for its notes and bonds.

The final act in Cleveland's fiscal tragedy came in December 1978, when $14 million in short-term notes came due. Pressure mounted for the city to sell its debt-ridden Municipal Electric Light and Power Plant (Muny Light) to the investor-owned Cleveland Electric Illuminating Company (CEI), thereby following Mayor Perk's example of paying expenses through divestment of assets. A fiery populist dedicated to ensuring lower utility rates, young Mayor Kucinich refused point-blank to eliminate CEI's one competitor, telling the city council president: "I'm not going to give in on Muny Light. I'll go to hell first."[138] Local banks, however, would not rollover the city's notes unless Cleveland sold Muny and otherwise set its financial affairs in order. Without funds to refinance its short-term notes, closed out of national credit markets, and caught in a stalemate with local banks, on December 16 the city defaulted, the first major municipality to do so since the Great Depression of the 1930s.[139] In February 1979 Cleveland voters finally approved a 50 percent increase in the municipal income tax, thus providing funds necessary to relieve the city of its immediate embarrassment. But its well-publicized default certainly reinforced the image of Cleveland as a community well on the way to total collapse.

From New York City's debacle in 1975 to Cleveland's default in 1978, fiscal crisis spread like an epidemic through the nation's central cities. The experience in one city was not a carbon copy of that in another, for local factors distinguished the various financial emergencies. Undermining Boston's financial position was its excessive reliance on the property tax; political stalemate between a confrontational mayor and an exasperated business community helped bring Cleveland to its knees; and Mayor Beame's extraordinary refusal to recognize the severity of the approaching crisis and to take drastic measures to slash expenditures contributed to New York City's problems.

But underlying the varied local circumstances was the common factor of shrinking resources. Mayor Flaherty's fiscal restraint may have spared Pittsburgh the humiliation of near bankruptcy in the mid-1970s. But Flaherty in the early 1970s was simply recognizing the bitter facts that the Municipal Assistance Corporation was to make clear to New Yorkers a few years later. The older hubs of urban America no longer had the money to maintain such an extensive army of employees or such expansive services. Central cities had to face up to their relative poverty and lay off thousands of workers and divest themselves of traditional responsibilities. Cincinnati could no longer maintain a university, and New York could no longer offer free tuition. Saint Louis and Detroit would have to relinquish their roles as patrons of the arts to regional authorities or to the states. And none of the cities could employ as many police, firefighters, or garbage collectors. The fiscal problems of the 1970s had imposed limits on what the cities could realistically achieve and had once again reminded Americans that New York and Cleveland were not the cities they once had been.

In fact, the fiscal crisis elicited an unprecedented outpouring of gloomy rhetoric about the seemingly moribund cities. Lewis Mumford, the venerable critic of urban planning and architecture, offered the following prescription for bankrupt New York: "Make the patient as comfortable as possible; it's too late to operate."[140] Economist Robert Zevin was equally pessimistic, claiming, "New York is not quite dead, but death is clearly inevitable."[141] Default or near default had branded the older central cities with one more mark of decline, and no amount of federal money or urban boosterism appeared able to eradicate this latest badge of failure.

Return to the Rails

Though central cities seemed to be hitting bottom in the early 1970s, there were many optimists who still believed that rebirth was possible and whose minds were fertile with schemes and projects to reverse the long decline. By the 1970s, however, most observers believed that the road to renaissance was headed in a different direction from that taken by previous boosters. Whereas the urban leaders of the 1940s and 1950s had emphasized highway building and new construction in their plans for reviving the central city, the planners and promoters of the 1970s turned to mass transit and the traditional neighborhood as essential components of a vigorous urban hub. Transit lines had been the skeleton of America's healthy urban body during the early twentieth century, and vital neighborhoods had been its flesh and blood. These elements had made the central cities great, and by bolstering these sources of strength, central cities could again become decent places in which to live and work. No longer should the older cities attempt to beat the suburbs at their own game by emphasizing automobile transportation and gleaming new projects. Instead, the revitalization philosophy of the 1970s held that the urban core should nurture its historical roots, restoring mass transit to a place of preeminence and rehabilitating its established neighborhoods.

Encouraging this return to urban roots was the overwhelming disenchantment with previous projects. Each city could point to its own example of urban renewal's failure, to the plots of land where weeds rather than buildings grew. Critics could recount ample stories of poor families displaced and the homes of elderly pensioners mowed down by bulldozers. In the early 1960s renewal was already beginning to lose its appeal; by the early 1970s it had become a dirty word, and because of this stigma many urban renewal agencies were changing their names to departments of community development. Similarly, highway projects had threatened too many neighborhoods and provided too little traffic relief. The disruptive consequences of the ribbons of concrete and asphalt seemed too great to warrant further construction.

Moreover, for the first time in decades the economic and cultural trends of American society seemed to give new hope for urban living. With the advent of the energy crisis in 1973–74, the price of gasoline doubled and tripled, and lines at service stations extended for blocks, testing the patience of harried drivers. The age of the automobile was possibly coming to a close, ushering in a new era of mass transit and restoring the transportation advantage of the central city. The higher cost and greater inconvenience of the automobile might finally give Boston, New York City, and Chicago a competitive edge over the suburbs. Older neighborhoods close to centers of employment might again flourish once the automobile was relegated to a subordinate position. In addition, changing lifestyles seemed to promise new vitality for the central city. The baby boom was over; people were marrying later, and more were childless. Thus child-oriented suburbia had less appeal, and the central city's maligned schools would prove less of a detriment in the competition with outlying communities. For decades the central city had been struggling against the prevailing tides of society. Now the flow seemed to be reversing, and the aging hubs could catch the new current if they restored their transit systems and neighborhoods.

This shift in policy preference is evident in the mounting rebellion against highway projects. Learning the lesson taught by militant municipal employees and civil rights activists, highway opponents were becoming increasingly belligerent, heightening the pressure on public officials to abandon plans for new roads. In Chicago the Anti-Crosstown Coalition scuttled plans to construct a circumferential expressway linking the superhighways radiating from the central business district. Opponents claimed the giant swath of highway cutting through the city's southwest and west sides would displace more than ten thousand people, and one angry resident expressed the views of many when he said: "This is just Mayor Daley's way of rerouting trucks from downtown and destroying our neighborhoods, our churches, and our schools."[142] In the 1972 guber-natorial race, the Democratic victor, Daniel Walker, was firmly committed to halting the scheme and the Republican incumbent, Governor Richard Ogilvie, said that the project was "frozen" and insisted that he was "com-pletely free" of any obligation to Mayor Daley to implement the plan.[143] To ensure that politicians did not yield to Daley's arguments, the coalition organized a giant demonstration and parade in May 1972. Thousands gathered for the one-mile march, motorcade, and rally with Walker tell-ing the crowd, "Today we walk again in an effort to put people ahead of concrete."[144]

Philadelphia residents likewise battled against a Crosstown Express-way that was to run from the Delaware to Schuylkill rivers on the south side of the central business district. Long planned, the project had a pub-lic hearing in 1964, and final design and property acquisition were under way when militant community opposition halted further work in 1969. Again the chief complaint was displacement of residents, and in 1972 the opposition was sufficient to finally defeat the scheme.[145] Moreover, in 1971 Pennsylvania's governor personally intervened to halt activity on Philadelphia's Northeast Freeway, which had been in the design process for over a decade. That same year the Chief Engineer of the Philadelphia Department of Streets lamented, "The carefully developed Major High-way program planned for over 10 years and about to be implemented in all elements has, over the past 18 months[,] been reduced to one project . . . slowly creeping along."[146] Then from 1972 to 1975 the Neighbor-hoods Preservation Coalition mobilized to block proposed exit ramps from the Delaware Expressway that would channel traffic into the streets of Queen Village, a district south of Society Hill that was becoming popular with middle-class Philadelphians who sought an inner-city home. Though business and civic groups believed the ramps were necessary for down-town development and especially for the stalled Penns Landing project, Queen Villagers organized protest demonstrations, including a motorcade to city hall led by a hearse and a neighborhood street festival that was intended, in the words of its organizer, to say, "This street is not dead, and the ramps would kill it—would kill what is alive and well."[147] Echoing Chicago expressway foes, one opponent of the ramps argued, "Highway departments throughout the nation, had to be made aware of the fact that you just can't build highways through people's homes."[148]

By the early 1970s Baltimore's East-West Freeway was still not com-pleted, and in 1969 a group had brought suit to prevent it from destroying much of the historic Fell's Point neighborhood.[149] And in 1971, after four years of controversy, the Minnesota Highway Department was conducting yet another public hearing to determine whether Interstate 55 should run through Minneapolis's Minnehaha Park or bypass it and level eighteen homes.[150]

Nowhere were highway foes more active and successful, however, than in Boston. The bone of contention there were the proposed Inner Belt designed to pass through Boston's South End and the inner suburbs of Cambridge and Somerville and the Southwest Expressway that was to run from downtown through the city's largely black area of Roxbury and the predominantly white district of Jamaica Plain. In January 1969 hundreds of expressway opponents confronted incoming Governor Francis Sargent with a "People before Highways" demonstration on the Boston Common. Sargent promised the crowd, "Never, never will this administration make decisions that place people below concrete," but said that he would have to study further the road proposals before taking action.[151] By December 1969 Boston's Mayor Kevin White was asking Sargent to halt all highway construction in the city because of the "anguished objections of neighborhood residents."[152] Yet the Greater Boston Chamber of Commerce together with the *Boston Globe* rebuked Mayor White, claiming, "Failure to complete the highway network would lead to increased congestion of existing roads and economic deterioration as the core becomes less accessible."[153] Both White and neighborhood opponents emphasized the loss of housing and the increase in air pollution that would result from the proposed expressways. Moreover, a leading member of the local antihighway coalition commented: "Building a road destroys more than housing. It destroys a way of life that can never be replaced, no matter how much housing is built."[154] Thus highway foes juxtaposed an image of asphalt speedways belching noxious fumes against a picture of happy, close-knit neighborhoods and came to the obvious conclusion. Expressway construction had to cease.

Faced with opposition from the mayors and city councils of Boston, Cambridge, and Somerville and with resistance from state legislators representing those cities, in February 1970 Governor Sargent declared a moratorium on the building of the Inner Belt and Southwest Expressway and reopened consideration of possible alternative routes for the arteries.[155] For more than two years the governor procrastinated, and pressure mounted to permanently shelve the highway proposals. Finally, at the end of 1972 Sargent announced that plans for both the Southwest Expressway and the Inner Belt would be abandoned.[156] The ten-mile Southwest Expressway was intended to close the last gap in the Maine-to-Florida route of Interstate 95. But highway foes had ensured that this gap would remain, a testimony to Boston's revolt against the automobile.

In Boston as in Philadelphia and Chicago, highway engineers were left with a diminishing body of allies by the early 1970s. In the 1940s and 1950s many of those threatened with displacement had also protested road construction but to little avail. During that earlier era, the urban consensus favored new expressways, and governors, mayors, newspapers, and the general body of motorists and voters dismissed neighborhood foes of road construction as selfish parochials unwilling to suffer inconvenience for the greater good of the metropolis. By the 1970s, however, neighborhood opponents had grown shriller and better organized, and they had attracted a mounting corps of sympathizers who themselves could empathize with the frightful consequences of highway construction. Mayors like Kevin White and governors like Daniel Walker and Francis Sargent had deserted the highway camp, and the general electorate also had seemingly strayed from their past devotion to six-lane motorways. Some business groups like the Greater Boston Chamber of Commerce and newspapers like the *Boston Globe* remained allies of the road builders and continued to present familiar arguments about improving accessibility to the urban core. But even within the business community, support was wavering and the big newspapers were beginning to defect. The age of the automobile may not have passed, but the era of urban highway construction had. Highway engineers would not be able to complete the ambitious plans of the 1940s and 1950s with their radiating highway spokes and multiple rims of inner and outer belts. Instead, city maps showed only a few expressway spokes open to traffic, and beltway rims serviced suburbia but did not cut through the central city.

The militance of antihighway forces certainly encouraged politicians and others to forsake their fondness for freeways. But another factor in the desertion from the pro-road cause was the renewed attractiveness of alternate modes of transportation. During the 1960s and early 1970s, Congress stepped up aid to mass transportation, thereby enticing city leaders throughout the nation to investigate the possibilities of the mass transit approach. In 1964 Washington lawmakers had approved a program of capital grants to cities for construction of mass transit facilities and for the purchase of existing transit lines. As a result, public authorities or municipalities were able to buy out remaining private bus and commuter rail companies. Moreover, urban leaders began to dream about construction of such highly touted panaceas for transit problems as automated people movers, monorails, and sky buses. Just as the Housing Act of 1949 had given birth to a myriad of drafting-board schemes of salvation, so the Mass

Transportation Act of 1964 stirred the imagination of planners and public officials, nurturing Buck Rogers visions of future transit.

Even more important, however, was the federal legislation of the early 1970s. The Urban Mass Transportation Assistance Act of 1970 increased considerably Washington's financial commitment to transit projects, and the Federal Aid Highway Act of 1973 permitted cities to trade earmarked interstate highway construction money for an equal amount of mass transit funds. A city like Boston could thus abandon highway building without losing its federal bounty. It could simply exchange road funds for transit money. Then in 1974 Congress authorized federal operating subsidies to relieve budget pressures on transit systems that faced mounting deficits.[157] In other words, Washington was now offering to foot much of the bill for transit, so why not eschew highway plans and head off in a new direction. Expressway proposals had not saved the aging central cities; maybe mass transit would.

As disillusionment with highways mounted and federal funding for mass transit increased, a number of older central cities launched new and expensive rapid transit ventures. One city that sought to catch the wave of transit euphoria was hard-pressed Buffalo. In 1971 the Niagara Frontier Transportation Authority (NFTA) announced its plans for a 12.5-mile rapid transit rail line linking downtown Buffalo and the state university campus in suburban Amherst. Together with a huge downtown covered mall, the rapid transit system would supposedly provide the needed elixir to revive the dying central business district. Expressing the thoughts of all Buffalo boosters, Mayor Frank Sedita hoped the plan would "capture the imagination of the entire community and . . . spur continuing support for downtown by bringing back residents, shoppers, retail merchants, and most importantly, private investors."[158]

The NFTA proposed an aerial structure for the line, but the thought of an overhead railroad immediately stirred strong opposition and the organization of a protest coalition NOT (No Overhead Transit) that spoke for more than sixty community groups.[159] During the next few years, debate on the project continued with the authority eventually agreeing to place the bulk of the system underground. Meanwhile, cost estimates soared, forcing the NFTA to revise its proposal and offer a more modest project. Whereas in 1971 the authority was sponsoring a 12.5-mile line with an estimated cost of $239 million, by the time of the ground-breaking ceremony in late 1978, it was building a 6.4-mile system with an expected price tag of $440 million. Despite the diminished proportions, Buffalo leaders still dreamed that the new rail line might mark the dawn of the city's renaissance. NFTA's public relations manager proclaimed the line "the biggest transit project in Buffalo since the completion of the Erie Canal," and he and others were hoping it would have the same impact on the city's fortunes as the renowned waterway.[160]

Elsewhere central-city leaders were also counting on dramatic transit ventures to lift their communities out of the doldrums of urban decay. Backed by such downtown boosters as the Greater Baltimore Committee, in the early 1970s Baltimore's transit authority drafted plans for a 65-mile rapid transit system reaching out in all directions from the central business district. As in Buffalo, neighborhood groups challenged proposed routings, and only in 1977 were construction contracts awarded for a single 7.5-mile line running northwest from downtown along the right-of-way of the Western Maryland Railway to the city limits.[161]

Detroit's Southwestern Michigan Transportation Authority was making even bigger plans than its counterparts in Buffalo and Baltimore. In 1971 it proposed six rail routes, totaling 148 miles, with air-conditioned cars zooming along at speeds of up to eighty miles per hour. A reporter for the *Detroit News* commented, "The grand plan for rapid transit in the Detroit region reads like an impossible dream.[162] Indeed, the scheme proved impossible, but by 1977 the authority and Detroit boosters were still planning a rapid rail subway running under the city's main street, Woodward Avenue, and extending into the northern suburbs. A people mover operating on an overhead structure looping through the central business district was to supplement the rapid transit line and convey the new throngs converging on downtown speedily and comfortably between the stores, hotels, and office buildings.[163]

Cities that already boasted of a rapid transit system were also taking advantage of the new federal funding and revived interest in public transportation. In 1968 New York City's Board of Estimate approved a major rapid transit expansion program, including construction of a $2 billion Second Avenue subway running from lower Manhattan through the Bronx and the building of lines linking midtown Manhattan with outlying sections of the Queens. The fiscal crisis of the mid-1970s, however, brought much of the construction to a standstill and most notably halted work on the Second Avenue project.[164] In Greater Boston the Massachusetts Bay Transportation Authority (MBTA) funded a program of modernization largely with federal money. In fact, total federal grants and loans to the MBTA soared from $57.5 million for 1965–68 to $757.8 million for 1975–78 with much of the rise owing to the trade-in of interstate highway funds.[165] Moreover, between 1973 and 1976 the authority assumed ownership of all the commuter rail lines entering Boston, thereby completing its monopoly of transit in the region.[166] In 1972 the Chicago Transit Authority proudly announced a $283 million modernization plan permitting the purchase of much-needed new cars.[167] Three years later Philadelphia voters approved by a two-to-one margin a $61 million municipal bond issue to help finance a downtown commuter rail tunnel and a high-speed rail line between the airport and Penn Center. Eighty percent of the funding of these projects, however, were to come from Washington.[168]

Though most of urban America seemed caught up in the new enthusiasm for costly rapid transit schemes, some cautious and sober persons shied away from the fancy packages proposed by planners. The residents of Saint Louis, for example, were cool toward the construction of high-speed rail lines. During the early 1970s, Mayor Alfonso Cervantes argued, "If the nation's commuters continue to clog our expressways at the rate of half an acre of car for one driver, there will never be enough roads or parking space until the whole country is paved over."[169] Like his colleagues in other cities he found the solution to this problem in mass transportation and in 1970 called for an immediate campaign to win public approval of a rapid rail transit project. A series of feasibility studies considered the question, and one issued in 1971 proposed a 100-mile system radiating from downtown Saint Louis.[170] By early 1974, however, this had been reduced to an initial $381 million, 11-mile subway line running from East Saint Louis, Illinois, through the city of Saint Louis, and terminating at Clayton in Saint Louis County. Boosters from the business community generally supported the scheme with the president of the downtown-oriented Civic Progress, Inc., claiming that without rapid transit the region would "continue expanding outwards, forever leaving blighted areas behind."[171] Likewise, the spokesman for the St. Louis Regional Commerce and Growth Association claimed that Saint Louis should not "settle for a third-rate urban transportation system of buses running on the clogged freeways of the future."[172]

But the general public remained largely indifferent, with only sixty persons attending a public hearing on the issue, and political leaders were generally hostile to the costly scheme. The president of the Saint Louis Board of Aldermen urged his fellow policymakers to "keep [their] feet on the ground" and support the more practical but less glamorous alternative of better bus service. "With crime rampant," the aldermanic leader asked, "who will ride in driverless coaches . . . underground?"[173] In contrast, Cervantes's successor, Mayor John Poelker, was "solidly behind moving ahead" with the project.[174] Despite Poelker's support, the regional planning council that had to approve any such proposal voted to shelve the 11-mile subway and chose to commission yet another study of mass transportation needs in the metropolitan area. In the words of one member of the planning body, the decision was "a step backwards in the right direction."[175]

Pittsburgh's tightfisted Mayor Peter Flaherty similarly thwarted the grand transit schemes sponsored by planners and business leaders. The Pittsburgh controversy centered on the proposed Skybus, a rubber-tired, computer-controlled vehicle operating on an exclusive guideway. Developed by Pittsburgh's Westinghouse Corporation, Skybus represented the most advanced transit technology available, and its adoption was supposedly to consolidate the city's reputation as a leader in urban revitalization. The big-business moguls of the Allegheny Conference endorsed a proposal for a 10-mile Skybus line from the prestigious South Hills suburbs to the Golden Triangle, but Mayor Flaherty balked. He claimed that the scheme was "a $228-million convenience for the suburban commuter . . . It would not do enough for those who live in the city." Flaherty advocated instead spending the money on more conventional transport. The mayor favored "taking our street cars off and replacing them with a steel rail system which was not quite as innovative as Skybus. This seemed to me more practical and less costly."[176] After much heated discourse, Flaherty won, and by 1974 the Skybus proposal was dead.

The caution of political leaders in Pittsburgh and Saint Louis, however, was unusual. Few urban areas were willing to be left behind in the rush for high-tech, federally funded transit systems. Moreover, such long-standing travelers along the road to urban renaissance as Pittsburgh's Allegheny Conference, the Greater Baltimore Committee, and Saint Louis's Civic Progress envisioned modern rapid transit systems as a means of achieving their long-term goals of boosting downtown business. A city without a subway seemed doomed to the same second-class oblivion as a city without a major-league sports team. High-speed rail lines were becoming an essential credential for big-city status. And the more innovative the rapid transit system, seemingly the better, for it would announce to the world that Buffalo, Baltimore, and Detroit were not relics of the past but metropolises of the future. People movers, sky buses, and computer-operated subways were the latest signs of renaissance, and without them an older central city might be dismissed as a dying backwater.

Yet the sober critics in Pittsburgh and Saint Louis had reason to question the prevailing mass transit hype. Cold figures in the ledger books showed that transit systems faced mounting deficits, and it was far from clear that thousands of urban commuters would abandon their automobiles for a seat on what was now called a "light rail vehicle" but which bore a striking resemblance to an old-fashioned trolley. In 1973 Saint Louis's Bi-State Development Agency actually defaulted on the principal and in-

terest payments on revenue bonds it had issued ten years earlier to purchase bus lines throughout the metropolitan area. Moreover, that same
year operating deficits seriously jeopardized continued bus service in
Saint Louis.[177] The operating costs of Cincinnati's newly purchased bus
system was far exceeding expectations, threatening to saddle that city
with new debt.[178] And in Boston the Massachusetts Bay Transportation
Authority operating deficit soared from $79 million in 1971 to $199 million in 1978.[179] Federal and state assistance helped bridge these budgetary gaps, yet it was obvious that investments in mass transit were burden-
ing fiscally strapped urban governments with just one more liability.
Rising gasoline prices did seem to draw a few additional riders to mass
transit during the mid-1970s, halting the long-term postwar decline in
patronage. But as yet there were mixed signals as to the duration of America's love affair with the automobile.

Reviving the Neighborhoods

During the 1970s, mass transit was one element in the movement to restore America's urban core, but another of even greater importance was
the emerging enthusiasm for neighborhood revival. According to prevailing urban folklore, lively but cohesive neighborhoods had been the sinew
of the traditional city, giving it strength and ensuring a quality of life unmatched in humdrum suburbia or sterile renewal projects. A return to
vital neighborhoods was, then, as essential to a restored city as a return to
the rails. Throughout the country political leaders mouthed the rhetoric of
the neighborhood movement and promised a new commitment to these
vital building blocks of urban society. As early as 1969 Pittsburgh mayoral candidate Peter Flaherty was vowing, "As mayor I will concentrate on
the neighborhoods rather than on the Downtown section," and four years
later Flaherty's opponent, city council president Richard Caliguiri, was
also presenting himself as the friend of neighborhoods, claiming to have
"moved extensively through the neighborhoods . . . long before it became fashionable."[180]

In 1970 Boston's Mayor Kevin White told the city council that "for too
long urban renewal in Boston has emphasized rebirth of the downtown
area at the expense of the neighborhoods." And the following year Mayor
Alfonso Cervantes of Saint Louis expressed the conventional wisdom of
the 1970s when he claimed that the "two pressing priorities" of city government were "the fight against crime and the fight to preserve our neighborhoods."[181] Similarly, in the 1975 election campaign Cincinnati's victorious city council candidates argued that "the emphasis [had] to be on

an attempt to preserve the neighborhoods," and the leading vote-getter warned, "We must keep our eyes on the stable neighborhoods which could start to decline."[182] In 1977, when asked by a local newspaper how they would distribute development funds in the city, most Minneapolis council candidates contended that the residential neighborhoods should take priority over downtown, claiming, "Strong neighborhoods are essential to the vitality of Minneapolis," and arguing, "Neighborhood development has been neglected in favor of downtown."[183]

Perhaps no city lavished praise on the neighborhood so loudly or with such panache as Baltimore. In September 1970 that city celebrated the opening of the First Annual Baltimore City Fair with the release of two thousand balloons and a Parade of Neighborhoods. At the fair each of the diverse neighborhoods of the city had a booth with exhibits extolling its merits. This first fair attracted 300,000 visitors but by 1972 the annual event was drawing 1.3 million people to the displays of sixty-eight participating neighborhood groups. According to Mayor William Donald Schaefer, "The focus of the fair is the neighborhoods of Baltimore," and "Every fairgoer, no matter who he is or what part of town he comes from, sees himself and his neighbors represented there."[184] It was, then, a celebration of Baltimore that graphically attributed the greatness of the city to its vital subdivisions. Like mayors Flaherty, White, and Cervantes and the council members of Cincinnati and Minneapolis, the Baltimore City Fair was proclaiming that neighborhoods were the strength of the metropolis and as such deserved nurture and support.

Any visitor to Baltimore's fair, however, was also made aware of the diversity of the neighborhood movement. Within the fair's circus tents were exhibits that boosted all-black, working-class districts, that praised gentrifying zones for middle-class professionals, and that advertised established blue-collar ethnic enclaves. This array of displays was indicative of the range of motives and concerns that underlay the common interest in neighborhood vitality. During the 1970s, perceived threats to ethnic ghettos mobilized some neighborhood groups that resorted to grass-roots militance. In these cases the prospect of highway construction or migrants of a different color might have been the catalyst for unwonted neighborhood enthusiasm. Other neighborhood advocates viewed community mobilization as a means of empowering and enriching the poor. For them the neighborhood was a prime staging ground for social revolution. Still others sought to rehabilitate deteriorating inner-city neighborhoods and attract middle-class residents. For these gentrifiers neighborhood organization could boost property values and ignite a real estate bonanza. And other neighborhood leaders saw community mobilization as a defensive tactic in the battle to keep middle-class districts middle-class. Rebels and realtors, workers and bosses, all were among those who saw grass-roots action in the neighborhood as the means to a desirable end.

Though a motley group, the various participants in the neighborhood movement did adhere to certain common tenets regarding urban revitalization. They all shared a respect for the existing physical structure of the urban core and generally wished to preserve the city's building stock. None favored large-scale clearance or redevelopment, and all viewed proposed superhighways that threatened to slash through the city's hub as the bane of urban America. Moreover, all sought both public and private reinvestment in central-city neighborhoods and fought such barriers to reinvestment as the adverse image of the inner city and the redlining practices of the loan departments of major financial institutions. Gargantuan urban renewal schemes, like Cleveland's Erieview or Saint Louis's Mill Creek Valley, were anathema to neighborhood organizers of every ilk. Instead, they glorified small-scale, modest rehabilitation ventures and could wax poetic when describing ordinary citizens working together at the neighborhood level to combat blight. Whether organizing community-run businesses to employ ethnic minorities or stripping the woodwork in townhouses for young professionals, they viewed small-scale grass-roots projects as the source of urban salvation. Only activated citizens at the neighborhood level could revitalize the city; without this local vitality the efforts of Washington or city hall were futile. The neighborhoods formed the essential foundation of the city, and they had to be protected, bolstered, and encouraged to take action.

Actually, this concern about the preservation of city neighborhoods was not new, but the 1970s did witness an unprecedented faith in the preeminent role of the neighborhood in urban renaissance. In the early 1940s foes of blight had backed neighborhood rehabilitation projects in Baltimore's Waverly district and Chicago's Woodlawn area. In the 1950s Baltimore's Fight-Blight program, the neighborhood projects in Philadelphia, and the Saint Louis community rehabilitation initiatives had all sought to halt the decline of neighborhoods. But these programs had never attracted the publicity or stirred the imagination like grandiose downtown renewal schemes. Because of the dramatic physical changes wrought by large-scale bulldozer projects, they were most evident to ordinary urban dwellers and experts alike, and urban renewal critics like Jane Jacobs reinforced the preoccupation with massive clearance and redevelopment by ignoring other urban revitalization ventures. Though neighborhood enthusiasts of the 1970s spoke as if their efforts were novel, they often were not. What was novel was the emphasis on the neighborhood as the primary path to renaissance. In the past it had played a supporting role in the revitalization drama. Now the neighborhood had become the star.

Many factors encouraged this new focus on the neighborhood. One of the most significant was the federal government's support for grass-roots community action during the late 1960s. Both the Economic Opportunity Act of 1964 and the Model Cities program launched in 1966 emphasized neighborhood organization and the encouragement of indigenous community leaders. Though neighborhood factionalism and battles with city hall stalled community action during much of the 1960s, by the early 1970s there were signs of some movement. Especially notable were the community development corporations authorized under an amendment to the original antipoverty law and funded by the federal Office of Economic Opportunity. These corporations were expected to mobilize the populace of poor, predominantly black neighborhoods in a battle to restore the economic vitality of their communities. With federal money and cooperative community effort, burned-out, devastated ghettos were supposedly to pull themselves up by their proverbial bootstraps. Neither city hall nor the urban renewal authority would be the engine of revitalization. Instead, black neighborhood leaders with dollars from Washington would resurrect the moribund inner city.

Throughout the nation community development corporations attempted to perform the miracle of rebirth. For example, in 1967 black residents formed the Hough Area Development Corporation (HADC) to revive the riot-scarred ghetto on Cleveland's east side. Receiving over $9 million from the federal government from 1968 through 1974, HADC founded Community Products, Inc., a manufacturer of rubber parts for automobiles, and also operated two McDonald's fast-food outlets. Moreover, it constructed a $3.5 million shopping mall, Martin Luther King Plaza, and started a supermarket to serve as the mall's key tenant. A subsidiary, Homes for Hough, was also expected to construct new housing for low- and moderate-income Clevelanders.[185]

In 1969 the Office of Economic Opportunity approved the funding of the Union Sarah Economic Development Corporation (USEDC) to boost the economy of a depressed black neighborhood in Saint Louis. Like HADC, USEDC founded a variety of local businesses, including an equipment rental company and a firm to manufacture and market African art objects. It also invested in a black-controlled plastics company and planned to construct housing for low-income neighborhood residents.[186] In New York City the Bedford-Stuyvesant Restoration Corporation and Harlem Commonwealth Council were attempting to realize similar economic revitalization projects as was the North Lawndale Development

Corporation of Chicago and the Roxbury Action Program of Boston.[187] For each of these groups grass-roots neighborhood action seemed the solution to the devastating problems of disinvestment and decay. With federal funds and some financing from private philanthropic agencies, these black ghettos could supposedly stanch the economic hemorrhaging of recent years and reestablish themselves as viable communities.

By the second half of the 1970s, however, faith in community development was waning as too many of the neighborhood corporations had foundered or retreated before the continuing onslaught of abandonment, crime, and physical deterioration. Internal conflict weakened some community corporations; for example, in 1972 the HADC board fired its executive director while he was out of town, the director having publicly attacked the black political organization of former mayor Carl Stokes and his brother Congressman Louis Stokes. One board member summed up the situation when she complained, "There is a struggle for power in Hough and it is tearing this community apart."[188] Meanwhile, the Hough corporation was recording few successes. Neither the McDonald's outlets nor the supermarket were profitable, and the bookkeeper of Community Products was using considerably more red ink than black. Martin Luther King Plaza had difficulty signing tenants, a problem shared by other inner-city retailing projects sponsored by community development corporations.[189] As early as 1972 the *Wall Street Journal* reported, "The cards are so stacked against black centers, in fact, that the International Council of Shopping Centers is abandoning a three-year effort to help get them started."[190] By the close of 1975 Union Sarah's plastics factory had failed and its African artifacts firm was bankrupt. Moreover, the Saint Louis group had failed to construct any new low-income housing, and its neighborhood supermarket had quickly folded. Chicago's North Lawndale corporation had made no headway by the mid-1970s, and in 1976 an observer of the Roxbury project found it was "moving ahead (slowly)."[191]

New York City's Bedford-Stuyvesant received the highest marks of all the neighborhood development corporations, and in the mid-1970s one commentator enthusiastically noted that "what was once regarded as the most hopeless community in America [was] now turning around—due largely to a talented, smart and hard-working Restoration Corporation."[192] Critics acclaimed the Bedford-Stuyvesant corporations' commercial center, which opened in 1976 with both retail and office space; the project supposedly gave the area "a heart, a focus, a sense of place."[193] IBM's new assembly plant in the Brooklyn ghetto was providing the more tangible benefit of jobs, putting paychecks in the pockets of four hundred workers. But given the magnitude of the problems in the Bedford-Stuyvesant area, some questioned whether these achievements would have a significant impact.

By the second half of the 1970s, then, the optimism of many neighborhood development boosters was waning. In the United States any small business faced unfavorable odds, with a 70 percent failure rate among such concerns during the 1970s. But neighborhood-sponsored enterprises in black ghettos like Hough or Union Sarah faced the additional problems of high crime rates, soaring insurance costs, unskilled and undisciplined workers, and obsolete facilities. The community development corporations were trying to build businesses in areas where these adverse factors had forced previous investors to close shop. To succeed at this formidable task would require more skill, luck, and money than many of the groups could provide. Conceding defeat, in 1977 a veteran of the Union Sarah project concluded that the community development corporation concept "should be set aside, funding should be denied, and the legislators should look for a new approach to improving the quality of life for the poor of the United States."[194]

While some activists sought to rebuild the poorest ghetto neighborhoods, others struggled to defend still-viable white working-class areas. Predominantly white blue-collar neighborhoods had not suffered the ravages of rioting and upheaval in the 1960s, and consequently, the social fabric of these communities was less frayed than in Hough or Harlem. But many neighborhood leaders perceived that the policies of the business and government establishment were accelerating the forces of blight and decay in aging working-class districts. Especially threatening were the trinity of evils: highway construction, urban renewal, and redlining by financial institutions. The first and second would kill the neighborhoods through a quick blow from the bulldozer. The third would slowly cut off the financial lifeblood of the community by denying mortgages and home improvement and business loans in neighborhoods that bankers deemed undesirable. Either way public and private policymakers seemed ready to commit urbicide if neighborhood activists did not rise to the defense.

Across the country, community groups attempted to triumph over all three evils, and one of the most publicized efforts was in southeast Baltimore. Beginning in the late 1960s the Southeast Council against the Road led the battle against building the East-West Expressway through the historic Fell's Point neighborhood, and it successfully kept up the fight through the early 1970s even though Mayor William Donald Schaefer was committed to completing the long-stalled superhighway. This antihighway crusade encouraged further community action and resulted in 1971 in the formation of the Southeast Community Organization (SECO), a coalition of more than ninety neighborhood groups.[195]

The ideas of radical neighborhood organizer Saul Alinsky influenced SECO. Alinsky had begun organizing in Chicago in the late 1930s, and throughout his career he favored militant confrontations with people of power; according to this outspoken proponent of neighborhood clout, intimidation and demands gained much more than petitions and pleas.[196] Applying the Alinsky approach, during the 1970s SECO members forced the city to investigate redlining by local savings and loan associations, and when the city's findings confirmed SECO's suspicions, the community group won an agreement from financial institutions to halt the discriminatory practice. Dedicated to rehabilitation rather than clearance, SECO also prevented destruction of three blocks in the Washington Hill neighborhood. A local social worker expressed the group's philosophy when she said, "We wanted to stop the city from even *planning* to demolish anything."[197] Moreover, SECO mobilized a corps of mothers, who with their baby carriages blocked residential streets in protest against truck traffic on the thoroughfares, and protests also kept a local branch library open.[198] SECO supplemented these confrontational tactics with an economic development program that helped finance home purchases and housing repairs for neighborhood residents and that also nurtured a company producing and marketing crafts made by elderly and handicapped persons from the community. In marked contrast to the gloomy Union Sarah veteran, an observer of SECO's activities enthusiastically reported in 1977 that the group had "restored community pride" and that "southeast Baltimore [had] become a classic model for reviving the inner city."[199]

Southeast Baltimore was a multiethnic community including persons of Southern and Eastern European ancestry as well as some black residents, and SECO sought to arouse citizens of every background to the common threat from the bulldozer and banker. But some emerging neighborhood groups of the 1970s focused their attention on preserving and promoting the cultural heritage of a single ethnic group. Economic decline was not the primary factor in the mobilization of these neighborhoods. Rather, threats to the survival of the ethnic culture of the community motivated many neighborhood crusaders to battle bureaucrats, politicians, developers, and other outsiders. Catholic priests seeking to preserve their diminishing flocks and save their parishes often led such neighborhood movements. But they were joined by others who likewise were unwilling to see their ethnic heritages paved under by superhighways or ravaged by the forces of decay and abandonment.

One ethnic neighborhood that gained national attention was Saint Louis's Italian enclave, the Hill. Leading the mobilization of that neighborhood was Father Salvatore Polizzi, the local parish priest. As early as 1965 the community had inaugurated Hill Day, an annual ethnic festival of grape stomping, fireworks, Italian delicacies, and costumed old-country dancers that was drawing 150,000 visitors by 1974. Proceeds from Hill Day benefited Hill 2000, Inc., a community improvement organization founded in 1970 to ensure that the tightly knit Italian community remained just as tightly knit and Italian in the year 2000 as thirty years earlier.

Toward this end, in 1971 Hill 2000 and Father Polizzi conducted a hard-hitting campaign to reunite 150 families north of Interstate 44 with the heart of the Hill by constructing a new overpass across the superhighway. State officials did not respond favorably, so Polizzi took the fight to Washington, where the Italian-American Secretary of Transportation John Volpe (soon to be named ambassador to Italy) authorized the desired overpass.[200] To protect the community from unwanted newcomers like the "Hoosiers" and "farmioli" (rural whites) who rented housing there in the 1950s, Hill 2000 purchased available properties to sell to "attractive buyers" and subsidized home improvements by neighborhood residents.[201] By 1975 the Hill was being lauded as "a perfect example of a neighborhood that has fought to maintain its character, and won."[202] Though hardly an unbiased observer, the Italian consul in Saint Louis expressed the views of many when in 1973 he stated: "I don't say that the Hill will save urban America . . . but still it's a good example. Downtowns are going to hell, but little downtowns like the Hill are helping . . . [in the] return to urban life."[203]

Moreover, the Hill was not unique. Confronted by the threatening expansion of adjacent Chinatown, residents of New York City's Little Italy neighborhood formed an improvement association with the purpose "of restoring the soul and atmosphere of Little Italy, fanning a spark in the coal to keep it alive."[204] In 1974 this group, aided by city planners, prepared the Risorgimento Plan for the renewal of the community. Within a few years business at the Italian restaurants and food shops along Mulberry Street was up markedly, and colorful new banners advertised the neighborhood's economic and social vitality.

Cincinnati's Urban Appalachian Council was mobilizing migrants from Appalachia in the Over-the-Rhine area, relying heavily on neighborhood organization. One of the council's leaders observed: "If you want to deal with city people, you have to start in neighborhoods . . . People don't live in cities. They live in neighborhoods."[205] Polish leaders in Buffalo seconded this view. In 1976 Polish-Americans in the Broadway-Fillmore area established the Polish Community Center, an act that one local leader characterized as "a last-ditch effort to stabilize the neighborhood and to stop the blight that was rapidly destroying the area." Two years later the center's director boasted, "We have arrested the exodus of families from the area[,] . . . have become a focal point of activities in the area and have seen a rebirth of the pride of our citizens in themselves, their community, and their city." In fact, this enthusiastic neighborhood activist claimed, "Centers like ours, well run, full of pride and dedication, will undoubtedly help to stabilize and to bring about a renewal of our cities."[206] For the Italian-Americans of Saint Louis and New York City, the Appalachians of Cincinnati, and the Polish-Americans of Buffalo, renewed pride in their cultural heritage and their neighborhoods was the supposed potion that would produce the long-sought goal of urban renaissance. Rebirth was to begin at the city's roots, in its diverse but purportedly lively neighborhoods.

In some cases, however, neighborhoods mobilized not to preserve a cultural or ethnic heritage but simply to maintain the advantages of middle-class community life. Though working-class grass-roots organizations won much publicity, in each of the older central cities middle-class neighborhood groups also viewed preservation of the fragment as the best means of creating a better whole. For example, the North Park community of Chicago exercised its clout in a battle to defend itself from commercial development sponsored by the city. A predominantly white area of single-family brick homes, in 1970 North Park ranked tenth in a status rating of the eighty-four communities within Chicago. But in 1973 a private developer announced plans to build a shopping center and high-rise apartment complex on the 155-acre site of the city's abandoned tuberculosis sanitarium in the heart of North Park. Led chiefly by the North River Commission, residents fought the proposal, which some opponents claimed would draw sixty thousand cars into the quiet neighborhood as well as level the handsome trees on the sanitarium's stately grounds. The movement included the community meetings, handbills, and visits to the mayor's office that were becoming standard routine as neighborhoods fought back across the nation. In North Park as in Fell's Point and the Hill, the residents demanded an end to ambitious building projects that would disrupt neighborhood life, and flyers expressed the urgency of action when they warned: "They're Going to Build a SHOPPING CENTER at the TUBERCULOSIS SANITARIUM unless . . . You and Your Neighbors Come to a Public Meeting."[207] The North Park community won its case, for the city would eventually preserve much of the sanitarium grounds as parkland and use the rest for senior citizens apartments and an outpatient health facility.

Some middle-class communities even rallied behind militant Alinsky-oriented organizers in their struggle to protect neighborhood interests. For example, in 1973 an organizer trained in Alinsky's methods launched the Shadyside Action Coalition in one of Pittsburgh's more affluent districts. Traditionally, Shadyside had been one of the few areas in the city to provide a dependable corps of Republican voters, but now Shadyside residents threatened the Mellon Bank, played hardball with city hall, and adopted the tough and angry approach favored by Alinsky. For example, the Shadyside Action Coalition forced the noisy and rowdy Fantastic Plastic night spot to close, attacking it as "a massive gangster-controlled club."[208] Moreover, like North Parkers the Pittsburgh residents battled local government officials over use of vacant public land and remained on the watch for developments that might increase traffic on quiet Shadyside streets. The citizens of Shadyside wanted to save their neighborhood from detrimental influences, thus maintaining the desirable residential status of at least one fragment of the aging central city, and they were ready to take tough action to attain their goals.

The Hill opposed any threat to its ethnic culture, and Shadyside and North Park sought to preserve their tranquil middle-class residential identities. For each community, neighborhood mobilization was a protective device to defend a desired lifestyle from the incursions of city, state, and federal policymakers and big-time private developers. Still others sought to refashion central-city neighborhoods into social enclaves for single people, childless couples, or those who did not savor the middle-class conventionality of North Park. This desire for environments congenial to alternative, non–family-oriented lifestyles fired much of the rehabilitation in the highly publicized gentrifying neighborhoods of the 1970s.

In most of the older central cities during the 1970s, certain neighborhoods attracted young, middle-class, childless residents who were rehabilitating townhouses, boosting property values, and raising hopes that the long-expected back-to-the-city movement had arrived. For example, the gentrification of Boston's Bay Village began when the neighborhood became a refuge for gays, who, according to one local banker, "had been pushed out of Beacon Hill."[209] Though the community was to become more diverse in its sexual preference, it would remain attractive primarily to the young childless professional. Moreover, as the more affluent migrated to the district, they found it necessary to organize to protect their new turf from perceived undesirables. Two bars on the edge of the neighborhood seemed to nurture street violence and were responsible for a string of homicides. To combat these threats to the economic and social upgrading of the community, Bay Villagers mobilized for a neighborhood campaign and after a five-year battle succeeded in closing the bars. Just as North Park had organized to fight commercial intrusion and the Hill had sought to preserve its ethnic identity, Bay Villagers were applying political pressure and exploiting the media to eliminate enemies along their neighborhood's fringes.[210]

Elsewhere a similar pattern was developing with young, childless, middle-class residents carving out a fragment of the city for themselves. The Allentown area was winning a reputation as "the Greenwich Village of Buffalo," and Cincinnati's Mount Adams neighborhood was assuming a prosperous but bohemian air unusual in that conservative city.[211] By the 1960s and 1970s gentrification was also spilling over the southern boundary of Society Hill into Queen Village as the young and affluent moved into that traditionally working-class Philadelphia neighborhood.[212] In each case the newly renovated fragment was proclaimed a seed of the long-awaited urban rebirth.

Bay Village, North Park, the Hill, and Bedford-Stuyvesant were districts with little in common but a shared faith in the promise of central-city neighborhoods and a belief in the right of neighborhoods to pursue their own goals. Through neighborhood associations and community development corporations, they had defended their ways of life and had sought to promote their individual interests. Moreover, such community efforts seemed to represent the brightest hope for urban revitalization in the otherwise dismal central cities of the early and mid-1970s. Community development efforts in Union Sarah had faltered, but the Hill appeared more vital than had downtown Saint Louis with its misfired urban renewal projects, its empty storefronts, and vacant offices. New York City as a whole was bankrupt, but Little Italy was supposedly making a comeback. Similarly, most of Buffalo seemed doomed except for "artsy" Allentown and the purportedly revived Polish community. Some of the reports from the neighborhood battlefield may have been overly optimistic, claiming victory prematurely and ignoring signs of defeat. But for many urban observers neighborhoods offered the only semblance of success.

Encouraged by these signals from the neighborhoods, a number of urban leaders and experts sought to regularize community mobilization and create a formal voice for neighborhoods within the governing structure. "Planning with people" became a popular slogan among guilt-ridden city planners, whose professional predecessors had plowed highways through homes and businesses and had drafted proposals for clearing acres of inner-city real estate. Mayors and city councils spoke with increasing enthusiasm about community participation, regarding it both as a cure for ghetto unrest and as a means of stirring a revitalizing neighborhood pride. Government channels had to be created for the expression of neighborhood opinion and the presentation of community goals. The grass-roots had to have a place in city government.

In a number of the older central cities, mechanisms were developing to realize this goal of heightened neighborhood participation in policy-making. For example, under Peter Flaherty, Pittsburgh adopted a community planning program. The city was divided into seven districts with each district assigned a community planner who was to hear neighborhood complaints, consult with community organizations about land-use planning, identify neighborhood needs, and encourage communities to organize. Moreover, in 1974 Pittsburgh's voters approved a new city charter providing for an elected community advisory board in each neighborhood that would have a formal role in advising the city council and mayor on local planning issues and the provision of public services.[213]

In 1971 a coalition of reform council members won control of Cincinnati's government, rallying around the theme "Forty-four Neighborhoods, One Great City."[214] Dedicated to empowering the various neighborhoods within the city, this governing faction supported a community planning program that assigned professional planners to work with local councils to draft plans for the individual communities. A planner expressed the prevailing opinion in Cincinnati's city government when he asserted that "community ideas should come first."[215] The Clifton Town Meeting, which spoke for one upper-middle-class neighborhood, certainly seconded this view, and its community plan exemplified the emphasis on neighborhood autonomy and distinctiveness. Reflecting community attitudes, a former Clifton Town Meeting president insisted that "Clifton's overall plan must strengthen its unique 'village within the city character.'"[216] During the early 1970s, Cincinnati also increased the role of community councils in defining city budget priorities and in distributing federal development funds. Then in 1976 city hall created Community Assistance Teams that were to serve as liaisons between each community and the municipal departments.

Suffering from the nation's most severe case of municipal giantism, New York City seemed to face an especially urgent need to decentralize authority and obtain neighborhood input. In the 1960s Mayor John Lindsay had advocated and created neighborhood city halls to establish a link between the municipal bureaucracy and the grass-roots citizenry. But in 1970 Lindsay went one step further when he formed the Office of

Neighborhood Government, and his spokesman proudly announced that this reform would launch the "year of the neighborhoods."[217] Then in June of that year the mayor unveiled a plan for neighborhood government intended to make "city agencies more responsive and accountable at the neighborhood level" and "to reduce the alienation and distance that citizens feel toward a remote City government."[218]

A series of other decentralization proposals followed, culminating in the city charter amendments of 1975. Under the new charter provisions, advisory community boards appointed by the borough presidents would appoint district managers to ensure greater coordination and responsiveness in the delivery of city services. For example, a district manager and his or her cabinet would supposedly ensure that the public works department was not operating at cross-purposes with the sanitation department at the neighborhood level, and this manager would also guarantee that both departments responded to neighborhood needs. Moreover, the charter amendments required the City Planning Commission to refer all zoning and planning proposals to the board for the community affected, and departments also had to consult with the boards when preparing their budget requests. Though the boards had only an advisory role in planning and budgetary questions, the charter amendments of 1975 clearly demonstrated an unprecedented concern for giving the grass roots a voice in the charting of the city's future.

Unfortunately, in 1975 New York City's future appeared decidedly dreary. Bankrupt, with thousands of square feet of empty office space and scores of vacant factories, the city had fallen to a new low after three decades of descent. Yet as the charter amendments indicated, the city's neighborhoods remained a source of hope. In New York City as in Cincinnati, Chicago, and Saint Louis, perhaps new life in the local communities and a new sense of neighborhood pride would accomplish what miles of concrete and acres of cleared slums had not. Visitors to Hill Day did not feel the city was dead nor did those attending the annual San Gennaro festival in Little Italy. The white-collar residents of Clifton were successfully defending their village within the city as were their counterparts in North Park. The older central cities may have been hitting bottom, but possibly the vitality of the surviving urban subdivisions might result in a renewed if more fragmented metropolis.

CHAPTER SEVEN ○ **Messiah Mayors and the Gospel of Urban Hype**

On August 26, 1976, Boston's Mayor Kevin White joined with entrepreneur James Rouse in opening the Rouse-developed Quincy Market, a festive collection of boutiques, gourmet groceries, trendy restaurants, and colorful pushcarts occupying the city's 150-year-old recycled public market. Located in the supposedly crime-ridden city core with insufficient parking facilities and no department-store anchor, the marketplace seemed to defy all conventional retailing wisdom. Neither White nor Rouse was confident of success, but when they arrived on opening day, more than fifty thousand customers were already on the scene to launch what one observer described as "a gigantic four-day party, with mimes and steel bands and dancing into the night."

The enthusiasm did not wane during the following months and years. In 1978 one national magazine claimed that at night the marketplace became "a huge, floating cocktail party for singles, suburbanites, and partying businessmen." By 1979 Quincy Market's promoters were boasting that it attracted more foot traffic than Disney World, and according to one Bostonian the marketplace was "Disney World with class," "a glittering rebuke to the notion that inner cities could not attract tourists and shoppers with their cameras, their appetites, and their money." On the tenth anniversary of the auspicious opening, the market's designer reminisced about the joyous event, proclaiming that "it was the day the urban renaissance began."[1]

Across the nation many commentators agreed with this assessment. A longtime veteran of the urban revitalization war with service in the Fight-

Blight campaign and the Greater Baltimore Committee offensive, James Rouse himself was to become the guru of the festival marketplace, claiming that its appearance represented a turning point in the seemingly endless battle to revive the city. After decades of effort, Rouse perceived victory at hand. Though some were less enthusiastic than was the ebullient developer, the birth of the festival marketplace certainly marked the beginning of a fresh optimism about central cities. The emerging downtown real estate boom of the late 1970s and early 1980s lent further support to hopes for revival, and the gentrification of inner-city neighborhoods also seemed to offer proof that the cities were coming back. For Rouse and many like-minded urbanites the portents of recovery were increasingly clear.

Moreover, in case anyone failed to perceive these hopeful signs, journalists, local officials, and business leaders worked full time to fashion a new upbeat image for their central cities. The late 1970s and the 1980s was an era of unprecedented urban hype with the bad-mouthing of the past yielding to rosy prognostications and positive publicity. Older hubs needed to shed their blighted reputations; with a fresh promotional face the expected renaissance would arrive on schedule. Festival marketplaces, waterfront fairs, and big-league sports teams were among the flourishes that would brighten the city's image. If only a city could boast of a World Series team, an ethnic carnival with thousands of suburbanites munching on ribs, ravioli, and matzo balls, and a local version of Quincy Market, then municipal bond ratings would supposedly improve, local employment increase, and national recognition as a comeback city soon follow.

The age of doomsayers had passed, and everywhere urban boosters trumpeted the new positive message that central cities could be fun and profitable. Even signs of blight and social disorder could be repackaged in positive language favorable to the city. The vandalism of New York City's subways by spraycan-wielding youths was proclaimed "graffiti art," a blossoming of indigenous urban culture rather than a symptom of decay and lawlessness. Those praising graffiti art now glorified the burned-out ruins of Bronx as the "cradle of Hip Hop culture," where the numerous subway trains running through the neighborhoods provided residents "with a constant exposure to the latest works of art and the young kids . . . with the models of what they might one day achieve."[2] Urban junk, likewise, was no longer junk. Describing the "aging inner ring" of Minneapolis, one writer claimed, "Nowhere else in the entire metropolitan area can such exotic backyards be found," complete with "everything from complex mechanical gadgets or whimsical playthings to oversized objets d'art."[3]

No publicists or pollyannas, however, were more positive than were the new wave of big-city mayors. They preached a message of revival, and every new office tower, behemoth convention center, and lively Quincy Market represented a glittering incarnation of their words of redemption. Moreover, they were not reluctant to attribute the city's improved fortunes to their own leadership and political acumen. In fact, they were the messiahs of their own gospel of urban hype. Endlessly, they presented the same message: the cities were coming back, and they were the saviors responsible for this rebirth.

Even sober and often pessimistic scholars believed that the worst had passed. By the mid-1980s scholarly articles were appearing that asked "Where Has Urban Crisis Gone?" "Whatever Happened to the Urban Crisis?" and "What Urban Crisis?"[4] Though these commentators recognized that problems persisted, "crisis" no longer seemed an appropriate description for the state of urban America. The crisis was over, and many older central cities appeared to have stemmed their decline.

Thus after more than four decades of intensive debate over how to revive the faltering central city, the prevailing rhetoric was positive, and morale in the once-beleaguered hubs seemed to be high. Whether reality matched the rhetoric was another question that many mayors, journalists, and even some scholars chose to ignore. The evangelists of urban hype had declared victory, and at urban festivals and marketplaces throughout the nation's northeastern quadrant there was literally dancing in the streets.

The Mayors and Their Message

In 1985 political scientist Barbara Ferman published a study titled *Governing the Ungovernable City.*[5] It told of mayors who had overcome the barriers to effective urban leadership that had seemed so insuperable just a decade earlier. And it testified to the new spirit in city hall. In the late 1960s and early 1970s big-city mayors like John Lindsay had appeared to be at the mercy of the chaotic events of the time. They did not govern the city; they reacted to the myriad crises that wracked the metropolis. By the late 1970s and early 1980s, however, the messiah mayors did seem to be in control, confidently charting the urban course rather than being pushed helplessly to and fro. They easily won reelection, remained in the mayor's seat year after year, and effectively hobbled opposition. Their electoral successes rested largely on their reputations as urban saviors. They had redeemed their cities from the fiscal doom of the mid-1970s and bolstered municipal credit ratings. They had created a more favorable business climate and thus had nurtured a new downtown building boom.

Moreover, they had supposedly kept a lid on social disorder, and their cities had not suffered a recurrence of rioting. In other words, they could claim to have saved the central city from the endemic crises of the past, and they could count on the voters' gratitude.

Perhaps the most lauded of the messiah mayors was Baltimore's William Donald Schaefer. Thomas D'Alesandro III, Schaefer's immediate predecessor, had retired in exasperation in 1971 after only one frustrating term in the mayor's office. By contrast, Schaefer was to win four terms as mayor, survive fifteen years in that position, and would step down only to assume the higher office of Maryland governor. Though he was a white man in a predominantly black city, in the 1983 Democratic primary Schaefer was able to defeat his black mayoral opponent, outpolling him among voters of both races. Schaefer's foe had recruited Martin Luther King III and Atlanta's Mayor Andrew Young as well as other black leaders from throughout the country to campaign for him, but a majority of Baltimore's blacks seemed unimpressed. Speaking to over two thousand paying guests at a "Blacks for Schaefer" dinner, a former black mayoral candidate lauded the incumbent as a modern Joshua "bringing down the walls that separate people in Baltimore," and one seasoned observer reported that in the early 1980s "Schaefer had an approval rating of ninety percent throughout the city" with the figure "higher among blacks than among whites."[6]

Even the national media lavished praise upon the triumphant Baltimore executive. One magazine proclaimed Schaefer "the best mayor in America," a man who had "become his city" and with "single-minded determination [had] pulled the city of Baltimore out of red into the pink."[7] A bald, double-chinned bachelor who had lived all his life in an ordinary rowhouse with his mother Tululu, Schaefer was a far cry from the sexy, young wunderkinds of the Lindsay era. In the new age of the late 1970s and early 1980s, however, Lindsayesque good looks and wit counted for less than in the late 1960s. Writing in 1984 about Schaefer, one journalist observed, "Most cities learned hard in the last twenty years [that] you don't need a charming, wavy-haired talker for mayor." Instead, "You need the toughest, canniest, most obsessive sonofabitch in town. You need someone who's going to make it his life."[8] The messiah mayors of the 1980s were not matinee idols but feisty character actors who had battled their way into the starring role.

Schaefer's counterpart in New York City was another plump, bald bachelor, Edward Koch. Elected the city's chief executive in 1977, by 1980 *New York* magazine was describing him as "the most popular mayor in memory."[9] The following year Koch won both the Democratic and Republican mayoral primaries, carrying more than 60 percent of the vote in each contest, and he went on to triumph in the general election with a 75 percent majority, the largest in modern New York history. Like Schaefer, Koch was a "character," about whom innumerable stories circulated. He was outspoken, often tactless, and unlike the Baltimore mayor he especially alienated black political leaders. Moreover, he suffered from a serious case of egomania. But just as Schaefer's life was Baltimore, Koch seemed to work unceasingly with an undeniable love for his city. And his quirks were appealing to an electorate satiated by the smooth charm of Lindsay and the colorless ineffectuality of Beame. According to *Time*, Koch was "New York's nut uncle, the bachelor workhorse with opinions on everything [and] who will not stop talking."[10]

Elsewhere the messiah mayors had less media appeal but were equally attractive to the voters. In 1977 Richard Caliguiri became mayor of Pittsburgh and launched Renaissance II. According to Caliguiri, "[Pittsburgh's residents] had allowed the flame to die which had ignited our civic pride and enabled Pittsburgh to rank with the best of America's cities in its commitment to urban progress and renewal." "But it was not too late," the mayor claimed, "to regain that drive, to restore that pride and to rededicate ourselves to the future of this City."[11] To recapture the glory of the Lawrence-Mellon collaboration of the 1940s and 1950s, Caliguiri adopted a low-key, conciliatory style rather than an attitude of confrontation. In fact, *Time* described him as an "unobtrusive" person who had "the muzzy charm of a maître d' " and who "avoid[ed] controversies as if they were fatal diseases."[12] This style worked with the voters who reelected him in 1981 and 1985, the latter year with a 77 percent majority.

Another conciliatory, low-profile mayor was winning a reputation as the savior of beleaguered Cleveland. Campaigning with the slogan "Together we can do it," in 1979 George Voinovich defeated the controversial incumbent Dennis Kucinich, garnering a majority among both blacks and whites in the racially divided city.[13] Two years later he won reelection with a 77 percent majority, carrying all the city's wards. Conceding defeat, even his opponent admitted that "Mayor Voinovich [had done] a remarkable job in pulling the pieces back together" since 1979.[14] Then in 1985 Cleveland's mayor won a third victory, this time with 72 percent of the vote. One political observer summed up the prevailing attitude when he claimed that Voinovich "could be mayor into the 21st century. There's nobody around who can beat him."[15]

In other aging hubs strong executives were also perpetuating their control of city hall. For example, in 1985 Buffalo voters were awarding a third term to James Griffin, who the *Buffalo Evening News* described as "an honest, tough, scrappy independent politician committed to fiscal conservatism."[16] Like his New York City counterpart, Griffin worked hard to restore his city's financial standing and upgrade its reputation, and his efforts earned him the title of "the Ed Koch of western New York."[17] In 1985 Saint Louis also returned its renaissance mayor to office. With 72 percent of the primary vote and 85 percent of the general election ballots, Vincent Schoemehl, Jr., was replicating the victories of Voinovich, Caliguiri, Koch, and Schaefer. And his triumph rested on similar claims. Schoemehl boasted: "I have done a lot of things in this city that have never been done before. There's a real sense of momentum in this town."[18] Like the other messiah mayors, Schoemehl was in control and appeared to have led his city down the road to revival.

Detroit's perennial savior was the black mayor Coleman Young. First elected in 1973, Young won reelection in 1977, 1981, and 1985, capturing over 60 percent of the vote in the latter two contests. In 1981 a *Detroit Free Press* commentator observed, "Coleman Young continues to dominate Detroit politics as few leaders in the city's history have done."[19] Year after year he somehow put together deals that saved his city from financial debacle, and he never ceased to preach of Detroit's coming renaissance. Though a former labor radical and a representative of rising black power, like his white counterparts Young was not a confrontational politician. He told the *Free Press:* "I think the only future for black people in this country has got to be in coalition, not in head-to-head conflict with the white majority, or else it would be counter-productive."[20] Reflecting the success of Young's coalition building with the white business establishment, auto tycoon Henry Ford II proclaimed that without Young, "this city would be dead."[21]

Only one of the glamorous crusaders of the late 1960s was able to adapt to the new age and assume the trappings of a messiah mayor. A political chameleon par excellence, Boston's Mayor Kevin White fashioned a new image for himself in the second half of the 1970s. No longer Boston's Lindsay, he was now that city's Koch, an unbeatable mayor who could cope with financial emergencies and father such monuments of revival as Quincy Market. His arrogance offended some Bostonians, and one city council member complained, "Kevin thinks he's the one true God."[22] But after his fourth victory in 1979 the *Boston Globe* correctly identified the longtime mayor as "one of the most powerful in Boston's history."[23]

Less sympathetic observers labeled the perennial Boston mayor a "boss" and attacked his efforts to build a personal machine. After his reelection in 1975, White established a permanent campaign organization with precinct captains and ward coordinators who between elections were expected to identify and answer neighborhood complaints. On election day, however, they were to make sure that the voters turned out for the mayor. As a reward, the White administration granted these lieutenants city jobs and promotions. Though it was a personal organization dedicated to one man rather than to a party, White's arrangement was a throwback to the machine politics of an earlier era.[24] In 1979 White's mayoral opponent tried to capitalize on this, using the slogan "We Can Beat the White Machine" and calling for a "change from the politics of fear and spoils to the politics of access and openness."[25] But White defended his attempt to restore the power of urban political leaders. "Since 1970," the mayor argued, "there's been an unstructured assault on the political profession's right to govern, to lead. Until we recapture a very diffuse political process, nobody can do anything!" According to the embattled chief executive, "When I'm faced with this kind of situation, you bet your life I'm going to pull together all the scraps of power I can assemble."[26]

Other messiah mayors would have seconded White's views, and a number of them shared the Boston leader's appreciation for the merits of machine politics. Baltimore's Mayor Schaefer was an admirer of Boss-Mayor Richard Daley and praised Daley's ability to make Chicago work in contrast to John Lindsay's politics of perpetual crisis. The Maryland politician reportedly mused: "When you need to get to the airport in Chicago you're there in fifteen minutes. In fifteen minutes, Lindsay's still trying to find the phone on his desk."[27] Though he had entered politics as a reform foe of Tammany boss Carmine DeSapio, Mayor Koch of New York City also expressed little admiration for such crusading opponents of party politics as his handsome predecessor in city hall. After winning the mayor's office, Koch made peace with the regular Democratic organizations in New York City's boroughs, winning their support in both 1981 and 1985.[28]

In Saint Louis, Mayor Schoemehl was building his political clout and eliciting criticism similar to that aimed at Boston's Kevin White. Appointing some of his staunchest supporters to the city Civil Service Commission, Schoemehl gained control over the municipal bureaucracy to a degree unprecedented in recent Saint Louis history. A critical alderman asserted that the civil service idea "that the people worked for the city, not the mayor, [was] out the window." Claiming that Schoemehl was "building a new political machine," another foe argued that the mayor had "utilized his position to really set up a citywide operation in the grand style of the old days."[29]

For the messiah mayors, power concentrated in the hands of canny politician-executives seemed a necessary ingredient to the urban revival formula. Medicis spawned renaissance, not Lindsays. Diatribes against power brokers and machines were momentarily out of fashion. Once regarded as a remnant of a benighted past, after his death Chicago's Richard Daley became a mayor one could learn from. He had made Chicago work, and others could make their cities work as well if they adhered more closely to the rules of practical politics. The terms "practical" and "politics," in fact, summed up the attitude of the postcrisis era of the late 1970s and early 1980s. According to the Whites, Schaefers, Kochs, and Schoemehls, revival would be a product of pragmatic government partnerships with business, sensible budget making, and hardheaded deals with labor and neighborhoods.

In Boston, Detroit, Saint Louis, Buffalo, Cleveland, Pittsburgh, New York, and Baltimore, then, the scenario was much the same. Powerful and perennial executives seemed to be disproving the notion of the ungovernable city. Moreover, all of these executives were dedicated to restoring their cities' financial reputations, brightening their business climates, and strengthening their municipal governments through the application of practical politics. Even in other cities with weaker mayors, these same goals were evident. For example, in Cincinnati and Minneapolis, with their weak-mayor structures of government, the city councils were adopting much the same approach as the messiah mayors. Moreover, in Philadelphia, where no strong executive was able to seize control and stay in office for term after term, the aims were still economic revitalization, fiscal caution, and a conciliatory, achievement-oriented politics rather than a confrontational or crusading political style. After one term, ineffectual Mayor Green yielded to the even less effective Mayor Goode, ensuring that no messiah mayor would reign in the City of Brotherly Love, but the perceived goals of these lukewarm executives differed little from those of their more dynamic colleagues. Likewise, in Chicago, snow-clogged streets turned the electorate against Mayor Bilandic; a shrewish personality crippled Mayor Byrne; and political infighting hobbled Mayor Washington, preventing any of them from gaining long-term control of the Windy City. Thus weakened, they were either unable or unwilling to establish any significant alternatives to the policy agenda of the messiah mayors.

Of first priority on this agenda was the pressing question of restoring the financial health of city government. In the wake of the crisis of the mid-1970s, each of the messiah mayors recognized the necessity of balancing budgets and upgrading municipal credit ratings. Virtual bankruptcy and near default had been the ultimate humiliation for the aging central cities, and not until the cities erased this financial blot from their records could they ever seriously claim the renaissance title.

Exacerbating the mayors' problems were the cutbacks in federal aid that began during the Carter administration and deepened with the coming of Ronald Reagan to power. As is evident in table 20, in each of the older central cities the percentage of general revenues derived from Washington dropped sharply between 1977–78 and 1984–85. In most of the cities the proportion coming from the federal government fell by approximately one-half, and a number of states tried to close the resulting revenue gap and shouldered a heavier burden of municipal costs. Yet only in Boston did the combined state and federal share in 1984–85 surpass that in 1977–78. In eleven of the twelve hubs, city governments had to rely more on local resources with the long-term shift from property to nonproperty taxes continuing. Clearly by the 1980s, federal fiscal power was no longer ascendant, and most of the older cities were increasingly on their own.

The messiah mayors did not accede quietly to these cuts but instead kept up the traditional calls for more aid from Washington. Pittsburgh's Democratic Mayor Caliguiri complained of "social programs abandoned so callously by the Reagan Administration" and called on the Republican President to seek increased federal funding for municipal public works projects aimed at restoring the crumbling streets, bridges, water mains, and sewer systems.[30] Likewise, Mayor Koch argued, "Washington has an obligation to help local governments rebuild their deteriorating physical plants," and in the words of one journalist, Baltimore's Mayor Schaefer "went to Capitol Hill . . . and tore ass into Ron Reagan's cuts in aid to the cities."[31]

Yet in certain unacknowledged ways the tightfistedness of the Reagan administration, combined with fresh memories of financial debacle, actually benefited the mayors. The grim fiscal realities ushered in an era of diminished public-sector expectations and offered mayors a convincing excuse for not solving urban problems. Whereas Mayor Lindsay and the largesse of the Johnson administration had raised citizens' hopes unrealistically, fiscal stringency and Reagan's cutbacks caused voters and municipal employees to expect little. By 1980 a big-city mayor was a success if he or she could just keep the city from going bankrupt. Minor achievements could win plaudits and earn the mayor laurels. It was easy for mayors to be messiahs in an age when nobody expected them to walk on water. If faced with demands, waving the red-inked ledgers of fiscal crisis could prove a useful tactic. Thus deficit and debt figures were more powerful answers to police officers threatening to strike or neighborhood groups demanding improved services than was all the Lindsayesque rhetoric.

Table 20. Sources of General Revenue, 1977–1978 and 1984–1985

City	Property Taxes (%)		Nonproperty Taxes (%)		Federal Intergovernmental Aid (%)		State Intergovernmental Aid (%)	
	1977–78	1984–85	1977–78	1984–85	1977–78	1984–85	1977–78	1984–85
New York	22.8	18.5	20.0	27.6	7.8	6.7	38.4	33.5
Chicago	21.8	18.3	26.0	35.3	27.4	14.7	10.2	14.3
Philadelphia	14.0	11.5	38.8	46.1	19.8	7.7	12.5	14.4
Detroit	17.4	12.7	18.3	22.1	23.2	12.2	21.7	26.1
Baltimore	19.8	22.5	9.5	11.7	20.0	6.2	42.1	44.3
Cleveland	13.0	10.0	19.7	39.3	32.5	19.9	10.3	10.3
Boston	53.7	32.2	0.5	2.0	13.4	6.6	21.8	44.6
Saint Louis	10.1	6.7	41.8	44.0	22.9	14.2	10.0	8.7
Pittsburgh	26.0	27.1	24.0	34.0	24.0	12.7	15.5	9.8
Buffalo	24.0	19.3	1.1	2.4	25.6	13.9	32.8	41.0
Cincinnati	10.4	8.1	29.5	34.0	24.0	15.5	8.4	6.5
Minneapolis	32.3	18.7	5.1	3.8	21.2	9.2	24.4	18.5

Sources: U.S. Bureau of the Census, *City Government Finances in 1977–1978* and *City Government Finances in 1984–1985* (Washington, D.C.: U.S. Government Printing Office, 1980 and 1986).

Washington and the bankers left big-city mayors with little financial lee-way in the late 1970s and early 1980s, and everyone knew that demonstra-tions and diatribes would yield relatively little in cash. The cash just was not in the city coffers.

Faced with federal cutbacks and a recent history of fiscal debacle, city leaders from Boston to Saint Louis adopted a strategy of belt-tighten-ing. Slashing expenditures was the hallmark of the era, and since most city outlays went for labor costs, cutting payrolls was a prime means to the end of financial security. As seen in table 21, between 1977 and 1985 the number of municipal employees dropped in ten of the twelve older central cities, with nine of the municipalities recording a decline of more than 10 percent and three slashing their personnel by over 20 percent. Pittsburgh inched upward from the already low level that had existed at the close of Mayor Peter Flaherty's frugal administration. The figures for New York City also rose, but only because in 1977 the near-bankrupt city had al-ready cut payrolls drastically. A comparison of precrisis figures in 1974 with the numbers for 1985 would show a loss for New York as well.

Part of this drop in the municipal work force was owing to federal cuts, but the decline was also a product of local attempts to pare away costly personnel. Carter's reduction of funding for programs initiated under the Comprehensive Employment and Training Act (CETA) forced municipal layoffs, and the repeal of the CETA public service jobs scheme under the

Table 21. Number of City Employees, 1977 and 1985

City	No. of Employees		% Change 1977–1985
	1977	1985	
New York	349,306	393,290	+ 12.6
Chicago	47,261	45,260	− 4.2
Philadelphia	38,593	32,854	− 14.9
Detroit	24,174	20,332	− 15.9
Baltimore	38,003	31,420	− 17.3
Cleveland	11,109	9,348	− 15.9
Boston	27,617	20,704	− 25.0
Saint Louis	14,995	8,719	− 41.9
Pittsburgh	5,984	6,152	+ 2.8
Buffalo	13,653	12,021	− 12.0
Cincinnati	7,986	6,186	− 22.5
Minneapolis	6,080	5,394	− 11.3

Sources: U.S. Bureau of the Census, *City Employment in 1977* and *City Employment in 1985* (Washington, D.C.: U.S. Government Printing Office, 1978 and 1986).

Reagan administration induced further cuts in the work force. But local attempts to improve productivity and eliminate expendable employees ensured additional slashes in the payroll. For example, the shift from three-person to two-person collection crews on New York City garbage trucks meant that the average daily number of sanitation workers assigned to the trucks dropped from 3,207 in 1978 to 2,670 in 1984.[32] Elsewhere sanitation crews also shrank, and city budget makers came to regard park and recreation employees as unaffordable luxuries. Though citizens continued to identify crime and violence as the chief banes of urban living, even the number of police employees dropped in ten of the twelve cities, with only New York City and Cleveland increasing their law enforcement personnel.[33]

Though labor leaders protested loudly in the press about the personnel cuts, fiscal crisis had made them more amenable than in the past. This was especially evident in New York, where union chiefs recognized that imminent bankruptcy and the resulting outcry against supposedly overpaid municipal employees threatened hard-won collective bargaining privileges and jeopardized labor's role in city government. The chairman of New York City's Office of Collective Bargaining expressed the prevailing belief that "the survival of the city as well as the collective bargaining process necessitated compromise and conciliation and an abandonment of the traditionally adversarial relationship between the city and the unions."[34]

Moreover, given the harsh financial realities, a confrontational approach seemed likely to reap few benefits. As the president of the United Federation of Teachers observed: "A strike is a weapon you use against the boss who has money. This boss has no money."[35] Consequently, in 1977, 1978, and 1979 there were no labor actions against New York, and the most powerful union chief, Victor Gotbaum, proved cooperative with the Emergency Financial Control Board. Wall Street banker Felix Rohatyn, who was the chief architect of the control board's policies, developed a personal friendship with the normally tough-talking, expletive-prone Gotbaum and lauded the labor boss as "one of the people who probably did as much as anyone to help save the city in 1975 and the period afterwards."[36] Harmony did not invariably prevail between labor and the cities. Gotbaum developed a strong aversion for Koch and attacked the mayor's administration because it "didn't give a damn about the poor."[37] In addition, in 1980 a New York City transit strike and a Chicago firefighters walkout seemed to augur for a return to the tumult of earlier times. Yet in the late 1970s and early 1980s labor politics in New York City and the other aging metropolises was not a repeat performance of the late 1960s.

Gotbaum and others grumbled and civil servants occasionally walked off the job, but in the end they had to accede to personnel cutbacks as cities attempted to balance their books.

In one city after another the municipal ledgers testified to the belt-tightening of local government leaders. Between 1977–78 and 1984–85 the consumer price index soared 68 percent, yet as seen in table 22, the general expenditures of ten of the twelve older cities rose less than this figure. With the exception of Minneapolis and Pittsburgh, when measured in constant dollars, city spending actually declined in the aging hubs. Moreover, with spending increases in current dollars of less than 20 percent, Baltimore, Cleveland, and Boston also seem to have been especially thrifty during those inflationary years.

Such fiscal probity was among the proudest boasts of messiah mayors throughout the northeastern quadrant of the United States. Though New York City did not rank among the most frugal of the older municipalities, Mayor Koch never ceased to brag of his courageous budget cuts and of his supposed role in the financial salvation of his metropolis. Summing up his first six years in office, Koch proclaimed that he was able "to take a city on the edge of bankruptcy and make it bankable[,] . . . to lead a citizenry in total disarray, shaken by what had occurred in the financial debacle in 1975, . . . turn them around so that they now have confidence in themselves and faith in their government."[38] In his autobiography he described how he had battled to close the budget gap by facing down the transit workers union and by eliminating a redundant city hospital despite vigorous protests from the city's blacks.[39] The authors of a more critical account of the Koch administration agreed that "fiscal management, first and foremost, became the watchword of his City Hall" and observed that

Table 22. Increase in General Expenditures, 1977–1978 to 1984–1985

City	% Increase	City	% Increase
New York	66.5	Boston	17.1
Chicago	59.8	Saint Louis	50.7
Philadelphia	33.6	Pittsburgh	79.3
Detroit	28.5	Buffalo	44.5
Baltimore	15.1	Cincinnati	33.9
Cleveland	13.8	Minneapolis	121.0

Sources: U.S. Bureau of the Census, *City Government Finances in 1977–1978*, and *City Government Finances in 1984–1985* (Washington, D.C.: U.S. Government Printing Office, 1980 and 1986).

"after years of profligate spending, Koch emerged as the mayor who would say no." Moreover, they found that "the public actually seemed to like taking Dr. No's bitter medicine."[40] Koch kept warning of the need for sacrifices and seemingly repentant New Yorkers rewarded the demanding mayor with ever higher ratings in the polls.

If anyone doubted his fiscal mastery, Koch could point to a series of landmark achievements. After six years of being shut out, in 1981 New York City again entered the long-term money markets and borrowed for capital purposes. Two years later Moody's Investor Service raised the city's credit rating from speculative grade to medium grade. Then in 1985 Koch announced that within the year the city planned to retire virtually all of the remaining federally guaranteed debt incurred during the crisis era of the late 1970s. The mayor boasted, "There is no better symbol of the city's turnaround than its ability to pay off these loans faster and more efficiently than anyone had expected."[41]

Mayors elsewhere were also building their reputations as fiscal redeemers. Mayor George Voinovich successfully backed Cleveland away from bankruptcy. Attempting to improve the city government's efficiency, Voinovich established the Operations Improvement Task Force, a body of eighty local private-sector executives who reviewed municipal operations. The Task Force made 650 recommendations that supposedly would save the city $57 million a year, and by 1984 approximately 75 percent of the suggestions had been implemented.[42] In 1980 the mayor also negotiated a $36.2 million loan from area banks, thereby ending twenty-two months of default. To avoid renewed catastrophe, Voinovich proposed an austerity program that included a hike in taxes and utility rates and layoffs of up to 650 municipal employees. Responding to the mayor's rhetoric of sacrifice, in February 1981 Cleveland voters approved a 33 percent raise in the city income tax rate. Together with continued budget paring, in 1983 this tax boost allowed the city to reenter the national bond market after an absence of five years. And in 1987 Cleveland finally paid off the last of the $110 million debt that it had owed at the time of its default. The state commission created to oversee Cleveland's finances was then disbanded, and in a ceremony at city hall Mayor Voinovich set fire to facsimiles of notes that Cleveland had defaulted on nine years earlier. Summing up the feelings of many of his fellow citizens, the mayor said: "This ends one of the saddest segments of Cleveland's history."[43]

Meanwhile, in Saint Louis, Mayor Vincent Schoemehl was slashing payrolls with unprecedented vigor, cutting about five thousand positions between 1981 and 1987. During this same period, the membership of the municipal employees union dwindled from 2,500 to 900.[44] Through privatization of public facilities, Schoemehl also reduced expenses and rid the city of overpaid civil servants. For example, the Schoemehl administration assigned operation of a city-owned nursing home to a private contractor. Since it was no longer administering the home, the city laid off the facility's employees, but the private operator then hired many of them back at much lower salaries.[45] Moreover, Schoemehl closed the city's public hospital and entered into a pact with suburban Saint Louis County for the joint funding of a regional medical center. A nonprofit corporation and private management company would actually operate the new hospital, thus avoiding continued reliance on civil service employees.[46] By divesting itself of full responsibility for health services and through increased privatization, the Schoemehl administration trimmed Saint Louis government and ensured that the city stayed within its means.

Other mayors were less fortunate than Voinovich and Schoemehl, facing recurrent fiscal crises all too similar to those of the dire days of the mid-1970s. But somehow they patched together solutions and in the process enhanced their reputations as miracle workers and as seemingly indispensable leaders. For example, Coleman Young was able to skirt a financial debacle in Detroit in 1981. In 1980 the Michigan Supreme Court had upheld a 1978 arbitration settlement that awarded an additional $50 million in wages to the city's police and firefighters. As a result, the city recorded a $80 million deficit in 1980 and a $120 million shortfall in 1981. Faced with the likelihood of even deeper debts in the future and confronting a recession in the automobile industry that cut local income tax receipts by $30 million, Mayor Young fashioned a bailout package, or "survival plan," for his sinking domain. Central to the plan was a 50 percent increase in the municipal income tax rate for city residents and a 200 percent hike for nonresident commuters. Against seemingly insuperable odds, Young secured state legislative permission for the increase and also won voter approval for the raise in a city referendum. At the height of the crisis Young declared, "Our situation is one where we have to choose between extreme pain and agony."[47] But the mayor persevered, saving Detroit from the humiliation that New York City and Cleveland had earlier suffered. In late 1981 the *Detroit Free Press* editorialized, "[Young's] leadership in resolving this year's fiscal crisis was little short of genius."[48]

Similarly, in Boston, Mayor Kevin White confronted persistent budget problems, yet he kept the city from bankruptcy. Exacerbating White's budget woes was passage of a statewide tax limitation, Proposition $2\frac{1}{2}$, in November 1980. Massachusetts voters mandated that local property taxes could not exceed 2.5 percent of the fair market value, a restriction that could mean the loss of 75 percent of Boston's property tax revenues.

Within a month after the proposition's passage, Standard and Poor's, the bond-rating firm, lowered Boston's credit rating because the tax ceiling might have "a severe impact on the city and the quality of life" there. The glum city treasurer admitted, "If I was in their shoes, I might have done the same thing."[49] At the same time, Mayor White's ten-member committee charged with examining possible budget cuts submitted its report proposing a 25 percent reduction in police and fire budgets, a 50 percent drop in the allocation for hospitals and health, and the slashing of 60 percent from park and recreation funds.[50] White proceeded to lay off unprecedented numbers of municipal employees, but fortunately direct financial aid from the state increased markedly. Moreover, the city sold its convention center to the state, adding $40 million to the municipal account and saving Boston taxpayers from the necessity of alone having to shoulder the center's deficits.[51] Throughout the remaining White years, the budget crunch continued to be front-page news, but as in Detroit the mayor was able to salvage his city by taking tough measures.

The messiah mayors did not, then, usher in a new era of abundant funds and fiscal ease. Boston and Detroit narrowly skirted disaster, and the fortunes of New York and Cleveland only appeared rosy in comparison to the bankruptcy of the 1970s. In 1984 the *Wall Street Journal* reported that Standard and Poor's had "nudged Buffalo's credit rating up a notch, from triple-B to triple-B-plus," which was "not exactly a gold-plated endorsement." But the business journal described the gesture as "a kind word for Buffalo, which has enjoyed precious few of them lately."[52]

This same judgment was easily applicable to Buffalo's sister cities. By the early 1980s the older central cities were not suddenly basking in good fortune, but through a policy of fiscal restraint the messiah mayors were coaxing some kind words from credit-rating agencies and wary bankers. The mayors' gospel was one of sacrifice and austerity, not of expanded services or a bountiful, benevolent public sector. They fashioned fiscal survival through layoffs, tax hikes, privatization, and divestment of functions to the state or to joint city-suburban authorities. Repeatedly they told the city electorate that the citizenry had to pay more and to get less in return. And the chastened voters generally seemed to buy this message. Achieving this popular tolerance for a policy of higher taxes and fewer police was probably the messiah mayors' most miraculous accomplishment.

Yet the mayors' message was not only one of deprivation and self-denial. Sweetening their rhetoric was a heavy strain of ballyhoo about the long-awaited arrival of the central-city renaissance, a rebirth that supposedly would soon fatten starved budgets and relieve residents of some of their tax burden. Aiding the mayors in realizing this dream was the federal government's Urban Development Action Grant Program (UDAG). Initiated in 1978, UDAG offered distressed central cities money to stimulate economic development. Moreover, the program was highly flexible, allowing municipalities to use the grants in virtually any manner so long as they nurtured private investment that created new jobs and taxes. Though overall federal funding was declining, this relatively unencumbered grant of cash was just what the mayors wanted. Now the public sector could enter into partnerships with private developers and leverage billions of dollars of needed investment. The city could, for example, use the money to provide public infrastructure improvements to facilitate private construction projects, and it could subsidize interest payments on loans or offer direct subsidies to developers. With such financial lures older central cities might well attract new development dollars.[53]

Especially encouraging to public officials attempting to foster economic development was the boom in office construction in many central business districts during the late 1970s and early 1980s. As early as August 1977 the trade journal of the Building Owners and Managers Association (BOMA) was reporting that "office building occupancy rates in the U.S. have improved substantially in the past six months," and a year later this same publication ran the headline "Office Market Making Recovery: Squeeze on Space Predicted."[54] Whereas in the mid-1970s new office buildings in the New York City had stood empty because of slack demand, in 1978 the BOMA reported "an extreme shortage of new office space" in America's largest metropolis and predicted "an extremely tight market for new office space" in the nation as a whole.[55] In other words, the market for downtown offices had revived, and developers were ready to fill this demand. Across the country, power shovels and bulldozers were again gouging huge holes for the foundations of new skyscrapers, and cranes were lifting steel beams into place as structures rose thirty, forty, and fifty stories. To the messiah mayors each towering edifice was evidence of the revitalization of the city, and they were not hesitant to publicize this renaissance. A revived office market meant a revived city. This was the simple formula for success that many urban boosters preached.

New York City especially reveled in the office boom of the late 1970s and early 1980s. From a high of 20 percent in late 1973, the midtown Manhattan office vacancy rate dropped to only 4 percent by the close of 1978.[56] His spirits buoyed by this low figure, the city's biggest private developer proclaimed, "We're at the beginning of one of the largest booms in real-estate history." "We've been in the starting gate for five years," he told a reporter, "now we're off and running."[57] By 1981, 2.7 million square feet of new office space were ready for tenants; the next year thirteen newly completed buildings with a total of 6.3 million square feet opened their doors; in 1983 the office harvest was up to seventeen buildings with 9.5 million square feet.[58] From 1981 through 1986 Manhattan acquired approximately 45 million square feet of new commercial space, a quantity equal to the combined total space in Boston and San Francisco.[59]

Feeding this boom was a marked rise in the number of office employees. In a laudatory article on the "New York Colossus," *Business Week* reported that employment in business services such as law and accounting had risen 41 percent in New York City between 1977 and 1983, the number of jobs in the securities industry was up 64 percent, and real estate employment had grown 25 percent.[60] Thousands of new office workers crowded the streets and subways of midtown Manhattan, forcing the Koch administration to adopt policies aimed at dispersing development. Though the bumptious mayor embraced every new office structure, no matter how gargantuan or ungainly, as a freshly found treasure for his city, in 1981 his planning commission did recommend a program of tax and zoning incentives that would encourage new construction on the underutilized West Side of midtown Manhattan and draw it away from the overcrowded East Side.[61] By the early 1980s fears of overbuilding had supplanted anxieties about vacancies and lack of construction. New York City seemed to be struggling with the enviable problem of too much success.

In Pittsburgh, office construction in the Golden Triangle was also on the upswing, giving substance to Mayor Caliguiri's Renaissance II rhetoric. Demands for space gradually mounted during the late 1970s, and by 1980 the downtown occupancy rate was a tight 99.3 percent.[62] Such figures could only produce broad smiles and a heightened pulse rate among profit-hungry private developers, and between 1980 and 1987 an estimated $2.3 billion was spent on Golden Triangle commercial projects.[63] With approximately 6 million square feet of office space added between 1978 and 1985, the increment for this seven-year period was almost as great as that constructed during the entire previous two decades.[64] Fifty-three-story Grant Street Plaza and forty-six-story One Oxford Centre joined the Pittsburgh skyline, but the crown jewel of Renaissance II was the six-building PPG Place complex with its glass-sheathed 635-foot neo-Gothic tower. A monument worthy of the Land of Oz, PPG Place not only reflected the sunlight of the now smoke-free Pittsburgh; its gleaming facades also flashed the message to all onlookers that the former steel city had come back.[65]

In Cleveland the mammoth bulk of the new forty-five-story Sohio

Building and in Cincinnati the construction of a new Procter and Gamble headquarters announced boldly the same encouraging news.[66] Giant corporations were not abandoning the central cities but were investing hundreds of millions of dollars in the aging downtowns and committing themselves to a continued stay in the urban core. Likewise, the *Chicago Tribune* reported happily, "Chicago's downtown building boom will hit record levels in 1986, after an eight-year investment binge that has produced a 'Super Loop' of new offices, hotels and apartment buildings."[67] The following year a local magazine entitled its lead article "BOOM!" and proclaimed, "More construction has taken place in central Chicago during the last eight years than at any time since the Great Fire."[68] In Boston, 3.2 million square feet of downtown office space was scheduled for completion in 1987, but still analysts claimed that the New England metropolis was not overbuilt.[69] Instead, every new office tower seemed to engender new optimism about the onset of a permanent renaissance. Similarly, the *Baltimore Sun* proclaimed 1984 the "year of the crane" since "the sky above the central business district was full of them" with work proceeding "on nearly a dozen high-rise office, hotel and housing projects."[70]

Even when by all objective standards a downtown office project proved a failure, messiah mayors and their booster allies could use their ample powers of hype and transform it into a symbol of success. For example, Detroit's mammoth Renaissance Center was both the city's most noteworthy debacle and its most ballyhooed landmark of revitalization. When it opened in 1977, with 2.2 million feet of office space and a seventy-three-story hotel, the *Detroit Free Press* described it as "the towering symbol of what is hoped to be Detroit's new lease on life." At the lavish dedication ceremony with free champagne for all eight hundred people present, its principal developer, Henry Ford II, was confident of the invigorating qualities of the center, claiming that it and other construction projects were indications "that the flow of business and commercial operations to the suburbs [had] slowed down very considerably and might well be in the process of reversing itself."[71] In his 1979 state of the city address, Mayor Coleman Young similarly asserted, "The Renaissance Center has led the way in bringing our downtown area back to life," and supposedly because of the project, "new restaurants [were] popping up like wild flowers" and the adjacent area was "blossoming into an exciting entertainment district."[72]

In fact, the center drew tenants from existing downtown office buildings, the main target of the rental agents' sales pitch being firms already located in the central business district. Thus, by 1978 the occupancy rate of the forty-story Cadillac Tower was down to 40 percent, and its woes were not unusual.[73] Moreover, the Renaissance Center itself suffered serious financial ills, losing $140 million by 1983, when its debt and ownership had to be restructured.[74] Adding to the center's problems were a barrage of complaints from architecture critics. Attacking the center's isolation from the rest of downtown and its lack of regard "for the intricacy of the urban fabric," one critic claimed, "The skyscraping bundle of glass tubes on the Detroit River is really a counter–Renaissance Center."[75]

Yet the carping from planners, architects, journalists, and book-keepers did not stifle the enthusiasm of Mayor Young or other downtown boosters. Ten years after the center's opening, Young proclaimed: "What-ever you may think about the architectural integrity . . . , there's no question that Renaissance has had an impact that's felt all over downtown Detroit." The mayor attributed "the development that [had] taken place" to "the impetus and the catalytic force of Renaissance."[76] A leading downtown real estate broker concurred, saying, "[The center] has helped and hurt Detroit, but it has helped far more than it has hurt . . . Detroit is moving again."[77] In 1985 a spokesman for the Young administration summed up the prevailing attitude when he said: "Give me two million square feet of office space; give me a 73-story hotel with 1,500 rooms; . . . give me a total of $400 million of private sector investment in place— and I'll take it any day, complaints, criticisms and all."[78] After the dire days of the early 1970s, any construction was by definition good and any new office tower, no matter how much a violation of the urban fabric, was an encouraging sign.

Similarly, any signs of retail life downtown fueled the hype of messiah mayors and their ilk. Especially encouraging were the new shopping malls and festival marketplaces that arose in some central business dis-tricts during the late 1970s and early 1980s. In 1976 Boston's Quincy Mar-ket led the way, but other well-publicized signals of retail revitalization soon appeared elsewhere. For example, in August 1977 Quincy Market's developer, James Rouse, opened his Gallery at Market East in Phila-delphia. A four-level enclosed shopping mall with 125 stores and restau-rants as well as an 850-car garage, it was a clone of the latest in suburban retailing. As its public relations director observed, "It's like a suburban mall in an urban area, but it also has some good food."[79] Yet according to the city's press office, the Gallery was a symbol of "the New Philadelphia, a Philadelphia that is vibrant and progressive." And at its opening the mayor claimed that the Gallery "reestablishe[d] Market Street East as the most vital downtown shopping area in the United States."[80]

What firmly secured James Rouse's title as the savior of downtown retailing, however, was the inauguration of Baltimore's Harborplace in 1980. Part of Mayor Schaefer's Inner Harbor project to revitalize an area of rotting wharves and warehouses, Harborplace applied the Quincy Market formula with enormous success. According to police estimates, four hundred thousand people jammed the Inner Harbor area on the marketplace's opening day, and during the next year, its forty-five specialty shops, twenty food markets, and thirty-seven restaurants served eighteen million visitors, more than the total number attracted to Walt Disney World, and its sales were more than twice those of a typical regional mall. Moreover, it seemed to realize Rouse's goal for the inner city, making it "a warm and human place, with diversity of choice, full of festival and delight."[81]

Especially blessed was Saint Louis, for it was soon to enjoy a double boost to its downtown retailing, acquiring both a Rouse-developed festival marketplace in the mold of Harborplace and a downtown shopping mall reminiscent of suburbia and Philadelphia's Gallery. Early in August 1985, St. Louis Centre opened with four levels of two hundred shops anchored on either end by the city's major department stores. After only three weeks of business, a sales clerk in the mall expressed the prevailing euphoria in Schoemehl's Saint Louis when he observed: "For years we've been hearing about what a dead city this is, and now, suddenly, it's had new life breathed back into it."[82] Meanwhile, that same month Rouse's Union Station welcomed its first customers, appealing to the shoppers' nostalgia for the railroad just as Harborplace cashed in on the romance of Baltimore's bygone seafaring tradition. Within the mammoth headhouse and train shed of Saint Louis's ninety-year-old rail depot, Rouse carved out space for eighty shops, twenty-two restaurants, and a 550-room hotel. "This is a remarkable structure and place that people really have a deep affection for," rhapsodized a member of the Schoemehl administration. But he continued on a more practical note: "Having it come back to life means an immense amount of economic activity that simply would not have happened otherwise."[83]

Union Station, Harborplace, and Quincy Market were especially welcome to the messiah mayors, for these popular attractions fit into the city leaders' long-term goal of boasting tourism and convention business. Repeatedly, economic development experts spoke of the postindustrial economy and the growth of the service sector. In other words, the future of urban America was not in factories but in service, and one of the service industries most pregnant with possibilities was tourism. Unlike the steel mills and hog-butchering establishments, it was a clean industry without environmental drawbacks. In fact, tourism and convention goers meant glittering hotels, posh restaurants, and an aura of fun and excitement to counter the long-standing grim images of the older hubs. If the messiah mayors wished to repackage their domains in glitzy new wrappings, tourism and the convention trade would provide the necessary materials. Moreover, the hospitality industry employed large numbers of unskilled workers, something the older central cities had in abundance. In one city after another, then, festival marketplaces, convention centers, and hotels were all ingredients of a new formula for revitalization success. Older cities could come back if they became exciting magnets for the tourist dollar.

To aid their quest for the visitor's dollar, older cities throughout the Northeast and Midwest built ever larger convention centers. In 1977 Saint Louis opened a new convention facility, the tenth largest in the nation; within the next five years Baltimore and Pittsburgh likewise launched up-to-date meeting centers.[84] Nine days of festivities marked the inauguration of Pittsburgh's David L. Lawrence Convention Center; climaxing the ceremonies, industrial exhibits, and free entertainment was the arrival of almost two dozen Nobel laureates, imported especially to draw attention to a city that Mayor Caliguiri called "the best kept secret in the East."[85] But at its completion in 1986, New York City's Jacob Javits Convention Center outshone the lesser facilities of Pittsburgh, Baltimore, and Saint Louis. With almost four times the exhibit area of the Saint Louis center, New York's behemoth sprawled across twenty-two acres and could accommodate ninety thousand people.[86]

By the mid-1980s the race for ever bigger and better facilities was escalating. A new annex to Chicago's McCormick Place ensured that the Windy City's facility would retain first place in the nation, with twice the exhibit space of Javits Center.[87] By 1986 Mayor Vincent Schoemehl was decrying the failure of Saint Louis's convention center to keep up with the pack, having dropped from tenth largest in 1977 to nineteenth nine years later with an anticipated fall to twenty-fifth by 1990. Schoemehl pushed for a doubling of the exhibition space, arguing that "the payoff for such an investment is enormous."[88] Meanwhile, Cincinnati was expanding its convention center by 70 percent, and the director of sales at a major downtown hotel reported excitedly, "Cincinnati is on the brink of emerging as a convention city."[89] Cleveland's Convention Center was undergoing a $28 million rejuvenation, Detroit's Cobo Hall was expanding at a cost of $200 million, a newly created state convention authority was pouring an estimated $500 million in Boston's Hynes Convention Center, and Minneapolis was laying plans for an expanded facility with more than double the area than in the old.[90]

To fill this space, however, public officials and convention bureaus had to sell an upbeat image of their cities. Cleveland's George Voinovich summed up the feelings of his fellow messiah mayors when he said: "Everything we can do to put our best foot forward means that we're better off as a city."[91] The director of Baltimore's Office of Promotion and Tourism agreed, arguing, "Image ends up being real dollars and cents."[92] To ensure that convention planners saw only the best side of the city, public relations campaigns were essential. Financed by state or local tourism offices, chambers of commerce, or other booster groups, the repackaging of a city could supposedly pay off. Officials believed that New York State's "I Love New York" promotion with television ads blitzing the nation helped New York City to recover from its fiscal debacle. Boston's "Bright from the Start" proved less successful as did Detroit's "Super City USA," though a promotion with the Four Tops singing "Do It in Detroit" may have worked better. Chicago's "My Kind of Town" purportedly brought in the dollars, and Philadelphia broadcasters donated $2.5 million of air time for "Get to Know Us" commercials aimed at boosting their city's drooping self-image and even its national reputation.[93] The Buffalo Area Chamber of Commerce realized the growing need to sell the western New York metropolis as a tourist destination and convention site, boosting marketing funds from $75,000 in 1980 to $800,000 in 1985.[94]

A standout in the public relations battle to capture convention business was Saint Louis. Headed by John G. Walsh and financed by a local hotel room tax, the St. Louis Convention and Visitors Commission put its city on the map with the slogan "St. Louis—The Meeting Place." Devised by the Benton and Bowles agency, "The Meeting Place" campaign paid off, with visitor expenditures doubling within the first three years of the advertising barrage and a four-thousand-room hotel building boom soon following.[95] A leading marketing analyst observed, "A city lucky enough to get its slogan established will find itself with enormous credibility," and the Saint Louis experience testified to the wisdom of his words.[96] Walsh and his commission trumpeted their message enough that thousands of meeting planners soon believed it. But the commission did not rely solely on slogans; the personal touch also proved effective. To attract the Lions Club convention with its twenty-five thousand attendants, Walsh flew the club's inspection team by private plane to the city, arranged a lavish dinner for them, and made sure that Mayor Schoemehl, as well as baseball great Stan Musial, stopped by their table, the latter proving the coup de grace for the fervent baseball fans among the Lions' contingent.[97]

Essential in these efforts to bolster the image of an older central city was a big-league sports team. If a city lacked a professional baseball or football franchise, local boosters and messiah mayors feared that out-siders would label it second-rate. A big city had to have big-time sports, and a giant domed stadium could supposedly lure business and visitors just like an up-to-date convention center. Mammoth sports arenas, elabo-rate meeting facilities, and vibrant festival marketplaces all seemed to spell visitors' dollars and a fun reputation for a traditionally begrimed ur-ban core. They were all part of the promotional package of the late 1970s and the 1980s, and urban leaders sought to ensure that each element of this winning combination was in place.

As in the case of the battle for conventions, the struggle to secure and retain major-league sports franchises required massive investment and constant vigilance. Faced with the supposedly imminent departure of the baseball Twins and football Vikings, in the late 1970s Minneapolis boos-ters fought for approval and financing of a downtown domed stadium. A Chamber of Commerce spokesman asserted, "Minneapolis is truly one of the great cities in the United States," but commenting on the possible departure of the sports teams, he warned, "The second you begin to lose an asset, a slide from the top can begin."[98] The proposed stadium, how-ever, would not only ensure Minneapolis's status as a "major-league com-munity," it would also be a vital prop in the long-term effort to lift the sagging fortunes of the central business district. The executive vice presi-dent of the Chamber assured his members, "A downtown stadium will generate much needed economic activity that will result in new con-struction and help to stabilize business already in the downtown area." Moreover, he explained, "Minneapolis, like other large cities . . . , needed all the economic generators it can get since it is facing competi-tion from the suburbs."[99] Convinced by the Minneapolis entreaties, Min-nesota's legislature authorized a metropolitan agency to issue bonds for construction of a domed giant, the bonds to be repaid from operating reve-nues and Minneapolis city excise taxes on liquor sales and hotel rooms.[100]

Minneapolis kept its teams and thus did not slip from its position at the top of the urban hierarchy. That most ballyhooed renaissance city of the 1980s, Baltimore, proved less fortunate. In 1984 rumors were spread-ing that Robert Irsay, owner of the Baltimore Colts football team, was se-riously negotiating a move of his franchise to Indianapolis. A concerned Mayor Schaefer met privately with Irsay and said point blank to the owner: "I want you to tell me what you want me to do." Irsay responded by asking for a $15 million loan, improvements to the city's stadium, and a few other sweeteners while the usually irascible but now compliant mayor took notes and uttered reassurances.[101] Meanwhile, Maryland legislators were pushing through an eminent domain law permitting the city of Baltimore to seize the Colts. Before Schaefer and his city could act, however, Irsay packed his team's belongings in moving vans and in the dead of the night sneaked out of town to a new home in Indianapolis.

Galvanized by Baltimore's humiliating fall from the big-league football galaxy, Schaefer's administration set to work to prevent any further slippage. In June 1984 Schaefer's negotiators agreed to hand over to the Orioles nearly $2 million in concessions income as well as ballpark parking and scoreboard advertising revenues, all of which had formerly gone to the city treasury. Moreover, they promised $1.6 million in stadium improvements.[102] Soon planning began for a new $235-million, two-stadium complex, one for the Orioles baseball team and the other for a professional football franchise that the unrelenting mayor hoped to lure to his city.[103] Writing in the *Baltimore Business Journal,* one local commentator lauded the stadium project, claiming, "New skyscrapers are built in major U.S. cities every year, but when the Hoosierdome or the Metrodome goes up, people take notice." According to this observer, "The city that builds complexes such as these has a right to swagger in economic development and business circles."[104] Yet fears of sliding one more rung down the urban ladder tormented Baltimore boosters, and by early 1988 the *Baltimore Sun* was warning Schaefer's successor of the dangers of losing the Blast, the city's professional soccer team. In words repeated in one aging city after another, the *Sun* argued, "The Blast enlivens an otherwise dreary part of downtown[,] . . . [which] means money to the city."[105]

At the same time the *Sun* was editorializing on behalf of the Blast, now-Governor Schaefer was continuing his city's pursuit for big-league glory by making seductive offers to William Bidwell, owner of the St. Louis Cardinals football team. Yet neither Schaefer nor Saint Louis Mayor Schoemehl won this battle. Bidwell chose Phoenix, causing the *St. Louis Post-Dispatch* to lament, "The departure of the football Cardinals . . . is a blow to the area's economy as well as its pride."[106] But Schoemehl like Schaefer continued his unflagging crusade for a professional football team, proposing the sale of half of the city's airport to the suburban county government in exchange for county financial aid in building a downtown domed stadium.[107]

In early 1988 Detroit's Mayor Coleman Young was also urging construction of an inner-city stadium with a retractable roof to replace the seventy-six-year-old, city-owned Tiger Stadium.[108] The same message was heard in Cleveland as well. "What you need downtown more than anything else," Ohio superdeveloper Edward J. DeBartolo, Sr., told the *Cleveland Plain Dealer,* was for Clevelanders "with some help from the city, the county and the state" to join together to "invest in a huge domed stadium that would be located downtown, that would more or less be the heart of a lot of future development and excitement."[109] Meanwhile, Chicagoans struggled with the demands of the owners of the football Bears and baseball White Sox for new stadiums that would make these franchises more profitable.[110]

Perpetually hanging over the heads of messiah mayors and chamber-of-commerce boosters was the threat that a sports team would shift to playing fields on the suburban fringe or even worse would head for Sunbelt cities eager to offer any inducements to acquire major-league status. Advocates of domed gargantuans repeatedly pointed to the economic rewards of sports franchises and their role as an essential component in the revitalization of the central city. Minneapolis officials claimed that the Twins brought $30 million annually to the local economy, and Baltimore leaders asserted that the Colt's departure cost their city an equal amount.[111] Even more important was the psychological impact of a city losing its claim to big-league status. As Cleveland's Mayor Voinovich had noted, cities had to put their best foot forward and convince the world that they were coming back and regaining their dynamism. Favorable images manufactured by high-priced advertising firms had to be nurtured and protected if conventions, tourists, and businesses were to flock to the older central cities. And few events could tarnish a reputation for renaissance as readily as the departure of a sports franchise for sunnier climes.

But sports teams and convention centers were not the only magnets for drawing entertainment dollars to downtown. A number of older cities also hoped to cash in on renovated 1920s movie palaces that would anchor "culture" in the central business district and bring much-needed people to the empty nighttime streets. In Buffalo the city's department for community development was establishing a downtown cultural district centering on Shea's Theater but which was intended to include "artists' lofts, . . . restaurants, and a nightclub."[112] The multimillionaire owner of the Little Caesar's pizza chain purchased Detroit's massive Fox Theater complete with decaying plaster gargoyles and in early 1988 announced plans to build a small shopping mall between the Fox and State theaters as part of a scheme to restore the defunct Woodward Avenue entertainment district. Ever-optimistic Mayor Coleman Young responded to the pizza king's plans by boasting, "I think within two or three years, you'll see a transformation along Woodward Avenue." And one journalist observed that with the "grand rebirth" of the Fox "the slow and unsteady revitalization of the Motor City may be ready to move into high gear."[113]

Meanwhile, the Heinz Endowment was putting together a public-private partnership for the development of a mixed-use cultural district in

Pittsburgh's Golden Triangle. The city was to obtain federal funding for the scheme and the city-county auditorium authority was to contribute the proceeds from a bond issue, but private investors would provide 90 percent of the financing. The first stage of the project would transform a 2,800-seat 1920s movie palace into a center for the performing arts and produce an adjacent thirty-four-story office complex. Ultimately, the 1,600-seat Fulton Theater was to become another element in the cultural package, and ideally, creation of three smaller spaces for local and experimental dramatic groups was to follow.[114]

Not to be outdone by the former steel city, Cleveland was also fashioning a multitheater complex from the derelict remnants of three movie houses along Playhouse Square. Just as the Heinz Endowment spearheaded Pittsburgh's project, a bastion of local philanthropy, the Cleveland Foundation, financed much of the Ohio project, though in Cleveland as in Pittsburgh the city government served as intermediary in obtaining federal funds. Although largely intended to stimulate downtown business, the Playhouse Square project rested on a solid foundation of local nostalgia. "I courted my wife at Playhouse Square," Mayor Voinovich observed. "The rehabilitation of the theaters is a labor of love for me."[115]

The theaters, however, were only one tactic in the new entertainment strategy of Cleveland's boosters. In 1983, at the request of Mayor Voinovich, the city planning department drafted a plan for the downtown lakefront including an aquarium, a maritime museum, a festival marketplace, and a winter garden.[116] At the same time, a weed-ridden collection of decaying industrial structures and warehouses known as the Flats was being touted as a new center of downtown nightlife. Once dismissed as a commercial slum, now the Flats and the adjacent Cuyahoga River were evoking hyperbole. One urban design professional observed, "The boating experience up the seven-bend Cuyahoga and under its 22 bridges compares favorably in dramatic impact to boating on the canals of Berlin or Paris," and another wrote of the sunlight "sending tangential stabs of gold through the gaunt lattices of railroad bridges" making the Flats "so evocative that in a moment you are drawn into its sights and sounds and smells and your own personal musings."[117] To attract the leisure dollars of visitors less moved by romantic visions of industrial decay, Voinovich and Cleveland promoters achieved perhaps their greatest coup when they secured for the city the Rock and Roll Hall of Fame. In January 1988 famed architect I. M. Pei unveiled plans for the structure to be located in the Flats; the *Plain Dealer* described it as a "glittering glass tent." The enthusiastic architect predicted, "It will kick off tremendous development of this part of Cleveland," and a beaming Mayor Voinovich effused: "It's a fantastic building . . . People will travel from all over the world to see the architecture."[118]

No mayor proved more successful at drawing new tourists to his town than did Baltimore's William Schaefer. His Inner Harbor project included the oldest American warship, a science museum, and the National Aquarium as well as Harborplace. Opened in 1981, the National Aquarium attracted four million visitors during its first three years, offering such tourist delights as a shark tank, a tropical rain forest with thirty species of fish and almost one hundred colorful tropical birds, as well as an outdoor seal pool. And to publicize the aquarium, the irrepressible Mayor Schaefer donned a bathing suit and with appropriate ceremony dove into the seal tank.[119]

The Schaefer administration adopted a conscious policy of creating "animation" in the city, organizing a constant round of ethnic festivals, farmers' markets, concerts, street performers, and children's programs. To stir excitement during one promotion campaign, it even painted the curbs pink. The head of the city's Office of Promotion and Tourism said that the festivities were intended to make Baltimoreans "begin to feel good about themselves, so that then they would feel good about their city." Moreover, she boasted, "Everything we do is called 'common denominator entertainment'—things that will bring people together and not pull them apart."[120] Through this policy of perpetual circuses, Baltimore's messiah mayor thus hoped to patch over the divisions within the city and boost spirits depressed by the decades of decline. Further, if Baltimoreans felt good about their city, so would outsiders, thereby bringing additional profits to the city's cash registers.

Throughout the Northeast and Midwest, mayors and urban boosters were pursuing the Baltimore philosophy. In the postindustrial city, anything and everything must be done to draw outside dollars. Unlike in the early twentieth century, excellent port facilities or ready access to supplies of iron ore and coal were no longer sufficient for urban success. Now Coleman Young, mayor of America's once-supreme industrial giant, was advocating casino gambling as a substitute for the fortunes that Chrysler, General Motors, and Ford had formerly generated. Answering critics of the idea, Young observed, "I don't believe that any enterprise that offers the prospect of 50,000 jobs can be cavalierly dismissed."[121] If roulette wheels could boost beleaguered Detroit, then the city should permit them. And if diving into seal pools and painting curbs pink worked, then why not dive and paint?

Though downtown was the showpiece of any renaissance city of the late 1970s and the 1980s, urban boosters could also identify encouraging signs in some of the core residential neighborhoods. In fact, gentrifying districts in a number of cities seemed to provide strong evidence that the tide had turned and the urban comeback was genuine. Especially in New York City, a tight housing market sent upper-middle-income urbanites scurrying for homes in neighborhoods that they would not have dared visit a decade earlier. A wave of so-called yuppies engulfed Manhattan's Upper West Side in the late 1970s and the 1980s, turning former slums into prime real estate. In 1976 a middle-class couple bought an Upper West Side brownstone for $65,000. "This block was a hellhole," according to the wife, "it was terrible to walk down the street." Eight years later the brownstone was worth $400,000 and was within a stone's throw of an ample supply of gourmet delicatessens and trendy boutiques.[122]

With housing costs soaring in Manhattan, Brooklyn also acquired a new allure. The Park Slope neighborhood welcomed chic migrants from the overcrowded island across the East River. In 1986 one Brooklyn resident observed, "When you see Bloomingdale's head-to-toe going to the park, then you know Park Slope is changing."[123] Meanwhile, the Greenpoint section of Brooklyn seemed to be taking off as well, becoming the possible site for a real estate binge. "In Greenpoint certain blocks have gone nuts," a resident exclaimed in 1986. "One house in this neighborhood just sold for $250,000."[124]

Some other cities also could claim new residential wealth in older neighborhoods. Philadelphia's Spring Garden seemed to be following the path of Society Hill to renewed fortune. A local restoration contractor observed that in 1968 Spring Garden "was a territory ruled by drug addicts, alcoholics, [and] pyromanics."[125] But by 1984 the former president of the Spring Garden Civic Association was boasting: "Spring Garden is going up. We've had all the government housing programs, and all they do is drain tax money. What we've done [in Spring Garden] is resurrect the tax base."[126] This was the type of language that cheered budget makers in city hall. Townhouses appreciating 500 percent in a decade meant added funds for central-city treasuries as well as needed support for claims of urban renaissance.

Yet messiah mayors and city functionaries also had to deal with residential districts less attractive to yuppies and gentrifying restorationists. In the early 1970s a proliferation of feisty neighborhood organizations had forced municipal officials to take notice of their demands, and in order for the Caliguiris, Schaefers, and Voinovichs to achieve some semblance of harmony and perpetuate their long reigns in city hall, they had to recognize these neighborhoods and tout them almost as loudly as the central business district. Critics of the messiah mayors complained of their downtown orientation, writing of the "corporate center strategy" that dominated renaissance efforts.[127] But the popular executives of the 1980s were generally too smart politically to fall prey to downtown tunnel vision. A Cincinnati city councilman expressed the political reality facing many urban leaders when he observed: "Politicians in this town don't want to be accused of being anti-neighborhood, so you keep groups quiet by feeding them dollars."[128] Revitalized neighborhoods had to be part of the new message of salvation; voters demanded it. Thus messiah mayors included some neighborhood programs in their packages of revitalization initiatives, though their professions of faith in the neighborhood gospel were perhaps less sincere than their gung ho preaching on the rebirth of downtown.

One city that seemed especially dedicated to a balanced program of neighborhood and downtown revitalization was Pittsburgh. Whereas big business operating through the Allegheny Conference had monopolized the city's attention during Renaissance I, Mayor Caliguiri did seek a broader scope for his Renaissance II. His public pronouncements on Renaissance II regularly included mention of the neighborhoods, and in 1987 he told reporters, "[I work] a lot closer with . . . community organizations than I do with the business organizations."[129] During the early 1980s, neighborhoods received three-fourths of the city's federal funds, with the Golden Triangle garnering only the remaining quarter. Moreover, 80 percent of the city's capital investment in the late 1970s and 1980s went for infrastructure improvements and revitalization programs in the neighborhoods.[130] In 1979 the city, in cooperation with community groups, created the North Side Revitalization Program, which provided below-market-rate mortgages to homeowners and investors in six neighborhoods to encourage the purchase and rehabilitation of decaying residential properties. Caliguiri's administration also sponsored a commercial revitalization program in the business district of the depressed East Liberty community. And together with private philanthropic foundations, in 1983 the city initiated the Pittsburgh Partnership for Neighborhood Development to help five community development corporations to undertake housing construction and rehabilitation projects as well as neighborhood retail redevelopment and job creation programs.[131]

Elsewhere "comeback" cities were also attempting to spread some of the good fortune of their central business districts to the older neighborhoods. For example, in New York City during the 1980s, the Koch administration granted tax abatements to firms willing to locate in the outer boroughs surrounding Manhattan. New office structures were crowding onto the little island at New York's core, and city officials hoped to divert more business to Brooklyn or Bronx, especially the back-office operations of banks and insurance companies and industrial concerns still willing to remain in the metropolis but squeezed out of Manhattan by high rents. Meanwhile, Mayor Schaefer established a neighborhood commercial revitalization program to prop up older retailing districts scattered through his city. Baltimore's Department of Housing and Community Development secured loan packages for neighborhood merchants to finance the repair of their properties, the restoration of their building facades according to city design standards, and the adoption of uniform signs to replace the tasteless array that generally characterized inner-city commercial strips. One of the earliest projects was Old Town Mall, the nation's first mall in a poor, black, central-city neighborhood. Moreover, the same department initiated a "shopsteading" program, turning over vacant shops for only $100 to investors willing to rehabilitate the buildings and open businesses.[132]

Typical of Schaefer's Baltimore, however, a heavy dose of hoopla was included in the formula for neighborhood revival. Baltimore's City Fair flourished during the late 1970s and the 1980s, and its chief theme remained the glorification of the "city of neighborhoods." Each subdivision of the city was able to boast of its accomplishments and gain recognition. Moreover, Mayor Schaefer was always ready to laud Baltimore's neighborhoods as "the City's most precious resource."[133] Similarly, the Caliguiri administration through its Neighborhoods for Living Center organized NeighborFair, an annual festival to promote the diverse communities within Pittsburgh. And ethnic festivals abounded throughout the Northeast and Midwest, all dedicated to praising the cultural heritage of each fragment of the central-city population.

Some mayors appeared less solicitous of neighborhoods, however, and perhaps no city pursued a more downtown-oriented policy than Coleman Young's Detroit. City councilman Mel Ravitz attacked Young's "obsession with the development of the Detroit riverfront and occasional industrial projects to the virtual exclusion of planning for the conservation and revitalization of the city's sagging neighborhoods." Moreover, he claimed that the mayor's policy was resulting in two cities, "one shiny new city being developed downtown and aimed at the upper middle class, and the rest of the city—old, deteriorating, and lacking adequate city services—from which residents are quietly leaving."[134] Though much evidence supported Ravitz's charges, even Coleman Young doled out money to neighborhoods that were organized and needed to be mollified. Dollars from the city's Neighborhood Opportunity Fund quieted some groups, and beginning in 1981 the Alinsky-style Michigan Avenue Community Organization received approximately $500,000 a year in federal development funds from the city.[135] In the words of one local observer, this was proof of the old adage that "the squeaky wheel gets the grease."[136]

Festivals and mayoral lip service as well as rehabilitation programs and community infrastructure improvements eased relations between city hall and the neighborhoods. But other factors also helped the dynamo mayors to maintain a semblance of peace with neighborhood groups. Among these factors were fiscal stringency and diminishing federal funds. Money problems discouraged the creation of large-scale disruptive programs that would bulldoze neighborhoods, thus rendering city hall less of a threat. In the past nothing had galvanized neighborhood forces so readily as freeway and urban renewal plans. By the 1980s, however, such costly schemes were largely completed or abandoned, lessening the opportunity for major sins of commission against central-city communities. Sins of omission never aroused as much furor, especially if the alternative to neglect was higher taxes or displacement of residents and businesses. Thus funding problems ushered in an era of diminished intervention by city hall, and fears of fiscal crisis likewise lowered the expectations of community residents.

Moreover, by the late 1970s and the 1980s many of the neighborhood organizations were eschewing earlier confrontation strategies and placing new emphasis on housing and economic development. Realizing that the financially strapped city governments could not by themselves implement neighborhood panaceas and that Reagan's Washington would not do so, a number of community activists assumed the task of creating their own revitalization programs. Piecing together grants from the federal and city governments and from private foundations, churches, and businesses, organizers who had formerly confronted mayors and angrily demanded action from city hall now took action for themselves. For example, in the late 1970s Baltimore's Southeast Community Organization shifted its focus from organizing neighborhoods for the purpose of direct confrontation and increasingly devoted its energies and funds to community development, especially housing rehabilitation.[137]

Throughout the Northeast and Midwest, community groups were inordinately dedicated to extending the opportunity of home ownership to low- or moderate-income families. In 1981 nine of Cleveland's nonprofit neighborhood housing development corporations joined together in the Cleveland Housing Network, a group committed to the rehabilitation of abandoned dwellings for resale to buyers of modest means.[138] At the same time, in New York City the Nehemiah Program in Brooklyn built new houses for moderate-income families, many of whom had formerly lived in public housing.[139] Similarly, in Minneapolis a group known as Project for Pride in Living (PPL) was rehabilitating hundreds of dwellings in inner-city districts for sale to those unable to afford new suburban homes. PPL had grown out of Advocate Services, an organization founded by a parish priest in the late 1960s to help poor residents confront indifferent bureaucrats in city hall and discriminatory bankers downtown. But by the mid-1980s, PPL was definitely in the real estate business, having bought and sold properties in older neighborhoods throughout the Twin Cities, and it was even the landlord for some rental units.[140] In the late 1970s eleven Chicago neighborhood housing development organizations formed the Chicago Rehab Network also to provide dwellings for low-income residents, though the Windy City program emphasized rental housing as opposed to home ownership.[141] Yet as in Minneapolis, New York City, Cleveland, and Baltimore, development rather than protest was the focus of activity. The neighborhood development corporations did not eschew the use of pressure tactics, but such tactics were no longer the primary means to their ends.

In fact, some feared that the new emphasis on neighborhood economic development meant a sellout to the establishment, an abandonment of the community advocacy of the early 1970s. A Pittsburgh resident who had participated in community organizations expressed a typical concern when he said: "Talent is now channeled into development; we've lost the ability to be good organizers. We're all on the gravy train."[142] In 1987 a planning journal article on the transformation of neighborhood groups was appropriately titled "Off the Barricades, into the Boardrooms." In this essay a neighborhood organizer working with Cleveland's Buckeye Woodland Community Development Corporation admitted: "When you have your banks walk in and be partners, it's a little more difficult to say to them, 'Stop redlining.' "[143] A year later *Community Capitalism* described the revitalization efforts of Chicago's Illinois Neighborhood Development Corporation, an organization that owed as much to Adam Smith as to Saul Alinsky.[144] The founder of the PPL summed up the change in attitude between the early 1970s and the 1980s when he told an interviewer: "I felt all the advocacy work, well, temperamentally wasn't all that great. I felt more comfortable being a 'cooperator.' "[145]

As cooperators became more numerous than old-fashioned community advocates, the aging central cities became more manageable for the messiah mayors. Some rehabilitation programs, a little jawboning of the private sector to obtain money for neighborhoods, and a good deal of lip service about revitalizing communities and "balanced development" were generally sufficient to keep a lid on the city and to ensure neighborhood support for the mayor's reelection campaign. Moreover, given the diminished expectations of the 1980s, inexpensive, largely symbolic projects could prove an effective substitute for more notable development. Thus mayors and community groups applauded neighborhood garden projects, citing them as symbols of new life in the central cities. In the South Bronx, the Roxbury section of Boston, and on Cleveland's East Side, neighborhood residents were transforming the large number of vacant lots cleared of abandoned homes and apartments into vegetable gardens. With a mere $45,000 in federal funds, Mayor Voinovich's administration financed the Summer Sprout Program with 170 neighborhood garden sites producing over fifty tons of vegetables for the inner-city residents who cultivated the patches. Community gardeners in Boston even organized a Wake Up the Earth Festival held each spring, a festival being a necessary ingredient of every revitalization effort in the age of urban hype.[146]

More cynical observers might have viewed such back-to-the-land initiatives as the final nail in the coffin of urban life, a grim attempt to cover the wounds left by the depopulation of the central city and the demolition of its structures. But community groups and messiah mayors regarded the neighborhood gardens like the festival marketplaces and the convention centers as a sign of renaissance. At summer's end, Mayor Voinovich surrounded by a bounty of produce would pose for photographers, celebrating the fact that the once great industrial dynamo of Cleveland was being transformed into a farm.

Mayor Voinovich's exhilaration at the sight of squash, corn, and beans was representative of the attitude of the age. No matter what was happening in Cleveland, Baltimore, Detroit, or Saint Louis, the messiah mayors were dedicated to perpetuating the public relations hype and putting on happy faces. Thinking positive was the philosophy of urban leaders of the late 1970s and the 1980s, and the mission of city hall was to spread this positive message throughout the land. New office buildings, hotels, and meeting facilities as well as city-sponsored "animation" and neighborhood gardens were all purported signs of a revival of life in the city. Old movie theaters were reopening as performing arts centers, downtown shopping malls were welcoming throngs of customers, and community groups were rehabilitating blocks of residential structures. The age of urban decline was supposedly over; renaissance had arrived, and every mayor was ready to organize a festival to make sure the nation knew of the rebirth.

Beyond Hype

In 1986 a poll conducted by the *Wall Street Journal* and NBC News found that among residents of New York City's five boroughs, "only Manhattanites felt their quality of life had improved over the past five years," and "overall, about four in 10 residents would move if they could." According to the *Wall Street Journal*, typical New Yorkers agreed that Mayor Koch's supposedly revitalized "Big Apple [was] getting wormier" with streets "trashier than ever" and schools in which "the grossly underpaid do battle with the wildly undisciplined."[147] That same year the *Detroit Free Press* published a similar poll on the image of its city. Only 53 percent of Detroit residents thought of Detroit as a city that they would like to stay in, and a mere 15 percent of suburban residents and 9 percent of Michiganders expressed a willingness to move to the Motor City. Though a majority of respondents in all three categories believed that Detroit had improved over the previous ten years, when asked "What comes to mind when you think of Detroit?" by far the most frequent response of city, suburban, and state residents was crime and violence.[148]

A survey of urban and suburban residents in metropolitan Saint Louis found that 88 percent of suburbanites believed conditions in the central city of Saint Louis were improving, but only 6 percent of the outlying residents replied that they would prefer to live in the city whereas 31 percent of the urban dwellers desired a suburban residence.[149] In the most ballyhooed renaissance city of Baltimore, in 1987 a local foundation released a report concluding that such flashy creations as Harborplace and the National Aquarium simply masked the "rot beneath the glitter." The study predicted that Baltimore in the year 2000 would be both a poorer and smaller city.[150] During Mayor Schaefer's fourth term in office, one neighborhood activist summed up lingering doubts when she said, "The biggest problem in Baltimore is that people won't admit we have severe problems."[151]

In Koch's New York, Young's Detroit, Schoemehl's Saint Louis, and Schaefer's Baltimore, there was a world beyond the hype issuing from city hall, a world of continuing decay and distress not mentioned in the glossy publicity tracts produced in the offices of promotion and tourism. Amid the enthusiasm for resurgent urban vitality, it was a side of the older central cities most Americans chose to ignore, but the residents of New York City, Detroit, Saint Louis, and Baltimore knew it was there and knew that life in the aging hubs was actually no festival. Many metropolitan residents admitted that the central city had improved since the dismal days of the mid-1970s. Yet it still was not a mecca for those seeking the good life.

To many who had to grapple with the problems of persistent central-city deterioration, the renaissance was mere rhetoric. Central cities were not reborn; they were simply putting on an act.

Nowhere were the persistent economic problems of the central city more evident than in the field of manufacturing. Throughout the late 1970s and the 1980s, the once-great industrial centers continued to lose factories and thousands of industrial jobs. As seen in table 23, manufacturing employment dropped sharply in each of the older central cities between 1972 and 1982, and during the "renaissance" years of 1977 to 1982, the decline was just as pronounced as in the dismal mid-1970s. Nationwide the number of manufacturing jobs remained almost unchanged in 1972, 1977, and 1982, fluctuating between 19.0 million and 19.6 million. Yet in the single five-year span from 1977 to 1982, Chicago, Philadelphia, Detroit, Cleveland, Saint Louis, and Buffalo each lost more than 20 percent of their manufacturing jobs, and industrial employment in New York City, Baltimore, and Minneapolis dropped more than 10 percent. In 1982 the nation was in the midst of a serious recession, but even after the economy turned upward in the mid-1980s, the hemorrhaging of manufacturing jobs in the central cities continued. By the close of 1987 New York City could claim only 377,000 factory jobs, having lost 20,000 in 1985, 15,000 in 1986, and 7,000 in 1987.[152] During the 1980s, Boston could

Table 23. Number of Manufacturing Employees, 1972, 1977, and 1982

City	No. of Employees (1,000)		
	1972	1977	1982
New York	757.5	609.7	529.0
Chicago	430.6	366.0	277.0
Philadelphia	202.6	157.5	125.0
Detroit	180.4	153.3	105.7
Baltimore	90.6	72.9	59.3
Cleveland	131.2	120.8	92.5
Boston	59.0	50.9	47.4
Saint Louis	97.3	92.6	68.9
Pittsburgh	62.3	55.3	52.3
Buffalo	53.2	46.4	36.9
Cincinnati	68.2	64.4	62.0
Minneapolis	57.9	52.0	46.0

Sources: U.S. Bureau of the Census, U.S. censuses of manufactures for 1972, 1977, and 1982 (Washington, D.C.: U.S. Government Printing Office, 1976, 1981, and 1985).

boast of the most robust economy of any older central city, yet by 1985 it had only 42,500 manufacturing employees, a drop of more than 10 percent in only two years.[153]

Throughout the Northeast and Midwest the industrial sectors in the central cities were collapsing. New York City, the traditional garment capital, lost 36,000 apparel jobs during the first three quarters of the 1980s; in 1984 the *Wall Street Journal* reported that after the recent closings of blast furnaces "no steel is poured anymore" in Pittsburgh proper and "the city's most famous neon sign—a big mosaic of a steelworker pouring the metal—is no longer being lit."[154] Municipal industrial development programs financed with federal funds and industrial revenue bonds failed to stem the outward flow of manufacturing jobs. In 1976 Mayor Schaefer's administration created the Baltimore Economic Development Corporation (BEDCO) to foster business growth and particularly industrial development. It laid out industrial parks for manufacturing firms, which at the beginning of 1987 employed 5,800 persons, and converted empty factory buildings into multitenant space for smaller concerns employing a total of almost 1,000. Yet between 1970 and 1985 Mayor Schaefer witnessed the net loss of nearly 40,000 industrial jobs in his renaissance city, a drop of 45 percent.[155] In Detroit, Mayor Coleman Young leveled 319 acres of the Poletown neighborhood, displacing more than 3,800 residents, to create the Central Industrial Park as a site for a new Cadillac assembly plant.[156] But even such drastic measures could not push the Motor City's employment figure upward.

Public officials and business analysts might dismiss the job losses as a necessary consequence of the shift from a manufacturing to a service economy characteristic of the postindustrial city. Such explanations for the flight of manufacturing jobs from the supposed renaissance cities, however, were little consolation to the thousands of people who found themselves unemployed or working for much lower wages. A survey of hundreds of Chicagoans who had lost their jobs in the city's steel mills found that 26 percent had been forced to move because of reduced income, 44 percent had no health insurance, and 15 percent had had one or more cars repossessed. Expressing the attitude of many, the president of the steelworkers local said, "My feeling is one of tragedy."[157]

Though the decline in manufacturing was the most marked economic shortcoming of older central cities, almost equally discouraging were the figures on retailing. Despite all the publicity about festival marketplaces and revitalized shopping areas, the aging hubs continued to lose stores, retailing jobs, and customer dollars. The central cities had not eclipsed the supremacy of suburban malls. Instead, the trend toward peripheral shopping areas remained unabated. In the late 1970s and the 1980s, retailing data reflected the same phenomena as in the 1950s and 1960s.

This is apparent in a comparison of the retail census figures for 1977 and 1982. As table 24 indicates, during this five-year period, retail employment declined in nine of the twelve older central cities of the Northeast and Midwest, remained constant in Baltimore, and increased only in Boston and Pittsburgh. By comparison, for the nation as a whole the number of retail jobs rose 12 percent. The data was more dismal for the central business districts (CBDs). In every one of the twelve downtown areas, retail employment declined, with a drop of more than 20 percent in seven of the twelve. Though business was supposedly booming at Baltimore's Harborplace in 1982, the number of retail jobs in the city's downtown had plummeted 29 percent. During the first five years of Renaissance Center's existence, downtown Detroit lost 27 percent of its retail jobs, and six years of lucrative business at Quincy Market did not prevent the Boston central business district from suffering a 15 percent decline in retailing employment.

The sales data when corrected for inflation offered even fewer signs of revitalization. Nationwide retail sales in constant dollars decreased by 7 percent between 1977 and 1982, but in eleven of the twelve older cities

Table 24. Change in Retail Employment and Sales, 1977–1982

City	% Change in Employment		% Change in Sales (adjusted for inflation)	
	CBD	Total	CBD	Total
New York	− 5.9	− 2.1	− 3.0	− 10.2
Chicago	− 26.5	− 9.7	− 24.7	− 20.6
Philadelphia	− 8.7	− 1.1	− 22.8	− 18.6
Detroit	− 26.9	− 21.9	− 42.6	− 38.2
Baltimore	− 28.5	+ 0.1	− 22.7	− 17.4
Cleveland	− 17.7	− 16.3	− 16.3	− 25.1
Boston	− 15.3	+ 1.9	− 14.5	− 4.9
Saint Louis	− 29.0	− 7.2	− 39.1	− 22.2
Pittsburgh	− 15.8	+ 10.8	− 29.0	− 8.7
Buffalo	− 28.4	− 16.5	− 35.5	− 28.7
Cincinnati	− 36.1	− 7.5	− 30.7	− 17.4
Minneapolis	− 29.3	− 3.4	− 24.6	− 11.4

Sources: U.S. Bureau of the Census, U.S. censuses of retail trade for 1977 and 1982 (Washington, D.C.: U.S. Government Printing Office, 1980 and 1984).

sales dropped at an even sharper rate with only Boston outperforming the nation. Retail business declined more than 20 percent in Chicago, Detroit, Cleveland, Saint Louis, and Buffalo. In nine of the twelve central business districts, sales were off more than one-fifth, and in Detroit, Saint Louis, Buffalo, and Cincinnati the drop was greater than 30 percent. The Motor City enjoyed the dubious distinction of suffering the worst decline, with downtown business plummeting an extraordinary 43 percent during the five-year span.

Much of this drop in sales was a result of the decline of the downtown department store. Big department stores had always been the foundation of central business district retailing, but by the late 1970s and the 1980s many of these establishments were dinosaurs threatened with extinction. Not only did fewer Americans shop downtown, an increasing number of shoppers were buying from specialty stores rather than from the giant emporiums. In both the central city and suburbia the department store had problems adapting to changing consumer patterns, but the effect was especially devastating for the downtown outlets. In 1977 Baltimore's Hochschild Kohn closed its downtown flagship, as did Lit Brothers in Philadelphia and Crowley's in Detroit. Crowley's president expressed the sentiment of management in all of the doomed stores when he said, "The continuing decline in sales downtown has resulted in an operating loss that we in no way could continue."[158] Along the much-vaunted Nicollet Mall in downtown Minneapolis, Powers Dry Goods went out of business in late 1985, and a few months later J. C. Penney moved out of an adjacent block-long building, leaving a dismal expanse of empty retail space. According to the Minneapolis city council president, the departures "were disastrous."[159] Meanwhile, during the 1980s Cincinnati lost both the downtown Elder Beerman and L. S. Ayres outlets, reducing the number of department stores in the central business district from four to only two. At the closing of Ayres, the president of a rival retail firm admitted, "I just hate to see all these things happen to downtown Cincinnati."[160]

Perhaps most disheartening was the closing of Detroit's mammoth J. L. Hudson's store in early 1983. For ninety-one years Hudson's had been a Detroit landmark, and its massive fifteen-story block-square downtown flagship had ranked among the nation's best-known department stores. But its closing proved that even the greatest retail outlets were not immune from the continuing threat of urban blight. And when management chained its doors for the last time, it was proof of the hollowness of Coleman Young's renaissance rhetoric. Detroit was still declining, and nothing announced that fact so loudly as the demise of the downtown Hudson's. As one customer of forty years said in response to its closing, "For me, Hudson's *was* Detroit and when it is gone, there will be nothing left."[161]

The decline of the downtown department store was also evident in the scaling down of outlets. Across the nation older department stores were closing sections and reducing sales space in order to operate more efficiently. In some cases this shrinking accompanied the construction of new downtown shopping complexes. Thus in 1977 Gimbel's abandoned its outdated mammoth structure in downtown Philadelphia and built a smaller store with about half the sales space as part of the Gallery at Market East project. Hailed at the time as the first new downtown department store in forty years, the relocated Gimbel's was actually a means for reducing the chain's personnel, overhead expenses, and its real estate commitment in the Philadelphia central business district.[162]

Other retailers also successfully masked their downsizing of downtown stores by participation in well-publicized commercial projects. As its contribution to the St. Louis Centre, the adjoining Stix, Baer, and Fuller department store planned to reduce its retail space to only the first three floors of its building, converting the top six floors into a hotel. Eventually the store was sold to the Dillard chain, which located its Saint Louis flagship in the suburbs, leaving the shrunken downtown store as a branch outlet.[163] Meanwhile in Baltimore, Hutzlers' closed its old store, but to the delight of the Schaefer administration, in 1985 the retailer moved into a new building adjacent to its previous location. The new outlet, however, was no larger than a suburban mall branch, and by 1987 to keep the downtown Hutzlers' open, the store's landlord had to cut the rent by almost 60 percent. The *Baltimore Sun* characterized the revised rent agreement as "a last-ditch attempt to save the much-ballyhooed but unprofitable" store "that was once touted as a savior for the city's flagging downtown retail district." According to the newspaper, Hutzlers' was "the victim of grandiose, overly optimistic expectations for the still depressed Howard Street shopping area."[164] A stroll along the once-bustling retail thoroughfare offered ample testimony to the truth of this statement. In 1988 the sprawling old Hutzlers' stood empty as did the bulk of space in the former Stewart's department store across the street.

Elsewhere other new downtown retail developments also faced problems. Chicago's "Magnificent Mile" along North Michigan Avenue was booming, serving convention goers willing to splurge on luxury items, but the traditional center of downtown retailing was faltering despite the creation of a much-publicized mall. Begun in 1978, the construction of State Street Mall converted nine blocks of the retailing thoroughfare into a pedestrian-oriented transit mall open only to buses and emergency vehicles. Financed jointly by State Street merchants, the city of Chicago, and the federal Department of Transportation, the project entailed the widening of sidewalks, the planting of trees, and the installation of planters and new lighting fixtures. Moreover, the planners of the project had specified that "fountains, sculpture, sidewalk cafes, or art display cases might be placed at midblock locations or other activity areas."[165]

Soon after its completion, however, many were ready to pronounce it a failure. At the end of 1981 the bankrupt Goldblatt Brothers chain closed its State Street department store, and in October 1982 Sears announced that it would shut down its State Street branch the following spring, claiming that the store had been losing money for seven years. Montgomery Ward shuttered its outlet along the street in early 1984, and Wieboldt's State Street flagship ceased operation in July 1987, leaving only two department stores along the mall. The Sears and Montgomery Ward stores alone comprised more than one million of the 6.5 million square feet of retail space along State Street.[166] By 1982 a leading real estate consultant concluded, "It's now clear even to skeptics that State Street is in deep trouble."[167] In fact, less than a decade after the mall's construction the southern end of the street was dead as a shopping area. The northern end centering on Marshall Field's survived, and some boosters even claimed that it flourished. But the figures made public by the State Street Council showed that from 1980 through 1986 sales in the Loop shopping area had increased at only half the rate of the nation as a whole.[168]

Philadelphia's transit mall project along one of its leading shopping streets proved, if anything, even less successful. In 1975 the city opened the Chestnut Street Transitway, complete with brick pavement, unique new street lights, and convenient benches supposedly for tired shoppers. Chestnut Street had long been the poshest retailing thoroughfare in downtown Philadelphia, but the mall seemed only to accelerate its decline. Between 1975 and 1987 there was an 83 percent turnover rate among the businesses on Chestnut.[169] By the mid-1980s Brooks Brothers and Bonwit Teller's still had outlets on the street, but scattered among these classy remnants were video game arcades, fast-food franchises, wig stores, and discount emporiums specializing in going-out-of-business sales. Derelicts filled the street benches intended for paying customers, and the manager of a nearby hotel complained, "There are times when the smell of marijuana is enough to get even the average pedestrian high."[170] Many criticized the filth along Chestnut, and as early as 1979 one Philadelphian observed, "It's pretty hard to find any of the brand new sodium lamp posts on Chestnut Street . . . which have not been plastered over with a sea of signs hawking tea readings, theatricals, yogi meditation, rock concerts and political candidates."[171] Despite the transit mall and the Gallery on Market East project, in 1986 an article in the *Philadelphia Inquirer* summed up the state of downtown shopping in the Pennsylvania metropolis, describing the city as "a department-store graveyard[,] . . . a burial ground for retailers."[172]

Even in the most prosperous of the renaissance cities, some of the new retailing initiatives failed. In 1979, for example, the city of Boston installed brick pavement, "old-fashioned acorn street lights," benches, bollards, and planters at Downtown Crossing, the heart of the shopping district. But just as the improvements were completed, the Crossing lost Gilchrist's department store and the following year Kennedy's likewise closed, leaving only Jordan Marsh and Filene's.[173] Meanwhile, to shore up the traditional retail hub, the city negotiated a special tax deal with the developers of a downtown shopping mall known as Lafayette Place. Lafayette Place opened in late 1984, but as late as March 1988 only a little more than 50 percent of the retail space was leased, and the third floor of the mall remained unoccupied. Expected to be Boston's version of the Gallery on Market East and St. Louis Centre, Lafayette Place was actually a $100 million fiasco. Part of the problem was its circular design, which left first-time shoppers wandering about in confusion. One retailer suggested: "Implode it. It looks like a prison . . . I don't know any retailer in Boston who would consider opening there."[174] But most local leaders focused on the success of Quincy Market and tried to forget the continuing problems plaguing the retail core.

To the extent that Lafayette Place lured customers, they were mainly downtown office workers seeking lunch at the second-floor food court. Food courts and fast-food outlets were, in fact, the most successful element in central-city retailing, for they filled the needs of the growing number of office employees. If one looked beneath the heavy mantle of hype produced by city administrations, one found that the true success story in the older hubs was in the office sector. That was the chief area of growth, and downtown retailers, for the most part, had to eschew traditional efforts to attract the suburban housewife and instead concentrate on the white-collar labor pool that might make purchases at lunchtime or after work.

In almost every downtown the vitality of the office sector was evident. From 1977 to 1987 the number of private sector jobs in New York City increased by 342,000, and finance and business services together were responsible for almost 70 percent of this rise. Growth was especially vigorous in the securities industry, with employment doubling.[175] In Boston, employment in professional services soared 62 percent between 1976 and 1985, whereas the number of business service jobs increased 55 percent, and the finance/insurance/real estate sector recorded a 32 percent gain.[176] Business was absorbing millions of square feet of new office space in the New England metropolis, and in Boston as in Manhattan there was growing concern about overbuilding and the resulting problem of increased congestion. Meanwhile, in Chicago's central business district the inventory of office space grew by 15 million square feet between 1980 and 1985 as compared with the construction of 21 million square feet for the entire decade of the 1970s.[177] Messiah mayors and other boosters had some justification for their pride in downtown office development. The number of office jobs in the older central cities was rising, and new towers were accenting the skyline.

Yet even the office sector was not altogether vibrant, and cynics could find signs of decline as well as symptoms of boom. Though such professional and business services as law, accounting, and advertising were adding much-needed dollars to the central-city economy, corporate headquarters continued to move out. Whereas the number of Fortune 500 corporate headquarters in New York City dropped 34 percent, from 128 to 84, between 1965 and 1976, from 1976 to 1986 the figure fell from 84 to 53, a decline of 37 percent.[178] The administrative offices of manufacturing companies employed fifty-nine thousand in New York City in 1977 but only thirty-five thousand by 1986.[179]

Other older central cities were experiencing the same phenomenon. Diamond Shamrock left Cleveland and moved its headquarters to Texas, and Dallas-based LTV Corporation absorbed the Cleveland-headquartered Republic Steel. Meanwhile, the fifty-seventh largest industrial corporation, TRW Inc., built a new home office in the Cleveland suburb of Lyndhurst, avoiding the central city and affirming its commitment to suburbia. By 1986 the executive offices of the Chessie System railroads were moving from Cleveland, and only 35 employees remained of a staff that had comprised 275 during the 1950s.[180] In fact, in 1986 only New York City, Chicago, and Pittsburgh could claim more Fortune 500 headquarters than did the suburban community of Stamford, Connecticut, or the Sunbelt centers of Dallas and Houston. Business decision makers were continuing to leave the aging urban core for suburbia or the South and Southwest, and there were few signs that the older central cities were becoming more central to the business of America.

Actually, during the 1980s, the older hubs were simply benefiting from a nationwide boom in office employment and business and professional services. Though new office buildings meant good news for central-city mayors in search of tax dollars, the inventory of suburban office space was expanding at a more rapid rate than that in the urban core, and the growth in suburban office employment far outpaced that of New York, Chicago, or Philadelphia. Many major corporations were relocating their back-office operations outside of the city, moving thousands of employees to suburbia or beyond.

For example, Citicorp shifted its credit card operations from New York City to South Dakota; Mutual of New York transferred back-office workers to suburban Westchester County; Bankers Trust likewise moved 1,200 to 1,400 employees to Jersey City; and Morgan Bank built its data processing and operations center on a 158-acre site in suburban Delaware.[181] Between 1977 and 1986 insurance companies cut the number of their employees in New York City from 75,000 to 65,000, whereas the surrounding suburban counties in New York State recorded a gain of 5,700 insurance jobs, and northeastern New Jersey had almost 7,000 additional workers in this industry.[182] Between 1982 and 1985 Manhattan's share of office space in the New York City metropolitan area dropped from 67 percent to 60 percent, and in 1986 developers added 16.1 million square feet of offices to the suburban supply whereas Manhattan gained 7.6 million square feet.[183] By the late 1980s Michigan's suburban Oakland County could claim more office space than the central city of Detroit. In fact, the two suburban communities of Southfield and Troy had a combined office inventory virtually equal to that of the Motor City.[184]

Overall employment figures also demonstrated that suburbia was outpacing the central cities during the late 1970s and the early 1980s. For example, employment in Mayor Koch's New York was growing at a considerably slower rate than in nearby suburbia. In 1977 New York City accounted for nearly half the jobs in the metropolitan area, but during the ensuing decade, it could claim only about 30 percent of the new employment.[185] Similarly, Boston proudly boasted of a 16 percent rise in employment between 1976 and 1985, but during these same years, New England as a whole recorded a 27 percent gain in the number of jobs and the national rate was 23 percent.[186] Meanwhile, between 1980 and 1986 the renaissance city of Baltimore recorded a net loss of 7,700 jobs, a weak showing compared with nearby Washington, D.C., or suburban Maryland.[187] Philadelphia's annual employment growth rate for 1980–86 was −0.6 percent compared with +1.2 percent for the metropolitan area as a whole and +1.5 percent for the United States.[188] The annual rate in Mayor Schoemehl's Saint Louis was −1.8 percent from 1980 through 1985, actually worse than the −0.9 percent average for the 1970s.[189]

America's urban renaissance was, then, only a relative phenomenon.

The central-city economy of the mid-1980s was generally better than it had been in the mid-1970s, but compared with suburbia or the nation as a whole, even the most prosperous of the older central cities seemed sluggish at best. Moreover, the central-city office construction boom of the 1980s was no greater than that of the late 1960s and early 1970s. At the close of the 1980s no soaring giants had topped such creations of the early 1970s as Chicago's Sears Tower or New York City's World Trade Center. Instead, the 1980s office construction bonanza could be seen as a continuation of an office boom that had been in progress since the late 1950s and had suffered only a momentary interruption in the mid-1970s. If new office towers and an expanding business and professional service sector were symptoms of urban rebirth, then the gestation period for this new life had begun at least a quarter of a century earlier.

But the office sector was not the only sign of economic hope for the central city. The much-publicized growth in tourism and convention business and the accompanying boom in hotel construction also signaled revitalization. In Boston more than 4,000 new hotel rooms opened for visitors between 1980 and 1985, more than the total constructed during the entire half century from 1930 to 1980. Moreover, Boston's hotel employment soared 109 percent between 1976 and 1985.[190] In downtown Baltimore the number of available hotel rooms tripled between 1980 and 1986 as did the figures for tourist visits and expenditures.[191] Unknown to convention goers prior to 1980, Baltimore was capturing an increasing share of the meeting business, and the Saint Louis "Meeting Place" campaign also seemed to be placing the Missouri metropolis on the convention map. With newly fashioned "fun" images, former models of dullness and despair like Baltimore and Saint Louis were reaping financial rewards.

But for every older central city winning in the convention game, there was a loser. For example, tourism and convention business was not fueling a rebirth in Philadelphia; instead, the hotel business in the City of Brotherly Love was as dismal as ever. In 1985 downtown Philadelphia had 6,200 hotel rooms compared with 6,300 a decade earlier. Despite charging the lowest room prices in the Northeast, the occupancy rate in 1985 dropped below 55 percent, the worst in the Boston-Washington megalopolis. Between July 1, 1984, and June 30, 1985, the fifteen major downtown hotels lost a total of $36.5 million, leading the *Philadelphia Inquirer* to pronounce the local lodging industry "desperately ill."[192] Moreover, the immediate future held little promise. An expert on the lodging business observed: "The city's hotel industry faces a bleak future. Some hotels are going to down-size or go out of business. Business is dead for the remainder of this decade."[193] Among the casualties was the historic Bellevue Stratford, which closed in 1986, only eight years after a $25 million remodeling.[194]

Many attributed the Bellevue Stratford's fate to the absence of a modern convention center in the Pennsylvania metropolis, and throughout the 1980s Philadelphia leaders fought over the construction of a new meeting facility to replace the outmoded Civic Center. After its formation in 1982, a convention-center steering committee proceeded to hire a consulting firm and in 1983 selected the site of the Reading Railroad terminal adjacent to the Gallery shopping mall as the best location for the new center. A successful campaign for state aid ensued, and construction of the facility seemed imminent in 1986. At that time a spokesman for the Philadelphia Convention and Visitors Bureau confidently reported, "Everything's in place . . . We're very optimistic."[195] But dispute over the site revived in 1987 with the architecture critic for the *Philadelphia Inquirer* attacking it, and a coalition of neighborhood groups brought suit to halt the project. In January 1988 one observer of the struggle reported, "Philadelphia is still far from having a new convention center."[196]

Philadelphia was not, then, to receive its fair share of the revitalizing bounty of America's convention business. And some visitors felt the city's ill fortune was well deserved. In the mid-1980s one participant at a beauty care and hair salon convention held in Philadelphia was so angered by the experience that he placed a full-page ad in a trade journal expressing his views. According to this outraged visitor: "Some of the hotels were without a doubt the worst we had encountered. If we had had a choice, we'd have picked tents and sleeping bags . . . The food at the Convention Center was right out of the Hanoi prison system." "What can I say about this city?" the ad continued. "Beirut is cleaner. There must be a city ordinance against cutting the grass and picking up the refuse."[197] Moreover, the editor of *Philadelphia* magazine agreed, responding to the complaints by calling the city "shabby, dirty and unappealing."[198] In a nationwide survey a convention-center consulting firm found that people throughout the country shared this impression. In the 1980s as in the 1940s, Philadelphia had a reputation as a "dirty, boring city."[199] Mayor Schaefer's Baltimore may have successfully repackaged itself in flashy new wrappings, but Philadelphia was still deemed dismal and deteriorating.

Philadelphia was not the only loser in the convention game. All the efforts of Mayor Voinovich and his fellow boosters could not transform Cleveland into a meeting mecca. In 1987 the owner of two of Cleveland's four downtown hotels attacked the local convention bureau for failure to attract meetings; he claimed that his establishments had only a 35 percent to 40 percent occupancy rate and had lost $3 million in the past four years. When asked by the *Plain Dealer* whether Cleveland was a come-back city, the hotel owner responded: "You might say that anyone who believes that . . . is either on marijuana or heroin. It's [that] far away from reality."[200] In reply, the convention bureau president admitted that his agency was not as successful in attracting conventions and hotel book-ings as it had been ten years earlier, but he blamed this partially on the lack of adequate hotel space for large meetings.[201] Actually, in the first half of the 1980s no major hotel chain had been willing to make a commit-ment to downtown Cleveland. Despite all the positive rhetoric and the attempts at image refurbishing, Hyatt and Hilton knew that investing in Cleveland would be a mistake.

Buffalo could boast a Hilton and a Hyatt, but it proved equally unat-tractive to convention planners. In 1979 the city constructed a $22 million convention center that four years later the *Washington Post* described as "something of an embarrassment." The facility attracted only four major events in 1982, losing $400,000 and drawing fewer than five thousand visitors. In 1983 a spokesman for the Chamber of Commerce admitted, "We have an image problem," but with the optimism of a good booster he proclaimed, "Without a doubt, conventions and tourism are the most en-couraging light on the horizon for this community."[202] Only in dismally depressed Buffalo could a $400,000 deficit rank as the most encouraging light on the horizon.

Overall, the older central cities were doing better than Buffalo, but they were not proving inordinately successful in the competition for the convention trade. By 1986 New York City and Chicago headed the list of convention destinations, hosting more delegates than any other cities. Not one of the ten other older central cities, however, ranked among the top ten gathering places. Instead, Sunbelt communities such as Dallas, Houston, Las Vegas, and Anaheim followed New York and Chicago on the list and were acquiring a growing share of meeting business.[203]

Not even the most applauded tourist draw of the older central cities proved a total success. Baltimore's Inner Harbor with its festival mar-ketplace and aquarium was the envy of places like Cleveland and Phila-delphia, but one element of Mayor Schaefer's complex proved a bomb. To add to the fun in downtown Baltimore, in 1985 the Six Flags corporation transformed a derelict power plant adjacent to the harbor into an attrac-tion that was billed as "the nation's first urban theme park."[204] According to the Urban Land Institute, it was "designed to attract affluent 25- to 40-year-old adults" and to provide employment for two hundred Baltimore residents.[205] The power plant's marketing director stated, "[I don't] think there's any way it won't work," and press releases proclaimed it "the most spectacular indoor entertainment facility ever imagined."[206] The theme park, however, never made money and closed in January 1987. Amid all the upbeat publicity, the failure of the Six Flags Power Plant received little notice. Just as the media hyped the success of Boston's Quincy Market and ignored the failure of nearby Lafayette Place, the shortcomings of Baltimore and the erroneous investments at Inner Harbor were overlooked. During the late 1970s and the 1980s, Cleveland had to be proclaimed a comeback city even if it was not, and Baltimore had to be painted pink by image makers even though much of it was dull gray.

Like convention centers, mass transit had been touted as a leading panacea for central-city woes in the 1970s, but by the mid-1980s transit realities also seemed to fall short of the promoters' hype. Generally, the much-awaited transit projects proved more expensive than expected, attracted less patronage, and reaped fewer benefits. Perhaps no city placed greater faith in the miracle-working propensities of rail transit than had Buffalo. Since the early 1970s, local advocates of a rail system envisioned it as the stimulus for a resurgent city. Optimism gradually waned, however, as the scheme's price soared, the miles of proposed trackage shrank, and construction delays mounted. Though Mayor Griffin continued to count on the new subway to ignite a downtown renaissance, in 1983 an expert at the Brookings Institution expressed less sanguine sentiments. He argued, "The main advantage of a subway is that it's a gigantic public works project," but he noted, "Once it's built, it doesn't pay for itself."[207]

This observation proved accurate, for in 1986 the *New York Times* reported that according to a state study group, "Buffalo's year-old rapid-transit line might be forced to shut down unless a new source of revenue is found to cover its operating deficits."[208] The Buffalo line was carrying only twenty-one thousand to twenty-three thousand riders per day as compared to the projected forty-five thousand, and fares covered less than 20 percent of operating costs. Confronted by budget woes, transit officials were forced to delay completion of the downtown pedestrian mall that was expected to be the capstone of the scheme. Instead, the chief retailing thoroughfare remained torn up, causing the transit authority's executive director to call downtown Buffalo "Beirut."[209] In 1986 the subway's superintendent still insisted, "There is all the potential in the world for this system to be a very big asset to Buffalo," and completion of the line to the south campus of the state university was expected to boost ridership. But others were fed up with the scheme. A suburban councilman organized Citizens Against Rapid Transit Extensions and argued that "the whole thing [had] been a perfect 10 in bad decision-making."[210]

Meanwhile, Detroit was the scene of an even more publicized and more troubled transit initiative. By the early 1980s Detroit's hopes for a regional rapid transit system had produced only plans for a 2.9-mile People Mover looping around downtown on an elevated track. Seemingly this mini-line should have proved a manageable endeavor, but its construction was fraught with difficulties. When it was discovered that the concrete guideway beams were cracking and prone to shattering, the whole project seemed threatened. By 1985 the chairman of the Southeastern Michigan Transportation Authority was admitting, "Ever since we began this project, all we have had is pain on top of pain," and the unsympathetic director of the federal Urban Mass Transportation Administration had nicknamed the costly scheme "the price mover."[211] Moreover, in 1986 a journalist with the *Detroit News* complained that the People Mover's $210 million expenditure "could have purchased 1,000 new buses, 12,000 vans for transporting the poor, elderly, and handicapped, or a new subcompact auto for every low-income household that now lacks a car."[212]

Finally, in the summer of 1987 Detroit's People Mover opened to passengers, a year and a half behind schedule and with a price tag that was $73 million above the original estimate. After a preview ride, a *Detroit Free Press* columnist called the Mover a "$200.3 million carnival ride," but his newspaper's editorial board looked forward to further transit projects, announcing optimistically, "The People Mover may get plans for rail transit back on track."[213] By the beginning of 1988, however, the People Mover was transporting only about eleven thousand people daily compared with the original prediction of seventy-five thousand. And a visiting Chicago journalist found that most of the passengers were not downtown workers as expected but "wide-eyed gawkers, curious tourists and nostalgic city residents."[214] Given the massive investment, eleven thousand curiosity seekers hardly seemed an adequate dividend. As one *Free Press* journalist commented: "The cost of this spiffy, super-tech transit system demands that it be much more than a tourist attraction."[215]

Elsewhere transit expenditures produced better returns but also reaped many critics. Baltimore opened its first rapid transit line without suffering Detroit's manifold embarrassments. But when Governor Schaefer sought state funding for an extension of the system, a *Baltimore Sun* poll found that only 15.7 percent of the respondents in the metropolitan area said they would ever use the proposed rail line. Moreover, representatives from the Maryland suburbs of Washington, D.C., attacked the scheme as a "boondoggle."[216] In fact, boondoggle was a word used increasingly when referring to rapid transit projects, and in 1983 *Harper's* printed an article that referred to rail schemes as "the billion-dollar boondoggle that can't beat the bus."[217] In some cities with long-established rapid transit systems, billions of additional dollars also did not solve transportation problems or end the chorus of criticisms. At the close of 1986 an article on New York's subways complained, "Cities like Toronto and Paris have quiet, clean trains, but New Yorkers have to endure delays, breakdowns, filth, crimes, fires, graffiti, faulty signs and air conditioners, and, now, a triple-digit fare."[218] When asked to compare the New York transit system in 1986 with that of ten years earlier, one New Yorker expressed a typical sentiment, "I don't care whether it's better or worse, but it's terrible the way it is."[219]

Though some cities were still attempting to dun the federal government for money to build rail systems, by the mid-1980s, the rapid transit boom seemed to have passed. Baltimore and Buffalo had completed functioning rail lines, but many questioned whether the benefits justified the costs. Boston and New York had made transit improvements, though not enough to satisfy their steadfast patrons or lure many additional passengers. Transit schemes might aid downtowns and reinforce the central-city economies, yet they would not revolutionize urban America. In 1985 Americans still lived in an automobile age just as they had in 1975 and 1965.

Thus in the 1980s the United States was not experiencing a transportation revolution, though it was in the midst of an economic transformation that had both positive and negative consequences for the older urban hubs. Those central cities fortunate enough to attract conventions could boast of new hotel and restaurant jobs, and the employment figures for financial institutions and business and professional services proved that one city after another did have some economic future. Jobs were being created in the central cities, and they were not doomed to be welfare wastelands. Yet the economic transformation of the late 1970s and 1980s also created employment problems. As central-city factories closed, blue-collar workers lost good-paying jobs and seemingly had little hope of success in the new service economy of the postindustrial city. The unskilled jobs in the convention hotels, burgeoning fast-food restaurants, or the expanding hospital complexes paid little more than minimum wage, far less than the manufacturing jobs that were migrating to the suburbs, the American South or Southwest, or to Asia. In addition, displaced factory workers had little chance of landing well-paying positions in business services or the professions. One could not move readily from the assembly line to the offices of Arthur Andersen. Accounting firms needed trained personnel as did law offices. Those workers who could operate a welding iron or wrench but not a computer seemed destined for unemployment or the counter of McDonalds.

This growing mismatch of skills between city residents and new job openings was especially serious because of the failure of central-city schools to adequately train youths and the high dropout rate among inner-city teenagers. In New York City the dropout rate was nearly 50 percent, in Chicago it was 45 percent, and in Boston 43 percent.[220] Moreover, on a typical day one-third of the students in Chicago's schools were absent. Judged by national standards, the central-city educational record was dismal with only one-third of Chicago's pupils reading at or above their grade level. By 1988 one-half of the Windy City's public high schools ranked in the lowest 1 percent in the performance of their students on the national ACT tests. That year a local journalist warned, "The situation has deteriorated so badly that exasperated businessmen . . . complain that Chicago students lack the basic reading and writing skills for even minimum-wage employment."[221] Neither the rising office towers downtown nor the newly opened Neiman-Marcus store on North Michigan Avenue offered any economic hope for these teenagers. The reborn city was a dead-end for them.

In fact, suburban commuters were the chief beneficiaries of the growing supply of downtown office jobs. The number of jobs in New York City rose 7 percent between 1977 and 1984, but the number of employed city residents increased only 1 percent.[222] Most of the new jobs were going to suburbanites with the requisite skills. The same trend was evident in other cities. Between 1969 and 1979 in downtown Baltimore the proportion of workers who lived in the city dropped from 58 percent to 46 percent, and the highest-paying positions went to suburban dwellers.[223]

Meanwhile, despite all the rhetoric of revitalization, central-city residents remained disproportionately poor. In 1984 after thirteen years of Mayor Schaefer's leadership, Baltimore's unemployment rate was 7.4 percent, or more than 40 percent higher that the state average of 5.2 percent.[224] Every year from 1977 through 1985 the unemployment rate for Boston stood well above the Massachusetts figure.[225] Moreover, the number of those falling below the poverty level fixed by the federal government was increasing in the New England metropolis. Sixteen percent of Bostonians had an income below the poverty line in 1970; by 1985 the figure was 20 percent, and the Boston Redevelopment Authority estimated that it would rise to 23 percent in 1990.[226] The fate of central-city minority groups was particularly gloomy. With too many dropouts and too few jobs in manufacturing, blacks and Hispanics did not benefit from the purported renaissance as much as non-Hispanic whites. In 1987 in New York

City the unemployment rate for non-Hispanic whites was 3.1 percent but for minorities it was 8.5 percent.[227] A year earlier an extraordinary 20 percent of Pittsburgh blacks were jobless compared with less than 4 percent of the city's whites.[228]

Everywhere the signs of continued decay vied with symptoms of revival. Infant mortality rates among inner-city blacks remained far above the national average. Violent crime was still a source of fear, and tales of muggings continued to keep city dwellers and suburbanites alike off many inner-city streets after dark. In the tenth year of Mayor Schaefer's reign, the *Baltimore Sun* reported that with only one-half the population of strife-torn Northern Ireland, Baltimore had three times as many murders.[229] Lamenting the decline of white blue-collar neighborhoods in Philadelphia and the departure of factory jobs, in 1985 a local journalist wrote: "The area east of Hunting Park is populated by zombie armies of crack dealers and users, by 15-year-old Puerto Rican Scarfaces who pump energy and money in the only remaining industry in the neighborhood: cocaine."[230] Such a description fit New York, Chicago, Boston, or Saint Louis as well as the City of Brotherly Love. One did not need to read a costly foundation report to discover there was "rot beneath the glitter." A drive through the city streets beyond the central business district would yield the same conclusion.

Moreover, slums persisted, and housing, if anything, was a more serious problem than it had been before. Public housing units were decaying, and the federal government was opposed to increasing appropriations for such projects. In Chicago, public housing was a perennial and seemingly insoluble problem. At the close of 1986 the *Chicago Tribune* ran a series of articles that referred to the projects' "crime, graffiti, garbage, urine-stained stairwells and broken elevators" and described the giant high-rise apartment buildings as "almost universally viewed as failures that devour human lives and tax dollars."[231] According to the *Tribune*, the local housing authority's finances were "falling apart as quickly as its buildings," and the newspaper concluded, "In the future, as in the past, all the stereotypes, all the fears, all the frustrations that have come to be associated with public housing in Chicago are likely to block significant change."[232]

Rehabilitation of housing was occurring in the older cities, but it produced more publicity than dwelling units. The neighborhood development corporations may have proudly turned out a few hundred housing units annually, but in the meantime thousands of dwellings were deteriorating and thousands of poor residents needed improved shelter. By the mid-1980s Chicago could claim 960 new or rehabilitated low-income units each year, yet 3,500 units, most of them inner-city slums, were demolished annually. The executive director of the Chicago Rehab Network admitted that his organization's efforts were "a Band-Aid approach to saving neighborhood housing," and the *Tribune* referred to the community development corporations' rehabilitation efforts as "drops of salvation in [a] housing drought."[233] A Cincinnati councilman expressed much the same opinion when he complained of appropriating money to neighborhood development corporations: "Three years pass, and you ask how many housing units they've produced and usually you can count them on one hand."[234]

Gentrification seemed to offer hope to middle- and upper-income Americans in search of central-city dwellings, and the media frequently focused on comeback neighborhoods with their renovated townhouses and charming boutiques. Yet there were only slight glimmers of gentrification in such cities as Cleveland and Detroit, and in revived Pittsburgh, city boosters could point to merely a few gentrified streets. Even where the return of the middle class seemed more pronounced, it was deemed a mixed blessing, driving up housing costs for the poor and displacing lower-income residents with few housing alternatives. To stem the supposed tide of gentrification in Baltimore, in 1986 working-class residents of Upper Fells Point banded together to block a proposal to add their neighborhood to the Fells Point Historic District. Designation as a historic district would ensure state and federal tax credits for people investing in the renovation or restoration of properties, and thus gentrification would probably ensue. The leader of the working-class opposition warned: "This is going to be nothing but another Georgetown. The rich are going to be in and the poor are going to be out."[235]

During the 1980s, Boston probably suffered the greatest housing pressure owing to an influx of middle-class residents. Conversion of rental properties to condominiums for the affluent was a leading political issue. In the 1987 municipal election mayoral challenger Joseph Tierney asked incumbent Raymond Flynn, "What has the city of Boston done under your leadership to provide and build and encourage the construction of affordable housing . . . your record speaks for itself and it's dismally poor."[236] Moreover, when the *Boston Globe* asked city council candidates "what [was] the single most critical issue facing the city of Boston," one respondent after another replied "affordable housing."[237]

Focusing attention on the low-income housing problem were frequent media reports on the homeless in America's cities. Though figures differed on the number of homeless, it seemed as if their numbers were increasing in many renaissance cities. This was in part owing to the deinstitutionalization of the mentally ill, a policy that added new recruits to the army of street people and "crazies" found in every central city. But especially troubling was evidence that a growing number of families, especially female-headed families, were without shelter. In 1984 New York City was caring for 2,354 homeless families in hotels and shelters, a 148 percent rise over July 1982, and by September 1986 the figure was up to 4,365 families, or about fifteen thousand people. As of 1986 New York City had sixty-five hotels, motels, and city-run shelters to house the homeless.[238] That same year Chicago authorities estimated that there were twenty-five thousand homeless in the Windy City, and to handle the problem, the city government provided 1,400 additional beds in the public shelters.[239] Whatever the reasons for this phenomenon, it was hardly a sign of renewed economic vitality in the older central cities.

Homelessness, continued poverty, the skills mismatch, and the high dropout rates all were evidence of the shortcomings of the supposed urban renaissance. Perhaps some were profiting from a revived Baltimore or Pittsburgh, but much seemed to remain the same for those at the bottom of the social ladder. Commenting on this inequitable distribution of the benefits of prosperity, some observers began to warn of the development of two cities within the central city, one rich and the other poor. In 1984 Robert F. Wagner, Jr., son of the former mayor and himself deputy mayor under Edward Koch, spoke of the emergence of "two New Yorks." The New York below Ninety-sixth Street in Manhattan was "made up of people with jobs and opportunities," whereas the other New York consisted of "blacks, Hispanics, and the elderly, who are often unemployed and poor."[240]

Moreover, three years later a commission on the city's future chaired by Wagner warned that "without a response to the problem of poverty, the New York of the 21st century [would] be not just a city divided, not just a city excluding those at the bottom from the fullness of opportunity, but a city in which peace and social harmony [might] not be possible."[241] Articles referred to life in New York as "a tale of two cities," and Irving Howe claimed, "The signs of social and economic polarization seem more visible, more gross than in earlier years." "Those sleek, dark-curtained limos," Howe wrote, "driving through streets in which thousands of people are homeless on winter nights" were among the signs, as was "the glitz of midtown contrasted with the devastation of large sweeps of Brooklyn and the Bronx."[242]

Such devotees of renaissance rhetoric as Baltimore's Mayor Schaefer would tolerate none of this carping; for him Baltimore was back, and he had an aquarium to prove it. Yet by the late 1980s it was apparent to any objective observer that America's older central cities had not yet triumphed wholly over the forces of blight and decentralization that they had been battling for five decades. Flashy new skylines proved that central-city downtowns had not died as the founders of the Urban Land Institute had feared they would. There were millions of feet of additional office space in the central business districts, and millions of workers congregated there each weekday. But in most of the older hubs suburban shoppers were a relatively rare sight, and the first-run movie houses had long before switched off their marquee lights. Some film palaces survived as performing arts centers, but most were gone as was much of the downtown nightlife. The function of the central business district had narrowed. In the 1980s it was the center of business and professional services and finance, but no longer the hub of shopping or amusement.

Moreover, beyond the central business districts, vacant lots and abandoned buildings were constant reminders of the scars inflicted by persistent blight and decentralization. Some neighborhoods were gentrified, but these were, in the words of one urban expert, "islands of renewal in seas of decay."[243] A number of residential areas had survived the preceding half century relatively unscathed, and others seemed to be sprouting new life after the long battle against decline. Yet no city lacked its wastelands that lent credence to the worst fears of those who had warned of urban decay decades before. A visitor to these no-man's-lands could only conclude that America's cities had taken a wrong turn along the road to renaissance and become irretrievably lost.

Yet, if nothing else, the messiah mayors had boosted the spirits of many urban dwellers and made them proud of their cities. They had also rehabilitated the bleak images of the older cities and convinced many Americans that places like Baltimore were fun and cities like Pittsburgh were highly livable. Further, the messiah mayors had seemingly overcome some of the political problems that had undermined the efforts of earlier executives. They had fashioned enough of an urban consensus to keep themselves in power year after year and had made the formerly ungovernable cities governable. Whereas the disruption of traditional political patterns had made the road to renaissance rougher for earlier mayors, the Kochs, Schaefers, and Youngs filled some of the dangerous potholes and eliminated some of the obstacles in the way of revitalization. These messiahs may not have worked as many miracles as they claimed, but they were generally adept enough at political sleight-of-hand to keep up the illusion of success.

CHAPTER EIGHT ○ **Coping in a New World**

In 1955 *Time* published an article entitled "Rebirth of the Cities" with four pages of photographs of the reborn urban core.[1] Seven years later the same magazine's cover story on cities was entitled "The Renaissance," which discussed nagging urban problems but also proclaimed that "never has the big city offered so much."[2] By 1981 *Time*'s cover featured a picture of James Rouse and the words "Cities Are Fun!"[3] And in November 1987 *Time* was still proclaiming the gospel of urban renaissance with a cover that announced "Bringing the City Back to Life."[4] In the pages of *Time* and myriad other publications the older central cities enjoyed more comebacks than did an aging Hollywood star. Though stories of "urban crisis," the "plight of the cities," and the "death of the city" told how Detroit, Cleveland, and Baltimore were down on their luck, with reassuring predictability reports would appear that announced the good news of stardom regained. From World War II to the 1980s the older central city's career was a rocky one with all-too-evident signs of financial distress and physical deterioration, but publicity about inspiring comebacks offered hope to fans of the urban hubs.

Yet were the reports of renaissance like so many Hollywood comebacks more journalistic puffery than accurate estimates of reality? After four decades of encouraging rhetoric was there any renaissance or had the central cities simply grown older, uglier, and more feeble? Were Philadelphia, Pittsburgh, and Saint Louis again box office hits or would they never again achieve anything more than featured parts in American life?

In some ways the very concept of central-city renaissance was mis-

308

leading, a bit of public relations hype unfortunately applied to urban problems. Rebirth implied that the older central cities had once died, but by the mid-1980s it was evident that rumors of their demise had been premature. Throughout the period 1940 to 1985 the urban core continued to serve a vital function in the American economy, remaining the focus of an expanding office sector. From the mid-1950s through the mid-1980s, office construction had flourished in the aging hubs with only a brief intermission in the mid-1970s. As urban boosters so often proclaimed, scores of new towers had transformed central-city skylines and provided millions of square feet of additional office space. Billions of dollars of private investment proved that in the 1950s and 1960s as well as in the 1970s and 1980s downtown was not washed up as a center of financial institutions and business and professional services. In 1985 as in 1945 New York's Wall Street was the center of the nation's securities industry, Boston's State Street was the hub of finance in New England, and Chicago's LaSalle Street was the mecca of commodity traders. Throughout the postwar decades these downtown locales had retained their preeminence and remained relatively immune to the supposed cancer of blight.

Similarly, many central-city residential neighborhoods had survived the four postwar decades largely unchanged. In 1945 Baltimore's Roland Park, Philadelphia's Chestnut Hill, Pittsburgh's Squirrel Hill, Cincinnati's Hyde Park and Mount Lookout, and Minneapolis's Lake District had been upper-middle-class neighborhoods, and they remained much the same in 1985. These and countless less affluent districts in older central cities had not suffered the much-publicized waves of blight, abandonment, gentrification, or displacement. Their histories included no dramatic tales of death or resurrection. Instead, they enjoyed a seemingly perpetual stability.

Though far from dead, it was true that the older cities were not the center of American life that they had once been, and there was little likelihood that they would regain that position in the near future. The central cities had not died; they had survived in a far different world than that which existed before World War II. In the postwar automobile-oriented world of decentralized residence and business, they were inevitably relegated to a lesser role. With an increasingly poor black population, they also grew increasingly out of sight and out of mind for many middle-class whites. Renewal proponents in the 1940s and 1950s had tried to overcome the central city's awkward disadvantages by advocating centripetal schemes of superhighway construction, dozens of additional parking garages, and new middle- and upper-income housing to draw paying customers closer to the downtown retailing core. But even the radical surgery of urban renewal clearance and highway construction had proved insufficient to keep the old central business district central to the American economy. The outer belts were to become the main streets of the late-twentieth-century metropolis. Suburbia was to draw not only residents but also the bulk of retailing and manufacturing as well as an increasing share of the new office buildings.

Thus the older central cities had not slipped into oblivion, but they had adapted to a changed world. In many ways their ability to adapt was admirable. For example, despite much publicity about fiscal crisis in the 1970s, the urban centers scored some notable financial triumphs during the period 1940 to 1985. Faced with a stagnant, and some claimed overburdened, property tax base, the cities successfully obtained new sources of revenue that kept most of them from bankruptcy. By the 1980s central cities had imposed income taxes, sales taxes, cigarette taxes, and a multitude of other levies. Though many people criticized the flat-rate income taxes as regressive and unduly burdensome for the wage earner, these earnings levies did enable central cities to reach into the pockets of commuters and recover some of the wealth that had migrated to suburbia. This success in diversifying the sources of local revenue was in marked contrast to the experience of Canadian cities, which continued to impose only property taxes.

Moreover, by the 1980s the central cities had successfully shifted some responsibilities to metropolitan authorities and the states, thus relieving themselves of unwanted financial burdens. They had also slashed municipal payrolls, reducing the number of city employees. And the urban core had tapped the federal treasury without becoming indigent wards of Washington policymakers. Federal largesse had lasted only a decade, from the late 1960s to the late 1970s, and the 1980s demonstrated that the big cities of the Northeast and Midwest could keep their financial houses in order despite federal cutbacks. In fact, the headlines of the mid-1980s warned of huge federal deficits rather than of yawning municipal budget gaps. Cities still wanted federal money and still needed it, but in the long run the greatest change in municipal financing was not the increase in federal payments but the diversification of local revenue sources. The cities had largely bailed themselves out of the fiscal hole created by excessive dependence on property taxes; the federal government had helped but only in a secondary role.

At the same time, the older cities had adapted their physical fabric to the changing needs of the postwar era. Some of the achievements were perhaps misguided but were achievements nonetheless. The central cities had cleansed their environments with effective smoke-control programs and improved sewage treatment systems. In the competition for a clean and healthy environment, they had narrowed the gap between the core and the suburbs. Central cities also had adapted to the transportation needs of the new age with freeways and mammoth airports. And the new-breed city executives of the 1950s and messiah mayors of the 1980s had fostered billions of dollars of new investment downtown.

In contrast, the older central cities had proved much less successful in adapting to the problems of the growing numbers of poor residents within their boundaries. Neighborhood conservation programs rarely halted blight, and slum areas spread across the cities in the 1950s and 1960s. Then in the 1970s abandonment of housing and demolition of structures reached unprecedented proportions. By 1980 costly and well-engineered highways and transit lines passed through ruined wastelands in many cities, linking the lucrative offices of downtown to prosperous suburbia. Whereas the economic heart of the city still beat strongly and the transportation skeleton had benefited from expensive treatments, a portion of the urban body's residential flesh had rotted away.

The human renewal schemes of the 1960s had produced no more miracles than had the physical revival efforts. Especially for thousands of black migrants, the central cities were too often not avenues of upward mobility but downhill grades, dead-ending in a seemingly permanent underclass. In too many cases, central-city schools failed in their mission to uplift both the black and white masses, and these "blackboard jungles" attracted mounting criticism. Fearful of sending their children to inner-city schools, many Americans sought a suburban home or paid a hefty tuition bill for private instruction. Meanwhile, crime rather than automobiles was now synonymous with Detroit, and security services did a booming business. The central cities were not dead, but many of their residents were scared to death.

Moreover, the older central cities had failed to retain manufacturing employment but instead had witnessed a seemingly irreversible erosion of their industrial base. Blue-collar jobs disappeared and factories closed down, seriously restricting the economic opportunities of the urban working class. Such industrial renewal schemes as Cincinnati's Kenyon-Barr, Philadelphia's Eastwick, or Saint Louis's Mill Creek Valley did not dam the outward migration of manufacturing nor did the efforts of Mayor Schaefer's BEDCO. After four decades, few seriously expected the aging hubs to regain their industrial significance.

The political adaptation of the older central cities had also proved fraught with difficulties. The decline in party politics and the emerging political autonomy of municipal employees and blacks had forced city officials to develop new means for patching together a governing coalition. John Lindsay and his ilk had hoped to mobilize the electorate into a governable whole through crusading rhetoric and a high sense of moral purpose. William Donald Schaefer and the leaders of the late 1970s and the early 1980s sought to build a consensus based on the fear of renewed crisis and the need for a strong leader to guide the urban populace toward prosperity. Without an established messiah like Schaefer at the helm, the city would supposedly founder once again; with his firm guidance it would be saved.

Meanwhile, the search for renaissance together with the weakening of the traditional party structure resulted in heightened political activism by a broad range of urbanites. In the late 1940s and the 1950s fears of economic decline aroused business leaders to organize in support of their policy objectives. Whereas in the past the Mellons had worked through the Republican party to achieve their policy goals, after World War II they opted for the politically independent Allegheny Conference to push through a long list of projects and to lobby both sides of the political aisle. Moreover, other Pittsburgh moguls, who had formerly contributed to campaign funds and occasionally telephoned the mayor to obtain favors, now mobilized behind the conference's full-fledged policy agenda and assumed a higher profile in public affairs. Likewise, the Greater Baltimore Committee and Civic Progress represented a new level of concerted activism among a business elite fearful of the consequences of continued decentralization and blight.

But others also soon opted for independent political activism, bypassing the no longer adequate party machinery in order to protect their interests in the renaissance struggle. Thus by the 1960s and 1970s a new level of neighborhood mobilization had developed as proposed freeways and clearance projects threatened homes and federally funded programs encouraged community-based revitalization schemes. Though the poorest residents were slow to rally behind the cause of community activism, policymakers in city hall had to face a new army of angry citizens from a multitude of working-class and middle-class neighborhoods who no longer could be mollified by partisan ward leaders. Similarly, the municipal employees unions demanded a stronger voice in personnel policy, white mothers left their kitchens to run for mayor and defend neighborhood schools, and anger about "Negro removal" schemes stirred heightened racial indignation among blacks and made them less compliant to the dictates of the Democratic party organization.

Thus the road to renaissance had bulldozed through existing political structures and aroused unprecedented independent action by a broad spectrum of urban residents and business figures. The political portrait of the older central cities was far different in the 1980s than it had been in the 1940s. Moreover, physically and financially, the aging hubs had changed markedly during the four decades after World War II. Though the never-dead cities did not enjoy the dramatic transformation implied by rebirth, they had adapted. They had coped with a different world than that which had spawned them, and they had muddled through four difficult decades. But they had never regained their stellar positions, and boosters never felt so confident of success that they were willing to permanently shelve plans for renaissance or cease to look for signs of comeback. Instead, there was in the late 1980s as in the late 1930s a ready market for urban panaceas. After more than forty years of planning and implementation, the concept of renaissance still charmed policymakers ready to continue the journey along the road toward that elusive goal.

ENVIRONMENTAL RENEWAL
Pittsburgh in the late 1940s

1. Downtown Pittsburgh street at 9:20 in the morning, darkened by the smoke pall that frequently engulfed the city.

2. To generate support for smoke control legislation, in 1946 these Pittsburgh women, at the behest of the Allegheny Conference, donned masks to protect them from the air pollution.

3

4

PITTSBURGH—The Renaissance Showcase of the 1950s

3. The Point in 1947 before the Renaissance.

4. The Point in 1958 after clearance and construction of Gateway Center.

5. Lower Hill area of Pittsburgh as seen in 1956, a dilapidated and densely populated black neighborhood.

6. Plan from the 1950s for rebuilding the Lower Hill with the proposed Civic Arena in the center. The sleek high-rises set amid ample open spaces were typical of urban renewal plans of the first two decades after World War II.

7

8

EARLY FEDERAL URBAN RENEWAL HOUSING PROJECTS
Cleveland in the mid-1950s

7. Blighted housing in Longwood area.

8. New apartments in Longwood project intended for moderate-income blacks.

9. New apartments in Cleveland's Garden Valley project. Like most of the early urban renewal housing schemes, this drab development did not win as much publicity or inspire as much enthusiasm as the downtown high-rise proposals.

INDUSTRIAL RENEWAL IN THE 1950s
Cincinnati's Kenyon-Barr Project

10. Densely-populated black residential area prior to clearing for Kenyon-Barr project.

11. Plan from 1956 for coordinating freeway construction and industrial renewal of Kenyon-Barr area.

12. Kenyon-Barr area after redevelopment, with expansive freeway interchange and low-rise industrial structures in the background.

KENYON-BARR INDUSTRIAL PARK

PREPARED BY

VOGT, IVERS, SEAMAN & ASSOCIATES
ENGINEERS   ARCHITECTS
CINCINNATI, OHIO   CHICAGO, ILLINOIS
OCTOBER 1956

11

12

13

14

15

DOWNTOWN RENEWAL IN THE 1960s
Cleveland's Erieview Project

13. Futuristic skyline of Erieview as envisioned by project planners.

14. Contrast between Erieview Plaza under construction and low-rise commercial structure to be cleared.

15. Erieview area in 1973, eight years after expected completion of redevelopment. This single tower in a sea of parking lots demonstrates why many in the early 1970s were disheartened by the slow progress of urban renewal projects.

NOTES

Introduction: The Road to Renaissance

1. Two of the best histories of federal urban policy are Mark I. Gelfand, *A Nation of Cities: The Federal Government and Urban America, 1933–1965* (New York: Oxford University Press, 1975), and Philip Funigiello, *The Challenge to Urban Liberalism: Federal-City Relations during World War II* (Knoxville: University of Tennessee Press, 1978).

2. Paul E. Peterson, *City Limits* (Chicago: University of Chicago Press, 1981). For a critique of Peterson's position, see Heywood T. Sanders and Clarence N. Stone, "Developmental Politics Reconsidered," *Urban Affairs Quarterly* 22 (June 1987): 521–39. See also Clarence N. Stone, "The Study of the Politics of Urban Development," in Clarence N. Stone and Heywood T. Sanders, eds., *The Politics of Urban Development* (Lawrence: University Press of Kansas, 1987), pp. 3–22.

3. John H. Mollenkopf, *The Contested City* (Princeton, N.J.: Princeton University Press, 1983).

4. See, for example, James O'Connor, *The Fiscal Crisis of the State* (New York: St. Martin's Press, 1973). Note also Larry Sawers, "New Perspectives on the Urban Political Economy," Nancy Kleiniewski, "From Industrial to Corporate City: The Role of Urban Renewal," Richard Child Hill, "Fiscal Crisis, Austerity Politics, and Alternative Urban Policies," and William K. Tabb, "The New York City Fiscal Crisis," all in William K. Tabb and Larry Sawers, eds., *Marxism and the Metropolis: New Perspectives in Urban Political Economy*, 2nd ed. (New York: Oxford University Press, 1984), pp. 3–17, 205–22, 298–345.

Chapter 1: The Problem Perceived

1. *Cleveland Plain Dealer*, 4 July 1940, p. 18.

2. *Saint Louis after World War II* (Saint Louis: City Plan Commission, 1942), pp. 12–13.

3. *City Record* 33 (11 January 1941): 25.

4. "Rebuilding the Cities," *Business Week*, no. 566 (6 July 1940): 40.

5. *Christian Science Monitor*, 25 July 1940, p. 20.

6. Walter S. Schmidt, *Proposals for Downtown Cincinnati* (Chicago: Urban Land Institute, 1941), p. 1.

7. Harland Bartholomew, "The American City: Disintegration Is Taking Place," *Vital Speeches* 7 (1 November 1940): 61.

8. *Urban Land Institute News Bulletin*, no. 2 (14 November 1941): 2.

9. Charles Edmundson, "Saint Louis: A City in Decay," *Forum* 102 (November 1939): 201.

10. Schmidt, *Proposals for Downtown Cincinnati*, p. 2.

11. Hugh R. Pomeroy, "Philadelphia's Planning Problems," in *National Conference on Planning, 1941* (Chicago: American Society of Planning Officials, 1941), pp. 238–39.

12. Bartholomew, "American City," p. 63. For similar findings for Boston, see William H. Ballard, *A Survey in Respect to the Decentralization of the Boston Central Business District* (Boston: Urban Land Institute, 1940), p. 58; and *Building a Better Boston* (Boston: City Planning Board, 1941), pp. 8–9.

13. R. B. Navin, William D. Peattie, and F. R. Stewart, *An Analysis of a Slum Area in Cleveland* (Cleveland: Cleveland Metropolitan Housing Authority, 1934), p. 16. See also *Waverly: A Study in Neighborhood Conservation* (Washington, D.C.: Federal Home Loan Bank Board, 1940), p. 2.

14. Leverett S. Lyon, "Economic Problems of American Cities," *American Economic Review* 32 (March 1942 Supplement): 313.

15. Mary C. Schauffler, *The Suburbs of Cleveland: A Field Study of the Metropolitan District outside the Administrative Area of the City* (Chicago: University of Chicago Press, 1945), p. 3.

16. *Urban Land Institute News Bulletin*, no. 2, p. 3.

17. Marquis W. Childs and John Coburn Turner, "The Real Philadelphia Story," *Forum* 103 (June 1940): 290.

18. Lyon, "Economic Problems of American Cities," p. 315.

19. *Saint Louis after World War II*, p. 24.

20. Urbanism Committee to National Resources Committee, *Our Cities: Their Role in the National Economy* (Washington, D.C.: U.S. Government Printing Office, 1937), p. 68.

21. For the effect of FHA policies on suburbanization, see Kenneth T. Jackson, *Crabgrass Frontier: The Suburbanization of the United States* (New York: Oxford University Press, 1985), pp. 203–17.

22. "Rebuilding the Cities," *Business Week*, p. 38.

23. Bartholomew, "American City," p. 64. See also *St. Louis Post-Dispatch*, 18 June 1940, p. 8A.

24. Bartholomew, "American City," p. 63. For data on the central business district's share of the total city assessment, see Richard J. Seltzer, *Proposals for Downtown Philadelphia* (Chicago: Urban Land Institute, 1942), p. 38; Carl S. Wells, *Proposals for Downtown Detroit* (Washington, D.C.: Urban Land Institute, 1942), pp. 7, 20; Milton C. Mumford, "A Review of the Parking Problem with Particular Reference to Chicago," *Urban Land* 6 (June 1947): 3; and *St. Louis Post-Dispatch*, 23 June 1940, p. 1C.

25. *St. Louis Post-Dispatch*, 23 June 1940, p. 1C; Donald H. McNeil, "Pittsburgh's Downtown Parking Problem," in *Proceedings Institute of Traffic Engineers, 1946* (New

Haven, Conn.: Institute of Traffic Engineers, 1947), p. 30; and Mumford, "Review of Parking Problem," p. 3.

26. Mumford, "Review of Parking Problem," p. 3.

27. Edmundson, "Saint Louis," p. 201.

28. H. M. Propper, "Saving Our Downtown Areas," *Nation's Business* 28 (May 1940): 20.

29. Seltzer, *Proposals for Philadelphia*, p. 5.

30. *St. Louis Post-Dispatch*, 23 June 1940, p. 1C; Park H. Martin, "Pittsburgh's Golden Triangle," *American Planning and Civic Annual, 1951* (Washington, D.C.: American Planning and Civic Association, 1952), p. 139; McNeil, "Pittsburgh's Parking Problem," p. 30; Wells, *Proposals for Detroit*, p. 10; and Seltzer, *Proposals for Philadelphia*, pp. 27, 30.

31. John R. Fugard, "What Is Happening to Our Central Business Districts?" in *National Conference on Planning, 1940* (Chicago: American Society of Planning Officials, 1940), p. 108; Seltzer, *Proposals for Philadelphia*, p. 20; Ballard, *Survey of Boston Central Business District*, p. 26; and *St. Louis Post-Dispatch*, 23 June 1940, p. 1C.

32. *St. Louis Post-Dispatch*, 23 June 1940, p. 1C.

33. "Traffic Jams Business Out," *Architectural Forum* 72 (January 1940): 64–65; Walter H. Blucher, "The Economics of the Parking Lot," *Planners' Journal* 2 (September–October 1936): 113; and Wells, *Proposals for Detroit*, p. 9.

34. Seltzer, *Proposals for Philadelphia*, pp. 20–21, 53. For information on demolition in downtown Boston, see Ballard, *Survey of Boston Central Business District*, pp. 15–16. Ballard found that for the period between 1930 and 1939 "the value of the properties demolished . . . more than offset new construction with the exception of the year 1930."

35. "Traffic Jams Business Out," *Architectural Forum*, p. 64.

36. Seltzer, *Proposals for Philadelphia*, pp. 27, 30.

37. Wells, *Proposals for Detroit*, p. 10.

38. Ballard, *Survey of Boston Central Business District*, p. 27.

39. "Boston Diagnosis," *Business Week*, no. 594 (18 January 1941): 62; and Ballard, *Survey of Boston Central Business District*, p. 49.

40. Seltzer, *Proposals for Philadelphia*, p. 38.

41. Wells, *Proposals for Detroit*, p. 10.

42. "Suburban Branch Stores in the New York Metropolitan Region," *Regional Plan Bulletin*, no. 78 (December 1951): 1–8.

43. "Employment Trends 1942–1951 in the New Jersey–New York–Connecticut Metropolitan Region," *Regional Plan Bulletin*, no. 84 (March 1954): 13.

44. Charles C. Colby, "Centrifugal and Centripetal Forces in Urban Geography," *Annals of the Association of American Geographers* 23 (March 1933): 5; and Lyon, "Economic Problems of American Cities," p. 311.

45. *Annual Report of the Chicago Plan Commission, 1943* (Chicago: Chicago Plan Commission, 1944), p. 27.

46. Ibid., p. 28.

47. Ibid.

48. *St. Louis Post-Dispatch*, 18 June 1940, p. 2C.

49. Ibid., 26 December 1940, p. 2B.

50. *Cleveland Plain Dealer*, 26 August 1940, p. 6.

51. "Urban Land Institute," *American Society of Planning Officials News Letter* 6 (June 1940): 42.

52. "Rebuilding the Cities," *Business Week*, p. 40.

53. The reports were: William H. Ballard, *Proposals for Downtown Boston;* Walter S. Schmidt, *Proposals for Downtown Cincinnati;* Carl S. Wells, *Proposals for Downtown Detroit;* A. J. Stewart, *Proposals for Downtown Louisville;* K. Lee Hyder and Howard J. Tobin, *Proposals for Downtown Milwaukee;* Robert H. Armstrong and Homer Hoyt, *Decentralization in New York City;* and Richard J. Seltzer, *Proposals for Downtown Philadelphia.* For a description of the Armstrong and Hoyt study, see *New York Times*, 20 April 1941, sec. 11, pp. 1–2.

54. For a planner's comments on the need to accommodate automobiles, see Gordon Whitnall, "Downtown Disease," *Planning and Civic Comment* 6 (October– December 1940): 23–24. Whitnall observed: "Today the capacity of a business district is in an increasing degree measured in terms of automobiles and not in persons."

55. Henry H. Saylor, "The Diary," *Architectural Forum* 74 (February 1941): 131.

56. *New York Times*, 15 December 1940, sec. 12, p. 3.

57. *St. Louis Post-Dispatch*, 23 June 1940, pp. 1C, 3C.

58. Ibid., 12 February 1941, p. 4A.

59. *Downtown Study—Baltimore* (Baltimore: Industrial Corporation, 1941), pt. 2, p. 1.

60. *New York Times*, 19 May 1940, sec. 4, p. 10.

61. "Approval of Neighborhood Unit Development Plan Advances Regional Program of Rehabilitation," *Regional Plan Bulletin*, no. 51 (1 July 1940): 1–8.

62. "Downtown Buffalo in 1949," *American City* 55 (February 1940): 57. See also *Urban Land Institute Bulletin*, no. 10 (October 1942): 3–4.

63. John T. Howard, *What's Ahead for Cleveland?* (Cleveland: Regional Association of Cleveland, 1941), p. 10. See also *Regional Association of Cleveland Plan Bulletin*, no. 7 (10 September 1941).

64. Howard, *What's Ahead for Cleveland?* pp. 24, 33.

65. *Annual Report of the City Planning Commission and Department of City Planning, the City of New York, 1940* (New York: City Planning Commission, 1941), p. 9.

66. *Saint Louis after World War II*, p. 25.

67. *Twenty-sixth Annual Report of the City Planning Board for the Year Ending December 31, 1939* (Boston: City of Boston Printing Department, 1940), p. 26.

68. *Christian Science Monitor*, 11 June 1940, pp. 1, 12.

69. Ibid., 12 June 1940, p. 1.

70. Robert A. Caro, *The Power Broker: Robert Moses and the Fall of New York* (New York: Alfred A. Knopf, 1974), pp. 639–47, 657–75; and Robert Moses, "The Changing City," *Architectural Forum* 72 (March 1940): 148–49. See also *Borough of Manhattan: A Report, July 1, 1939–June 30, 1940* (New York: City of New York, 1940), pp. 13–20, 27; *Borough of Manhattan: A Report, July 1, 1940–June 30, 1941* (New York: City of New York, 1941), pp. 13–18; and *Chicago Tribune*, 17 February 1940, p. 5; 20 February 1940, p. 14; 21 February 1940, pp. 12–13; and 22 February 1940, p. 7.

71. For a critical account of Philadelphia's water, see Thomas P. O'Neil, "Philadelphia: Where Patience Is a Vice," in Robert S. Allen, ed., *Our Fair City* (New York: Vanguard Press, 1947), pp. 61–63.

72. Raymond R. Tucker, "The Saint Louis Code and Its Operation," in *Air Pollution: Proceedings of the United States Technical Conference on Air Pollution* (New York: McGraw-Hill, 1952), p. 728.

73. *St. Louis Post-Dispatch*, 17 June 1940, p. 2C.

74. Ibid., 18 June 1940, p. 2C.

75. Ibid., 23 June 1940, p. 1C.

76. Ibid., 5 June 1941, p. 1C. See also Tucker, "Saint Louis Code and Its Operation," pp. 726–31; Raymond R. Tucker and J. H. Carter, "Some Legal Foundations for Air Pollution Control," *Proceedings of the Third National Air Pollution Symposium* (Los Angeles: National Air Pollution Symposium, 1955), pp. 211–15; *St. Louis Post-Dispatch*, 17 June 1940, p. 2C; and ibid., 2 February 1941, Pictures section, pp. 1–7.

77. Stefan Lorant, *Pittsburgh: The Story of an American City* (Garden City, N.Y.: Doubleday, 1964), p. 488. See also Joel A. Tarr and Bill C. Lamperes, "Changing Fuel-Use Behavior and Energy Transitions: The Pittsburgh Smoke-Control Movement, 1940–1950," *Journal of Social History* 14 (Summer 1981): 561–79.

78. *Smoke Abatement Activities of the Regional Association, 1937–1941* (Cleveland: Regional Association of Cleveland, 1941), pp. 1, 7.

79. Donald H. McNeal, "Waverly—A Study in Neighborhood Conservation," in *National Conference on Planning, 1941* (Chicago: American Society of Planning Officials, 1941), pp. 216–22; and "The Waverly Neighborhood Conservation Program," *American Society of Planning Officials News Letter* 6 (September 1940): 71.

80. *Waverly*, pp. 4, 65.

81. *Annual Report of the Chicago Plan Commission, 1940* (Chicago: Chicago Plan Commission, 1941), pp. 9–10; and *St. Louis Post-Dispatch*, 23 February 1941, p. 1C.

82. Robert C. Alberts, *The Shaping of the Point: Pittsburgh's Renaissance Park* (Pittsburgh: University of Pittsburgh Press, 1980), p. 55; and Robert C. Alberts, "The Shaping of the Point: Pittsburgh's Renaissance Park," *Western Pennsylvania Historical Magazine* 63 (October 1980): 295.

83. *Annual Report of the City Plan Commission, Saint Louis, Missouri, 1940–1941* (Saint Louis: City Plan Commission, 1941), pp. 31–32.

84. *Twenty-third Annual Report, City Plan Commission, Detroit, 1941* (Detroit: City Plan Commission, 1942), pp. 9–14.

85. *Twenty-seventh Annual Report of the City Planning Board for the Year Ending December 31, 1940* (Boston: City of Boston Printing Department, 1941), p. 4.

86. Ibid., p. 32.

87. *Building a Better Boston*, pp. 7–8.

88. Thomas S. Holden, "New York to Stimulate Urban Redevelopment," *American City* 56 (May 1941): 69; Arthur C. Holden, "Urban Redevelopment Corporations: A Legislative Victory in New York," in *National Conference on Planning, 1941* (Chicago: American Society of Planning Officials, 1941), pp. 222–30; "Private Slum Clearance Dawns," *Architectural Forum* 74 (June 1941): 54, 449; *Urban Plan Institute News Bulletin*, no. 1 (21 July 1941): 1; "Illinois Enacts Neighborhood Redevelopment Corpora-

tion Law," *American City* 56 (August 1941): 37; *Annual Report of the Chicago Plan Commission, 1941* (Chicago: Chicago Plan Commission, 1942), p. 15; and *Report City Plan Commission, Detroit, 1941*, pp. 10–11. For the response of Saint Louis leaders to the passage of the New York redevelopment law, see *St. Louis Post-Dispatch*, 22 December 1940, p. 1D.

89. *Urban Land Institute News Bulletin*, no. 9 (1 September 1942): 2; and *Twenty-fourth Annual Report, City Plan Commission, Detroit, 1942* (Detroit: City Plan Commission, 1943), p. 12.

90. *Report of Chicago Plan Commission, 1941*, pp. 16–17; "Neighborhood Redevelopment," *American City* 56 (December 1941): 39, 71; and *Urban Land Institute News Bulletin*, no. 3 (12 January 1942): 3.

91. "Private Slum Clearance Dawns," *Architectural Forum*, p. 54.

92. *Planning Cleveland in 1943: Annual Report of the Cleveland City Planning Commission* (Cleveland: City Planning Commission, 1944), p. 6.

93. *Proposed Postwar Works Program, the City of New York* (New York: City Planning Commission, 1942), pp. 6–8; and Rebecca B. Rankin, ed., *New York Advancing* (New York: Municipal Reference Library, 1945), p. 106.

94. Rankin, *New York Advancing*, p. 107.

95. *Postwar Works Program, New York*, p. 3.

96. *Proposed Postwar Works Program, the City of New York, Supplement A* (New York: City Planning Commission, 1942), p. iii.

97. Rankin, *New York Advancing*, p. 105.

98. *Report of Chicago Plan Commission, 1941*, pp. 8–9; and *Annual Report of the Chicago Plan Commission, 1942* (Chicago: Chicago Plan Commission, 1943), p. 23. See also "Hear Plans for Future Chicago," *City Club Bulletin* 38 (26 March 1945): 25–26.

99. *Planning Detroit 1943: The City Plan Commission of the City of Detroit Presents a Review of Its Work for the Year 1943* (Detroit: City Plan Commission, 1944), pp. 28–29; and *An Advance Plan Program for Detroit* (Detroit: City Plan Commission, 1942).

100. *Annual Report of the City Manager, Cincinnati, Ohio, 1943* (Cincinnati: City of Cincinnati, 1944), pp. 3–4; and *Annual Report of the City Manager, Cincinnati, Ohio, 1944* (Cincinnati: City of Cincinnati, 1945), p. 2.

101. *Saint Louis after World War II*, p. 3.

102. *City Record* 84 (10 January 1942): 33.

103. *City Planning in Philadelphia* (Philadelphia: Citizens' Council on City Planning, 1944), pp. 3–4. For information on attempts at postwar planning in Buffalo, see Philip J. Funigiello, *The Challenge to Urban Liberalism: Federal-City Relations during World War II* (Knoxville: University of Tennessee Press, 1978), pp. 178–80.

104. John T. Howard, "An Urban Rehabilitation Program for Cleveland," *Journal of the American Institute of Planners* 10 (Autumn 1944): 23.

105. Ibid., pp. 21–22.

106. Robert C. Weinberg, "A Technique for Urban Rehabilitation," *Journal of the American Institute of Planners* 10 (Autumn 1944): 23–24.

107. *Postwar Works Program, New York*, p. 8; and *Proposed Postwar Works Program, the City of New York, Supplement B* (New York: City Planning Commission,

1942), p. vi. Also for postwar plans for New York City, see *Twelve Years of Park Progress* (New York: Department of Parks, 1945), pp. 40–63.

108. *Postwar Works Program, New York*, p. 8; *Postwar Works Program, New York, Supplement B*, p. vi; *Office of the President of the Borough of Manhattan Annual Report, 1942–1943* (New York: Manhattan Borough President, 1943), pp. 4–17; and *Borough of Manhattan, a Report, 1944–1945* (New York: Manhattan Borough President, 1945), pp. 18–22.

109. *Annual Report Chicago Plan Commission, 1944* (Chicago: Chicago Plan Commission, 1945).

110. *St. Louis Post-Dispatch*, 2 August 1944, p. 10A; and *Annual Report of the City Plan Commission, Saint Louis, Missouri, 1944–1945* (Saint Louis: City Plan Commission, 1945), p. 24.

111. *Report of City Manager, Cincinnati, 1944*, pp. 6–7.

112. *Journal of Proceedings of the City Council of Baltimore at the Session of 1943–1947, Second Councilmanic Year, May 1944–May 1945* (Baltimore: King Brothers, 1944), pp. 401, 868.

113. *Planning in Philadelphia*, p. 11; and *News Letter, Citizens' Council on City Planning* 2 (April 1945): 4. See also John F. Bauman, "Visions of a Postwar City: A Perspective on Urban Planning in Philadelphia and the Nation, 1942–1945," *Urbanism Past and Present* 6 (Winter–Spring 1980–81): 1–11.

114. Alberts, "Shaping of the Point," pp. 300–331; and idem, *Shaping of the Point*, pp. 65–69.

115. *Journal of the City Council of Baltimore, May 1944–May 1945*, p. 745.

116. Ibid., p. 875.

117. Ibid., p. 419.

Chapter 2: Laying the Foundations for Renaissance

1. For La Guardia's views on federal aid for local public works, see *New York Times*, 23 February 1945, p. 13; 23 July 1945, p. 1; 20 August 1945, p. 11; and 17 September 1945, p. 21.

2. Jeanne R. Lowe, *Cities in a Race with Time: Progress and Poverty in America's Renewing Cities* (New York: Random House, 1967), p. 126; and Michael P. Weber, *Don't Call Me Boss: David L. Lawrence, Pittsburgh's Renaissance Mayor* (Pittsburgh: University of Pittsburgh Press, 1988), pp. 203–4.

3. "Pittsburgh's New Powers," *Fortune* 35 (February 1947): 73; and Roy Lubove, ed., *Pittsburgh* (New York: New Viewpoints, 1976), p. 184.

4. "Pittsburgh's New Powers," *Fortune*, p. 76; Lubove, *Pittsburgh*, p. 187; Weber, *Don't Call Me Boss*, p. 206; Lowe, *Cities in a Race with Time*, p. 122; and Roy Lubove, *Twentieth-Century Pittsburgh: Government, Business, and Environmental Change* (New York: John Wiley and Sons, 1969), p. 108.

5. Katharine Lyall, "A Bicycle Built for Two: Public-Private Partnership in Baltimore," in R. Scott Fosler and Renee A. Berger, eds., *Public-Private Partnership in American Cities* (Lexington, Mass.: D. C. Heath, 1982), p. 29.

6. James Neal Primm, *Lion of the Valley: Saint Louis, Missouri* (Boulder, Colo.: Pruett Publishing, 1981), p. 493.

7. *St. Louis Post-Dispatch*, 27 May 1955, p. 6A.

8. *Report on Urban Renewal in Cleveland* (Cleveland: Cleveland Advertising Club, 1955), p. 3. See also David D. Van Tassel and John J. Grabowski, eds., *The Encyclopedia of Cleveland History* (Bloomington, Ind.: Indiana University Press, 1987), p. 229.

9. *Report on Urban Renewal in Cleveland*, p. 4. See also *Progress Report 1962–1963, Cleveland Development Foundation* (Cleveland: Cleveland Development Foundation, 1963).

10. On the development of downtown organizations, see Laurence A. Alexander, *Downtown Associations: Their Origins, Development, and Administration* (New York: Downtown Idea Exchange, 1966).

11. Martin Millspaugh, ed., *Baltimore's Charles Center: A Case Study of Downtown Renewal* (Washington, D.C.: Urban Land Institute, 1964), p. 13.

12. Alan Altshuler, *The City Planning Process: A Political Analysis* (Ithaca, N.Y.: Cornell University Press, 1965), pp. 202–3; idem, *A Report on Politics in Minneapolis* (Cambridge, Mass.: Joint Center for Urban Studies, 1959), p. V-3; and *Economic Study of Downtown Minneapolis* (Chicago: Real Estate Research Corporation, 1959).

13. *Second Annual Report, Downtown in St. Louis, Inc., 1959–1960* (Saint Louis: Downtown in St. Louis, 1960), p. 1.

14. Ibid., p. 10.

15. Ibid., pp. 15–16.

16. Ibid., p. 18.

17. *City Planning in Philadelphia* (Philadelphia: Citizens' Council on City Planning, 1945), p. 8.

18. David A. Wallace, "Renaissancemanship," *Journal of the American Institute of Planners* 26 (August 1960): 173.

19. Ibid.

20. Aaron Levine, "Citizen Participation," *Journal of the American Institute of Planners* 26 (August 1960): 196.

21. John F. Bauman, *Public Housing, Race, and Renewal: Urban Planning in Philadelphia, 1920–1974* (Philadelphia: Temple University Press, 1987). p. 99.

22. Kirk R. Petshek, *The Challenge of Urban Reform: Policies and Programs in Philadelphia* (Philadelphia: Temple University Press, 1973), p. 26.

23. Ibid., p. 23.

24. *Newsletter, Citizens' Council on City Planning* 12 (October 1957): 1.

25. Frances H. Morton, "Clinic: Role of a Citizen Planning Agency," *Planning 1954: Proceedings of the Annual National Planning Conference* (Chicago: American Society of Planning Officials, 1954), p. 128.

26. Ibid., p. 127. See also Lyall, "Bicycle Built for Two," pp. 20–27.

27. *Report of the Urban Renewal Study Board to Mayor Thomas D'Alesandro, Jr.* (Baltimore: City of Baltimore, 1956), p. 63. The CPHA staff also served as advisers to the city's urban renewal policy and staff committees. See *Urban Renewal in Baltimore* (Baltimore: Planning Commission of Baltimore, 1955), p. 2.

28. Dorothy L. Rubel, "Clinic: Role of a Citizen Planning Agency," in *Planning 1954: Proceedings of the Annual National Planning Conference* (Chicago: American Society of Planning Officials, 1954), p. 123; " 'Star' Committee Drafts Standards for

Housing Code," *Tomorrow's Chicago* 8 (October 1954): 1; and "The Housing and Planning Council . . . ," *Tomorrow's Chicago* 8 (September 1954): 2.

29. Rubel, "Clinic," pp. 123–24.

30. "From the Mire," *Time* 54 (21 November 1949): 24; and Joseph R. Fink, "Reform in Philadelphia: 1946–1951," Ph.D. diss., Rutgers University, 1971, p. 136.

31. Roger Butterfield, "Revolt in Philadelphia," *Saturday Evening Post* 225 (8 November 1952): 106; and Fink, "Reform in Philadelphia," p. 175.

32. Butterfield, "Revolt in Philadelphia," p. 106; Fink, "Reform in Philadelphia," pp. 120, 175; and *Philadelphia Inquirer*, 15 September 1947, p. 3.

33. James Reichley, *The Art of Government: Reform and Organization Politics in Philadelphia* (New York: Fund for the Republic, 1959), pp. 13, 15; and Fink, "Reform in Philadelphia," pp. 164–65, 209–10. For an account of the movement for charter reform, see Joseph D. Crumlish, *A City Finds Itself: The Philadelphia Home Rule Charter Movement* (Detroit: Wayne State University Press, 1959).

34. For accounts of Bacon's work, see "The City: Under the Knife, or All for Their Own Good," *Time* 84 (6 November 1964): 60–72, 75; and Jonathan Barnett and Nory Miller, "Edmund Bacon: A Retrospective," *Planning* 49 (December 1983): 4–11.

35. Fink, "Reform in Philadelphia," p. 116. For election returns in the 1955 mayoral contest, see *Philadelphia Bulletin*, 9 November 1955, pp. 1–2. For background information on Dilworth, see ibid., 24 January 1974, pp. 3–4.

36. *Boston Herald*, 4 November 1951, sec. 1, p. 6.

37. Ibid., 6 November 1949, p. 2C.

38. Ibid., 9 November 1949, p. 16.

39. Ibid., 6 November 1951, p. 9. See also Lorin Peterson, *The Day of the Mugwump* (New York: Random House, 1961), pp. 259–60; *Boston Herald*, 24 September 1951, p. 14; Edward C. Banfield and Martha Derthick, eds., *A Report on the Politics of Boston* (Cambridge, Mass.: Joint Center for Urban Studies, 1960), p. II-6; and Lashley G. Harvey, "Boston's Mid-Century Revolt," *National Municipal Review* 40 (April 1951): 195–200. For the election returns from the 1951 and 1955 Curley-Hynes contests, see *Boston Herald*, 26 September 1951, pp. 1, 16; 7 November 1951, pp. 1, 18; and 28 September 1955, pp. 1, 6.

40. *St. Louis Post-Dispatch*, 1 March 1953, pp. 1A, 4A; 2 March 1953, p. 2B; 7 March 1953, p. 1A; 12 March 1953, p. 2B; 14 March 1953, pp. 1A, 8A; 1 March 1957, p. 1A; 2 March 1957, p. 1A; and 6 March 1957, pp. 1A, 4A, 2C.

41. Kenneth E. Gray, *A Report on Politics in Saint Louis* (Cambridge, Mass.: Center for Urban Studies, Harvard University, 1959), pp. II-15, II-16.

42. For typical statements of Celebrezze's programs, see *Cleveland Plain Dealer*, 2 October 1957, pp. 1, 10; and 6 November 1957, p. 12.

43. *Minneapolis Tribune*, 13 June 1957, p. 6. For the results of the 1957 election in Minneapolis, see ibid., 12 June 1957, pp. 1, 9, 13. For a discussion of the influence of the Central Labor Union in Minneapolis politics, see Altshuler, *Politics in Minneapolis*, pp. V-6, V-7; and Peterson, *Day of the Mugwump*, pp. 289–98.

44. Roger Biles, *Big City Boss in Depression and War: Mayor Edward J. Kelly of Chicago* (DeKalb: Northern Illinois University Press, 1984), pp. 133–51. Also *Chicago Tribune*, 2 April 1947, pp. 1, 3, 6; and 4 April 1951, pt. 1, pp. 1–3.

45. "New Strength in City Hall," *Fortune* 56 (November 1957): 157; and Weber, *Don't Call Me Boss.*

46. Warren Moscow, *The Last of the Big-time Bosses: The Life and Times of Carmine DeSapio and the Rise and Fall of Tammany Hall* (New York: Stein and Day, 1971), p. 131.

47. *Baltimore Sun*, 4 May 1947, p. 14.

48. Ibid., 6 May 1951, p. 14; and 7 May 1951, p. 10.

49. Ibid., 9 May 1951, pp. 1, 10.

50. Ibid., 1 May 1955, p. 1. See also ibid., 2 May 1955, p. 1; and 4 May 1955, p. 18.

51. *Pittsburgh Press*, 29 October 1945, p. 2; and Sally Shames, "David L. Lawrence, Mayor of Pittsburgh: Development of a Political Leader," Ph.D. diss., University of Pittsburgh, 1958, p. 155.

52. Alfred Steinberg, "Pittsburgh, a New City," *National Municipal Review* 44 (March 1955), p. 129; and Shames, "David L. Lawrence," p. 245.

53. *New York Times*, 4 September 1949, p. 27.

54. *Buffalo Evening News*, 1 November 1949, p. 18. For other comments on the "racial" issue in the 1949 election, see ibid., 2 November 1949, p. 40; and 9 November 1949, p. 58.

55. The cities with Republican mayors were Baltimore, Buffalo, Cincinnati, Philadelphia, and Saint Louis. Those having Republican-controlled councils were Buffalo, Cincinnati, Philadelphia, and Saint Louis. In Cleveland, Cincinnati, Chicago, and Minneapolis the council races were officially nonpartisan, but in each of these cities party slates actually vied for the council seats. In Minneapolis the slates were Liberals and Progressives (also known as Independents or Conservatives). The Liberals were adherents of the Democrat-Farmer-Labor party, and the Progressives were Republicans. The two cities with nonpartisan elections in fact as well as law were Boston and Detroit.

56. *St. Louis Post-Dispatch*, 4 April 1945, pp. 1A, 3A, 2B.

57. "Voting in Buffalo," *Just a Moment*, no. 873 (23 October 1947).

58. *Cleveland Plain Dealer*, 7 November 1945, pp. 1, 3.

59. Ibid., 5 October 1955, pp. 1, 10; 9 November 1955, p. 1; 2 October 1957, pp. 1, 10, 12; 6 November 1957, p. 1; 4 November 1959, pp. 1, 16; 5 November 1959, p. 12; and 8 November 1961, pp. 1, 20.

60. *St. Louis Post-Dispatch*, 3 April 1957, pp. 1A, 8A, 2C.

61. *Chicago Tribune*, 8 April 1959, pt. 1, pp. 1–2; and *Philadelphia Bulletin*, 4 November 1959, pp. 1, 3.

62. *Pittsburgh Post-Gazette*, 7 November 1945, pp. 1, 4; 9 November 1949, pp. 1–2; 10 November 1949, pp. 1–2, 12; and 4 November 1953, pp. 1, 4. Also *Pittsburgh Press*, 6 November 1957, pp. 1–2.

63. Frank Hawkins, "Lawrence of Pittsburgh: Boss of the Mellon Patch," *Harper's* 213 (August 1956): 57; Shames, "David L. Lawrence," p. 180; and Lubove, *Pittsburgh*, p. 202.

64. Charles J. Fox, "Municipal Revenues," *Municipal Finance* 19 (August 1946): 25.

65. Lewis B. Sims, "The Downward Trend of City Debt," in *The Municipal Year*

Book, 1947 (Chicago: International City Managers' Association, 1947), p. 196.

66. "Nineteenth Annual Study of Debts-Taxes-Assessments," *Civic Federation*, no. 404 (June 1952): 4.

67. "City's Debt Picture," *Citizens' Business*, no. 1979 (10 September 1951); "The Saint Louis Debt Picture," *Dollars and Sense in Government*, no. 58 (26 May 1948); "Buffalo's Borrowing Power," *Just a Moment*, no. 945 (10 March 1949); and *Greater Philadelphia Facts* (Philadelphia: Chamber of Commerce of Greater Philadelphia, 1953), p. 71.

68. *New York Times*, 19 September 1945, p. 27.

69. "City Bond Sale," *Just a Moment*, no. 1112 (22 May 1952); and *Cincinnati Progress* 3 (23 January 1956): 14.

70. "Nineteenth Annual Study of Debts," *Civic Federation*, p. 11.

71. "City Council Requested to Appropriate $194 Million," *Citizens' Business*, no. 2088 (11 October 1954); and *Financing Philadelphia's Future Capital Improvements, 1955–1960* (Philadelphia: Bureau of Municipal Research, 1954), Appendix C. See also "Greatly Improved Interest Picture," *Citizens' Business*, no. 1744 (26 February 1946); "City's Interest Charges Continue Downward," ibid., no. 1831 (2 March 1948); and "City's Interest Burden Continues to Lighten," ibid., no. 1780 (7 January 1947).

72. "Local Facts," *Just a Moment*, no. 840 (6 March 1947).

73. *St. Louis Post-Dispatch*, 12 March 1953, p. 1A.

74. Ibid., p. 6A.

75. Ibid., 10 March 1953, p. 2C; and 12 March 1953, p. 6A. See also ibid., 8 March 1953, Pictures section, p. 7; 9 March 1953, p. 1A; and 11 March 1953, p. 2D.

76. *St. Louis Post-Dispatch*, 14 March 1953, pp. 1A, 8A; and Raymond R. Tucker, "Saint Louis Gets a Bargain," *American City* 68 (December 1953): 107–8.

77. *St. Louis Post-Dispatch*, 22 May 1955, pp. 1A, 4A, 2B, and Pictures section, p. 3; 24 May 1955, pp. 1A, 14A; and 25 May 1955, p. 2C.

78. Ibid., 27 May 1955, pp. 1A, 6A, 2B.

79. *Capital Improvement Program, 1963–1968* (Cleveland: City Planning Commission, 1962), pp. 46–47.

80. *Philadelphia Bulletin*, 3 Nov. 1963, sec. 1, p. 9; and Robert L. Freedman, *A Report on Politics in Philadelphia* (Cambridge, Mass.: Joint Center for Urban Studies, 1963), p. III-5.

81. "Detroit Sewer Bond Proposition," *Council Comments*, no. 693 (10 February 1959): 1–2; "November Ballot Issues," ibid., no. 612 (27 October 1953): 1–2; and *Detroit Free Press*, 5 November 1947, p. 1.

82. *Baltimore Sun*, 7 May 1947, pp. 1, 6; 9 May 1951, pp. 1, 10, 38; and 4 May 1955, pp. 1, 8.

83. *Cleveland Plain Dealer*, 2 October 1957, p. 14; and 6 November 1957, pp. 1, 20.

84. Altshuler, *Report on Politics in Minneapolis*, p. VI-2.

85. "Where Does the City Stand Financially?" *Dollars and Sense in Government*, no. 74 (30 July 1952): 4.

86. *St. Louis Post-Dispatch*, 16 March 1950, p. 1A.

87. *Capital Improvement Program, 1958–1963* (Boston: City Planning Board, 1958), p. 2.

88. "The Mayor's Financial Review," *Just a Moment*, no. 868 (18 September 1947).

89. "The State of the City," *Just a Moment*, no. 938 (20 January 1949). For information on Buffalo's efforts to reduce its debt, see George W. Wanamaker, "Buffalo Improves Its Credit," *Municipal Finance* 19 (November 1946): 6–9.

90. Robert M. Haig and Carl S. Shoup, *The Financial Problem of the City of New York* (New York: City of New York, 1952), p. 119.

91. *Financial Report, Department of Revenue, City of Cleveland, Ohio, Year Ending December 31, 1959* (Cleveland: Department of Finance, 1960), p. 51; *Report of the Comptroller of the City of Saint Louis for Fiscal Year 1958–1959* (Saint Louis: City of Saint Louis, 1959), p. 82; and "Assessed Valuations at Peak," *Citizens' Business*, no. 2057 (4 May 1953).

92. George B. Merry, "Boston Reawakening," *National Municipal Review* 46 (June 1957): 283; *Fortieth Annual Report on the Statistics of Municipal Finances for the Year Ending December 31, 1945* (Boston: Commonwealth of Massachusetts, 1946), p. xxxi; *Forty-fifth Report on the Statistics of Municipal Finances for the Year Ending December 31, 1956* (Boston: Commonwealth of Massachusetts, 1957), p. 6; and *Forty-sixth Report on the Statistics of Municipal Finances for the Year Ending December 31, 1960* (Boston: Commonwealth of Massachusetts, 1961), p. 4.

93. Herbert Fallin and Theodore R. McKeldin, "Baltimore Faces the Postwar Period," *Municipal Finance* 18 (November 1945): 6.

94. *The Mayor of Baltimore Reports for 1949–1950* (Baltimore: City of Baltimore, 1950), p. 47; "Tax Rates in Buffalo," *Just a Moment*, no. 1149 (25 February 1954); and *Greater Philadelphia Facts*, p. 73.

95. *Annual Report of the City of Detroit, Michigan, by the Auditor General for the Fiscal Year Ended June 30, 1958* (Detroit: City of Detroit, 1958), p. 118; and *Annual Report of the Comptroller of the City of Saint Louis, Missouri, for the Fiscal Year Ended March 31, 1960* (Saint Louis: City of Saint Louis, 1960), p. 51.

96. Banfield and Derthick, *Report on Politics of Boston*, p. VI-4.

97. Altshuler, *Report on Politics in Minneapolis*, p. VI-2.

98. "The Upward Spiral," *Citizens' Business*, no. 2169 (27 October 1958).

99. Ibid.

100. *Greater Philadelphia Facts*, p. 69; and *Financial Statistics of Cities over 100,000 Population, 1939* (Washington, D.C.: U.S. Government Printing Office, 1943), p. 47.

101. Robert A. Sigafoos, *The Municipal Income Tax: Its History and Problems* (Chicago: Public Administration Service, 1955), pp. 78–79; and Mabel Walker, "Nonproperty Revenues and Service Charges," *Municipal Finance* 29 (August 1956): 43. See also Leon Jay Quinto, *Municipal Taxation in the United States* (New York: Mayor's Committee on Management Survey of the City of New York, 1952), pp. 9–30; Freedman, *Report on Politics in Philadelphia*, pp. VI-18–VI-19; Robert K. Sawyer, "Commuters Aid City Comeback," *National Municipal Review* 39 (June 1950): 273–77, 287; "City's Income Tax," *Citizens' Business*, no. 1974 (4 June 1951); and Alfred G. Buehler, "Philadelphia's Experience," in Robert H. Connery, ed., *Municipal Income Taxes* (New York: Academy of Political Science, 1968), pp. 27–29.

102. *St. Louis Post-Dispatch*, 23 April 1954, p. 2B; and William O. Winter,

"Mayor Stumps the State," *National Municipal Review* 44 (June 1955): 303. See also *St. Louis Post-Dispatch*, 4 April 1953, p. 1A; Sigafoos, *Municipal Income Tax*, pp. 78–79; and Quinto, *Municipal Taxation*, pp. 75–81.

103. Kenneth E. Gray, *A Report on Politics in Cincinnati* (Cambridge, Mass.: Joint Center for Urban Studies, 1959), pp. VI-9–VI-10; *Cincinnati Enquirer*, 20 December 1955, p. 1; Sigafoos, *Municipal Income Tax*, pp. 1–2, 4–5, 72; and Robert H. Wessel, "Cincinnati's Income Tax—An Emergency Financing Device," *National Tax Journal* 9 (March 1956): 84–90.

104. Sigafoos, *Municipal Income Tax*, pp. 71–72, 78–79; and Shames, "David L. Lawrence," p. 213. For more on the municipal income tax, see also Elizabeth Deran, "An Overview of the Municipal Income Tax," *Proceedings of the Academy of Political Science* 28 (January 1968): 441–48.

105. U.S. Bureau of the Census, *Financial Statistics of Cities over 100,000 Population, 1937* (Washington, D.C.: U.S. Government Printing Office, 1940); idem, *City Finances, 1945—Individual City Reports* (Washington, D.C.: U.S. Government Printing Office, 1947), p. 362; idem, *City Finances, 1945—Statistical Compendium* (Washington, D.C.: U.S. Government Printing Office, 1947), p. 13; and "What Has Happened to City Revenues? 1929–1946," *Dollars and Sense in Government*, no. 49 (16 July 1946).

106. U.S. Bureau of the Census, *Compendium of City Government Finances in 1958* (Washington, D.C.: U.S. Government Printing Office, 1959), pp. 17, 27.

107. Freedman, *Report on Politics in Philadelphia*, p. VI-19.

108. Temporary Commission on City Finances, *Better Financing for New York City* (New York: City of New York, 1966), p. 56.

109. *Chicago's Report to the People* (Chicago: City of Chicago, 1947), pp. 73–74, 76.

110. *Minneapolis Tribune*, 4 June 1947, pp. 4–5; 5 June 1947, p. 4; 6 June 1947, pp. 4–5; and 7 June 1947, p. 5.

111. Haig and Shoup, *Financial Problem of New York*, p. 21; and Wallace S. Sayre and Herbert Kaufman, *Governing New York City: Politics in the Metropolis* (New York: Russell Sage Foundation, 1960), p. 52.

112. *Financial Report, Department of Finance, City of Cleveland, Ohio, Year Ending December 31, 1958* (Cleveland: Department of Finance, 1959), sec. 1, p. 14.

Chapter 3: Progress or Decay

1. *St. Louis Post-Dispatch*, 5 March 1950, p. 1C.

2. George Sessions Perry, "Pittsburgh," *Saturday Evening Post* 219 (3 August 1946): 15.

3. "Pittsburgh's New Powers," *Fortune* 35 (February 1947): 187; and Roy Lubove, ed., *Pittsburgh* (New York: New Viewpoints, 1976), p. 196.

4. Charles O. Jones, *Clean Air: The Policies and Politics of Pollution Control* (Pittsburgh: University of Pittsburgh Press, 1975), p. 46; Ralph H. German, "Problems of Compliance with Air Pollution Ordinances in Allegheny County, Pennsylvania," in *Air Pollution: Proceedings of the United States Technical Conference on Air Pollution* (New York: McGraw-Hill, 1952), pp. 695–99; Michael P. Weber, *Don't Call Me Boss:*

David L. Lawrence, Pittsburgh's Renaissance Mayor (Pittsburgh: University of Pittsburgh Press, 1988), pp. 244–47; Joel A. Tarr and Bill C. Lamperes, "Changing Fuel-Use Behavior and Energy Transitions: The Pittsburgh Smoke-Control Movement, 1940–1950," *Journal of Social History* 14 (Summer 1981): 561–79; Theodore L. Hazlett, Jr., "Citizens Responsibility for Civic Planning: The Pittsburgh Story," *American Planning and Civic Annual* (1954): 187–88; F. E. Schuchman, "Pittsburgh—'Smokeless City,' " *National Municipal Review* 39 (November 1950): 489–93, 506; and "Pittsburgh's New Powers," *Fortune*, pp. 183–84.

5. Schuchman, "Pittsburgh—'Smokeless City,' " p. 489.

6. "Pittsburgh Comes Out of the Smog," *Newsweek* 34 (26 September 1949): 25–29.

7. "Pittsburgh Renascent," *Architectural Forum* 91 (November 1949): 59.

8. As quoted in Schuchman, "Pittsburgh—'Smokeless City,' " p. 506.

9. George Sessions Perry, "Cincinnati," *Saturday Evening Post* 218 (20 April 1946): 101.

10. "Cincinnati, Ohio, News Note," *Smoke: Official Bulletin Smoke Prevention Association of America, Inc.* 14 (January 1947): 2; and "Cincinnati News Note," ibid. 13 (September 1946): 2. The *Cincinnati Enquirer*'s "Platform for Cincinnati" printed each day on the editorial page included "abatement of the smoke nuisance."

11. "Cincinnati, Ohio, News Note," *Smoke*, p. 2.

12. *Bureau of Smoke Inspection, Activities for 1950* (Cincinnati: City of Cincinnati, 1951), p. 1. See also *1951 Annual Report of the Bureau of Smoke Inspection* (Cincinnati: City of Cincinnati, 1952), and Charles W. Gruber, *Air Pollution Control in Cincinnati* (Cincinnati: City of Cincinnati, 1964), pp. 24–25.

13. *Chicago's Report to the People, 1933–1946* (Chicago: City of Chicago, 1947), pp. 105–6. See also Harvey M. Karlen, *The Governments of Chicago* (Chicago: Courier Publishing, 1958), pp. 207–8.

14. "Twin Cities and Northwest News Note," *Smoke: Official Bulletin Smoke Prevention Association of America, Inc.* 14 (January 1947): 2; and "Minneapolis News Note," ibid. 15 (July 1948): 2.

15. "Smoke," *Citizens' Business*, no. 1809 (30 September 1947).

16. "Locomotive Smoke Reduced—A Progress Report," ibid., no. 1927 (9 May 1950). See also "The Record on Smoke Control," ibid., no. 1814 (4 November 1947); "First Steps toward Smoke Abatement," ibid., no. 1826 (27 January 1948); "A New Smoke Ordinance," ibid., no. 1835 (30 March 1948); and "Status of Air Pollution Control," ibid., no. 1872 (15 February 1949).

17. *New York Times*, 4 June 1948, p. 22; "New York City Adopts Smoke-Control Bill," *Smoke: Official Bulletin Smoke Prevention Association of America, Inc.* 16 (March 1949): 1; and "Smoke Costs New York 8 Million Dollars, Says Byrne," ibid. 16 (September 1949): 1. See also *New York Times*, 8 June 1948, p. 28; 15 June 1948, p. 26; 14 September 1948, p. 28; and 8 November 1948, p. 20.

18. "Smoke Bill Becomes Law," *Citizens Union News* 4 (May 1949): 1. See also "Smoke Gets in Your Hair," *Across from City Hall—Citizens Union News* 4 (December 1949); "Smoke Progress," ibid. 6 (June 1951); and "Smoke Screen," ibid. 6 (September 1951).

19. *Annual Report to the People of Cleveland, 1958–1959* (Cleveland: City of

Cleveland, 1959), p. 39. See also *Cleveland Plain Dealer*, 28 October 1947, pp. 1, 16.

20. Perry, "Cincinnati," p. 99.

21. Thomas P. O'Neil, "Philadelphia: Where Patience Is a Vice," in Robert S. Allen, ed., *Our Fair City* (New York: Vanguard Press, 1947), p. 62.

22. *New York Times*, 11 June 1948, p. 46.

23. Weber, *Don't Call Me Boss*, pp. 201–2, 238–40; and *Annual Report of the City Manager: 1947—Cincinnati, Ohio* (Cincinnati: City of Cincinnati, 1948), p. 1.

24. Edward J. Cleary, *The Orsanco Story: Water Quality Management in the Ohio Valley under an Interstate Compact* (Baltimore: Johns Hopkins University Press, 1967), p. 28.

25. Ibid., pp. 36–37.

26. *Little Miami Valley Sewage Disposal Works* (Cincinnati: City of Cincinnati, 1953), p. 3; and Arthur D. Caster, "The Cincinnati Sewage Disposal Program," *Sewage and Industrial Wastes* 27 (August 1955): 880.

27. John F. Laboon, "Pittsburgh Treatment Plan Commended for Design," *Water and Sewer Works* 101 (May 1954): 236–38; Stanley Dore, "The Allegheny County Sanitary Authority Project in Western Pennsylvania," *Journal of the Boston Society of Civil Engineers* 40 (April 1953): 103–19; Langdon Pearse, "Reviews and Abstracts," *Sewer and Industrial Wastes* 25 (December 1953): 1479; and "Allegheny Conference on Community Development," *Allegheny Conference on Community Development Presents Planning to Reality* (Pittsburgh: Allegheny Conference on Community Development, 1956), p. 21.

28. *The Saint Louis Region Water and Sewage Facilities* (Saint Louis: East-West Gateway Coordinating Council, 1971), pp. 111–13; and *The 125th Annual Report, Fiscal Year Ended June 30, 1977, Detroit Water and Sewerage Department* (Detroit: Detroit Water and Sewerage Department, 1977), p. 14.

29. *Department of Public Works, City of New York, Annual Report 1957* (New York: Department of Public Works, 1958), pp. 5, 46; *The Public Works Department Annual Report 1960 of the City of New York* (New York: Department of Public Works, 1961), pp. 30, 67; and *Department of Public Works, City of New York, Annual Report 1950* (New York: Department of Public Works, 1951), p. 14.

30. *Annual Report, Philadelphia Water Department, 1960* (Philadelphia: Philadelphia Water Department, 1961), p. 27.

31. "Our Glass House," *Citizens' Business*, no. 1780 (11 March 1947).

32. *Annual Report, Philadelphia Water Department, 1960*, pp. 27–28.

33. Elwood L. Bean, "Taste and Odor Control at Philadelphia," *Journal American Water Works Association* 49 (February 1957): 209. See also Samuel S. Baxter, "Management Reorganization of Philadelphia Water Department," ibid. 48 (October 1956): 1199–1208; "A New Water Commission," *Citizens' Business*, no. 1712 (15 May 1945); "Philadelphia's Water Supply Problem," ibid., no. 1745 (5 March 1946); "A Revised Waterworks Improvement Program," ibid., no. 1763 (10 September 1946); "Waterworks Improvements," ibid., no. 1971 (14 May 1951); Myron G. Mansfield, "Philadelphia Improvement Program," *Journal American Water Works Association* 42 (July 1950): 645–53; *Water Department, Annual Report 1955* (Philadelphia: Philadelphia Water Department, 1956); "Progress in Removing Tastes and Odors from City Water,"

Citizens' Business, no. 1799 (20 May 1947); and "Speed Up Water Treatment," ibid., no. 1867 (11 January 1949).

34. *Recommended Program of Public Improvements, 1950–1955* (Philadelphia: Philadelphia City Planning Commission, 1949), p. 4; and *Capital Program, City of Philadelphia, 1956–1961* (Philadelphia: Philadelphia City Planning Commission, 1955), p. 4.

35. George E. Flower, "Solving Metropolitan Cleveland's Sewerage Needs," *Sewage and Industrial Wastes* 29 (January 1957): 6. See also *1951–1952 City of Cleveland Annual Report to the People* (Cleveland: City of Cleveland, 1951), pp. 16–17.

36. Wilford W. DeBerard, "System Developed by Central City," *Journal American Water Works Association* 51 (November 1959): 1335.

37. Jerome B. Wolff, "City-County Cost Allocation for Capital Improvements at Baltimore," ibid. 57 (June 1965): 722; and Gerald J. Remus, "Detroit's Metropolitan Water Service—A New Dimension," ibid. 59 (October 1967): 1224–26. See also *Detroit's Water Development Program for the Metropolitan Area* (Detroit: Board of Water Commissioners, 1959).

38. DeBerard, "System Developed by Central City," pp. 1331–32.

39. Ibid., p. 1335.

40. Flower, "Solving Metropolitan Cleveland's Sewerage Needs," p. 12. See also *A Report of Cleveland's Public Utilities* (Cleveland: City of Cleveland, 1954), pp. 12–13.

41. Flower, "Solving Metropolitan Cleveland's Sewerage Needs," p. 13; Wolff, "Capital Improvements at Baltimore," p. 722; and DeBerard, "System Developed by Central City," p. 1333.

42. Remus, "Detroit's Metropolitan Water Service," p. 1226.

43. Doris D. Reed and Thomas H. Reed, *The Cincinnati Area Must Solve Its Metropolitan Problems* (Cincinnati: Stephen H. Wilder Foundation, 1953), p. 34.

44. Remus, "Detroit's Metropolitan Water Service," pp. 1223–24.

45. George M. Smerk, *Urban Transportation: The Federal Role* (Bloomington, Ind.: Indiana University Press, 1965), pp. 125–39; and Mark H. Rose, *Interstate: Expressway Highway Politics, 1941–1956* (Lawrence: Regents Press of Kansas, 1979), pp. 55–67.

46. *Historical Statistics of the United States, Colonial Times to 1970*, vol. 2 (Washington, D.C.: U.S. Department of Commerce, 1975), p. 772; and Ross D. Eckert, *Airports and Congestion: A Problem of Misplaced Subsidies* (Washington, D.C.: American Enterprise Institute for Public Policy Research, 1972), p. 3.

47. *The Basis for a Master Transportation Plan—Report One* (Baltimore: Planning Commission of Baltimore, 1949), pp. 2, 7; and *A Tentative Master Transportation Plan—Report Two* (Baltimore: Planning Commission of Baltimore, 1949), p. 6.

48. *Cleveland Today . . . Tomorrow: The General Plan of Cleveland* (Cleveland: City Planning Commission, 1950), p. 30.

49. "Kensington Expressway Project, a Bargain Deal for Buffalonians," *Buffalo Business* 29 (June 1954): 28–29.

50. *Plan and Program, 1955* (Philadelphia: Urban Traffic and Transportation Board, 1956), p. iv.

51. Thomas H. MacDonald, "The Case for Urban Expressways," *American City* 62 (June 1947): 93.

52. *Detroit Free Press*, 2 November 1949, p. 2.

53. *Cleveland Today . . . Tomorrow*, p. 31.

54. *Planning Detroit, 1946* (Detroit: City Plan Commission, 1947), p. 12; and *Detroit Free Press*, 1 November 1953, p. 2A.

55. Charles L. Crangle, "Philadelphia Tomorrow," *USA Tomorrow* 1 (October 1954): 24.

56. *Allegheny Conference Presents Planning to Reality*, p. 16.

57. "Progress in Expressways," *Cincinnati Progress* 3 (23 January 1956): 2.

58. Robert Caro, *The Power Broker: Robert Moses and the Fall of New York* (New York: Alfred A. Knopf, 1974), pp. 837–94; and Jill Jonnes, *We're Still Here: The Rise, Fall, and Resurrection of the South Bronx* (Boston: Atlantic Monthly Press, 1986), pp. 117–26.

59. *1957 Annual Report—Chicago Plan Commission* (Chicago: Chicago Plan Commission, 1957), pp. 10–11; and Wilfred Owen, *The Metropolitan Transportation Problem* (Washington, D.C.: Brookings Institution, 1956), p. 47.

60. *Chicago Tribune*, 17 February 1940, p. 5. See also ibid., 21 February 1940, pp. 12–13; and 22 February 1940, p. 7.

61. *St. Louis Post-Dispatch*, 24 May 1955, p. 14A.

62. Ibid., 27 May 1955, pp. 1A, 6A.

63. *Our Downtown Parking Headache and How We Can Cure It* (Cleveland: City Planning Commission, 1951), p. 1.

64. *A Comprehensive Parking Survey of the Saint Louis, Missouri, Central Business District* (Saint Louis: n.p., n.d.), p. ix.

65. *Cincinnati Enquirer*, 4 November 1945, News section, p. 6.

66. George F. Emery, "Urban Expressways," in *American Planning and Civic Annual* (1947), p. 128.

67. "Central Business District Panel Session—Freeways and Assessing Methods," *Urban Land* 6 (December 1947): 3.

68. *Parking Programs: Facts about Selected Urban Parking Programs in the United States* (Washington, D.C.: American Automobile Association, 1954), pp. 153–67; Edward G. Mogren, *Parking Authorities* (Saugatuck, Conn.: Eno Foundation for Highway Traffic Control, 1953), pp. 74–80; *The First Ten Years . . . 1947–1957* (Pittsburgh: Public Parking Authority of Pittsburgh, 1957), pp. 2–14; *Allegheny Conference Presents Planning to Reality*, pp. 9–10; Wilbur Smith and Associates, *Parking in the City Center* (New Haven, Conn.: Automobile Manufacturers Association, 1965), pp. 53–54; and Donald H. McNeil, "Pittsburgh's Downtown Parking Problem," in *1946 Proceedings, Institute of Traffic Engineers* (New Haven, Conn.: Institute of Traffic Engineers, 1946), pp. 28–40.

69. *Parking Programs*, pp. 91–104.

70. Ibid., pp. 17–27; Nathan L. Smith, "Baltimore's Parking Problem and How It Can Be Solved," in *1946 Proceedings, Institute of Traffic Engineers* (New Haven, Conn.: Institute of Traffic Engineers, 1946), pp. 7–13; Adrian Hughes, "The Transit Parking Lot for Baltimore," in ibid., pp. 14–21; and Smith and Associates, *Parking in the City Center*, pp. 51–52.

71. Mogren, *Parking Authorities*, pp. 84–86; "Parking Authority," *Citizens' Business*, no. 2059 (18 May 1953); Robert M. Mitchell, "Downtown Parking—Philadelphia's Experience," *1946 Proceedings, Institute of Traffic Engineers* (New Haven, Conn.: Institute of Traffic Engineers, 1946), pp. 22–27; and Leo Adde, *Nine Cities: The Anatomy of Downtown Renewal* (Washington, D.C.: Urban Land Institute, 1969), pp. 26–27.

72. *Parking Programs*, pp. 33–41; and "Buffalo's Public Parking Garages," *Just a Moment*, no. 1252 (22 January 1959).

73. *Parking Programs*, pp. 43–60.

74. *Plan and Program*, p. vii.

75. *The First Ten Years*, p. 10.

76. Charles M. Hall, "There Will Always Be a 'Downtown,' " *Buffalo Business* 33 (February 1958): 45.

77. *Historical Statistics of the United States*, pp. 769–70.

78. *Cleveland Region Airport Plan* (Cleveland: City of Cleveland, 1946), Introduction.

79. "Shall Our International Airport Come of Age?" *Citizens' Business*, no. 1846 (15 June 1948). See also "Philadelphia's Immediate Airport Needs," ibid., no. 1720 (11 September 1945).

80. *St. Louis Post-Dispatch*, 16 April 1950, p. 1-K.

81. *The Mayor of Baltimore Reports for 1949–1950* (Baltimore: City of Baltimore, 1950), p. 33.

82. Crangle, "Philadelphia Tomorrow," p. 28.

83. *St. Louis Post-Dispatch*, 23 February 1986, p. 5B; and "The Saint Louis Airport Becomes of Age," *Dollars and Sense in Government*, no. 76 (4 March 1953): 1–2.

84. *Annual Report to the People, City of Cleveland, 1951–1952* (Cleveland: City of Cleveland, 1951), p. 40.

85. *Chicago's Report to the People*, p. 197.

86. *Annual Report Department of Aviation, 1960* (Chicago: Department of Aviation, 1961), pp. 12, 18, 20.

87. *Chicago's Report to the People*, p. 198.

88. *Annual Report Department of Aviation, 1959* (Chicago: Department of Aviation, 1960); *Report Department of Aviation, 1960*, p. 14; and *Annual Report 1958: Department of City Planning, City of Chicago* (Chicago: Department of City Planning, 1959), p. 17.

89. George Scullin, *International Airport: The Story of Kennedy Airport and U.S. Commercial Aviation* (Boston: Little, Brown, 1968), pp. 30–86. See also *Citizens Union News* 1 (April 1946); and ibid. 2 (May 1947).

90. Dorothy Nelkin, *Jetport: The Boston Airport Controversy* (New Brunswick, N.J.: Transaction Books, 1974), pp. 47–49.

91. *Chicago's Report to the People*, pp. 191–96; Alan R. Lind, *Chicago Surface Lines: An Illustrated History* (Park Forest, Ill.: Transport History Press, 1979), pp. 468–73; and Edward C. Banfield and Martha Derthick, eds., *A Report on the Politics of Boston* (Cambridge, Mass.: Joint Center for Urban Studies, 1960), pp. VI-19–VI-24.

92. *Report to the Mayor of Baltimore by the Committee on Mass Transportation* (Baltimore: City of Baltimore, 1955), pp. 1, 20–25.

93. *Capital Program, City of Philadelphia, 1956–1961* (Philadelphia: Philadelphia City Planning Commission, 1955), pp. 9–15.

94. *Progress in Philadelphia*, pp. 24–26; and *Philadelphia Evening Bulletin*, 7 November 1955, p. 1.

95. *Eighth Annual Six-Year Capital Improvement Program* (Cleveland: City Planning Commission, 1950), p. 2. Only one-fourth of the $36.1 million for freeways was from city funds. The remainder was state and federal.

96. *The Future of Metropolitan Cleveland Depends on the Subway* (Cleveland: Cleveland Transit System, 1957), pp. 1–2; *Report on Transit Modernization Proposed in Ordinance 2758-45* (Cleveland: City Planning Commission, 1946), pp. 1–7; *Cleveland Transit System Annual Report for the Year Ended December 31, 1951* (Cleveland: Transit Board of Cleveland, 1952), pp. 5–6; *Cleveland Transit System 1953 Annual Report* (Cleveland: Transit Board of Cleveland, 1954), pp. 10–11; and *Cleveland Transit System 1955 Annual Report* (Cleveland: Transit Board of Cleveland, 1956), pp. 3–4, 6.

97. *Chicago's Report to the People*, pp. 191–96; and *Annual Report 1958: Chicago Department of City Planning*, p. 24.

98. Banfield and Derthick, *Report on Politics of Boston*, pp. VI-24–VI-32.

99. *Financing Transit in New York City* (New York: Citizens Budget Commission, 1971), p. 13.

100. Phillip Robinson, *Mass Transportation Study of Pittsburgh and Allegheny County* (Pittsburgh: Allegheny Conference on Community Development, 1949), pp. 26, 47.

101. Jack E. Schramm, William H. Henning, and Thomas J. Dworman, *Detroit's Street Railways* (Chicago: Central Electric Railfans' Association, 1980), vol. 2, *City Lines, 1922–1956*, p. 83.

102. *The City of New York Board of Transportation—Report for the Three and One-Half Years Ending June 30, 1949* (New York: Board of Transportation, 1949), pp. 3, 46–52.

103. *Chicago's Report to the People*, p. 192.

104. James D. Johnson, *A Century of Chicago Streetcars, 1858–1958* (Wheaton, Ill.: Traction Orange, 1964), p. 18.

105. Schramm, Henning, and Dworman, *Detroit's Street Railways*, p. 99.

106. George Sternlieb, *The Future of the Downtown Department Store* (Cambridge, Mass.: Joint Center for Urban Studies, 1962), p. 17.

107. *Urban Transportation and the Detroit Bus System* (Detroit: Detroit City Plan Commission, 1972), p. 31; Sternlieb, *Future of the Downtown Department Store*, p. 59; and *Financing Transit in New York City*, p. 26.

108. *Urban Redevelopment Legislation in the United States: A Comparative Analysis* (Chicago: American Society of Planning Offices, n.d.); "The Status of Urban Redevelopment: A Symposium," *Urban Land* 7 (October 1948): 1; and Jon C. Teaford, *The Twentieth-Century American City: Problem, Promise, and Reality* (Baltimore: Johns Hopkins University Press, 1986), p. 120.

109. "Status of Urban Redevelopment," *Urban Land*, pp. 1, 3.

110. Charles F. Edgecombe, Otto K. Jensen, and Clarence E. Moullette, "Urban Redevelopment Is Under Way," *Planning 1947: Proceedings of the Annual Meeting* (Chicago: American Society of Planning Officials, 1947), pp. 152–65.

111. Mark I. Gelfand, *A Nation of Cities: The Federal Government and Urban America, 1933–1965* (New York: Oxford University Press, 1975), pp. 138–55.

112. *Redevelopment Area Report—1961* (Pittsburgh: Pittsburgh City Planning Commission and Urban Redevelopment Authority, 1961).

113. *Allegheny Conference Presents Planning to Reality*, pp. 6–7; Park H. Martin, "Pittsburgh's Golden Triangle," *American Planning and Civic Annual, 1951* (Washington, D.C.: American Planning and Civic Association, 1952), pp. 141–42; John J. Grove, "Pittsburgh's Renaissance: Industry's Role in the Rebirth of a City," *USA Tomorrow* 1 (October 1954): 18–20; Lorin Peterson, *The Day of the Mugwump* (New York: Random House, 1961), pp. 280–86; Park H. Martin, "Rebuilding the Golden Triangle," in *Creating Better Cities: A Complete Report on the Third Businessmen's Conference on Urban Problems* (Washington, D.C.: Chamber of Commerce of the United States, 1950), pp. 173–77; Roy Lubove, *Twentieth-Century Pittsburgh: Government, Business, and Environmental Change* (New York: John Wiley and Sons, 1969), pp. 112–14, 122–27; "Pittsburgh Renascent," *Architectural Forum*, pp. 62–65; Hal Burton, ed., *The City Fights Back* (New York: Citadel Press, 1954), pp. 188–91; Shelby Stewman and Joel A. Tarr, "Four Decades of Public-Private Partnerships in Pittsburgh," in R. Scott Fosler and Renee A. Berger, eds., *Public-Private Partnership in American Cities* (Lexington, Mass.: D. C. Heath, 1982), pp. 73–75; and Jeanne R. Lowe, *Cities in a Race with Time: Progress and Poverty in America's Renewing Cities* (New York: Random House, 1967), pp. 138–48.

114. "Pittsburgh Renascent," *Architectural Forum*, p. 59.

115. Grove, "Pittsburgh's Renaissance," p. 14.

116. Herbert Kubly, "Pittsburgh: The City That Quick-Changed from Unbelievable Ugliness to Shining Beauty in Less Than Half a Generation," *Holiday* 25 (March 1959): 80–87, 152–56.

117. "Philadelphia's Redevelopment," *Architectural Forum* 103 (July 1955): 122–23; Crangle, "Philadelphia Tomorrow," pp. 25–28; Robert L. Freedman, *A Report on Politics in Philadelphia* (Cambridge, Mass.: Joint Center for Urban Studies, 1963), pp. VI-38–VI-43; *1955 Annual Report—Philadelphia City Planning Commission* (Philadelphia: City Planning Commission, 1956), pp. 32–33; *Annual Report 1956—Philadelphia City Planning Commission* (Philadelphia: City Planning Commission, 1957), p. 20; *Philadelphia Bulletin*, 5 November 1955, p. 3; Kirk R. Petshek, *The Challenge of Urban Reform: Politics and Programs in Philadelphia* (Philadelphia: Temple University Press, 1973), pp. 218–19; and Lowe, *Cities in a Race with Time*, pp. 331–32. The Citizens' Council on City Planning also intervened in the planning of Penn Center. See, for example, *Citizens' Council on City Planning, 1953–1954* (Philadelphia: Citizens' Council on City Planning, 1954), p. 11.

118. W. Hawkins Ferry, *The Buildings of Detroit: A History*, rev. ed. (Detroit: Wayne State University Press, 1980), pp. 360–62; Leo Adde, *Nine Cities: The Anatomy of Downtown Renewal* (Washington, D.C.: Urban Land Institute, 1969), pp. 233–34; *Planning Detroit, 1948* (Detroit: City Plan Commission, 1949), pp. 8–9; and *Detroit Free Press*, 4 November 1951, sec. B, p. 3.

119. George B. Merry, "Boston Reawakening," *National Municipal Review* 46 (June 1957): 282; and Pietro Belluschi, "Boston's Back Bay Center," *USA Tomorrow* 1 (October 1954): 8–13. See also *The Forty-third Annual Report of the City Planning Board for the Year Ending December 31, 1956* (Boston: City of Boston, 1957), pp. 3–4.

120. Martin Millspaugh, ed., *Baltimore's Charles Center: A Case Study of Downtown Renewal* (Washington, D.C.: Urban Land Institute, 1964), p. 30.

121. Ibid., pp. 29–31.

122. *Report on Urban Renewal in Cleveland* (Cleveland: Cleveland Advertising Club, 1955), p. 9. See also *Private Developments in Cleveland's Urban Renewal Areas* (Cleveland: Cleveland Urban Renewal Agency, 1957); *Planning in Cleveland, 1957* (Cleveland: Cleveland City Planning Commission, 1958), pp. 25–27; and *Annual Report to the People of Cleveland, 1958–1959* (Cleveland: City of Cleveland, 1959), pp. 33–34.

123. *Report on Urban Renewal in Cleveland*, pp. 12–16; *Private Development in Cleveland's Urban Renewal Areas; Planning in Cleveland, 1957*, pp. 28–29; Kermit C. Parsons, "Garden Valley: Ohio's First Renewal Project," *Ohio Planning Conference Newsletter* 4 (July 1955): 6–9; and "Cleveland: City with a Deadline," *Architectural Forum* 103 (August 1955): 135–36.

124. Talbot Jones, "Minneapolis Rebuilds," *Northwest Architect* 27 (January–February 1963): 21; and *Glenwood Redevelopment* (Minneapolis: Housing and Redevelopment Authority, 1959), p. 8.

125. *A New Philadelphia Rises: 1958 Annual Report Redevelopment Authority of the City of Philadelphia* (Philadelphia: Philadelphia Redevelopment Authority, 1959), p. 31. See also *Renewal Patterns 1957: Annual Report of the Redevelopment Authority of the City of Philadelphia* (Philadelphia: Philadelphia Redevelopment Authority, 1958), p. 8; and *Conservation: A Report to the Conservation Committee of the Metropolitan Housing and Planning Council by Its Conservation Study Staff*, vol. 1 (Chicago: Metropolitan Housing and Planning Council, 1953), pp. 117–18.

126. *A New Philadelphia Rises*, p. 38; and *Renewal Patterns*, pp. 20–21.

127. *Conservation: A Report to the Conservation Committee*, p. 118; and William W. Nash, *Residential Rehabilitation: Private Profits and Public Purposes* (New York: McGraw-Hill, 1959), pp. 80–81.

128. *New York Times*, 18 September 1955, sec. 8, p. 1. See also ibid., 31 January 1957, pp. 1, 16.

129. *Title I Progress—New York City: Quarterly Report on Slum Clearance Projects under Title I of the Housing Act of 1949 as Amended* (New York: Committee on Slum Clearance, 1959), pp. 1–25; J. Anthony Panuch, *Building a Better New York: Final Report to Mayor Robert F. Wagner* (New York: City of New York, 1960), pp. 51–56; Lowe, *Cities in a Race with Time*, pp. 45–109; *St. Louis Post-Dispatch*, 5 April 1953, p. 1F; and Norman I. Fainstein and Susan S. Fainstein, "The Politics of Urban Development: New York City since 1945," *City Almanac* 17 (April 1984): 7–9. Also *New York Times*, 21 May 1955, pp. 37, 40; 9 September 1957, p. 39; and 12 September 1957, p. 33.

130. *Title I Progress—New York City*, p. 3.

131. *Renewal and Revenue: An Evaluation of the Urban Renewal Program in Detroit* (Detroit: Detroit City Plan Commission, 1962), pp. 37–41; *Planning Detroit*,

1953–1955, pp. 20–23; Hawkins, *Buildings of Detroit*, pp. 375–77; Adde, *Nine Cities*, pp. 222–25; "Mies van der Rohe—Redevelopment Program for Detroit," *Architectural Record* 127 (April 1960): 170–73; "Urban Neighborhood Redevelopment," *Progressive Architecture* 36 (August 1955): 100; "First Design Award—Urban Redevelopment: Detroit, Michigan," ibid. 37 (January 1956), p. 76; and Joe T. Darden, Richard Child Hill, June Thomas, and Richard Thomas, *Detroit: Race and Uneven Development* (Philadelphia: Temple University Press, 1987), pp. 158–67.

132. Morton Hoffman, "The Role of Government in Influencing Changes in Housing in Baltimore: 1940 to 1950," *Land Economics* 30 (May 1954): 133–35; Coleman Woodbury, ed., *Urban Redevelopment: Problems and Practices* (Chicago: University of Chicago Press, 1953), pp. 332–39; *Baltimore Health News* 28 (March–May 1951): 89–103; Martin Millspaugh and Gurney Breckenfeld, *The Human Side of Urban Renewal: A Study of the Attitude Changes Produced by Neighborhood Rehabilitation* (Baltimore: Fight-Blight, 1958); and *Conservation: A Report to the Conservation Committee*, pp. 91–101.

133. Millspaugh and Breckenfeld, *Human Side of Urban Renewal*, pp. 3–64. For information on the neighborhood rehabilitation program in Baltimore's Mount Royal area, see Millspaugh and Breckenfeld, *Human Side of Urban Renewal*, pp. 66–89; and *Urban Renewal in Baltimore* (Baltimore: Planning Commission of Baltimore, 1955), p. 1.

134. *Renewal and Revenue*, pp. 57–67; Maurice Frank Parkins, *Neighborhood Conservation: A Pilot Study* (Detroit: Detroit City Plan Commission, 1958), pp. 1–98; *Detroit's Workable Program* (Detroit: City of Detroit, 1955), pp. 5–6, 97–101; *Planning Detroit, 1953–1955*, pp. 29–33; and *Handbook, Detroit City Plan Commission, 1959* (Detroit: Detroit City Plan Commission, 1959), pp. E3–E11.

135. *Your Hyde Park Area Rehabilitation Plan* (Saint Louis: City of Saint Louis, 1957).

136. Nash, *Residential Rehabilitation*, pp. 100–102. See also "Saint Louis Will Also Rehabilitate Local Neighborhoods," *American City* 68 (December 1953): 108.

137. *Fortieth Annual Report of the City Planning Board for the Year Ending December 31, 1953* (Boston: City of Boston, 1954), p. 9.

138. Ibid. See also *Forty-second Annual Report of the City Planning Board for the Year Ending December 31, 1955* (Boston: City of Boston, 1956), p. 9; and *Annual Address of Mayor John B. Hynes to the Honorable the City Council, January 4, 1954* (Boston: City of Boston, 1954), p. 4.

139. *Conservation: A Report to the Conservation Committee*, pp. 5, 71.

140. Ibid., p. 82.

141. Francis J. Lammer, "Rehabilitation Has Taken Three Forms in Philadelphia—Remodeling Found Best," *Journal of Housing* 12 (February 1955): 49. See also *Conservation: A Report to the Conservation Committee*, p. 117; and Nash, *Residential Rehabilitation*, pp. 79–81.

142. Lammer, "Rehabilitation," p. 47.

143. Ibid., pp. 47–48. See also *Conservation: A Report to the Conservation Committee*, pp. 115–16.

144. *A Citizen's Guide to Housing and Urban Renewal in Philadelphia* (Phila-

delphia: Philadelphia Housing Association, 1960), p. 10; and *Renewal Patterns, 1957*, p. 28.

145. *Workable Program for Urban Renewal—The Program in Practice, 1956* (Philadelphia: Office of Development Coordinator, 1957), p. 1.

146. *Renewal Patterns, 1957*, p. 28.

147. *Partnership for Renewal* (Philadelphia: Office of Development Coordinator, 1960); *Citizen's Guide to Housing in Philadelphia*, p. 22; *Workable Program—The Program in Practice*, pp. 10–12; Petshek, *Challenge of Urban Reform*, pp. 146–49; *Philadelphia Bulletin*, 6 November 1955, sec. 2, p. 8; and Germantown Settlement, *A Neighborhood Acts: An Experiment in Cooperative Neighborhood Rehabilitation* (New York: National Federation of Settlements and Neighborhood Centers, 1957).

148. Millspaugh and Breckenfeld, *Human Side of Urban Renewal*, p. 63.

149. Lammer, "Rehabilitation," p. 48.

150. *Partnership for Renewal*, pp. 16–17.

151. Ibid., pp. 19, 24.

152. Ibid., p. 13.

153. *Renewal and Revenue*, p. 57. See also *Partnership for Renewal*, p. 60.

154. *Conservation: A Report to the Conservation Committee*, p. 98.

155. Ibid.

156. Lammer, "Rehabilitation," p. 48.

157. *Your Cherokee Area: Rehabilitation Plan* (Saint Louis: City of Saint Louis, 1957); and *Your Hyde Park Area*. See also *Renewal and Revenue*, pp. 63–65.

158. Muriel Beadle, *The Hyde Park–Kenwood Urban Renewal Years* (Chicago: Author, 1967), p. 13.

159. *Hyde Park–Kenwood Urban Renewal Plan* (Chicago: City of Chicago, 1958), p. 1. For accounts of the Hyde Park–Kenwood effort, see Julia Abrahamson, *A Neighborhood Finds Itself* (New York: Harper and Brothers, 1959); Peter H. Rossi and Robert A. Dentler, *The Politics of Urban Renewal: The Chicago Findings* (New York: Free Press of Glencoe, 1961); Harvey S. Perloff, *Urban Renewal in a Chicago Neighborhood: An Appraisal of Hyde Park–Kenwood Renewal Program* (Chicago: Hyde Park Herald, 1955); James V. Cunningham, *The Resurgent Neighborhood* (Notre Dame, Ind.: Fides Publishers, 1965), pp. 69–85; Beadle, *Hyde Park–Kenwood Renewal Years*; and Arnold R. Hirsch, *Making the Second Ghetto: Race and Housing in Chicago, 1940–1960* (Cambridge: Cambridge University Press, 1983), pp. 135–70.

160. *Thumbs Up for the Conference: The First Annual Report West End Community Conference, May 1955 to May 1956* (Saint Louis: West End Community Conference, 1956).

161. *Thumbs Up for the Conference: Second Annual Report, May 1956 to May 1957* (Saint Louis: West End Community Conference, 1957).

162. Ibid.

Chapter 4: Bad News and Good

1. Mitchell Gordon, *Sick Cities* (New York: Macmillan, 1963); and E. A. Gutkind, *The Twilight of Cities* (New York: Free Press of Glencoe, 1962).

2. Ira Rosenwaike, *Population History of New York City* (Syracuse, N.Y.: Syracuse University Press, 1972), p. 138.

3. *Sixty-seventh Annual Report of the Superintendent of Schools, City of New York, School Year 1964–1965—Statistical Section* (New York: Board of Education, 1965), p. 3; and Robert L. Freedman, *A Report on Politics in Philadelphia* (Cambridge, Mass.: Joint Center for Urban Studies, 1963), p. VI-11.

4. Evelyn M. Kitagawa and Karl E. Taeuber, eds., *Local Community Fact Book, Chicago Metropolitan Area, 1960* (Chicago: City of Chicago, 1963), pp. 126–27, 154–55.

5. John P. Alevizos and Allen E. Beckwith, *Downtown and Suburban Shopping Habits Study of Greater Boston* (Boston: Boston Herald–Traveler, 1954), pp. 14–17, 20–23; Arthur D. Little, Inc., *Preliminary Research for Redevelopment of Boston's Retail District* (Boston: Boston City Planning Board, 1957), pp. 12–13; *Minneapolis Tribune*, 9 June 1957, p. 1E; and George Sternlieb, *The Future of the Downtown Department Store* (Cambridge, Mass: Joint Center for Urban Studies, 1962).

6. George Sternlieb, "The Future of Retailing in the Downtown Core," *AIP Journal* 24 (May 1963), as reprinted in Howard A. Schretter, *Downtown Revitalization* (Athens, Ga.: Institute of Community and Area Development, University of Georgia, 1967), p. 96.

7. Ibid., p. 95.

8. *New York Times*, 17 February 1957, sec. 3, pp. 1, 8. See also ibid., 18 January 1960, p. 23.

9. *A Plan for Pittsburgh's Golden Triangle* (Pittsburgh: Pittsburgh Regional Planning Association, 1962), p. 40; and *New York Times*, 16 June 1957, p. 58.

10. *Cleveland Plain Dealer*, 15 February 1962, pp. 1, 4. See also ibid., 17 December 1961, p. 9AA; and 23 March 1962, p. 18.

11. *A Proposed Shopping and Transit Concourse for Downtown Buffalo* (Buffalo: City Planning Commission, n.d.), p. 2.

12. *Plan for Golden Triangle*, p. 39.

13. Robert Moore Fisher, *The Boom in Office Buildings: An Economic Study of the Past Two Decades* (Washington, D.C.: Urban Land Institute, 1967), pp. 26–27; and Regina Belz Armstrong, *The Office Industry: Patterns of Growth and Location* (Cambridge, Mass.: MIT Press, 1972), pp. 46–47.

14. "Offices: Building Fast, Filling Fast," *Business Week*, no. 1351 (23 July 1955): 31; and "Offices: They Can't Catch Up," ibid., no. 1426 (29 December 1956): 25.

15. "New Office Towers Change Face of U.S. Cities," ibid., no. 1620 (17 September 1960): 186.

16. John McDonald, "The $2 Billion Building Boom," *Fortune* 61 (February 1960): 119. See also "Office Building Boom," ibid. 60 (September 1959): 156; and "Newsweek Spotlight on Business: New York Office Structures," *Newsweek* 55 (4 April 1960): 89–91.

17. *Office Building Construction, Manhattan, 1947–1963* (New York: Research Department, Real Estate Board of New York, 1962), pp. 1, 2, 22–23; and McDonald, "$2 Billion Building Boom," p. 119.

18. Carl W. Condit, *Chicago 1930–1970: Building, Planning, and Urban Technology* (Chicago: University of Chicago Press, 1974), pp. 302–3. See also *An Anal-*

ysis of Chicago Commercial Office Space (Chicago: Continental Illinois National Bank and Trust Company, 1975), pp. 3–13.

19. Jim Toman and Dan Cook, *Cleveland's Changing Skyline* (Cleveland: Cleveland Landmarks Press, 1984), pp. 7–11.

20. For office occupancy figures nationwide, see *Forty-fourth Annual Experience Exchange Report, Office Building Operations, Calendar Year 1963* (Chicago: National Association of Building Owners and Managers, 1964), p. 4.

21. "New Office Towers Change Face of U.S. Cities," *Business Week*, p. 196.

22. *New York Times*, 30 July 1961, p. 58.

23. "Manhattan Greets New Hotel," *Business Week*, no. 1664 (22 July 1961): 32.

24. *New York Times*, 14 January 1962, sec. 8, pp. 1, 4.

25. "Hotel and Motel Building Boom," *Greater Minneapolis* 15 (January 1963): 20–25, 73–77; and *New York Times*, 22 October 1961, sec. 8, pp. 1, 12.

26. *New York Times*, 6 January 1964, p. 71. See also ibid., 9 January 1961, sec. 1, p. 112.

27. Ibid., 13 August 1961, sec. 1, p. 91.

28. *Cleveland Plain Dealer*, 21 March 1962, p. 6. See also ibid., 22 March 1962, p. 42.

29. *New York Times*, 22 October 1961, sec. 8, p. 12.

30. Ibid., 7 July 1963, sec. 8, pp. 1, 3.

31. Ibid., 14 January 1962, sec. 8, p. 4.

32. Ibid., 29 January 1961, sec. 8, p. 8.

33. *Cleveland Plain Dealer*, 21 March 1962, p. 6.

34. Ibid., 16 February 1962, p. 13.

35. *Plan for Golden Triangle*, p. 9.

36. Management and Economics Research, *Economic Development Program: Saint Louis*, 2 vols. (Palo Alto, Calif.: Management and Economics Research, 1968) 1: 3. See also Edgar M. Hoover and Raymond Vernon, *Anatomy of a Metropolis: The Changing Distribution of People and Jobs within the New York Metropolitan Region* (Cambridge, Mass: Harvard University Press, 1959), p. 28; "Why Some Firms Migrate," *Regional Plan News*, no. 53 (March 1957): 1–2; J. R. Meyer, J. F. Kain, and M. Wohl, *The Urban Transportation Problem* (Cambridge, Mass: Harvard University Press, 1965), pp. 25–55; and John B. Rae, *The Road and the Car in American Life* (Cambridge, Mass.: MIT Press, 1971).

37. *Detroit Free Press*, 13 September 1957, pp. 1–2.

38. "Decline in Detroit," *Time* 78 (27 October 1961): 27.

39. *Municipal Record: Proceedings of the Council of the City of Pittsburgh* 100 (28 November 1966): 494. For Barr's reelection in 1961, see *Pittsburgh Post-Gazette*, 2 November 1961, p. 7; 3 November 1961, p. 5; and 9 November 1961, pp. 1, 4, 22. See also James V. Cunningham, *Urban Leadership in the Sixties* (Cambridge, Mass.: Schenkman Publishing, 1970), pp. 47–64.

40. *Philadelphia Evening Bulletin*, 24 January 1974, p. 24. Tate published his memoirs in a series of articles in the *Philadelphia Evening Bulletin* in January 1974.

41. Ibid., 1 November 1963, p. 14B.

42. For information on the election of Mayor Kowal, see *Buffalo Evening News*, 1 November 1961, sec. 3, p. 46; 2 November 1961, sec. 3, p. 37; 6 November 1961, sec.

3, p. 32; and 8 November 1961, sec. 1, p. 1. Also *New York Times*, 16 June 1965, p. 50; 17 June 1965, p. 17; and 18 June 1965, p. 20.

43. *St. Louis Post-Dispatch*, 8 March 1961, pp. 1A, 4A.

44. Seymour Freedgood, "The Vacuum at City Hall," *Fortune* 61 (February 1960): 126.

45. *New York Times*, 19 October 1961, p. 34.

46. For Collins's election in 1959, see *Boston Globe*, 21 September 1959, p. 9; 23 September 1959, pp. 1, 18–19; 1 November 1959, pp. 1, 8, A-3, A-7; 2 November 1959, pp. 1, 19; 4 November 1959, pp. 1, 14; and Murray B. Levin, *The Alienated Voter: Politics in Boston* (New York: Holt, Rinehart and Winston, 1960).

47. *Philadelphia Evening Bulletin*, 20 January 1974, sec. 1, p. 27.

48. For information on Detroit's fiscal problems, see David Greenstone, *A Report on the Politics of Detroit* (Cambridge, Mass.: Joint Center for Urban Studies, 1961), pp. VI-1–VI-9; Albert L. Warren, "Detroit's First Year's Experience with the City Income Tax," *Proceedings of the Fifty-sixth Annual Conference on Taxation, 1963* (Harrisburg, Pa.: National Tax Association, 1964), pp. 443–44; and Leonard D. Bronder, "Michigan's First Local Income Tax," *National Tax Journal* 15 (December 1962): 423–24.

49. *Municipal Record: Proceedings of the Council of the City of Pittsburgh* 92 (1 December 1958): 492.

50. Ibid. 94 (5 December 1960): 467, 469.

51. Ibid. 95 (27 November 1961): 507.

52. Ibid. 96 (26 November 1962): 463–67.

53. *New York Times*, 2 April 1958, pp. 1, 26–27, 30; and 1 April 1959, p. 31.

54. Ibid., 2 April 1958, p. 30.

55. *The Magic of Ideas: Citizens Budget Commission Twenty-seventh Annual Report, 1958* (New York: Citizens Budget Commission, 1958), pp. 8, 29.

56. *New York Times*, 2 April 1959, pp. 1, 23, 30.

57. Ibid., 1 April 1959, p. 1.

58. Ibid., 16 April 1963, pp. 1, 26, 27.

59. Ibid., 17 April 1963, p. 25.

60. Ibid., 16 April 1963, p. 34.

61. Temporary Commission on City Finances, City of New York, *Better Financing for New York City* (New York: City of New York, 1966), p. 33.

62. Warren, "Detroit's First Year's Experience with the City Income Tax," pp. 442–50; and Bronder, "Michigan's First Local Income Tax," pp. 423–31.

63. *Municipal Record: Proceedings of the Council of the City of Pittsburgh* 94 (5 December 1960): 469; ibid. 96 (26 November 1962): 466; and ibid. 97 (26 November 1963): 438.

64. *City of Philadelphia, 1961 Financial Program* (Philadelphia: City of Philadelphia, 1961), p. 22.

65. *City Journal* 42 (12 May 1959): 2–3; ibid. 43 (10 May 1960): 1; and Kenneth E. Gray, *A Report on Politics in Saint Louis* (Cambridge, Mass.: Center for Urban Studies, Harvard University, 1959), pp. VI-9–VI-10.

66. *City Journal* 46 (30 April 1963): 3, 6–8.

67. *Civic Federation Bulletin*, no. 552 (13 February 1959): 1. For changes in prop-

erty tax rates, see Civic Federation, *Thirty-third Annual Study of Debts-Taxes-Assessments* (Chicago: Civic Federation, 1966), p. 21.

68. For a list of new and increased taxes in New York City, see Temporary Commission on City Finances, *Better Financing for New York City*, p. 56.

69. *New York Times*, 16 April 1963, p. 27; and 17 April 1963, p. 24.

70. "Decline in Detroit," *Time*, p. 27. See also Greenstone, *Politics in Detroit*, pp. VI-5–V-7.

71. *Municipal Record: Proceedings of the Council of the City of Pittsburgh* 94 (5 December 1960): 472.

72. *New York Times*, 2 April 1959, p. 30.

73. Robert F. Wagner, "Help for Our Cities," *National Civic Review* 49 (January 1960): 6.

74. *New York Times*, 7 September 1958, sec. 8, pp. 1, 12; Jeanne R. Lowe, *Urban Renewal in Flux: The New York View* (New York: New School for Social Research, 1966), pp. 85–87; and idem, *Cities in a Race with Time: Progress and Poverty in America's Renewing Cities* (New York: Random House, 1967), pp. 80–81, 87–89. For a review of the New York City renewal projects proposed in the 1950s, see *Title I Progress, October 26, 1959* (New York: Committee on Slum Clearance, 1959), and J. Anthony Panuch, *Building a Better New York* (New York: City of New York, 1960).

75. Franklin Toker, *Pittsburgh: An Urban Portrait* (University Park, Pa.: Pennsylvania State University Press, 1986), pp. 234–35; and Roy Lubove, *Twentieth-Century Pittsburgh: Government, Business, and Environmental Change* (New York: John Wiley and Sons, 1969), pp. 130–32.

76. Martin Millspaugh, ed., *Baltimore's Charles Center: A Case Study of Downtown Renewal* (Washington, D.C.: Urban Land Institute, 1964).

77. Leo Adde, *Nine Cities: The Anatomy of Downtown Revival* (Washington, D.C.: Urban Land Institute, 1969), pp. 199–200; George McCue, *The Building Art in Saint Louis: Two Centuries* (Saint Louis: Knight Publishing, 1981), pp. 20–21; and Margaret Sheppard, "The Fight to Build the Arch," *St. Louis* 18 (July 1986): 68–71.

78. *The Official Plan, Minneapolis Planning Commission* (Minneapolis: Planning Commission, 1962), p. 71; and *Three Decades: 1947–1977, Renewal in Minneapolis* (Minneapolis: Minneapolis Housing and Redevelopment Authority, 1967).

79. *Urban Renewal Notes* (November–December 1961).

80. Eric Johannesen, *Cleveland Architecture, 1876–1976* (Cleveland: Western Reserve Historical Society, 1979), p. 223.

81. *Cleveland Plain Dealer*, 23 November 1960, p. 4.

82. Jim Toman and Dan Cook, *Cleveland's Changing Skyline* (Cleveland: Cleveland Landmarks Press, 1984), pp. 15–65; "Erieview Phase 1," *Ohio Architect* 20 (February 1962): 4–7; Johannesen, *Cleveland Architecture*, pp. 223–28; and *1960–1961 Annual Report to the People of Cleveland* (Cleveland: City of Cleveland, 1961), pp. 5–10.

83. *1960–1961 Annual Report to the People of Cleveland*, p. 5.

84. Walter Muir Whitehill, *Boston: A Topographical History* (Cambridge, Mass.: Harvard University Press, 1968), pp. 200–214; "Boston Makes a Comeback," *U.S. News and World Report* 57 (21 September 1964): 52–58; "Old Boston Spruces Up," *Business Week*, no. 1754 (13 April 1963): 130, 132; Charles W. Eliot, Donald M.

Graham, and David A. Crane, "Boston: Three Centuries of Planning," *ASPO Newsletter* 30 (April 1964): 43–48; and John Stainton, *Urban Renewal and Planning in Boston: A Review of the Past and a Look at the Future* (Boston: Greater Boston Chamber of Commerce, 1972).

85. *Boston Globe*, 20 December 1959, p. 14A.

86. *Preliminary Plans for Redevelopment of the Kenyon-Barr Urban Renewal Area* (Cincinnati: City Planning Commission, 1958); *Cincinnati Enquirer*, 5 November 1957, p. 7; *History of Progress—Annual Report 1965–1966* (Cincinnati: Department of Urban Development, 1966); "Queensgate of the 'Queen City,' " *Ohio Planning Newsletter* 12 (February–March 1963): 2; and David B. Carlson, "New Life for City Industries," *Architectural Forum* 114 (March 1961): 109.

87. *Annual Report 1964 Redevelopment Authority, City of Philadelphia* (Philadelphia: Redevelopment Authority, 1965), pp. 42–43.

88. Adde, *Nine Cities*, pp. 208–210; and Management and Economics Research, *Economic Development Program: Saint Louis* 2: 156–57.

89. *Progress Report, 1962–1963* (Cleveland: Cleveland Development Foundation, 1963), p. 9. For problems with the Gladstone project, see *Cleveland Plain Dealer*, 22 March 1962, p. 43; and *Cleveland Press*, 31 July 1964, p. B-4.

90. Valerie Sue Halverson Pace, "Society Hill, Philadelphia: Historic Preservation and Urban Renewal in Washington Square East," PhD. diss., University of Minnesota, 1976, p. 114.

91. *Philadelphia Bulletin*, 10 May 1959, sec. 4, p. 6.

92. *Neighborhood Conservation in New York City* (New York: Housing and Redevelopment Board, 1966), p. 4.

93. Lubove, *Twentieth-Century Pittsburgh*, pp. 129–30; and "The Harrison Project," *Greater Minneapolis* 13 (January 1962): 67, 134–36.

94. *St. Louis Post-Dispatch*, 3 January 1962, p. 2C. See also ibid., 7 March 1962, pp. 1A, 6A.

95. Ibid., 2 January 1962, p. 2B.

96. Jane Jacobs, *The Death and Life of Great American Cities* (New York: Random House, 1961), pp. 4–5.

97. *Philadelphia Evening Bulletin*, 31 July 1957, pp. 1–2. For the Eastwick controversy, see also ibid., 30 July 1957, p. 26; and 4 August 1957, p. 6.

98. Ibid., 29 April 1958, p. B-45.

99. *Boston Globe*, 20 December 1959, p. 14A.

100. Herbert Gans, *The Urban Villagers* (New York: Free Press of Glencoe, 1962), pp. 281–335; and Marc Fried, "Grieving for a Lost Home: Psychological Costs of Relocation," and Chester Hartman, "The Housing of Relocated Families," both in James Q. Wilson, ed., *Urban Renewal: The Record and the Controversy* (Cambridge, Mass.: MIT Press, 1966), pp. 306, 360.

101. William H. Hessler, "The Refugees from Civic Progress," *Reporter* 21 (9 July 1959): 29.

102. *Chicago Tribune*, 14 February 1961, pt. 1, p. 7; and George Rosen, *Decision-Making Chicago-Style* (Urbana, Ill.: University of Illinois Press, 1980), pp. 114–15.

103. J. Clarence Davies III, *Neighborhood Groups and Urban Renewal* (New York:

Columbia University Press, 1966), p. 89. See also *New York Times*, 27 February 1961, p. 29; and Lowe, *Cities in a Race with Time*, pp. 101–3.

104. Davies, *Neighborhood Groups and Urban Renewal*, pp. 110–46.

105. *St. Louis Post-Dispatch*, 24 January 1962, pp. 1A, 12A. See also ibid., 15 January 1962, pp. 1A, 6A.

106. Ibid., 7 March 1962, p. 6A.

107. Ibid., 5 March 1962, p. 2C.

108. *Philadelphia Evening Bulletin*, 29 April 1958, p. B-45; and *Cleveland Plain Dealer*, 22 November 1960, p. 54.

109. George Rasmussen, "The Reawakening," *Buffalo* 39 (April 1964): 19. See also *New York Times*, 29 July 1965, p. 58.

110. Rasmussen, "Reawakening," pp. 20–21.

111. *New York Times*, 4 August 1965, p. 52.

112. Ibid., 18 June 1964, p. 32.

113. *St. Louis Post-Dispatch*, 16 January 1962, p. 1A. See also ibid., 6 January 1962, p. 3A.

114. Robert C. Alberts, *The Shaping of the Point; Pittsburgh's Renaissance Park* (Pittsburgh: University of Pittsburgh Press, 1980), p. 163.

115. Lubove, *Twentieth-Century Pittsburgh*, pp. 131–32. Michael P. Weber, *Don't Call Me Boss: David L. Lawrence, Pittsburgh's Renaissance Mayor* (Pittsburgh: University of Pittsburgh Press, 1988), p. 274.

116. Lubove, *Twentieth-Century Pittsburgh*, p. 132. See also Weber, *Don't Call Me Boss*, p. 271, and Toker, *Pittsburgh*, pp. 234–35.

117. "Saint Louis Snaps Out of a Long, Costly Lull," *Business Week*, no. 1881 (18 September 1965): 202; and Adde, *Nine Cities*, p. 205.

118. *St. Louis Post-Dispatch*, 1 September 1965, p. 2B; "Saint Louis Snaps Out of a Long, Costly Lull," *Business Week*, p. 204; and Adde, *Nine Cities*, p. 205.

119. William W. Nash, *Residential Rehabilitation: Private Profits and Public Purposes* (New York: McGraw-Hill, 1959), p. 81.

120. *Cleveland Plain Dealer*, 30 April 1961, p. 1A.

121. Ibid., p. 9A. See also ibid., 1 May 1961, pp. 1, 13; and 2 May 1961, pp. 1–2.

122. Ibid., 24 March 1962, pp. 1, 8.

123. Ibid., 19 May 1964, as reprinted in *Cleveland's Workable Program, 1963–1964; Supplementary Documentation for the Program of Community Improvement* (Cleveland: Department of Urban Renewal and Housing, 1964).

124. *Cleveland Plain Dealer*, 30 April 1961, p. 9A.

125. Ibid.

126. Ibid., 23 November 1960, p. 4.

127. Ibid., 22 November 1960, p. 54.

128. *St. Louis Post-Dispatch*, 7 March 1962, p. 6A.

129. *Cleveland Plain Dealer*, 20 October 1963, p. 8-AA; and *Cleveland Press*, 6 November 1963, as reprinted in *Cleveland's Workable Program, 1963–1964; Supplementary Documentation*.

130. John C. Schmidt, "Inner Harbor: Progress Report," *Baltimore* 58 (July 1965): 34. See also Harold R. Snedcof, *Cultural Facilities in Mixed-Use Development* (Washington, D.C.: Urban Land Institute, 1985), p. 240; John C. Schmidt, "Rebirth

of Baltimore—Phase Two," *Baltimore* 59 (October 1966): 33–34, 37–38; and Jake Slagle, Jr., "Inner Harbor: A New View for Baltimore," in Lenora Heilig Nast, Laurence N. Krause, and R. C. Monk, eds., *Baltimore: A Living Renaissance* (Baltimore: Historic Baltimore Society, 1982), p. 46.

131. *Cleveland Plain Dealer,* 1 May 1961, p. 13.

132. Adde, *Nine Cities,* p. 205.

133. George M. Smerk, *Urban Transportation: The Federal Role* (Bloomington, Ind.: Indiana University Press, 1965), p. 136.

134. Richard A. Miller, "Expressway Blight," *Architectural Forum* 111 (October 1959): 159.

135. *New York Times,* 15 May 1961, p. 30.

136. "Expressways and Parks," *Planning: News and Comment* 15 (March 1963): 1.

137. Charles W. Gruber, *1961 Annual Report, Bureau of Air Pollution Control and Heating Inspection* (Cincinnati: Department of Safety, 1962), p. 1.

138. *Annual Report, the Greater Baltimore Committee, for 1962* (Baltimore: Greater Baltimore Committee, 1962).

139. John B. Lotz, Jr., "Expressway Delaymanship," *Baltimore* 58 (October 1965): 63.

140. *New York Times,* 19 June 1962, p. 37. See also ibid., 3 January 1961, p. 46; 13 February 1961, p. 29; 27 February 1961, p. 29; 5 April 1962, pp. 1, 25; 10 April 1962, p. 42; 27 June 1962, p. 37; 24 August 1962, p. 26; 29 October 1962, p. 31; and 7 December 1962, p. 32.

141. *City Journal* 43 (3 May 1960): 5.

142. *City Journal* 45 (23 April 1963): 5.

143. Michael N. Danielson, *Federal-Metropolitan Politics and the Commuter Crisis* (New York: Columbia University Press, 1965), p. 97.

144. *Rapid Transit System and Plan Recommended for Detroit and the Metropolitan Area* (Detroit: Rapid Transit Commission, 1958), pp. 3, 41.

145. "An Interview with Henry Barnes," *Metropolitan Transportation* 57 (March 1961): 24.

146. Donald C. Hyde, "Role of Local Mass Transit in Community Development," in *City Problems of 1961: The Annual Proceedings of the United States Conference of Mayors* (Washington, D.C.: United States Conference of Mayors, 1961), pp. 89, 94.

147. Gilbert Burck, "How to Unchoke Our Cities," *Fortune* 63 (May 1961): 120.

148. Charles H. Frazier, "Philadelphia Transportation Alternatives," in *Proceedings of the Fifty-first Annual Conference on Taxation, 1958* (Harrisburg, Pa.: National Tax Association, 1959), pp. 521–22; Smerk, *Urban Transportation,* pp. 144–45; and Danielson, *Federal-Metropolitan Politics,* p. 98.

149. Danielson, *Federal-Metropolitan Politics,* p. 102.

150. Ibid., pp. 101–3.

151. Ibid., p. 174; and Smerk, *Urban Transportation,* pp. 148–52.

152. *New York Times,* 5 July 1961, as quoted in Danielson, *Federal-Metropolitan Politics,* p. 174.

Chapter 5: Rebellion and Reaction

1. John V. Lindsay, *Journey into Politics: Some Informal Observations* (New York: Dodd, Mead, 1967), p. 135.

2. *New York Times*, 2 January 1966, p. 56.

3. Ibid., 15 October 1967, sec. 6, p. 32; and Nat Hentoff, *A Political Life: The Education of John V. Lindsay* (New York: Alfred A. Knopf, 1969), p. 84. See also *New York Times*, 1 January 1967, sec. 6, p. 18.

4. *New York Times*, 1 January 1967, sec. 6, p. 18; and Hentoff, *A Political Life*, pp. 108–9. For a perceptive analysis of Lindsay's leadership, see Clarence N. Stone, "Complexity and the Changing Character of Executive Leadership: An Interpretation of the Lindsay Administration in New York City," *Urban Interest* 4 (Fall 1982): 29–50.

5. Oliver Pilat, *Lindsay's Campaign: A Behind-the-Scenes Diary* (Boston: Beacon Press, 1968), p. 239.

6. *New York Times*, 2 January 1966, p. 56.

7. Lindsay, *Journey into Politics*, p. 138.

8. Ibid., p. 136.

9. Hentoff, *A Political Life*, p. 166.

10. Ibid., pp. 87, 166.

11. *New York Times*, 1 January 1967, sec. 6, p. 19.

12. Lindsay, *Journey into Politics*, p. 141.

13. *New York Times*, 2 January 1966, p. 56.

14. Lindsay, *Journey into Politics*, p. 142.

15. Ibid.

16. Hentoff, *A Political Life*, p. 138.

17. Lindsay, *Journey into Politics*, p. 144.

18. David A. Grossman, "The Lindsay Legacy: A Partisan Appraisal," *City Almanac* 8 (October 1973): 6.

19. Pilat, *Lindsay's Campaign*, pp. 236, 329.

20. *New York Times*, 4 November 1965, p. 50.

21. Charles R. Morris, *The Cost of Good Intentions: New York City and the Liberal Experiment, 1960–1975* (New York: W. W. Norton, 1980), p. 59.

22. Robert Conot, *American Odyssey* (New York: William Morrow, 1974), p. 447.

23. Ibid., p. 452; and William Serrin, "How One Big City Defeated Its Mayor," *New York Times*, 27 October 1968, sec. 6, pp. 134–35.

24. *Detroit Free Press*, 8 November 1961, p. 1.

25. Serrin, "How One Big City Defeated Its Mayor," p. 134. For election returns, see *Detroit Free Press*, 8 November 1961, pp. 1–2, 9–10.

26. B. J. Widick, *Detroit: City of Race and Class Violence* (Chicago: Quadrangle Books, 1972), p. 156.

27. "Why Cities Are Turning to Washington for Cash: An Interview with the Mayor of Detroit," *U.S. News and World Report* 59 (23 August 1965): 44. For additional information on the career of Jerome Cavanagh, see *Detroit Free Press*, 28 November 1979, pp. 1A, 17A.

28. Carl B. Stokes, *Promises of Power: A Political Autobiography* (New York: Simon and Schuster, 1973), p. 93.

29. *Cleveland Plain Dealer*, 2 November 1969, p. 1AA.

30. Philip W. Porter, *Cleveland: Confused City on a Seesaw* (Columbus: Ohio State University Press, 1976), p. 238. For additional information on Stokes and his campaigns for mayor, see *Cleveland Plain Dealer*, 29 September 1965, p. 9; 3 November 1965, pp. 1, 10–11; 1 October 1967, pp. 1AA–2AA; 4 October 1967, pp. 14–15; 1 November 1967, pp. 1, 8, 57, 66; 2 November 1967, pp. 1, 8; 3 November 1967, pp. 1, 8; 4 November 1967, pp. 1, 6; 5 November 1967, pp. 4A, 1AA–2AA; 6 November 1967, p. 1; 1 October 1969, pp. 1, 10; 2 November 1969, pp. 1A, 4A, 16A, 18A, 1AA–2AA, 4AA; and 5 November 1969, pp. 1A, 6A; "Cleveland: Promise Denied," *Time* 89 (9 June 1967): 34; William E. Nelson, Jr., and Philip J. Meranto, *Electing Black Mayors: Political Action in the Black Community* (Columbus: Ohio State University Press, 1977), pp. 67–165; Charles H. Levine, *Racial Conflict and the American Mayor: Power, Polarization, and Performance* (Lexington, Mass.: D. C. Heath, 1974), pp. 53–67; Stokes, *Promises of Power*; and Estelle Zannes, *Checkmate in Cleveland: The Rhetoric of Confrontation during the Stokes Years* (Cleveland: Press of Case Western Reserve University, 1972).

31. Serrin, "How One Big City Defeated Its Mayor," p. 139.

32. *Boston Globe*, 21 September 1967, p. 27; and 4 November 1967, p. 3. For other coverage of the White campaign, see ibid., 21 September 1967, pp. 1, 37; 1 November 1967, pp. 1, 22; 2 November 1967, pp. 1, 16, 33; 3 November 1967, pp. 1, 25; 4 November 1967, p. 1; 6 November 1967, p. 16; and 8 November 1967, pp. 1, 18–19, 22–23. See also Martha Wagner Weinberg, "Boston's Kevin White: A Mayor Who Survives," in Ronald P. Formisano and Constance K. Burns, eds., *Boston, 1700–1980: The Evolution of Urban Politics* (Westport, Conn.: Greenwood Press, 1984), pp. 213–39; and Eric A. Nordlinger, *Decentralizing the City: A Study of Boston's Little City Halls* (Cambridge, Mass.: MIT Press, 1972).

33. Dorothy Pula Strohecker, "Tommys Two: The D'Alesandros," in Lenora Heilig Nast, Laurence N. Krause, and R. C. Monk, eds., *Baltimore: A Living Renaissance* (Baltimore: Historic Baltimore Society, 1982), p. 232. For additional information on Baltimore politics in the 1960s, see Sharon Perlman Krefetz, *Welfare Policymaking and City Politics* (New York: Praeger Publishers, 1976), pp. 21–50.

34. *Municipal Record: Proceedings of the Council of the City of Pittsburgh* 98 (23 November 1964): 446.

35. Ibid. 101 (4 December 1967): 459.

36. Margaret Josten, "Decade of Decision," *Enquirer Magazine, Cincinnati Enquirer*, 9 October 1983, p. 19.

37. William J. McKenna, "The Negro Vote in Philadelphia Elections," in Miriam Ershkowitz and Joseph Zikmund II, eds., *Black Politics in Philadelphia* (New York: Basic Books, 1973), p. 78; Charles A. Ekstrom, "The Electoral Politics of Reform and Machine: The Political Behavior of Philadelphia's Black Wards, 1943–1969," in ibid., p. 101; and *Philadelphia Sunday Bulletin*, 20 January 1974, sec. 1, p. 27.

38. *New York Times*, 19 August 1953, p. 20; 16 September 1953, p. 24; and 4 November 1953, p. 1.

39. Ibid., 4 December 1964, p. 1. See also James Q. Wilson, *Negro Politics: The Search for Leadership* (New York: Free Press, 1960).

40. *St. Louis Post-Dispatch*, 17 November 1963, p. 3A; and Ernestine Patterson, "The Impact of the Black Struggle on Representative Government in Saint Louis, Missouri," Ph.D. diss., Saint Louis University, 1968, pp. 16, 160, 174–75.

41. Arnold R. Hirsch, *Making the Second Ghetto: Race and Housing in Chicago, 1940–1960* (Cambridge: Cambridge University Press, 1983), p. 126.

42. *New York Times*, 12 September 1957, p. 33.

43. John Hadley Strange, "Blacks and Philadelphia Politics: 1963–1966," in Ershkowitz and Zikmund, *Black Politics in Philadelphia*, pp. 112–13, 115–16. See also Paul Lermack, "Cecil Moore and the Philadelphia Branch of the National Association for the Advancement of Colored People: The Politics of Negro Pressure Group Organization," in ibid., pp. 145–60.

44. *Philadelphia Evening Bulletin*, 3 November 1967, p. 43.

45. Strange, "Blacks and Philadelphia Politics," p. 114.

46. Patterson, "Impact of the Black Struggle in Saint Louis," pp. 156–57. Also *St. Louis Post-Dispatch*, 29 October 1963, p. 3A; 4 November 1963, pp. 1A, 6A; 17 November 1963, p. 3A.

47. *Defender*, 6 January 1965, p. 4, and 18 March 1965, p. 2, as quoted in Patterson, "Impact of the Black Struggle in Saint Louis," pp. 215, 222.

48. Daniel P. Moynihan, *Maximum Feasible Misunderstanding: Community Action in the War on Poverty* (New York: Free Press, 1969), pp. 88–90; and Stephen M. David, "Welfare: The Community Action Program Controversy," in Jewel Bellush and Stephen M. David, eds., *Race and Politics in New York City: Five Studies in Policymaking* (New York: Praeger Publishers, 1971), p. 25.

49. Arthur B. Shostak, "Promoting Participation of the Poor: Philadelphia's Antipoverty Program," *Social Work* 11 (January 1966): 67.

50. Moynihan, *Maximum Feasible Misunderstanding*, p. 137; David, "Welfare," p. 47; and James A. Krausko, "New York City's Antipoverty Program," *City Almanac* 7 (December 1972): 9.

51. Neil Gilbert, *Clients or Constituents* (San Francisco: Jossey-Bass, 1970), p. 137.

52. Shostak, "Promoting Participation of the Poor," p. 66. For an additional overview of the politics of Philadelphia's antipoverty program, see Harry A. Bailey, Jr., "Poverty, Politics, and Administration: The Philadelphia Experience," in Ershkowitz and Zikmund, *Black Politics in Philadelphia*, pp. 168–87.

53. Gilbert, *Clients or Constituents*, p. 152. For additional information on the community action program in Pittsburgh, see Neil Gilbert, "Maximum Feasible Participation? A Pittsburgh Encounter," *Social Work* 14 (July 1969): 84–92.

54. Murray Seidler, "Some Participant Observer Reflections on Detroit's Community Action Program," *Urban Affairs Quarterly* 5 (December 1969): 196.

55. David, "Welfare," p. 48. For additional overviews of New York City's antipoverty program, see Krausko, "New York City's Antipoverty Program," and Bertram M. Beck, "Organizing Community Action," in Robert H. Connery and Demetrios Caraley, eds., *Governing the City: Challenges and Options for New York* (New York: Frederick A. Praeger, 1969), pp. 162–78.

56. Peter Bachrach, "A Power Analysis: The Shaping of Antipoverty Policy in Baltimore," *Public Policy* 18 (Winter 1970): 177.

57. Seidler, "Participant Observer Reflections," p. 197.

58. *New York Times*, 2 January 1966, p. 1. For more on the transit strike, see L. H. Whittemore, *The Man Who Ran the Subways: The Story of Mike Quill* (New York: Holt, Rinehart and Winston, 1968), pp. 265–98.

59. Hugh O'Neill, "The Growth of Municipal Employee Unions," *Proceedings of the Academy of Political Science* 30 (1970–72): 9.

60. Sterling D. Spero and John M. Capozzola, *The Urban Community and Its Unionized Bureaucracies: Pressure Politics in Local Government Labor Relations* (New York: Dunellen, 1973), p. 43.

61. W. Donald Heisel, "Anatomy of a Strike," *Public Personnel Review* 30 (October 1969): 227; and Spero and Capozzola, *Urban Community and Its Unionized Bureaucracies*, p. 51.

62. Raymond D. Horton, *Municipal Labor Relations in New York City: Lessons of the Lindsay-Wagner Years* (New York: Praeger Publishers, 1972), pp. 28–30; Spero and Capozzola, *Urban Community and Its Unionized Bureaucracies*, pp. 64–65; and Raymond D. Horton, "Municipal Labor Relations in New York City," *Proceedings of the Academy of Political Science* 30 (1970–72): 72–73.

63. Horton, *Municipal Labor Relations in New York City*, p. 83.

64. Leonard Ruchelman, *Police Politics: A Comparative Study of Three Cities* (Cambridge, Mass.: Ballinger Publishing, 1974), p. 40. See also David W. Abbott, Louis H. Gold, and Edward T. Rogowsky, *Police Politics and Race: The New York City Referendum on Civilian Review* (New York: American Jewish Committee, 1969); Edward T. Rogowsky, Louis H. Gold, and David W. Abbott, "Police: The Civilian Review Board Controversy," in Bellush and David, *Race and Politics in New York City*, pp. 59–97; *New York Times*, 9 November 1966, pp. 1, 23, 38; and ibid., 10 November 1966, p. 1.

65. Maurice R. Berube and Marilyn Gittell, eds., *Confrontation at Ocean Hill–Brownsville: The New York School Strikes of 1968* (New York: Praeger Publishers, 1969), p. 219. For a useful chronology of the decentralization struggle, see pp. 335–40.

66. *New York Times*, 16 December 1966, p. 43.

67. Ibid., 3 February 1968, p. 1; 11 February 1968, pp. 1, 77; 7 November 1968, p. 43; and 15 November 1968, p. 36.

68. Ibid., 22 October 1968, p. 1; 24 October 1968, p. 1; and 28 October 1968, p. 1.

69. "When Policemen Strike in a Big City," in Robert E. Walsh, ed., *Sorry . . . No Government Today: Unions versus City Hall* (Boston: Beacon Press, 1969), pp. 59, 61; and Robert M. Fogelson, *Big City Police* (Cambridge, Mass.: Harvard University Press, 1977), pp. 211, 213. Also *New York Times*, 18 May 1967, p. 33; 16 June 1967, p. 59; 20 June 1967, p. 20; and 21 June 1967, p. 26.

70. Marylys McPherson, "Minneapolis: Crime in a Politically Fragmented Arena," in Anne Heinz, Herbert Jacob, and Robert L. Lineberry, eds., *Crime in City Politics* (New York: Longman, 1983), p. 175.

71. *New York Times*, 4 August 1968, p. 29; and 16 August 1968, p. 15.

72. Ibid., 28 May 1968, p. 6.

73. Heisel, "Anatomy of a Strike," p. 230. See also Spero and Capozzola, *Urban Community and Its Unionized Bureaucracies*, pp. 55–56.

74. Peter C. Buffum and Rita Sagi, "Philadelphia: Politics of Reform and Retreat" in Heinz, Jacob, and Lineberry, *Crime in City Politics*, p. 126; Hervey Juris and Peter Feuille, "Police Union Impact on the Formulation of Law Enforcement Policy," in David Lewin, Peter Feuille, Thomas A. Kochan, and John Thomas Delaney, eds., *Public Sector Labor Relations: Analysis and Readings* (Lexington, Mass.: D. C. Heath, 1988), p. 546; reprinted from Hervey Juris and Peter Feuille, *Police Unionism* (Lexington, Mass.: D. C. Heath, 1973), pp. 151–63.

75. "Pension Bonanza Proposed for City Police and Firemen," *Citizens' Business*, no. 2330 (23 November 1966); and "How Would You Like These?" ibid., no. 2334 (15 February 1967).

76. *Philadelphia Sunday Bulletin*, 20 January 1974, sec. 1, p. 27. See also Buffum and Sagi, "Philadelphia: Politics of Reform and Retreat," p. 119; and Lennox L. Moak, "The Philadelphia Experience," *Proceedings of the Academy of Political Science* 30 (1970–72): 132.

77. Horton, *Municipal Labor Relations in New York City*, p. 86; and *New York Times*, 12 February 1969, p. 37.

78. Horton, *Municipal Labor Relations in New York City*, p. 87; idem, "Municipal Labor Relations in New York City," p. 75; and *New York Times*, 18 October 1969, p. 1.

79. *Philadelphia Evening Bulletin*, 8 November 1967, p. 6. See also "Binding Arbitration for Policemen and Firemen," *Citizens' Business*, no. 2347 (1 November 1967).

80. Moak, "Philadelphia Experience," p. 128.

81. *Municipal Record: Proceedings of the Council of the City of Pittsburgh* 102 (2 December 1968): 569, 571.

82. Neal R. Peirce, "Auto-Based Recession Clouds Rebirth," *PA Times* (15 July 1980): 2; and Richard C. Kearney, *Labor Relations in the Public Sector* (New York: Marcel Dekker, 1984), p. 263.

83. "Fire and Police Salaries and Personnel Expenditures," in *The Municipal Year Book 1970* (Washington, D.C.: International City Management Association, 1970), pp. 266, 268.

84. Computed on the basis of figures in ibid., pp. 271, 301. See also Robert M. Fogelson, *Pensions: The Hidden Costs of Public Safety* (New York: Columbia University Press, 1984).

85. *Minneapolis Tribune*, 1 October 1969, p. 4.

86. Ibid., 6 June 1969, p. 24.

87. Ibid.

88. Ibid., 8 June 1969, p. 5B.

89. Ibid., 6 June 1969, p. 24.

90. Ibid., 11 June 1969, p. 1. For the voting returns and an analysis of them, see ibid., pp. 1, 9.

91. McPherson, "Minneapolis," p. 177.

92. *Philadelphia Evening Bulletin*, 23 January 1974, p. 16. For a short summary

of Rizzo's career as police commissioner, see Buffum and Sagi, "Philadelphia: Politics of Reform and Retreat," pp. 122–26.

93. Fred Hamilton, *Rizzo* (New York: Viking Press, 1973), p. 178.

94. Ibid.

95. Ibid., p. 162.

96. Ibid., p. 179.

97. *Philadelphia Evening Bulletin*, 19 May 1971, pp. 1, 3–5; and 3 November 1971, pp. 1, 3–4, 6–7. For one analysis of the mayoral vote in 1971, see Henry Cohen and Gary Sandrow, *Philadelphia Chooses a Mayor, 1971: Jewish Voting Patterns* (Philadelphia: American Jewish Committee, 1972).

98. George V. Higgins, "Boston's Busing Disaster," *New Republic* 188 (28 February 1983): 19.

99. *Boston Globe*, 3 November 1967, p. 25.

100. Ibid., 2 November 1967, p. 16.

101. Ibid., 1 November 1967, p. 22; and 3 November 1967, p. 1.

102. Ibid., 3 November 1967, p. 25.

103. Ibid., 8 November 1967, p. 22.

104. Ibid.

105. *Buffalo Evening News*, 5 November 1969, sec. 1, p. 14.

106. *New York Times*, 15 July 1969, p. 34.

107. Ibid.

108. Ibid., 5 October 1969, p. 77.

109. *Buffalo Evening News*, 5 November 1969, sec. 1, pp. 1, 14; *New York Times*, 5 November 1969, p. 37; and Robert Huckfeldt, *Politics in Context: Assimilation and Conflict in Urban Neighborhoods* (New York: Agathon Press, 1986), pp. 78–82.

110. *Detroit Free Press*, 7 September 1969, p. 2A.

111. Ibid., 11 September 1969, p. 3A.

112. *Cincinnati Enquirer*, 4 November 1967, p. 27; and 6 November 1967, p. 47.

113. Zannes, *Checkmate in Cleveland*, pp. 184, 189.

114. *New York Times*, 13 May 1969, p. 37.

115. Ibid., 14 May 1969, p. 28.

116. Ibid., 18 June 1969, p. 46.

117. For complete election returns, see ibid., 6 November 1969, p. 40.

Chapter 6: Hitting Bottom

1. *New York Times*, 2 January 1966, p. 56.

2. Douglas Yates, *The Ungovernable City: The Politics of Urban Problems and Policymaking* (Cambridge, Mass.: MIT Press, 1977), p. xiv.

3. *New York Times*, 27 October 1968, sec. 6, p. 39. For Cavanagh's later career, see also *Detroit Free Press*, 28 November 1979, pp. 1A, 17A.

4. *New York Times*, 1 May 1971, p. 22.

5. See Martha Wagner Weinberg, "Boston's Kevin White: A Mayor Who Survives," *Political Science Quarterly* 96 (Spring 1981): 87–106. Weinberg's article was reprinted in Ronald P. Formisano and Constance K. Burns, eds., *Boston, 1700–1980: The Evolution of Urban Politics* (Westport, Conn.: Greenwood Press, 1984), pp. 215–

39. For information on the second White-Hicks contest of 1971, see *Boston Globe*, 1 November 1971, pp. 1, 11–12; and 3 November 1971, pp. 1, 15.

6. Michael C. D. MacDonald, *America's Cities: A Report on the Myth of Urban Renaissance* (New York: Simon and Schuster, 1984), p. 285.

7. *New York Times*, 31 January 1970, p. 19. See also *Cincinnati Enquirer*, 3 January 1970, p. 1; 5 January 1970, p. 1; and 6 January 1970, p. 1.

8. *Cleveland Plain Dealer*, 17 February 1972, pp. 1A, 6A; 18 February 1972, pp. 1A, 6A; and 24 February 1972, pp. 1A, 5A.

9. *St. Louis Post-Dispatch*, 4 March 1973, p. 3C.

10. *Washington Post*, 9 July 1974, pp. A1, A7.

11. *Cincinnati Enquirer*, 6 January 1970, p. 1.

12. George Sternlieb, "The City as Sandbox," *Public Interest*, no. 25 (Fall 1971): 14–21.

13. Norton E. Long, "The City as Reservation," ibid., no. 25 (Fall 1971): 33.

14. William C. Baer, "On the Death of Cities," ibid., no. 45 (Fall 1976): 3, 18–19.

15. See ibid., pp. 15–16, and *Hearings before the Committee on Banking, Currency, and Housing, House of Representatives, Ninety-fourth Congress* (Washington, D.C.: U.S. Government Printing Office, 1976), pp. 838, 878–85.

16. Jill Jonnes, *We're Still Here: The Rise, Fall, Resurrection of the South Bronx* (Boston: Atlantic Monthly Press, 1986), p. 265.

17. Robert Jensen, *Devastation/Resurrection: The South Bronx* (New York: Bronx Museum of the Arts, 1979), p. 54; "The Bronx Is Burning," *Newsweek* 85 (16 June 1975): 30; and Jonnes, *We're Still Here*, p. 251.

18. Frank Kristof, "Housing and People in New York City: A View of the Past, Present, and Future," *City Almanac* 10 (February 1976): 5.

19. *Abandoned Housing Research: A Compendium* (Washington, D.C.: U.S. Department of Housing and Urban Development, 1973), pp. 15, 18.

20. *Cleveland Plain Dealer*, 17 December 1972, p. 4A.

21. Ibid., 20 December 1972, p. 2D. See also ibid., 18 December 1972, pp. 1A, 10A; and 19 December 1972, pp. 1A–2A.

22. Mike Mallowe, "The Barren North," *Philadelphia* 72 (August 1981): 110. See also Michael J. Dear, "Abandoned Housing," in John S. Adams, ed., *Urban Policymaking and Metropolitan Dynamics: A Comparative Geographical Analysis* (Cambridge, Mass.: Ballinger Publishing, 1976), pp. 59–99.

23. Winston Moore, Charles P. Livermore, and George F. Galland, Jr., "Woodlawn: The Zone of Destruction," *Public Interest*, no. 30 (Winter 1973): 41, 45.

24. *The State of the City—Buffalo, N.Y., November 1976* (Buffalo: City of Buffalo, 1976), pp. 30, 33, 64.

25. Marv Gisser, "Downtown Has a Future," *Clevelander* 48 (January 1971): 31.

26. *Cleveland Plain Dealer*, 27 February 1972, p. 1B.

27. J. Thomas Black, Libby Howland, and Stuart L. Rogel, *Downtown Retail Development: Conditions for Success and Project Profiles* (Washington, D.C.: Urban Land Institute, 1983), p. 84.

28. Jay Scher, *Financial and Operating Results of Department and Specialty Stores of 1976* (New York: National Retail Merchants Association, 1977).

29. *Washington Post*, 24 December 1976, p. C5.

30. *Chicago Tribune*, 3 February 1975, sec. 2, p. 4.

31. *Variety*, 29 December 1976, p. 27. See also ibid., 9 January 1974, p. 32; and 27 November 1974, pp. 2, 86.

32. *Chicago Tribune*, 23 January 1975, sec. 1, p. 2; 24 January 1975, sec. 2, p. 1; and 26 January 1975, sec. 1, pp. 1, 26.

33. Ibid., 11 September 1977, sec. 6, p. 4. See also *Variety*, 20 April 1977, p. 6.

34. *Chicago Tribune*, 11 September 1977, sec. 6, pp. 4, 6.

35. *Variety*, 18 December 1974, p. 26.

36. *Minneapolis Tribune*, 18 December 1975, p. 1B; 28 December 1975, p. 1B; and 17 November 1978, p. 11A. For additional information on porno theaters on Hennepin Avenue, see *Minneapolis Star*, 16 January 1976, p. 7A; 3 April 1976, p. 6A; 9 April 1976, p. 1B; 17 April 1976, p. 11A; and 22 November 1977, p. 11A; and *Minneapolis Tribune*, 17 April 1976, p. 1A; 14 June 1977, pp. 1A, 4A; and 15 June 1977, p. 6A.

37. *Variety*, 28 September 1977, p. 32.

38. Sylvia Auerbach, "The World Trade Center: Where Does It Stand?" *Real Estate Review* 4 (Summer 1974): 53.

39. "Occupancy Dips Slightly in Survey," *Building Owner and Manager* 2 (February 1977): 1. For information on the World Trade Center, see Auerbach, "The World Trade Center," pp. 47–54; and Leonard I. Ruchelman, *The World Trade Center: Politics and Policies of Skyscraper Development* (Syracuse: Syracuse University Press, 1977).

40. Peter Hellman, "Towering Fiasco," *New York* 11 (31 July 1978): 25–30.

41. Wolfgang Quante, *The Exodus of Corporate Headquarters from New York City* (New York: Praeger Publishers, 1976), pp. 43, 49.

42. *New York Times*, 19 February 1967, p. 1. See also ibid., 11 February 1967, pp. 1, 19; 12 February 1967, p. 66; 14 February 1967, p. 42; and 16 February 1967, pp. 1, 25.

43. Ibid., 17 February 1967, p. 40.

44. Ibid., 16 February 1967, p. 25.

45. Ibid., 17 February 1967, p. 40.

46. Quante, *Exodus of Corporate Headquarters*, p. 61.

47. *St. Louis Post-Dispatch*, 4 April 1971, p. 7D.

48. Ronald R. Pollina, "Trends in Chicagoland Office Development," *Chicagoland Development* 5 (February 1975): 8; *An Analysis of Chicago Commercial Office Space* (Chicago: Continental Illinois National Bank, 1975), p. 5; and "Occupancy Dips Slightly in Survey," *Building Owner and Manager*, p. 1.

49. Katherine D. Miller, "The Office Space Market and Economics of Building," *Chicagoland Development* 5 (February 1975): 5.

50. Dale Dreischarf, "Overall View of Chicago Office Space," *Commerce* 75 (November 1978): 24.

51. Rachelle L. Levitt, ed., *Cities Reborn* (Washington, D.C.: Urban Land Institute, 1987), p. 20.

52. Armin K. Ludwig, *Radial Freeways and the Growth of Office Space in Central Cities* (Washington, D.C.: Department of Transportation, 1977), p. 120.

53. *Minneapolis Tribune*, 13 January 1974, p. 7s.

54. Andrew Marshall Hamer, *Industrial Exodus from Central City: Public Policy and the Comparative Costs of Location* (Lexington, Mass.: D. C. Heath, 1973), p. 6.

55. Harvey W. Schultz, Gail Garfield Schwartz, and Anne Fribourg, "Planning for Jobs: New York City Attempts to Retain and Create Blue-Collar Jobs," *Planners Notebook* 2 (February 1972): 3.

56. *Minneapolis Tribune*, 15 February 1971, p. 10A. See also ibid., 2 March 1971, p. 3A; and 9 July 1971, p. 6A.

57. Ibid., 1 November 1975, p. 7A; and 4 November 1975, p. 6A.

58. David Shama, "The Stadium Issue: Headed for a 'Photo Finish,' " *Greater Minneapolis* 28 (May–June 1976): 12–14, 16–17; and David Shama, "Stadium Bill to Keep Twin Cities 'Major League,' " ibid. 29 (July–August 1977): 14–15.

59. Judith Martin, *Recycling the Central City: The Development of a New Town-in Town* (Minneapolis: Center for Urban and Regional Affairs, University of Minnesota, 1978), pp. 121, 129, 155. See also Rodney E. Engelen, "A Case Study—Cedar-Riverside," *Practicing Planner* 6 (April 1976): 30–40.

60. Jim Toman and Dan Cook, *Cleveland's Changing Skyline* (Cleveland: Cleveland Landmarks Press, 1984), pp. 15, 44.

61. Todd Swanstrom, *The Crisis of Growth Politics: Cleveland, Kucinich, and the Challenge of Urban Populism* (Philadelphia: Temple University Press, 1985), p. 98.

62. Kirk R. Petshek, *The Challenge of Urban Reform: Policies and Programs in Philadelphia* (Philadelphia: Temple University Press, 1973), p. 165.

63. *Philadelphia Sunday Bulletin*, 20 January 1974, p. 13.

64. Ibid.

65. *St. Louis Post-Dispatch*, 31 July 1976, p. 3A.

66. Ibid., 3 August 1975, p. 3A; and 24 August 1975, p. 1B. See also ibid., 13 April 1975, pp. 1A, 22A; and 25 August 1975, p. 3C.

67. A. J. Cervantes, *Mr. Mayor* (Los Angeles: Nash Publishing, 1974), pp. 135–37.

68. Stefan Lorant, *Pittsburgh: The Story of an American City*, 3d ed. (Lenox, Mass.: Authors Edition, 1980), p. 452. See also idem, *Pete: The Life of Peter F. Flaherty* (Lenox, Mass.: Authors Edition, 1978), pp. 82–86.

69. Melvin R. Levin, "New Boston Grows Old," *Planning* 39 (June 1973): 27. See also Alan Rabinowitz, *Nonplanning and Redevelopment in Boston: An Analytic Study of the Planning Process* (Seattle: Department of Urban Planning, University of Washington, 1972), pp. 30–38.

70. "Saint Louis Refuses to Lie Down," *Business Week*, no. 2327 (20 April 1974): 56.

71. Barbara R. Williams, *Saint Louis: A City and Its Suburbs* (Santa Monica: Rand, 1973), pp. vi–vii.

72. Roger Starr, "Making New York Smaller," *New York Times Magazine* (14 November 1976), p. 106.

73. *Annual Financial Report of the City of Baltimore, Maryland, Fiscal Year Ended June 30, 1976* (Baltimore: City of Baltimore, 1976), p. 255; "Debts/Taxes, Assessments," *Civic Federation*, no. 926 (Fall 1980): 20; *Annual Financial Report of the City of Cleveland, Ohio, for the Fiscal Year Ending December 31, 1978* (Cleveland: Department of Finance, 1979), p. 68; *City of Detroit Budget* (Detroit: Budget Depart-

354 ∘ Notes to Pages 219–222

ment, 1979), p. viii; *City of Pittsburgh, Pennsylvania, Annual Report December 31, 1979* (Pittsburgh: City of Pittsburgh, 1980), p. 86; and *The City of Saint Louis Annual Report of the Comptroller for the Fiscal Year Ended April 30, 1981* (Saint Louis: City of Saint Louis, 1981), p. 199.

74. Walter L. Webb, "Government Manpower: An Overview," in *The Municipal Year Book 1971* (Washington, D.C.: International City Management Association, 1971), pp. 202–3; David Lewin, "Expenditure, Compensation, and Employment Data in Police, Fire, and Refuse Collection and Disposal Departments," in *The Municipal Year Book 1975* (Washington, D.C.: International City Management Association, 1975), pp. 50, 52–53; and Carol A. Pigeon, "Personnel, Compensation, and Expenditures in Police, Fire, and Refuse Collection and Disposal Departments," in *The Municipal Year Book 1976* (Washington, D.C.: International City Management Association, 1976), p. 103.

75. *St. Louis Post-Dispatch*, 2 April 1969, p. 1A.

76. Ibid., 5 April 1971, p. 1A.

77. *Annual Report of Saint Louis Comptroller 1981*, p. 194.

78. David W. Lyon, "The Financial Future of City and School Government in Philadelphia," *Federal Reserve Bank of Philadelphia Business Review* (March 1971): 3–4.

79. William A. Cozzens, "Philadelphia City and School District Budgets: A Year of Austerity," *Federal Reserve Bank of Philadelphia Business Review* (April 1975): 23.

80. *Washington Post*, 5 March 1974, pp. B1, B9.

81. Ibid., 5 March 1974, p. B9.

82. *New York Times*, 28 October 1974, p. 33.

83. *141st Annual Report of the Comptroller, City of Buffalo, N.Y., for the Fiscal Year Ended June 30, 1973* (Buffalo: Department of Audit and Control, 1973), p. 154.

84. *New York Times*, 28 October 1974, p. 62.

85. *Cleveland Plain Dealer*, 16 February 1972, pp. 1A, 5A; and 16 June 1972, p. 14C. Also Nancy Humphrey, George E. Peterson, and Peter Wilson, *The Future of Cleveland's Capital Plant* (Washington, D.C.: Urban Institute, 1979), p. 8.

86. Humphrey, Peterson, and Wilson, *Cleveland's Capital Plant*, p. 8; and Philip W. Porter, *Cleveland: Confused City on a Seesaw* (Columbus: Ohio State University Press, 1976), pp. 280–83.

87. *St. Louis Post-Dispatch*, 1 April 1971, p. 1A.

88. Ibid., 1 April 1971, p. 4A. See also ibid., 4 April 1971, pp. 6C–7C, 2D; 5 April 1971, p. 1A; and 7 April 1971, pp. 1A, 3A.

89. *Pittsburgh Press*, 9 January 1970, p. 1.

90. Lorant, *Pete*, p. 79.

91. *Municipal Record: Proceedings of the Council of the City of Pittsburgh* 104 (4 December 1970): 597.

92. *Pittsburgh Annual Report*, pp. 83, 85, 87.

93. *Pittsburgh Post-Gazette*, 14 May 1973, p. 12; and 17 May 1973, p. 6.

94. *Cleveland Plain Dealer*, 28 February 1972, pp. 1A, 6A; and 1 March 1972, p. 15A.

95. *Report of the Proceedings of the City Council of Boston for the Year Commencing January 4, 1971, and Ending December 27, 1971* (Boston: City of Boston, 1972), pp. 1, 3.

96. *Annual Address of Honorable Kevin H. White, Mayor of Boston* (Boston: City of Boston, 1973), p. 2.

97. *New York Times*, 28 October 1974, p. 33; and 27 May 1975, p. 14.

98. Charles R. Morris, *The Cost of Good Intentions: New York City and the Liberal Experiment, 1960–1975* (New York: McGraw-Hill, 1981), p. 202.

99. Attiat F. Ott and Jang H. Yoo, *New York City's Financial Crisis: Can the Trend Be Reversed?* (Washington, D.C.: American Enterprise Institute for Public Policy Research, 1975), p. 19.

100. Joan K. Martin, *Urban Financial Stress: Why Cities Go Broke* (Boston: Auburn House Publishing, 1982), p. 125.

101. Humphrey, Peterson, and Wilson, *Cleveland's Capital Plant*, p. 6; and *Cleveland Plain Dealer*, 3 August 1978, p. 13A.

102. Ott and Yoo, *New York City's Financial Crisis*, p. 19.

103. *Financial Report of Baltimore, 1976*, p. 256; *141st Annual Report of the Comptroller, City of Buffalo, N.Y., for the Fiscal Year Ended June 30, 1973* (Buffalo: City of Buffalo, 1973), p. 152.

104. Boston Municipal Research Bureau, *Boston's Fiscal Crisis: Origins and Solutions* (Boston: Boston Municipal Research Bureau, 1976), p. 21.

105. Nonna A. Noto and Donald L. Raiff, "Philadelphia's Fiscal Story: The City and the Schools," *Business Review Federal Reserve Bank of Philadelphia* (March–April 1977): 4–5.

106. *Financial Report of Cleveland for 1978*, p. 68.

107. *City of Chicago Message of the Mayor to the City Council Submitting the Executive Budget for the Fiscal Year 1972* (Chicago: City of Chicago, 1971), p. 4; and "1972 City of Chicago Budget—The Budget in Brief," *Civic Federation*, no. 790 (November 1971): 1.

108. *City Journal* 54 (11 May 1971): 2.

109. Ibid. 53 (28 April 1970): 5.

110. *Report of Proceedings of the City Council of Boston for the Year Commencing January 3, 1972, and Ending December 26, 1972* (Boston: City of Boston, 1973), p. 3.

111. *New York Times*, 28 October 1974, p. 33.

112. Paul A. Gilje, "Sharing of Tax Growth—Redefinitions," *Governmental Finance* 6 (November 1977): 38.

113. Ibid. See also Ted Kolderie, "Governance in the Twin Cities Area of Minnesota," in Gary Helfand, ed., *Metropolitan Areas, Metropolitan Governments* (Dubuque, Ia.: Kendall/Hunt Publishing, 1976), pp. 194–95; Peter Nye, "Minnesota Helps Its Metropolis Share the Tax Base," in Dean Tipps and Lee Webb, eds., *State and Local Tax Revolt: New Directions for the Eighties* (Washington, D.C.: Conference on Alternative State and Local Policies, 1980), pp. 192–97.

114. Katharine C. Lyall, "Tax Base Sharing: A Fiscal Aid Toward More Rational Land-Use Planning," *Journal of the American Institute of Planners* 41 (March 1975): 90–100; *Washington Post*, 5 March 1974, p. B9; and Nye, "Minnesota Helps Its Metropolis," p. 197.

115. Thomas J. Anton, *Federal Aid to Detroit* (Washington, D.C.: Brookings Institution, 1983), p. 27.

116. *New York Times*, 18 February 1975, p. 28; and Morris, *Cost of Good Intentions*, p. 226.

117. Roger E. Alcaly and Helen Bodian, "New York's Fiscal Crisis and the Economy," in Roger C. Alcaly and David Mermelstein, eds., *The Fiscal Crisis of American Cities: Essays on the Political Economy of Urban America with Special Reference to New York* (New York: Vintage Books, 1977), p. 33.

118. Boston Municipal Research Bureau, *Boston's Fiscal Crisis*, pp. 8–9.

119. Mary John Miller, J. Chester Johnson, and George E. Peterson, *The Future of Boston's Capital Plant* (Washington, D.C.: Urban Institute Press, 1981), p. 5; and Martin, *Urban Financial Stress*, pp. 125–26.

120. Boston Municipal Research Bureau, *Boston's Fiscal Crisis*, p. 10.

121. Miller, Johnson, and Peterson, *Future of Boston's Capital Plant*, p. 5.

122. Robert P. Inman, "Anatomy of a Fiscal Crisis," *Federal Reserve Bank of Philadelphia Business Review* (September–October 1983): 17; and Noto and Raiff, "Philadelphia's Fiscal Story," pp. 15–18.

123. John Guinther, "Thinking the Unthinkable," *Philadelphia* 67 (April 1976): 112, 114.

124. Anton, *Federal Aid to Detroit*, p. 14.

125. Ibid., p. 15.

126. Ibid., p. 27; and the Citizens Research Council of Michigan, "Financing the Local and Regional Public Sector in Southeast Michigan: Past and Present," in Kent Mathewson and William B. Neenan, eds., *Financing the Metropolis* (New York: Praeger, 1980), pp. 282–85.

127. *New York Times*, 27 May 1975, p. 14.

128. Ibid.

129. Ibid., 8 October 1975, p. 21; and 9 October 1975, p. 49.

130. *Cincinnati Enquirer*, 14 November 1975, p. 1.

131. Ibid., 11 November 1975, p. 6.

132. Charles H. Levine, Irene S. Rubin, and George G. Wolohojian, *The Politics of Retrenchment: How Local Governments Manage Fiscal Stress* (Beverly Hills: Sage Publications, 1981), pp. 102, 105–107. See also *Cleveland Plain Dealer*, 18 December 1978, pp. 1A, 16A.

133. *Cleveland Plain Dealer*, 3 August 1978, p. 13A.

134. Ibid., 7 November 1977, pp. 1A, 3A.

135. Ibid., 25 July 1978, p. 8A.

136. Ibid., 25 July 1978, p. 8A; and 10 December 1978, sec. 1, p. 18. Also Swanstrom, *Crisis of Growth Politics*, p. 161; and Humphrey, Peterson, and Wilson, *Future of Cleveland's Capital Plant*, p. 10.

137. *Cleveland Plain Dealer*, 3 December 1978, sec. 7, p. 2. See also Alberta M. Sbragia, "Politics, Local Government, and the Municipal Bond Market," in Alberta M. Sbragia, *The Municipal Money Chase: The Politics of Local Government* (Boulder, Colo.: Westview Press, 1983), p. 82.

138. *Cleveland Plain Dealer*, 17 December 1978, sec. 1, p. 10.

139. For a summary of the events during the week prior to default, see *Cleveland Plain Dealer*, 17 December 1978, sec. 1, pp. 10–11. For an analysis of the Cleveland

situation, see John H. Beck, "Is Cleveland Another New York?" *Urban Affairs Quarterly* 18 (December 1982): 207–16.

140. "Urban Experts Advise, Castigate, and Console the City on Its Problems," in Alcaly and Mermelstein, *Fiscal Crisis of American Cities*, p. 10.

141. Robert Zevin, "New York City Crisis: First Act in a New Age of Reaction," in ibid., p. 11.

142. *Chicago Tribune*, 22 May 1972, sec. 1, p. 3. See also ibid., 11 May 1972, sec. 3, p. 17.

143. Ibid., 9 May 1972, sec. 1A, p. 4.

144. Ibid., 22 May 1972, sec. 1, p. 3. See also ibid., 14 May 1972, sec. S10, p. 10. For more on the Crosstown Expressway, see Milton Pikarsky, "Chicago's Crosstown Expressway: The Team Concept in Action," in *The Engineer and the City* (Washington, D.C.: National Academy of Engineering, 1969), pp. 63–77; and Elliott Arthur Pavlos, "Chicago's Crosstown: A Case Study in Urban Expressways," in David R. Miller, ed., *Urban Transportation Policy: New Perspectives* (Lexington, Mass: D. C. Heath, 1972), pp. 57–65.

145. James W. McPhillips, "Planning and Construction of Urban Expressways—1971," *Rural and Urban Roads* 9 (September 1971): 32; and Paul R. Levy, *Queen Village: The Eclipse of Community* (Philadelphia: Institute for the Study of Civic Values, 1978), pp. 63, 69.

146. McPhillips, "Planning and Construction of Expressways," p. 32.

147. Levy, *Queen Village*, p. 64.

148. Ibid, p. 65.

149. *New York Times*, 8 April 1969, p. 22.

150. *Minneapolis Tribune*, 7 June 1971, p. 5A.

151. *Boston Globe*, 26 January 1969, p. 29; and Alan Lupo, Frank Colcord, and Edmund P. Fowler, *Rites of Way: The Politics of Transportation in Boston and the U.S. City* (Boston: Little, Brown, 1971), p. 43.

152. *Boston Globe*, 18 December 1969, p. 7.

153. Ibid., 19 December 1969, pp. 6, 14.

154. Ibid., 1 February 1970, p. 2A; and Lupo, Colcord, and Fowler, *Rites of Way*, p. 264.

155. *Boston Globe*, 4 February 1970, pp. 1, 22; 5 February 1970, pp. 1, 8; and 6 February 1970, p. 12.

156. Ralph Gakenheimer, *Transportation Planning as Response to Controversy: The Boston Case* (Cambridge, Mass.: MIT Press, 1976), pp. 167–69; and *Thinking Small: Transportation's Role in Neighborhood Revitalization* (Washington, D.C.: U.S. Department of Transportation, 1978), p. 79. For more on the Boston controversy, see Allan K. Sloan, *Citizen Participation in Transportation Planning: The Boston Experience* (Cambridge, Mass.: Ballinger Publishing, 1974), and "Balanced Transportation—Boston Style," *Going Places* (Second Quarter, 1972): 8–9.

157. For an overview of federal legislation, see Edward Weiner, *Urban Transportation Planning in the United States: An Historical Overview* (New York: Praeger, 1987), pp. 24–25, 43–51.

158. William F. Callahan, "Downtown Buffalo Renaissance Plan Unveiled by Mayor," *Going Places* (Second Quarter, 1971): 3.

159. "LRRT System Planned for Niagara Frontier," *Metro* 74 (November–December 1978): 30.

160. Ibid., p. 31. See also *Center-City Environment and Transportation: Local Government Solutions* (Washington, D.C.: Public Technology, 1977), pp. 26–31; William D. Middleton, "LRRT Brightens Buffalo," *Railway Age* 185 (December 1984): 74–75; "Buffalo Opens Its LRRT," *Metro* 81 (March–April 1985): 54, 56, 58; and Kenneth G. Knight, "Buffalo's Light Rail Rapid Transit System," in *Light Rail Transit: Planning and Technology* (Washington, D.C.: National Academy of Sciences, 1978), pp. 32–38.

161. "Baltimore: We'll Start to Dig in '73," *Going Places* (Third–Fourth Quarter, 1971): 10; "Getting a City Moving Again," *Metro* 79 (May–June 1983): 22–24; and Harold C. Juram, "Planning Baltimore's Metro," *Metro* 80 (July–August 1984): 46–48, 52.

162. Ted Douglas, "Detroit's Rapid Transit System: Dream or Necessity?" *Going Places* (Third–Fourth Quarter, 1971): 7. See also "Metro Transit Plans Tie South Oakland County to Detroit Subway," *Going Places* (Second Quarter, 1971): 9.

163. *Center City Environment and Transportation*, pp. 6–13.

164. *Standards for Rapid Transit Expansion: A Report to the Mayor and the New York City Board of Estimate* (New York: City of New York, 1968); Masha Simreich, *New York, World City* (Cambridge, Mass.: Oelgeschlager, Gunn and Hain, 1980), p. 187; and Stan Fischler, *Uptown, Downtown: A Trip through Time on New York's Subways* (New York: Hawthorn Books, 1976), p. 72.

165. *1979 Annual Report* (Boston: MBTA, 1980), p. 34; and Miller, Johnson, and Peterson, *Future of Boston's Capital Plant*, pp. 63, 65.

166. Miller, Johnson, and Peterson, *Future of Boston's Capital Plant*, p. 56.

167. "Chicago Embarks on $283 Million Modernization Plan," *Going Places* (Second Quarter, 1972): 4; "Downtown Chicagoans Vote Transit District, Tax, for a New Subway," *Going Places* (Fourth Quarter, 1970): 8.

168. *Philadelphia Evening Bulletin*, 5 November 1975, p. 3B.

169. Cervantes, *Mister Mayor*, p. 153.

170. Andrew M. Hamer, *The Selling of Rail Rapid Transit: A Critical Look at Urban Transportation Planning* (Lexington, Mass.: D. C. Heath, 1976), pp. 217–46. See also "Saint Louis Gearing Up Plans for Rapid Transit," *Going Places* (Fourth Quarter, 1970): 9.

171. *St. Louis Post-Dispatch*, 3 March 1974, p. 2D.

172. Ibid., 12 February 1974, p. 3A.

173. Ibid., 8 March 1974, p. 4A.

174. Ibid., 11 March 1974, p. 1A.

175. Ibid., 14 March 1974, p. 1A.

176. Lorant, *Pete*, p. 84. See also *Municipal Record: Proceedings of the Council of the City of Pittsburgh* 105 (6 December 1971): 472; and Theodore C. Hardy, "Light Rail Transit in Pittsburgh," in *Light-Rail Transit: Planning and Technology*, pp. 38–42.

177. *St. Louis Post-Dispatch*, 1 March 1973, pp. 3A, 1B. See also ibid., 26 February 1974, p. 3A.

178. *Cincinnati Enquirer*, 6 November 1973, p. 4.

179. Miller, Johnson, and Peterson, *Future of Boston's Capital Plant*, p. 62.

180. *Pittsburgh Post-Gazette*, 11 May 1973, pp. 23, 31.

181. *Report of Proceedings of the City Council of Boston for the Year 1970* (Boston: City of Boston, 1971), p. 3; and *City Journal* 54 (4 May 1971): 11.

182. *Cincinnati Enquirer*, 4 November 1975, pp. 32–33.

183. *Minneapolis Tribune*, 4 November 1977, "Voter's Guide."

184. William Donald Schaefer, "Come to the City Fair!" *Nation's Cities* 11 (June 1973): 10. See also Nast, Krause, and Monk, *Baltimore: A Living Renaissance*, pp. 12–16.

185. Harry Edward Berndt, *New Rulers in the Ghetto: The Community Development Corporation and Urban Poverty* (Westport, Conn.: Greenwood Press, 1977), pp. 119–20; *Cleveland Plain Dealer*, 11 June 1972, p. 8A; ibid., 17 December 1972, pp. 1A, 4A; and Eric Johannesen, *Cleveland Architecture, 1876–1976* (Cleveland: Western Reserve Historical Society, 1979), pp. 231–32. See also Geoffrey Faux, *CDCs: New Hope for the Inner City* (New York: Twentieth Century Fund, 1971), pp. 67–70.

186. Berndt, *New Rulers in the Ghetto*, pp. 41–103.

187. Ibid., pp. 110–27; Edward K. Carpenter, "Good News from Bed-Stuy," *Design and Environment* 7 (Summer 1976): 34–39; *Chicago Tribune*, 9 May 1972, p. 2; and Jane Holtz Kay, "Moving Ahead (Slowly) in Highland Park," *Design and Environment* 7 (Summer 1976): 40–41, 48.

188. *Cleveland Plain Dealer*, 11 June 1972, p. 8A.

189. Berndt, *New Rulers in the Ghetto*, p. 120.

190. *Wall Street Journal*, 1 May 1972, as quoted in ibid., p. 89.

191. Kay, "Moving Ahead (Slowly) in Highland Park," p. 40.

192. Carpenter, "Good News from Bed-Stuy," p. 34.

193. Edward K. Carpenter, *Urban Design Case Studies: Second Awards Program* (Washington, D.C.: RC Publications, 1977), p. 12. See also Faux, *CDCs*, pp. 71–74.

194. Berndt, *New Rulers in the Ghetto*, p. 139.

195. Robert Cassidy, "A Lesson in Neighborhood Pride," *Planning* 45 (September 1979): 29–33; Geno Baroni, "The Neighborhood Movement in the United States: From the 1960s to the Present," in Phillip L. Clay and Robert M. Hollister, eds., *Neighborhood Policy and Planning* (Lexington, Mass.: D. C. Heath, 1983), pp. 183–85; Norman G. Rukert, *The Fells Point Story* (Baltimore: Bodine and Associates, 1976), pp. 91–99; and Robert Fisher, *Let the People Decide: Neighborhood Organizing in America* (Boston: Twayne Publishers, 1984), pp. 143–48.

196. See Saul D. Alinsky, *Rules for Radicals* (New York: Random House, 1971); Robert A. Slayton, *Back of the Yards: Making a Local Democracy* (Chicago: University of Chicago Press, 1986); and Patricia Mooney Melvin, ed., *American Community Organizations: A Historical Dictionary* (New York: Greenwood Press, 1986), pp. 5–6.

197. Cassidy, "A Lesson in Neighborhood Pride," p. 31.

198. Fisher, *Let the People Decide*, p. 144.

199. Ibid., pp. 146–47. For information on a similar neighborhood effort in the East Humboldt Park area of Chicago, see Ed Marciniak, *Reviving an Inner-City Community* (Chicago: Loyola University of Chicago, 1977), and Marcia C. Kaptur, "East Humboldt Park Copes with the Chicago 21 Plan," *Planning* 43 (August 1977): 14–16.

200. Robert Cassidy, "The Hill Builds for Tomorrow," *Planning* 41 (August 1975): 16–18; Gary Ross Mormino, *Immigrants on the Hill: Italian-Americans in Saint Louis, 1882–1982* (Urbana: University of Illinois Press, 1986), pp. 233–58; Sandra Perlman Schoenberg and Patricia L. Rosenbaum, *Neighborhoods That Work: Sources for Viability in the Inner City* (New Brunswick, N.J.: Rutgers University Press, 1980), pp. 49–64; and James Neal Primm, *Lion of the Valley: Saint Louis, Missouri* (Boulder, Colo.: Pruett Publishing, 1981), pp. 444–45.

201. Mormino, *Immigrants on the Hill*, pp. 240, 250.

202. Cassidy, "The Hill Builds for Tomorrow," p. 16.

203. Mormino, *Immigrants on the Hill*, p. 253.

204. Raquel Ramati, *How to Save Your Own Street* (Garden City, N.Y.: Doubleday, 1981), p. 50.

205. *Hearings before the Subcommittee on Housing and Community Development of the Committee on Banking, Finance, and Urban Affairs—House of Representatives, August 8, 9, and 10, 1978* (Washington, D.C.: U.S. Government Printing Office, 1978), p. 529.

206. Ibid., pp. 540, 542.

207. Jeffrey R. Henig, *Neighborhood Mobilization: Redevelopment and Response* (New Brunswick, N.J.: Rutgers University Press, 1982), p. 91.

208. James V. Cunningham and Milton Kotler, *Building Neighborhood Organizations* (Notre Dame, Ind.: University of Notre Dame Press, 1983), p. 54. See also Melvin, *American Community Organizations*, pp. 162–63.

209. Timothy Pattison, "The Stages of Gentrification: The Case of Bay Village," in Clay and Hollister, *Neighborhood Policy and Planning*, p. 78.

210. Ibid., p. 87.

211. Robert H. McNulty and Stephen A. Kliment, eds., *Neighborhood Conservation: A Handbook of Methods and Techniques* (New York: Waston-Guptil Publications, 1976), pp. 203–6.

212. Levy, *Queen Village*.

213. Billie Bramhall, "Planners Advocate for Communities within Planning Department," *Planners Notebook* 4 (June 1974): 1–8; James V. Cunningham, Roger S. Ahlbrandt, Jr., Rose Jewell, and Robert Hendrickson, "The Pittsburgh Atlas Program: Test Project for Neighborhoods," *National Civic Review* 65 (June 1976): 284–89; and James V. Cunningham, "Drafting the Pittsburgh Charter: How Citizens Participated," ibid. 63 (September 1974): 410–15.

214. McNulty and Kliment, *Neighborhood Conservation*, p. 201; John Clayton Thomas, *Between Citizen and City: Neighborhood Organizations and Urban Politics in Cincinnati* (Lawrence: University Press of Kansas, 1986), p. 76.

215. Thomas, *Between Citizen and City*, p. 76.

216. Kenneth E. Corey, *The Clifton Community Plan: Existing Conditions and Analysis of the Clifton Community* (Cincinnati: Clifton Town Meeting, 1977), p. 1–16. See also Henry D. Shapiro and Zane L. Miller, *Clifton: Neighborhood and Community in an Urban Setting: A Brief History* (Cincinnati: Laboratory in American Civilization, 1976), p. 43.

217. John Mudd, *Neighborhood Services: Making Big Cities Work* (New Haven, Conn.: Yale University Press, 1984), p. 65.

218. John V. Lindsay, *A Plan for Neighborhood Government for New York City* (New York: City of New York, 1970), p. 1. See also Edward N. Costikyan and Maxwell Lehman, *Restructuring the Government of New York City: Report of the Scott Commission Task Force on Jurisdiction and Structure* (New York: Praeger Publishers, 1972).

Chapter 7: Messiah Mayors and the Gospel of Urban Hype

1. Benjamin Thompson, "Making a Marketplace," *Boston Magazine* 78 (August 1986): 111; Gurney Breckenfeld, "Jim Rouse Shows How to Give Downtown Retailing New Life," *Fortune* 97 (10 April 1978): 90; and Michael Ryan, "Boston Learns to Love the Great American Marketplace," *Boston Magazine* 71 (April 1979): 120, 124. See also Morton S. Stark, "Mixed-Use and 'Theme' Centers," *Stores* 62 (April 1980): 50–52; and Michael Demarest, "He Digs Downtown," *Time* 118 (24 August 1981): 42, 44–48, 53.

2. Henry Chalfant and James Prigoff, *Spraycan Art* (London: Thames and Hudson, 1987), p. 28.

3. Judith A. Martin and David A. Lanegran, *Where We Live: The Residential Districts of Minneapolis and Saint Paul* (Minneapolis: University of Minnesota Press, 1983), p. 11.

4. Alexander Ganz, "Where Has the Urban Crisis Gone? How Boston and Other Large Cities Have Stemmed Economic Decline," *Urban Affairs Quarterly* 20 (June 1985): 449–68; M. Gottdiener, "Whatever Happened to the Urban Crisis?" ibid. 20 (June 1985): 421–27; and Eric Monkkonen, "What Urban Crisis? A Historian's Point of View," ibid. 20 (June 1985): 429–47.

5. Barbara Ferman, *Governing the Ungovernable City: Political Skill, Leadership, and the Modern Mayor* (Philadelphia: Temple University Press, 1985).

6. *Baltimore Sun*, 7 July 1983, p. D12; and Kevin O'Keeffe, *Baltimore Politics, 1971–1986: The Schaefer Years and the Struggle for Succession* (Washington, D.C.: Georgetown University Press, 1986), p. 94.

7. *Esquire* 102 (October 1984): 4.

8. Richard Ben Cramer, "Can the Best Mayor Win?" ibid. 102 (October 1984): 62.

9. Rinker Buck, "How Am I Doing? An In-Depth Look at Mayor Koch's Record," *New York* 13 (8 September 1980): 18.

10. Roger Rosenblatt, "A Mayor for All Seasons," *Time* 117 (15 June 1981): 24.

11. *Municipal Record: Proceedings of the Council of the City of Pittsburgh* 114 (10 November 1980): 993.

12. "Copious Coping: How Other Mayors Fare," *Time* 117 (15 June 1981): 31. For the Caliguiri election victory of 1977, see *Pittsburgh Post-Gazette*, 9 November 1977, pp. 1, 6, 12; and 10 November 1977, pp. 1, 11.

13. *Cleveland Plain Dealer*, 7 November 1979, p. 15A. See also ibid., 1 November 1979, pp. 1A, 6A; 2 November 1979, pp. 1A, 18A, 34A; 4 November 1979, pp. 1A, 22A; 5 November 1979, pp. 1A, 14A, 29A–30A; 7 November 1979, pp. 1A, 14A; and 8 November 1979, p. 4C; and Todd Swanstrom, *The Crisis of Growth Politics: Cleveland, Kucinich, and the Challenge of Urban Populism* (Philadelphia: Temple University Press, 1985), pp. 210–24.

14. *Cleveland Plain Dealer,* 4 November 1981, p. 3C. See also ibid., 2 November 1981, pp. 4A, 13A.

15. Ibid., 6 November 1985, p. 3C. See also ibid., 2 November 1985, pp. 1A, 9A, 6B; 3 November 1985, pp. 1A, 11A; 6 November 1985, p. 1A; and 7 November 1985, pp. 1A, 18A, 30A.

16. *Buffalo Evening News,* 9 November 1977, p. 44. See also ibid., 4 November 1977, p. 4; 5 November 1977, p. C4; and 9 November 1977, p. 1.

17. *New York Times,* 17 December 1980, p. B3. See also "A New Breed of Mayors Takes Over," *U.S. News and World Report* 91 (23 November 1981): 63–64.

18. *St. Louis Post-Dispatch,* 29 March 1987, p. 1B. For coverage of the Schoemehl campaigns and election victories, see ibid., 4 March 1981, pp. 1A, 8A; 5 April 1981, pp. 1L, 11L; 8 April 1981, pp. 1A, 11A–12A; 3 March 1985, p. 6B; 6 March 1985, pp. 1A, 16A; 7 March 1985, pp. 3A, 2B; and 3 April 1985, pp. 1A, 5A.

19. *Detroit Free Press,* 5 November 1981, p. 11A.

20. Ibid., 10 November 1977, p. 8A.

21. "Copious Coping," *Time,* p. 30.

22. Howie Carr, "Kevin versus the Council: Case History of a Feud," *Boston Magazine* 72 (December 1980): 98.

23. *Boston Globe,* 7 November 1979, p. 1.

24. Ferman, *Governing the Ungovernable City,* pp. 92–95.

25. *Boston Globe,* 3 November 1979, p. 1; and 7 November 1979, p. 22.

26. Ferman, *Governing the Ungovernable City,* p. 92.

27. Cramer, "Can the Best Mayor Win?" p. 66.

28. Martin Shefter, *Political Crisis/Fiscal Crisis: The Collapse and Revival of New York City* (New York: Basic Books, 1985), pp. 176–78.

29. *St. Louis Post-Dispatch,* 29 March 1987, pp. 1B, 4B.

30. *Municipal Records: Proceedings of the Council of the City of Pittsburgh* 116 (8 November 1982): 1190–91.

31. Edward I. Koch with William Rauch, *Mayor* (New York: Simon and Schuster, 1984), p. 322; and Cramer, "Can the Best Mayor Win?" p. 62.

32. Citizens Budget Commission, *The State of Municipal Services, 1978–1985* (New York: Citizens Budget Commission, 1985), p. 34.

33. *City Employment in 1977* (Washington, D.C.: Bureau of the Census, 1978), pp. 12–18; *City Employment in 1985* (Washington, D.C.: Bureau of the Census, 1986), pp. 12–21.

34. Arvid Anderson and Marjorie A. London, "Collective Bargaining and the Fiscal Crisis in New York City: Cooperation for Survival," *Fordham Urban Law Journal* 10 (1982): 374.

35. *New York Times,* 17 September 1975, p. 28; and Anderson and London, "Collective Bargaining and the Fiscal Crisis," p. 391.

36. *New York Times,* 25 November 1986, p. B4; and Mark H. Maier, *City Unions: Managing Discontent in New York City* (New Brunswick, N.J.: Rutgers University Press, 1987), pp. 173, 189.

37. *New York Times,* 25 November 1986, p. B4.

38. Koch, *Mayor,* pp. 346–47.

39. Ibid., pp. 169–223.

40. Arthur Browne, Dan Collins, and Michael Goodwin, *I, Koch: A Decidedly Unauthorized Biography of the Mayor of New York City, Edward I. Koch* (New York: Dodd, Mead, 1985), p. 181.

41. Alair A. Townsend, "Institutionalized Reform: The Fiscal Process Today in New York City," *City Almanac* 18 (Spring 1985): 11. See also Freda Stern Ackerman, Daniel N. Heimowitz, and Colleen Woodell, "The Restoration of New York City's Credit since the Fiscal Crisis," ibid. 18 (Spring 1985): 2–5.

42. Mark Weinberg, "The Urban Fiscal Crisis: Impact on Budgeting and Financial Planning Practices of Urban America," *Journal of Urban Affairs* 6 (Winter 1984): 41; and Swanstrom, *Crisis of Growth Politics*, p. 247.

43. *New York Times*, 26 June 1987, p. A10. See also ibid., 9 October 1980, p. A22; Weinberg, "Urban Fiscal Crisis," p. 43; Swanstrom, *Crisis of Growth Politics*, p. 247; and "Belt-Tightening Time for Big-City Mayors," *U.S. News and World Report* 88 (10 March 1980): 77–78.

44. *St. Louis Post-Dispatch*, 29 March 1987, p. 4B.

45. Ibid. Also see ibid., 9 February 1987, p. 2B.

46. Ibid., 25 August 1985, pp. 1B, 6B; and 26 August 1985, p. 1B.

47. "Copious Coping," *Time*, p. 30.

48. *Detroit Free Press*, 1 November 1981, p. 2B. On Detroit's financial problems, see also Bette Woody, *Managing Crisis Cities: The New Black Leadership and the Politics of Resource Allocation* (Westport, Conn.: Greenwood Press, 1982), pp. 22–32; Thomas J. Anton, *Federal Aid to Detroit* (Washington, D.C.: Brookings Institution, 1983), pp. 14–15; "Behind the Fiscal Bind That Plagues Detroit," *Business Week*, no. 2694 (29 June 1981): 55, 58; and Joan K. Martin, *Urban Financial Stress: Why Cities Go Broke* (Boston: Auburn House Publishing, 1982), pp. 53–99.

49. *Boston Globe*, 3 December 1980, p. 21.

50. Ibid., 4 December 1980, pp. 1, 40.

51. Richard P. Nathan, Fred C. Doolittle, and Associates, *The Consequences of Cuts: The Effects of the Reagan Domestic Program on State and Local Governments* (Princeton, N.J.: Princeton Urban and Regional Research Center, 1983), pp. 133–35; Mary John Miller, J. Chester Johnson, and George E. Peterson, *The Future of Boston's Capital Plant* (Washington, D.C.: Urban Institute Press, 1981), p. 5; and John Strahinich and J. William Semich, "The Money Pit," *Boston Magazine* 78 (September 1986): 154, 157.

52. *Wall Street Journal*, 10 April 1984, p. 31.

53. J. Thomas Black, Allan Borut, Robert M. Byrne, and Michael J. Morina, *UDAG Partnerships: Nine Case Studies* (Washington, D.C.: Urban Land Institute, 1980), pp. 100–108.

54. Michael Thoryn, "U.S. Occupancy Rates Rise Substantially," *Building Owner and Manager* 2 (August 1977): 1; and "Office Market Making Recovery: Squeeze on Space Predicted," ibid. 3 (July 1978): 2.

55. "Office Market Making Recovery," *Building Owner and Manager*, p. 2.

56. Fergus M. Bordewich, "Real Estate: How High the Boom?" *New York Magazine* 11 (11 December 1978): 66.

57. Ibid., pp. 62, 71.

58. Robert Ponte, "Manhattan's Real Estate Boom," *New York Affairs* 8, no. 4

(1985): 21. Emanuel Tobier, "Manhattan Emerges as 'World City,' " *Real Estate Review* 4 (Spring 1984): 49.

59. Jim Sleeper, "Boom and Bust with Ed Koch," *Dissent* 34 (Fall 1987): 438.

60. "The New York Colossus," *Business Week*, no. 2852 (23 July 1984): 111; and Ponte, "Manhattan's Real Estate Boom," p. 19.

61. *Midtown Development* (New York: City Planning Commission, 1981). See also Susan S. Fainstein, ed., "The Redevelopment of Forty-second Street," *City Almanac* 18 (Summer 1985); and Ponte, "Manhattan's Real Estate Boom," p. 22.

62. Stefan Lorant, *Pittsburgh: The Story of an American City*, 3d ed. (Lenox, Mass.: Authors Edition, 1980), p. 553; Brian J. L. Berry, Susan W. Sanderson, Shelby Stewman, and Joel Tarr, "The Nation's Most Livable City: Pittsburgh's Transformation," in Gary Gappert, ed., *The Future of Winter Cities* (Newbury Park, Calif.: Sage Publications, 1987), p. 180; and Shelby Stewman and Joel A. Tarr, "Four Decades of Public and Private Partnerships in Pittsburgh," in R. Scott Fosler and Renee A. Berger, eds., *Public-Private Partnership in American Cities* (Lexington, Mass.: D. C. Heath, 1982), p. 97.

63. "Pittsburgh's Liberty Center: Both an End and a Beginning," *Urban Land* 46 (September 1987): 28.

64. Berry et al., "The Nation's Most Livable City," p. 182; and Stewman and Tarr, "Public and Private Partnerships in Pittsburgh," p. 98.

65. Jonathan Barnett, "Designing Downtown Pittsburgh," *Architectural Record* 170 (January 1982): 92; Robert H. McNulty, R. Leo Penne, Dorothy R. Jacobson, and Partners for Livable Places, *The Return of the Livable City: Learning from America's Best* (Washington, D.C.: Acropolis Books, 1986), p. 52; and Franklin Toker, *Pittsburgh: An Urban Portrait* (University Park, Pa.: Pennsylvania State University Press, 1986), pp. 32–33.

66. Daralice D. Boles and Jim Murphy, "Cincinnati Centerpiece," *Progressive Architecture* 66 (October 1985): 71–87.

67. *Chicago Tribune*, 22 October 1986, p. 1.

68. Patrick Barry, "Boom!" *Chicago Times* 1 (September–October 1987): 27.

69. *Boston Globe*, 17 September 1985, pp. 1, 12.

70. *Baltimore Sun*, 6 January 1985, p. 14D.

71. *Detroit Free Press*, 16 April 1977, pp. 1A, 4A.

72. Tom Gorton, "Detroit Reborn," *Planning* 45 (July 1979): 15.

73. *Detroit Free Press*, 16 April 1977, p. 2A; and 12 April 1987, p. 10A.

74. Ibid., 12 April 1987, p. 10A; Tod A. Marder, ed., *The Critical Edge: Controversy in Recent American Architecture* (Cambridge, Mass.: MIT Press, 1985), p. 184; *Detroit News*, 12 January 1983, p. A10; and *New York Times*, 13 January 1983, p. A18.

75. Wolf Von Eckardt, *Back to the Drawing Board! Planning Livable Cities* (Washington, D.C.: New Republic Books, 1978), p. 167. For other criticisms, see Marder, *The Critical Edge*, pp. 178–82.

76. *Detroit Free Press*, 12 April 1987, p. 10A.

77. Ibid.

78. Ann Breen and Dick Rigby, eds., *Urban Waterfronts, 1985: Water Makes a Difference!* (Washington, D.C.: Waterfront Press, 1986), p. 20. For more on Renais-

sance Center, see Stephen A. Horn, "Detroit's Renaissance: Redevelopment Rescues City Symbol," *Urban Land* 46 (July 1987): 6–11.

79. *Philadelphia Evening Bulletin*, 11 August 1977, p. 52.

80. Ibid., 12 August 1977, p. 50. See also ibid., 7 August 1977, p. 26; ibid., 11 August 1977, p. 20; Jurgen F. Haver, "Philadelphia Story—Ongoing Renewal," *Stores* 62 (April 1980): 53–57; Morton S. Stark, "Shopping Center Futures—Tide Turning?" ibid. 62 (March 1980): 20; and *New York Times* 25 March 1978, pp. 25–26.

81. Demarest, "He Digs Downtown," p. 42. For further accounts of Harborplace, see Douglas M. Wrenn, *Urban Waterfront Development* (Washington, D.C.: Urban Land Institute, 1983), pp. 152–55; McNulty et al., *Return of the Livable City*, pp. 23–33; Harold R. Snedcof, *Cultural Facilities in Mixed-Use Development* (Washington, D.C.: Urban Land Institute, 1985), pp. 243–45; Joseph D. Steller, Jr., "An MXD Takes Off: Baltimore's Inner Harbor," *Urban Land* 41 (March 1982): 14–15; "A New Market Complex with the Vitality of an Old Landmark: Harborplace in Baltimore," *Architectural Record* 168 (October 1980): 100–105; David A. Wallace, "An Insider's Story of the Inner Harbor," *Planning* 45 (September 1979): 20–24; and Jacques Kelly, "The Master Builders," *Baltimore Magazine* 78 (June 1985): 90–103, 167.

82. *St. Louis Post-Dispatch*, 26 August 1985, p. 3A. See also Jacquelyn Bivens, "Full Steam Ahead in Saint Louis," *Chain Store Age Executive* 59 (May 1983): 80, 85, 87–90.

83. *St. Louis Post-Dispatch*, 29 August 1985, p. 7F. See also ibid., pp. 1F–6F; ibid., 30 August 1985, pp. 1A, 18A–19A; ibid., 10 January 1988, pp. 1I–2I; Edmund Faltermayer, "How Saint Louis Turned Less into More," *Fortune* 112 (23 December 1985): 44–46, 50, 54, 58; "Spirit of Saint Louis," *Progressive Architecture* 66 (November 1985): 84–93; and Charlene Prost, "Comeback City," *Planning* 51 (October 1985): 4–10.

84. Jay Nussbaum, "Saint Louis Regains Meetings Biz after Five Years of Rebuilding," *Meeting News* 11 (September 1987): 147–49; George McCue, *The Building Art in Saint Louis: Two Centuries*, 3d ed. (Saint Louis: Knight Publishing, 1981), p. 36; *St. Louis Post-Dispatch*, 12 February 1986, pp. 1A, 5A; "Baltimore Gains Meetings Momentum, Contemplates Center Expansion," *Meeting News* 11 (July 1987): 109–10; *New York Times*, 25 January 1981, sec. 1, p. 22; *Staff Report to the Committee on General Plans of the Pittsburgh City Planning Commission Describing the Basic Conditions of the Convention Center Study Area* (Pittsburgh: City of Pittsburgh, 1979), p. 1; "New Image Draws Delegates to a Renewed Pittsburgh," *Meeting News* 10 (February 1986): 101, 110; "Pittsburgh Changes Image from Iron City to Cultural Hub," ibid. 12 (February 1988): 121; and William Roberts, "New Hotel, Renovated Center, Draw Groups to Pittsburgh," ibid. 11 (June 1987): 124.

85. *New York Times*, 13 February 1981, p. 10.

86. Sidney Zion, "New York Is in a Conventional Dither," *New York* 11 (29 May 1978): 8–10; Adam Blair, "Celebrations Polish City's Image, Boost Hotel Occupancy," *Meeting News* 10 (December 1986): 107, 110; Erica Meltzer, "NYC Center Opens in Spring 1986; Plans Expansion," ibid. 9 (March 1985): 3; and *Christian Science Monitor*, 31 December 1986, p. 6.

87. Leah Krakinowski, "Chicago Defends Title as Top Convention Site," *Meeting News* 11 (April 1987): 89–90.

88. *St. Louis Post-Dispatch*, 12 February 1986, pp. 1A, 5A, 2B.

89. "Cincinnati Gears Up for Larger Facility," *Meeting News* 9 (September 1985): 183; *Cincinnati Enquirer*, 10 August 1987, pp. D1, D4; Mary Ann McNulty, "Cincinnati Spends $62M to Double Convention Center," *Meeting News* 11 (November 1987): 121–22; and idem, "Bicentennial Festivities Change Cincinnati's Face and Future," ibid. 12 (March 1988): 159.

90. "Convention Hall Modernization Promises Development Spur," *Meeting News* 9 (September 1985): 178; "Cleveland Revamps Facilities, Attracts Regional Meetings," ibid. 11 (May 1987): 148–49; Mary Ann McNulty, "Detroit Revs Up for Big Convention Dollars," ibid. 11 (July 1987): 119, 124; Strahinich and Semich, "The Money Pit," pp. 154–57, 215–20, 222, 224; John King, "Boston," *Meetings and Conventions* 20 (July 1985): 143–48; Julie Cohen, "Boston Awaits January 1988 Debut of Hynes Center," *Meeting News* 11 (June 1987): 117; Carol Bialkowski, "Boston Unveils New Hynes Center as City's Delegate Demand Increases," ibid. 11 (December 1987): 79–81; Susan E. B. Kossoy, "Twin Cities Outgrow Centers, Eye Expansion Plans in 1986," ibid. 9 (December 1985): 153, 156; and Mary Ann McNulty, "Minneapolis Plans New Center; Meetings Biz Blooms Statewide," ibid. 11 (November 1987): 129.

91. Robert Guskind, "Bringing Madison Avenue to Main Street," *Planning* 53 (February 1987): 10.

92. McNulty et al., *Return of the Livable City*, p. 32.

93. Susan Crystal, "I Love Slogans," *Meetings and Conventions* 22 (February 1987): 41; and Guskind, "Bringing Madison Avenue to Main Street," pp. 5, 8.

94. Ellen Wlody, "Rochester's New Center Threatens Other Cities' Business," *Meeting News* 9 (March 1985): N-7.

95. Crystal, "I Love Slogans," p. 44; and Mel Hosansky, "John G. Walsh," *Meetings and Conventions* 20 (February 1985): 113.

96. Crystal, "I Love Slogans," p. 44.

97. June Goldman, "Saint Louis: The Meeting Place Gains Momentum with New Attractions," *Meetings and Conventions* 20 (July 1985): 107.

98. David Shama, "Stadium Bill to Keep Twin Cities 'Major League,' " *Greater Minneapolis* 29 (July–August 1977): 14.

99. Ibid. See also *Minneapolis Tribune*, 2 December 1978, pp. 1A, 6A.

100. Lawrence D. Shubnell, John E. Petersen, and Collin B. Harris, "The Big Ticket: Financing a Professional Sports Facility," *Government Finance Review* 1 (June 1985): 9.

101. Jeffrey Kluger, "The Seduction of the Colts," *New York Times Magazine*, 9 December 1984, p. 106.

102. Arthur T. Johnson, "Economic and Policy Implications of Hosting Sports Franchises," *Urban Affairs Quarterly* 21 (March 1986): 415.

103. *Baltimore Sun*, 26 January 1988, pp. 1A, 6A.

104. Bob Leffler, "Camden Yards Project Will Spark Downtown Business," *Baltimore Business Journal* 5 (23–29 May 1988): 13.

105. *Baltimore Sun*, 23 January 1988, p. 8A.

106. *St. Louis Post-Dispatch*, 17 January 1988, p. 2C. See also ibid., 10 February 1987, pp. 1A, 7A; 16 January 1988, p. 11C; and 17 January 1988, pp. 1A, 5A.

107. Ibid., 28 January 1988, pp. 1A, 7A; 30 January 1988, pp. 1A, 5A; and 31 January 1988, p. 2B. For more on the pursuit of the Cardinals, see *Baltimore Sun*, 17 January 1988, pp. 1K, 5K.

108. *Detroit Free Press*, 7 February 1988, pp. 1A, 12A.

109. *Cleveland Plain Dealer*, 5 January 1988, pp. 1A–2A.

110. George Hinds, "A New Home for the Bears," *Inland Architect* 32 (January–February 1988): 68–74; and Ruth Eckdish Knack, "Stadiums: The Right Game Plan?" *Planning* 52 (September 1986): 6–11.

111. Shubnell, Petersen, and Harris, "The Big Ticket," p. 7.

112. George Clack, "Footlight Districts," in Kevin W. Green, ed., *The City as a Stage: Strategies for the Arts in Urban Economics* (Washington, D.C.: Partners for Livable Places, 1983), p. 12. See also Harvard Business School, "Cultural Revitalization in Six Cities," in ibid., pp. 26–28.

113. *Christian Science Monitor*, 14 July 1987, pp. 3, 6. See also *Detroit Free Press*, 23 February 1988, pp. 1A, 14A.

114. Snedcof, *Cultural Facilities*, pp. 216–35; and Rachelle L. Levitt, ed., *Cities Reborn* (Washington, D.C.: Urban Land Institute, 1987), pp. 130–35.

115. Mark Fadiman, "Break a Leg, Cleveland," *Forbes* 134 (2 July 1984): 74. See also Jane Kirkham, "Playhouse Square Theatre Restoration," *Urban Design International* 4 (Summer 1983): 14–15; Eric Johannesen, "Cleveland's Circle and Square," in Green, ed., *City as Stage*, pp. 86–88; and Clack, "Footlight Districts," pp. 12–15.

116. Hunter Morrison, "Revitalizing the Lakefront," *Urban Design International* 4 (Summer 1983): 32–33.

117. "Redeveloping Cleveland," ibid., p. 16; and David Lewis, "Reinforcing History," ibid., p. 18.

118. *Cleveland Plain Dealer*, 21 January 1988, pp. 1A, 14A. For more on plans for rebuilding downtown Cleveland, see Cynthia Davidson-Powers, "Cleveland," *Inland Architect* 32 (July–August 1988): 30–37.

119. Todd Englander, "Big-League Mayors Who Pitch for Their Cities," *Meetings and Conventions* 21 (May 1986): 52; and *Baltimore Wow!* (Baltimore: City of Baltimore, 1984), pp. 35–36.

120. Sandra Hillman, "Leveraging Prosperity in Baltimore," in Green, *City as Stage*, p. 98; and McNulty et al., *Return of the Livable City*, pp. 31–32.

121. *Detroit Free Press*, 13 February 1988, p. 7A. For a similar proposal for Cincinnati, see *Cincinnati Enquirer*, 8 November 1979, p. C1.

122. Amy Singer, "When Worlds Collide," *Historic Preservation* 36 (August 1984): 32.

123. Jane Peterson, "Anguish and Joy in a Changing Neighborhood," ibid. 35 (July–August 1983), p. 26.

124. Linda Greider, "Secrets of Great Old Neighborhoods," ibid. 38 (February 1986): 29. See also *New York Times*, 13 September 1987, sec. 12, pp. 4–7.

125. Singer, "When Worlds Collide," p. 38.

126. Ibid., p. 39.

127. See, for example, Marc V. Levine, "Downtown Redevelopment as an Urban

Growth Strategy: A Critical Appraisal of the Baltimore Renaissance," *Journal of Urban Affairs* 9, no. 2 (1987): 103–23; Joe R. Feagin, "The Corporate Center Strategy," *Urban Affairs Quarterly* 21 (June 1986): 617–28; and Richard Child Hill, "Crisis in the Motor City: The Politics of Economic Development in Detroit," in Susan S. Fainstein, Norman I. Fainstein, Richard Child Hill, Dennis R. Judd, and Michael Peter Smith, eds., *Restructuring the City: The Political Economy of Urban Redevelopment* (New York: Longman, 1983), pp. 80–125.

128. Susan Morse, "Neighborhood Spirit Shapes a City," *Historic Preservation* 40 (July–August 1988): 27.

129. *Pittsburgh Press*, 15 November 1987, p. A12; and Alberta Sbragia, "The Pittsburgh Model of Economic Development: Partnership, Responsiveness, and Indifference," in Gregory Squires, ed., *Unequal Partnerships: Urban Economic Development in Postwar America* (New Brunswick, N.J.: Rutgers University Press, forthcoming).

130. Sbragia, "The Pittsburgh Model"; Stewman and Tarr, "Public-Private Partnerships in Pittsburgh," p. 96; Robert H. Lurcott and Jane A. Downing, "A Public-Private Support System for Community-Based Organizations in Pittsburgh," *Journal of the American Planning Association* 53 (Autumn 1987): 459; and Roger S. Ahlbrandt, Jr., "Public-Private Partnerships for Neighborhood Renewal," *Annals of the American Academy of Political and Social Science* 488 (November 1986): 127.

131. Ahlbrandt, "Public-Private Partnerships for Neighborhood Renewal," pp. 128–30; Stewman and Tarr, "Public-Private Partnerships in Pittsburgh," pp. 100–101; Lurcott and Downing, "Public-Private Support System," pp. 459–68; and Sbragia, "The Pittsburgh Model."

132. Bernard L. Berkowitz, "Economic Development Really Works: Baltimore, Maryland," in Richard D. Bingham and John P. Blair, eds., *Urban Economic Development* (Beverly Hills: Sage Publications, 1984), pp. 217–19; Lenora H. Nast, Laurence N. Krause, and R. C. Monk, eds., *Baltimore: A Living Renaissance* (Baltimore: Historic Baltimore Society, 1982), p. 11; *Baltimore Wow!* pp. 26–27; and Bill Struever, "Market Revitalization Spurs Reinvestment in Baltimore Neighborhood Commercial Area," *Journal of Housing* 36 (January 1979): 31–34.

133. *Baltimore Wow!*

134. Mel Ravitz, "Perils of Planning as an Executive Function," *Journal of the American Planning Association* 54 (Spring 1988): 165.

135. Joe T. Darden, Richard Child Hill, Jane Thomas, and Richard Thomas, *Detroit: Race and Uneven Development* (Philadelphia: Temple University Press, 1987), p. 198.

136. Suzanne Dolezal, "The Squeaky Wheel Gets the Grease," *Detroit Free Press Magazine*, 2 August 1981, p. 7.

137. Geno Baroni, "The Neighborhood Movement in the United States: From the 1960s to the Present," in Phillip L. Clay and Robert M. Hollister, eds., *Neighborhood Policy and Planning* (Lexington, Mass.: D. C. Heath, 1983), pp. 183–85; and Patricia Mooney Melvin, ed., *American Community Organizations: A Historical Dictionary* (New York: Greenwood Press, 1986), pp. 165–67.

138. Beth Weiksnar, "The Cleveland Housing Network," *Urban Land* 47 (April 1988): 2–5.

139. *Reauthorization of Housing and Community Development Programs, Hearings before the Subcommittee on Housing and Urban Affairs of the Committee on Banking, Housing, and Urban Affairs, United States Senate, 100th Congress* (Washington, D.C.: U.S. Government Printing Office, 1987), pp. 287–93, 339–51.

140. Neal St. Anthony, *Until All Are Housed in Dignity* (Minneapolis: Project for Pride in Living, 1987).

141. *Development without Displacement: A Theme for the Eighties* (Chicago: Chicago Rehab Network, 1980).

142. Sbragia, "The Pittsburgh Model."

143. William Fulton, "Off the Barricades, into the Boardrooms," *Planning* 53 (August 1987): 11.

144. Richard P. Taub, *Community Capitalism* (Boston: Harvard Business School Press, 1988).

145. St. Anthony, *Until All Are Housed in Dignity*, p. 90.

146. *Nation's Cities Weekly*, 8 November 1982, p. 2; and 7 January 1985, p. 3. Also Sam Bass Warner, Jr., *To Dwell Is to Garden: A History of Boston's Community Gardens* (Boston: Northeastern University Press, 1987), pp. 36–38.

147. *Wall Street Journal*, 9 May 1986, p. 1.

148. *Detroit Free Press*, 12 January 1986, p. 1A.

149. Levitt, *Cities Reborn*, p. 150.

150. *Baltimore Sun*, 28 January 1987, pp. 1A, 8A, 1C, 4C; *Washington Post*, 28 January 1987, p. C3; and Marc V. Levine, "Response to Berkowitz, Economic Development in Baltimore: Some Additional Perspectives," *Journal of Urban Affairs* 9, no. 2 (1987): 133.

151. *Washington Post*, 24 November 1984, p. A8.

152. Samuel M. Ehrenhalt, "New York City's Economy: New Risks and a Changing Outlook," *Citizens Budget Commission Quarterly* 8 (Winter 1988): 3.

153. Levitt, *Cities Reborn*, p. 18.

154. Ehrenhalt, "New York City's Economy," p. 3; and *Wall Street Journal*, 18 October 1984, p. 1.

155. Levine, "Downtown Redevelopment," p. 107. See also *Baltimore Evening Sun*, 21 March 1985, pp. A1, A4–A5; and Eric Garland, "The End of Baltimore as a Blue-Collar Town," *Baltimore Magazine* 73 (December 1980): 52–58.

156. Katharine Warner, John Ehrmann, Luther Jackson, and Jerry Lax, "Detroit's Renaissance Includes Factories," *Urban Land* 41 (June 1982): 3–14; and David Fasenfest, "Community Politics and Urban Redevelopment: Poletown, Detroit, and General Motors," *Urban Affairs Quarterly* 22 (September 1986): 101–23.

157. *Wall Street Journal*, 16 April 1986, p. 23.

158. *Detroit Free Press*, 5 January 1977, p. 3A. See also *Philadelphia Bulletin*, 1 May 1977, sec. 1, p. 3; Thomas Hine, "Prospects Good for Renovation of Philadelphia Department Store," *Architecture* 75 (January 1986): 14, 16; *Baltimore Sun*, 22 January 1977, pp. A1, A8; and ibid., 23 January 1977, pp. B1–B2.

159. Ford S. Worthy, "The Could-Do City Could Do It Again," *Fortune* 115 (19 January 1987): 84.

160. *Cincinnati Enquirer*, 10 March 1988, p. A-20.

161. "The Death of a Landmark," *Newsweek* 100 (27 December 1982): 54. Also

Detroit Free Press, 4 January 1983, p. 4C; 17 January 1983, pp. 1A, 11A; and 19 January 1983, pp. 1A, 5A, 8A.

162. J. Thomas Black, Libby Howland, and Stuart L. Rogel, *Downtown Retail Development: Conditions for Success and Project Profiles* (Washington, D.C.: Urban Land Institute, 1983), pp. 32–34. Also *Philadelphia Bulletin*, 1 May 1977, sec. 2, pp. 1–2; 7 August 1977, p. 26; 11 August 1977, pp. 20, 52; and 12 August 1977, pp. 47, 50.

163. Black, Howland, and Rogel, *Downtown Retail Development*, pp. 45–48; and William Maher, Henriette McHugh, and Sandra Stern, "New Downtown Department Stores: A Tough Deal to Make," *Urban Land* 45 (September 1986): 24–27.

164. *Baltimore Sun*, 24 September 1987, pp. 1C, 4C. See also *Washington Post*, 24 November 1984, p. A9; and 28 September 1987, Business section, p. 28.

165. *State Street Transit Mall Before-After Study—Phase One Final Report* (Chicago: Department of Planning, 1981), p. II-5.

166. *Chicago Tribune*, 12 May 1982, sec. 1, pp. 1, 12; 30 October 1982, sec. 1, p. 1; and 30 August 1987, sec. 7, p. 1.

167. Ibid., 16 May 1982, sec. 2, p. 1.

168. Ibid., 30 August 1987, sec. 7, p. 1.

169. Mike Mallowe, "The Life and Death of Chestnut Street," *Philadelphia Magazine* 78 (October 1987): 142.

170. Ibid., p. 229.

171. D. Herbert Lipson, "Off the Cuff," ibid. 70 (April 1979): 1.

172. D. Herbert Lipson, "Off the Cuff," ibid. 77 (September 1986): 1.

173. Jane Algmin, "Boston's Downtown Crossing: Its Effects on Downtown Retailing," *Transit Journal* 6 (Spring 1980): 15, 18, 22.

174. *Boston Globe*, 29 March 1988, p. 48. See also ibid., 2 February 1988, pp. 1, 37; and 26 March 1988, pp. 35, 39.

175. Ehrenhalt, "New York City's Economy," p. 2.

176. Levitt, *Cities Reborn*, p. 18.

177. Richard Kateley, "Bull Market for Design," *Urban Design International* 6 (Summer 1985): 12.

178. Matthew Drennan, "Local Economy and Local Revenues," in Charles Brecher and Raymond D. Horton, eds., *Setting Municipal Priorities, 1988* (New York: New York University Press, 1987), p. 25.

179. Ehrenhalt, "New York City's Economy," p. 3.

180. *Cleveland Plain Dealer*, 20 April 1986, pp. 1A, 16A.

181. Marilyn Rubin, "Back-Office Activity—An Overview," *City Almanac* 18 (June–August 1984): 3; and "Back-Office Locations: Some Corporate Views," ibid. 18 (June–August 1984): 20–21.

182. Ehrenhalt, "New York City's Economy," p. 3.

183. Christopher B. Leinberger and Charles Lockwood, "How Business Is Reshaping America," *Atlantic Monthly* 258 (October 1986): 48.

184. Darden et al., *Detroit*, p. 34.

185. Ehrenhalt, "New York City's Economy," p. 3.

186. Levitt, *Cities Reborn*, p. 18.

187. *Washington Post*, 25 January 1988, p. WB3.

188. Anita A. Summers and Thomas F. Luce, *Economic Development within the Philadelphia Metropolitan Area* (Philadelphia: University of Pennsylvania Press, 1987), p. 13.

189. Levitt, *Cities Reborn*, p. 153.

190. Ibid., pp. 18, 21.

191. Levine, "Downtown Redevelopment," p. 109.

192. Gregory R. Barnes, "Philly Hotels Face Survival Struggle," *Hotel and Motel Management* 201 (13 January 1986): 3, 48.

193. Ibid.

194. Bill Gillette, "Philly Bids Adieu to Historic Bellevue," ibid. 201 (7 April 1986): 1, 22–23; Susan Kossoy, "Bellevue Closes; Staff Scrambles to Move Groups," *Meeting News* 10 (April 1986): 10; and Edward Watkins, "Philadelphia's Fairmont: The New Grand Dame of Broad Street," *Lodging Hospitality* 36 (May 1980): 32–34.

195. Gillette, "Philly Bids Adieu," p. 23; Loren Feldman, "Center of the Storm," *Philadelphia Magazine* 75 (April 1984): 142–46, 177–93.

196. Patrick Starr, "Philadelphia: Reading Reevaluated," *Planning* 54 (January 1988): 28.

197. D. Herbert Lipson, "Off the Cuff," *Philadelphia Magazine* 78 (March 1987): 1.

198. Ibid.

199. Feldman, "Center of the Storm," p. 146.

200. *Cleveland Plain Dealer*, 7 November 1987, pp. 1A, 12A.

201. Ibid., p. 12A.

202. *Washington Post*, 18 April 1983, p. A4.

203. *Wall Street Journal*, 16 September 1987, p. 37.

204. *Washington Post*, 12 January 1987, Business section, p. 10.

205. Snedcof, *Cultural Facilities*, pp. 248–49.

206. Tim Wheeler, "The Tourists Are Coming!" *Baltimore Magazine* 78 (May 1985): 72.

207. *Washington Post*, 18 April 1983, p. A4.

208. *New York Times*, 1 June 1986, sec. 1, p. 39.

209. Michael Desmond, "Trying to Make Buffalo's Ends Meet," *Mass Transit* 13 (October 1986): 28.

210. *New York Times*, 1 June 1986, sec. 1, p. 39.

211. Katharine Blood, "The Price Mover," *Forbes* 135 (22 April 1985): 76. See also Ed Bas, "Detroit's Troubled People Mover," *Mass Transit* 13 (October 1986): 8–9, 56–57; "A Railway That Won't," *Maclean's* 98 (24 June 1985): 57; and Luther Jackson, "Detroit's People Mover Finally off the Ground," *Mass Transit* 11 (September 1984): 112–13, 115–16.

212. Tony Snow, "The Great Train Robbery," *Policy Review* 36 (Spring 1986): 44.

213. *Detroit Free Press*, 26 July 1987, p. 7G; and 9 August 1987, p. 2C.

214. *Chicago Tribune*, 7 January 1988, sec. 1, p. 28.

215. *Detroit Free Press*, 26 July 1987, p. 7G.

216. *Washington Post*, 23 January 1988, p. D5; and 10 February 1988, p. C6.

217. Michael Berryhill, "Railroading the Cities," *Harper's* 267 (December 1983): 2, 8, 10, 12, 14, 16.

218. Marilyn Webb, "Paradise Postponed," *New York* 19 (17 November 1986): 46.

219. Ibid., p. 50. See also Michael C. D. MacDonald, *America's Cities: A Report on the Myth of Urban Renaissance* (New York: Simon and Schuster, 1984), pp. 357–62.

220. *Boston Globe*, 24 January 1988, p. 23.

221. Ben Joravsky, "The Chicago School Mess," *Illinois Issues* 14 (April 1988): 13.

222. Daniel E. Chall, "New York City's 'Skills Mismatch,' " *Federal Reserve Bank of New York Quarterly Review* 10 (Spring 1985): 21.

223. Levine, "Downtown Redevelopment," pp. 113–14.

224. *Washington Post*, 24 November 1984, p. A8.

225. Levitt, *Cities Reborn*, p. 19.

226. *Boston Globe*, 24 January 1988, p. 23.

227. Ehrenhalt, "New York City's Economy," p. 5.

228. Sbragia, "The Pittsburgh Model."

229. Hal Riedl, "Don Schaefer's Town," *New Republic* 185 (25 November 1981): 27.

230. Mike Mallowe, "Notes from the New White Ghetto," *Philadelphia Magazine* 77 (December 1986): 245.

231. *Chicago Tribune*, 2 December 1986, sec. 1, pp. 1, 12.

232. Ibid., 5 December 1986, sec. 1, p. 1; and 30 November 1986, sec. 1, p. 11. See also ibid., 1 December 1986, sec. 1, pp. 1, 9; 4 December 1986, sec. 1, pp. 1, 11; 10 December 1986, sec. 1, pp. 1, 8; and 12 December 1986, sec. 1, pp. 1, 8.

233. Ibid., 8 December 1986, sec. 1, pp. 1, 10.

234. Morse, "Neighborhood Spirit Shapes a City," p. 27.

235. *Washington Post*, 19 June 1986, p. Md1. See also Mark Cohen, "The Most Complicated Neighborhood in America," *Baltimore Magazine* 81 (August 1988): 44–49, 93–94; *Washington Post*, 31 May 1986, p. A23; and ibid., 8 June 1986, p. H7.

236. *Boston Globe*, 27 October 1987, p. 8.

237. Ibid., 26 October 1987, p. 20.

238. Thomas J. Main, "The Homeless Families of New York," *Public Interest*, no. 85 (Fall 1986): 4.

239. *Chicago Tribune*, 12 December 1986, sec. 1, p. 8.

240. *Christian Science Monitor*, 12 October 1984, p. 10.

241. Commission on the Year 2000, *New York Ascendant* (New York: City of New York, 1987), p. 7.

242. David Blum, "One Block: A Tale of Two Cities on West Eightieth Street," *New York Magazine* 20 (9 February 1987): 24–32; and Irving Howe, "Social Retreat and the Tumler," *Dissent* 34 (Fall 1987): 409.

243. Brian J. L. Berry, "Islands of Renewal in Seas of Decay," in Paul E. Peterson, ed., *The New Urban Reality* (Washington, D.C.: Brookings Institution, 1985), p. 69.

Chapter 8: Coping in a New World

1. "Rebirth of the Cities," *Time* 66 (5 December 1955): 25–28.
2. "The Renaissance," ibid. 79 (23 March 1962): 16.
3. Ibid. 118 (24 August 1981).
4. Ibid. 130 (23 November 1987).

INDEX

Abandonment, 206–8

Air pollution: in Chicago, 85–86; in Cincinnati, 85, 163; in Cleveland, 32, 86; in Minneapolis, 86; in New York City, 86; in Philadelphia, 86; in Pittsburgh, 31, 84–85; in Saint Louis, 31

Airports, 99–100, 101

Alinsky, Saul, 246, 249, 285

Allegheny Conference on Community Development, 48–51, 53, 111, 282, 312; and air pollution, 84; description of, 46–47; and Flaherty, 216; and Lawrence, 60; and mass transit, 104, 239; and the Point redevelopment, 108–9, 157; postwar plans, 41

American Federation of State, County, and Municipal Employees, 184, 188–89

American Institute of Architects, 27

American Society of Planning Officials, 107

Anti-Crosstown Coalition, 232

Anti-4 Per Cent Sales Tax Committee, 143

Apartment and Home Owners Association, 160

Appalachian whites, 4, 15, 45, 126–27, 247–48

Association of Philadelphia Settlements, 51

Bacon, Edmund, 57, 109

Baer, Sidney, 49, 81

Baer, William, 202

Bailey's department store, 130, 134

Baltimore, 2, 4, 9, 286, 306–8; airport, 100; assessed valuation, 19, 218; blacks, 125–26, 129, 203–4; business support for renewal, 47–49; community organization and neighborhoods, 32, 113, 117, 181–83, 241–42, 245–46, 283–84, 309; convention trade, 274–75, 297; crime, 304; employment, 296, 303; highways and traffic, 41–42, 94, 97, 164, 233–34, 245; hotels, 297; labor relations, 188, 202; manufacturing, 24, 135, 213, 288–89, 311; mass transit, 102, 166–67, 237, 239, 301–2; mayors,

60–61, 137, 176–77, 201, 256, 259–60; municipal finances, 70–72, 74, 76, 80, 144, 218–20, 223–26, 261–63, 265; office buildings, 132, 271; parking, 98; planning organization, 52–53; police strength, 218; population, 123–24, 128, 204; redevelopment legislation, 106; rehabilitation and conservation, 32, 113–14, 116–17, 119, 152–53, 283–84, 305; retailing, 129–30, 208, 273, 290–92; sports, 276–77; study of decline, 28, 287; tourism, 280, 299–300; urban redevelopment, 106–7, 110, 146–47, 160–61; water and sewerage, 89, 91; wealth compared to suburbs, 14, 125, 205

Baltimore Chamber of Commerce, 160, 164

Baltimore City Fair, 241, 283

Baltimore Economic Development Corporation, 289, 311

Baltimore Planning Council, 129

Barnes, Henry, 166

Barr, Joseph, 136–37, 140, 142–43, 145, 177, 191

Bartholomew, Harland, 13, 16, 18

Bay Village, 249–50

Beame, Abraham, 227, 230, 257

Beck, Mary, 198

Bedford-Stuyvesant Restoration Corporation, 243–44

Bidwell, William, 277

Bilandic, Michael, 260

Blacks: and community organization, 115, 181–82, 243–45; economic status of, 45, 125–26, 303–4; and John Lindsay, 173–74; and municipal employees, 185–86, 188; political power of, 175–81; population increase of, 4, 15, 125–27, 129, 203–4; and urban renewal, 110–12, 155–56, 158–59, 162, 178–79; and "white backlash," 193–99

Boston, 2, 12, 18, 232, 270, 300, 304, 309; airport, 101; assessed valuation, 19, 22, 74; blacks, 126, 204; community organization

The Rough Road to Renaissance

George F. Thompson, *Project Editor*

Designed by Ann Walston.

Composed by Brushwood Graphics
in Bodoni Book with Poster Bodoni display.

Printed by Arcata Graphics
on 50-lb. S. D. Warren's Sebago Cream.